THE PHILOSOPHER FISH

Also by RICHARD ADAMS CAREY

Against the Tide
Raven's Children

THE
PHILOSOPHER
~FISH~

STURGEON, CAVIAR, AND
THE GEOGRAPHY OF DESIRE

RICHARD ADAMS CAREY

COUNTERPOINT
A MEMBER OF THE PERSEUS BOOKS GROUP
NEW YORK

Published by Counterpoint
A Member of the Perseus Books Group

Counterpoint books are available at special discounts for bulk purchases in the United States by corporations, institutions, and other organizations. For more information, please contact the Special Markets Department at the Perseus Books Group, 11 Cambridge Center, Cambridge, MA 02142; or call (617) 252-5298 or (800) 255-1514; or e-mail special.markets@perseusbooks.com.

Set in 11.5-point Goudy by the Perseus Books Group

Library of Congress Cataloging-in-Publication Data

Carey, Richard Adams.
    The philosopher fish : sturgeon, caviar, and the geography of desire / Richard Adams Carey. — 1st ed.
        p.   cm.
    Includes bibliographical references and index.
    ISBN 1-58243-173-6 (hardcover : alk. paper)
    1. Sturgeons—History. 2. Caviar—History. I. Title.
QL638.A25C355 2005
597'.42—dc22

                                                                    2004028209

05 06 07 / 10 9 8 7 6 5 4 3 2 1

For Susan Atwood Carey

And her hair was a folded flower
And the quiet of love in her feet.

One thinks of the sturgeon as a kind of philosopher among fishes, as if its ancient lineage had bred, over the thousands of centuries, a curious old wisdom and a quiet acceptance of change. The sturgeon has seen more years when it first spawns than many fish see in a lifetime.

—HOWARD WALDEN,
Familiar Freshwater Fishes of America

Who hears the fishes when they cry? It will not be forgotten by some memory that we were contemporaries.

—HENRY DAVID THOREAU,
A Week on the Concord and Merrimack Rivers

CONTENTS

Prologue	*xi*
1. The Hero Descending	1
2. The World Is Not Enough	31
3. Flavors of the Divine Horizon	55
4. The People of the Sturgeon	75
5. Situation Unpleasant	95
6. A City of Water	121
7. Poor Man's Lobster	145
8. Russian California	165
9. A Poetry of Place	183
10. The Iron in the Garden	203
11. Thieves World	225
12. The Blood of the Earth	241
13. A Capacity for Wonder	265
14. The Gilded Morsel	285
Epilogue	*301*
Acknowledgments	*303*
Bibliography	*307*
Index	*321*

PROLOGUE

I'll call her Heather.

She came from the Emma Willard School and already knew how to live away from home. Her names—first, middle, and last—were homogeneously Scottish. Her skin was the color of oatmeal and milk freckled with chaff. I saw her as the Hollywood version of a Highland lassie—clad in a tartan, the wind coursing through her hair as she carried secret messages from the clans to Bonnie Prince Charlie, whose ship lay at anchor in the Firth of Forth.

I remember watching her brush that hair in her dormitory room at Radcliffe. She fell forward at the waist, letting its length drop in a tangled column to the floor. It was at once brutally thick and luxuriously fine, a twining of tree roots and silk. She didn't so much stroke as chip at it with her brush, impatient with both its texture and its prettiness. Then she straightened, flicking it back. There was something of the tomboy in the way she did that, and something of the vamp as well. I remember her looking at me then with a faint smile and an expression compounded of all that I loved about her: her frankness, her self-possession, her air of simultaneous invitation and remoteness.

There was a lot of "both" and "at once" and "simultaneous" in Heather. She was both—or at once, or simultaneously—contradictory and coherent. She was hard to figure out and impossible not to desire. Men stopped and stared at her in the street. I never stopped staring myself.

During my first couple of years at Harvard, I walked to the Radcliffe campus to eat dinner with Heather two or three times a month.

Sometimes, if it got late and if her roommate was gone, I might spend the night, though we never slept together. My best chance that way probably came the first night I went with her to her dorm after our freshman drama class. She introduced me to James Taylor, playing his first album on her phonograph. We listened to "Something in the Way She Moves" and "Rainy Day Man." Then we traded her guitar back and forth and played songs we had written ourselves. She particularly liked one song of mine about homesickness and being apart from my girlfriend. Out of loyalty to that girlfriend, I went back to my dorm and slept alone that night.

One afternoon later that year I happened to meet her on the sidewalk outside a delicatessen near Harvard Square. She had bought a small tin of caviar, and she was eating it right there on the sidewalk with crackers. Or maybe not, because I also remember that she scooped the eggs out of the container and into her mouth with her fingers. The caviar lay as smooth and dark in its tin as blackberry jam, except where her fingers, or a cracker, had gone in. She told me she came here every once in a while when she was in the mood for caviar. She asked me if I wanted some.

Well, I wasn't sure. I had never seen caviar before, though I had my prejudices and received notions. I had been raised Roman Catholic, and my family avoided meat on Fridays, and sometimes ate fish. This was penance, as I understood it, for the sins we were about to commit on the weekend. I had my reservations about that as an ecclesiastical policy, but if it was my duty as a Catholic not to like fish, to suffer and gag through every white and crumbling mouthful, then I held up my end. Only rarely did the weekend provide enough opportunity to justify my penance.

This caviar was something that looked like jam but smelled faintly like fish—that alone made it an abomination to me. I had also heard that caviar, like good wine, was an acquired taste. I supposed that meant that it would take many expensive repetitions to reach a point where I might begin to like it. I didn't see the point of that in a world where Junior Mints were plentiful and cheap. I knew Heather's family had money and guessed that for her this snack was affordable, if not thrifty. But the Scottish portion of my own blood rebelled at wasting her money. The Irish portion, maybe, rebelled at throwing up in the street, but that would be unlikely. In any event, I declined.

All my opinions about fish would change, however, in the summer after my freshman year at Harvard. While Heather joined the company of the Harvard Summer School Repertory Theater, I drove to Alaska in an old school bus with a lot of other Harvard students, some from MIT, and a few Cambridge street people. Our idea was to form a firefighting crew. We knew that frequent mass call-ups had occurred during previous summers around Fairbanks, and having our own bus, we reasoned, would enable us to get to the site of the fire ahead of other eager recruits. But this was the summer the state of Alaska professionalized its firefighting and ended the mass call-ups. It was also the summer that the Alaska Pipeline project, which would bring North Slope oil to the Lower 48, was scheduled to begin but didn't, held up as it was in environmental and Native land claims litigation. The school bus got sold and somebody pocketed the money. Most of the Harvard kids flew home. I was stranded in Fairbanks along with hundreds of roustabouts from Texas and Oklahoma whose jobs had also fallen through.

A buddy and I camped for three weeks in a vacant lot opposite Alaskaland, a theme park where you could pan for gold or dine on mooseburgers. We couldn't afford the mooseburgers. Instead we made a breakfast each day of oatmeal boiled over a campfire and then joined the immigrant throng marching up and down the Chena River looking for work. Finally we hitchhiked down Route 3 to Anchorage, where we spent three more weeks camped outside the city on Rabbit Creek. Each morning we thumbed in to make our rounds of the hiring agencies, and also to make the soup kitchen at the Salvation Army. Our money was running out, and for the first time in my life I learned what it felt like to finish a meal, still be hungry, and go to sleep that way. At the end of July, we gave up on Anchorage and hitched down the Kenai Peninsula. When we arrived in Homer, the very last town on the peninsula, we tried to book passage on a boat to Kodiak Island, but instead were lucky enough to find jobs at last at the Alaska Seafoods cannery perched at the end of Homer Spit, a long fishhook of sand curling into Kachemak Bay.

We finned and gutted red, silver, and chum salmon as they came at us in hordes down a conveyor belt. At night we slept under a wrecked fishing boat stranded on the beach, and after our shifts, prowling beneath the delivery dock, found salmon that had missed the chute and fallen to the rocks, or else checked homemade traps that we set for

Dungeness crabs down the spit where the fishing boats were moored. We boiled the crabs and cut the salmon into steaks that we fried over a campfire. I had never dared imagine that anything, least of all this fish, could taste so good and feel so satisfying.

I worked for almost a month at the cannery, quitting when it was time to go back to school. I made just enough money to buy my airfare home and repay my mother the money she had loaned me to get up there.

I continued to visit with Heather throughout our years in school, though less and less as time went on. She had several boyfriends, one after another, all more glamorous than I was: the hot young actor who pulled down lead roles in all the Loeb Drama Center productions; the swaggering All-American soccer player from Greece; the successful Boston psychologist who acted occasionally in Harvard shows and who already had a wife. She majored in psychology and starred on Radcliffe's basketball and tennis teams. She described her men in terms at once romantic and dispassionate. That complexity disappeared when she raptly described an evening she spent with a Radcliffe professor, a woman: a long talk on most everything important, some marijuana, an overnight stay because it got so late, a marriage of souls.

I didn't see Heather at commencement in 1973, and I never got to say good-bye to her. I knew she wanted to give the women's professional tennis tour a try. She became one of many friends from college with whom I lost touch. I went west again, this time to work at a sawmill in the Cascade Mountains, but within a few years I was back in Alaska. I taught school in Yupik Eskimo villages along the Kuskokwim River and the Bering seacoast. In villages such as Kongiganak, Quinhagak, and Chefornak I lived in one of the most unfrequented portions of the Alaskan Bush and among America's last pure hunter-gatherers. They lived mostly on salmon, supplementing that with seal, walrus, waterfowl, tundra berries, greens, and the occasional moose or bear. There was no sturgeon native to that part of Alaska, and no caviar—just bitter dishes made from salmon or whitefish eggs. But I thought most of the Eskimo diet was tasty, and the fish nearly as delicious as the salmon I had eaten in Homer.

The Native corporation stores in each village offered a narrow sampling of the mainstream American diet, the Shop 'N' Save alternative to these wild foods: frozen beef and chicken, canned vegetables, dry goods, Chef Boyardee spaghetti, Hamburger Helper—even Junior Mints. People liked these foods, with their added salt and sugar and engineered flavorings, and also their ease of preparation. But they were available only for cash, and in these villages very few people had jobs. No great loss: Although the work of foraging could be hard and dangerous and cold, people knew that it was more fun to hunt and fish for their meals than to work in an office and buy them, and that wild foods were more filling and provided more warmth.

The more I learned about that way of living and that way of eating, and the more I saw it weakened from within by dwindling salmon runs up the Kuskokwim River, and assaulted from without by the seductions of the cash economy and consumerism, the harder it became for me—as a teacher—to preach the McDonald's way of life, to encourage my Eskimo students to go to college and train for an office job and do their hunting at Safeway or Shop 'N' Save.

So after ten years I came back East, to rural New Hampshire, where salmon runs up the rivers had disappeared more than a century ago, but where New Englanders were part of a spectacular rise in demand for seafood in Europe and North America. There had always been plenty of cod in New England, but in the late 1980s the cod stocks of Georges Bank, the richest such fishery in the history of the world, began to dwindle and then collapse. Yet the price of cod, while higher per pound than chicken or beef, remained pretty stable on the supermarket shelves. In 1995, after fisheries regulations had been toughened and a lot of New England fishermen had gone out of business, I went to Cape Cod to fish for a year with four survivors, men who went out occasionally for cod but also fished for lobsters, shrimp, flounders, dogfish, scallops, and quahogs, risking their skins and their mortgages in pursuit of the world's last wild food source.

John Muir, the founder of the Sierra Club, understood all that was implicit in that word "wild." "In God's wildness lies the hope of the world—the great fresh unblighted unredeemed wilderness," he wrote in 1890. That would be even more literally true for our seas and rivers than for our forests, considering, say, the importance of the world's wild fisheries as a source of protein in both developed and undeveloped nations; or the role of fish meal in the production of fertilizer and animal feed, and as food for salmon and trout grown in fish farms; or the linchpin status of wild fish stocks in the health of marine ecosystems.

But what about the many hunters in that wilderness now, and all those who are fed by them? Fish are hard to count except after they have been caught. They move as they please across geographical boundaries, tempting people on one side of a line to catch what they can now before the greedy bastards on the other side take them all. Whether to feed a hungry baby or pay off some investors, people in the business of fishing cannot help but hope, and finally believe, that there are plenty of fish out there, and they don't need catch limits, thank you, or gear limitations. And sometimes fish just get caught in the crossfire when somebody wants something different from a river: hydroelectric power, say, or waste disposal.

But the loss of a fishery anywhere is an ominous sign. In some cases, those with money can just pay to have that same fish, or something like it, imported. Sometimes it doesn't even cost more than the local product, as has been the case with New England cod versus its facsimiles from Norway, Chile, or Alaska. And sometimes this is a good thing for the local product. The law of supply and demand is itself a force for conservation, the first line of defense for fish populations since the original hemp net went into the water. As supply goes down, price goes up, and eventually people who chase fish, or who buy them, start looking for cheaper alternatives. Local fishing pressure relaxes, and stocks begin to recover.

But in a world with no new frontiers and no remaining unexploited fisheries, this has become another way to rob Peter to pay Paul. The shrimp in the frozen foods section, the roughy on the restaurant menu, the caviar behind the delicatessen counter: It all has to come from somewhere, and getting it from far away or even from aquaculture does not obviate the question so much as restate it in different terms. And the question is the same for forests, farmlands, clean water, clean air, and energy sources: How do we reach a point where demand, ultimately, exists in an equilibrium with supply? How do we discipline ourselves to measure our desires against finite means? How do we harness the engines of commerce and the comforts of consumerism to the economy-class ideals of stewardship? However it is phrased, nowhere is the question more difficult than it is with fisheries, and nowhere the need for an answer so pressing.

Henry David Thoreau observed in 1849 that he had not yet met the philosopher who could show him in any conclusive way the difference between a man and a fish. In fact, lost and extinguished fisheries are graves in our own family plot, the mortal consequence of our reluctance so far in confronting this question. There is a headstone for the lost and lamented Atlantic salmon of the East Coast, and an unmarked plot of grass for America's forgotten sturgeon fisheries of the Hudson River, Delaware Bay, and Great Lakes: fisheries that once supplied the world with its best caviar, as the Caspian Sea does today. These provide morbid tales that are either shouted aloud in the political marketplace of wildlife conservation, as with the salmon; or else not, as with the Atlantic sturgeon, whose caviar fed mostly immigrants and foreigners, and so expired unmourned.

The caviar that Heather offered me some thirty years ago almost certainly came from the Caspian, the waters of either the Soviet Union or Iran. Today five squabbling nations ring that sea, and the sturgeon harvest is largely given over to organized crime. International initiatives in conservation and law enforcement seek to stop the slaughter while scientists scramble to understand the ancient fish's biology and behavior before it's too late. As the Caspian populations wane, more attention accrues to sturgeons surviving elsewhere in the world, particularly in American waters. The black market has found these fish as well, and today the caviar marketplace in the United States is a kaleidoscopic bazaar of money, politics, and intrigue. In this instance, less supply will not make the hunters go away. The sturgeon's legendary egg will become only a more compelling object of desire.

I think back to a time before such circumstances, to my refusal to dip my fingers into Heather's tin of caviar in Cambridge, and see in that moment a microcosm of my relationship with her. I was, after all, being offered just a taste, but it was a taste of something rich and strange and rare. I stood before that tin of eggs, and before that extraordinary girl, like J. Alfred Prufrock confronted by a peach. I remember watching her smile, clamp the tin shut, and disappear into the throng on the sidewalk. There was something in the way she moved, and through many rainy days afterward I wondered what might have happened instead.

Later I heard she tore up her knee and had to quit the tennis tour. Then I heard she was going back to school in psychology. The years flew by. There was never anything from her in the Harvard/Radcliffe class reports until recently. She wrote that she had become a clinical psychologist in private practice in a city on the West Coast, and also a political activist. She spoke out against the sort of oppression commonly exerted against people of minority races, but that had also attacked her in her own identity, she said, as a woman and a lesbian. For exercise she went ocean kayaking, and she had paddled up much of the Northwest coast and into Alaska. She sent in a photo as well. She was still beautiful, but in a different way, unrelated to age. Her hair was short, and she wore the face of someone who'd long since stopped wondering what was expected of her and what her duties were to that. Her smile was easier, less enigmatic.

I have no idea whether she still snacks on caviar. But I know that if she ever takes her kayak near the mouths of the Columbia or the Fraser rivers, and if she does that in the spring, then not only are Pacific salmon coursing beneath her paddles, surging upriver to spawn, but sturgeon as well, white sturgeon, *Acipenser transmontanus*. Some of them bear eggs, a blackberry jam of tiny globes, each of them bursting with a flavor I know now to be the distilled essence of wildness and the sea, with sparkling connotations of money and beauty and style and adventure—and also with a wonderful natural undertone, I think, of peach.

~ 1 ~

THE HERO DESCENDING

i.

Daryl Parkyn's pants were rumpled and stained and cinched at the knees by dirty kneepads. Frank Chapman settled into the forward thwart of the flat-bottomed motor skiff and pointed at those pads. They were spattered with what looked like drops of ink, as though someone had flicked a fountain pen in their direction. "You see that, Rick? You know what that is?" Frank's smile brimmed with laughter. "That's caviar, man. That's your first glimpse of caviar."

Daryl had come down from Dead Boy Eddy to pick us up here at the mouth of the river. He glanced down at his pants, smiled wearily, shrugged. He pointed the skiff past Hog Island and up East Pass. He had caught fifty-nine sturgeons over the past two weeks, and he didn't have time or energy, he explained, to make himself altogether presentable. "Sometimes you can't get from one end of the net to the other without a fish coming in behind you," he sighed.

This was a strange place to look for sturgeon. Well, it was a strange place, period: The Suwannee River, a 250-mile pathway to nowhere that trickles out of Georgia's Okefenokee Swamp, winds through the pine flatwoods of north Florida, arcs through the tidal marshes of Lafayette and Gilchrist and Dixie counties, widening as it goes, until finally, at a blank spot on the Florida map midway between Tallahassee

1

and Tampa Bay, in an area known as the Big Bend coast, it not so much empties as soaks into the Gulf of Mexico.

A century and a half ago, composer Stephen Foster made the Suwannee a household name. Archie Carr, the Florida naturalist who first studied the river, observed in one of his essays that its fame came "not from its many intrinsic merits nor its very lively history, but from the fact that 'Suwannee' is a trisyllable that can be slurred into a disyllable which, when stressed on the first syllable, fit the meter of a song Foster was trying to write." That 1851 song is about wanting to go home, but no matter how you say the river's name, it's because so few people ever went home to the Suwannee that Frank Chapman was there that day in March 2001. We had driven down from Gainesville, riding Route 349 through scattered farms and ranch houses and rows of live oak hung with Spanish moss. As we neared the river the houses disappeared, the live oak giving way to straight bundles of slash pine jammed like matchsticks into the ground.

The road followed the river to the delta village of Suwannee, once known as Demory Hill, and considered by Archie Carr to be the most isolated community in Florida. Carr first came there in the 1930s, when Route 349 was an occasional pair of wheel tracks, and when fishermen went after mullet with sticks of dynamite on short fuses. "You could hear the thumping boom of underwater explosions all up and down the river," he wrote in *A Naturalist in Florida*, published posthumously in 1994. "There used to be more missing fingers on the Suwannee, it seemed, than anywhere else." He was looking for information on the Suwannee chicken, a turtle species new to science, so called from the taste of its meat, and was surprised to learn from fishermen that there were sturgeons in the river.

We drove past houses on stilts with motorboats berthed on tributary creeks. Jaybirds and red-winged blackbirds squabbled in banks of red-bay, cabbage palmetto, and red cedar. The air was already as moist and warm as an exhaled breath. We went over a small bridge to a slate-blue cottage on the southern shore of East Pass, one of the river's three main outlets to the gulf. Rented by the University of Florida, this cottage also was on stilts, crouching like a mother crab over a pair of 30-foot fiberglass water tanks—swimming pools, maybe, for the photophobic—that sprawled on the dock beneath its bottom floor. Daryl, with caviar on his knees, had been waiting for us at that dock.

Our destination was a houseboat anchored several miles upriver. There Daryl and a contingent of other university researchers, supervised by Frank Chapman, had strung a gillnet for one of the rarest and most mysterious fishes in North America, the Gulf of Mexico sturgeon, *Acipenser oxyrinchus de sotoi*. Frank stretched his great length across the thwart, gazed at the banks of bald cypress and black tupelo speeding past, and drank in the air. It smelled like the beginning of time, in a place that looked like that as well, as tropical, rank, and unpeopled as it was.

"You'll listen, write this up, and then forget about it," Frank shouted to me above the motor's rattle. "But I'll still be here. I love it here, man. I'll never leave."

ii.

We tend to dismiss the sturgeon, if we think of it at all, as a primitive fish, and allow that to account for its rarity. In our collective memory we forget that as recently as 1890 the biomass of Atlantic and short-nosed sturgeons in Delaware Bay was in the neighborhood of 48 million pounds; that at the same time fishermen in Washington's Columbia and Baker rivers were unable to use their gillnets in the spring because hordes of white sturgeon would have burst through them; that in Austria, on the Danube River, members of the Viennese royal court amused themselves by firing cannonballs into fleet-sized squadrons of migrating beluga sturgeons.

Until just the last fraction of a second in geologic time, sturgeons were the dominant large fish in every major river system on all three continents of the temperate northern hemisphere, unassailable (except from artillery) and prolifically abundant.

But the sturgeon is geologic time made flesh, and the length of its tenure on earth is impossible to comprehend. The fossil record presents completely modern forms of sturgeon dating back to the Upper Cretaceous, 100 million years ago. The family roots of the Acipenseriformes go back a lot further, by most estimates between 200 million and 300 million years ago, to the dawn at least of the Jurassic, or possibly even the Pennsylvanian Age. Some trace those roots to the Devonian, 400 million years ago. In any event, this is a fish that took shape with or before the earliest dinosaurs, remaining unscathed—and probably unperturbed—by the several climate shifts, meteor impacts, and wholesale extinctions since then.

The Russian caviar expert Vulf Sternin has worked out a calendar for this. If we count back only as far as the Paleozoic and the appearance of the first marine invertebrates, and collapse that time into a single calendar year, he explained, then Acipenseriformes punched in on the 25th of July at 4 A.M.; salmon on the 29th of December at 11:30 A.M.; and *Homo sapiens* just three and half minutes before midnight.

But even this evokes a complicated response. The phrase "living fossil" is often assigned to the sturgeon, suggesting both the wonder of its longevity and some small contempt that a model so outmoded hasn't already been removed from nature's assembly line. One of the current debates in sturgeon biology hinges on whether the evolution of the fish has been driven primarily by peramorphosis—which is to say, the development of new or altered physical structures, such as an opposable thumb, to put it into primate terms—or paedomorphosis, which is the retention of juvenile physical characteristics into adulthood. Modern forms of adult sturgeon, for example, have skeletons that are less bony than their ancestors' and more like their juvenile forms. This is cited by some as an example of paedomorphosis, which is fine, we suppose, if that helps somehow, but it just doesn't seem so clever or forward-thinking as peramorphosis. The suspicion lingers that a sturgeon is not only primitive, but degenerate; that it has sojourned a few million years too long, maybe, in rural backwaters.

We have never really known what to make of this fish, and that would include our scientists. Frank Chapman and his colleagues now agree that Acipenseriformes first took shape in what is now western Europe, began to diversify into separate species in the freshwater basins of central and northern Asia, and then spread throughout the temperate latitudes of the Northern Hemisphere. Then where do they fit on the fish family tree? In 1758, the Swedish taxonomist Carolus Linnaeus considered their cartilaginous skeletons, heterocercal tails (where the upper lobe is larger than the lower), and jaws that may be protruded from their snouts. These, he decided, made them cousins to sharks.

A century later, however, naturalist Louis Agassiz discovered a fossil of a fish from the Jurassic that had a bony skeleton, but the same tail and body shape as a sturgeon, and the same projectile jaw system. On the credentials of that ancestor, the sturgeon was sundered from the cartilaginous shark and welcomed, with some reservation, into the higher family of bony fish. That lack of boniness in modern sturgeons? Paedomorphosis at work. That remarkable jaw, which in less than an eye-blink can shoot out like a sawed-off elephant's trunk to suck organisms off the bottom, or a fish out of midwater? That would be peramorphosis, and a feature developed independently from the operations of a shark's jaw.

To be sure, the sturgeon looks like something dredged from the Lower Triassic. The fish's maximum size is one of those things nobody can be certain about, since several species never really stop growing, but Atlantic sturgeon—of which the gulf sturgeon is a subspecies—have been known to reach 14 feet and 800 pounds. The white sturgeon of California and the Pacific Northwest is bigger: A Canadian newspaper in 1897 reported a 1,400-pound Fraser River specimen. And the beluga of the Caspian Sea is the world's largest freshwater fish. In 1736, a beluga pulled from the Volga River near the Russian city of Astrakhan measured 28 feet and 4,570 pounds. An 1898 German encyclopedia claimed that a beluga twice that weight was once taken from the Volga, though it doesn't provide the date or location. It's possible that some of our famous lake monsters—Nessie in Loch Ness, Champ in Lake Champlain, and so forth—are (or were) really sturgeons.

I recall a photograph of a white sturgeon hung from its head on block-and-tackle outside a Fraser River fish-packing plant in the 1950s. The fish was 14 or 15 feet long, and the cameraman had to forgo the head in order to get the tail, framing the top of his picture at the gill plate. Three men in ties, sport jackets, trench coats, wingtips, and fedoras stand around the fish. One smiles for the camera, another glances to the side, and a third looks at the fish towering above them, stretching his right hand out to touch its flank. The scene looks like the coda to an Eisenhower-era horror film: the beast from another time, dead now, thank God, and surrounded by the eggheads from the Smithsonian who found its weak spot just in time.

It's not just the sturgeon's size that's disconcerting, and apparently primeval. With its long snout and dangling barbels, its lines of armor and its scythe-like tail, the fish suggests the result of a night in which whales, sharks, catfish, and—somehow—armadillos all spawned together. Elsewhere the sturgeon has been described as a chain saw with fins. It has an unfinished and experimental look to it. Taxonomists find other signs. They see that its dorsal fin is located not at the peak of the spine, but down near the tail. They see that it has few scales, and these are not round and thin like a salmon's, but rhomboid, with peg-like extensions overlapped by the adjoining scale. And there is the armor plating itself, which in sturgeons runs in five rows of horny plates, called scutes, down the length of its body. These are all characteristics of primitive fish.

So in developmental terms, has the sturgeon simply been treading water, so to speak, since the Upper Cretaceous, 100 million years ago, when its modern form was fixed? Yes, but only because treading water has paid such handsome dividends. And only because the sturgeon learned that trick so early and so well.

Ancestral sturgeons were pelagic piscivores, like salmon, swimming at midwater levels and feeding on other fish. But at some point leading up to the Cretaceous an extraordinary series of changes took place: The sturgeon's palate began to break up into separate plates of cartilage; as these became mobile, opposable, and finally protrusible, the sturgeon shed its teeth (though juvenile sturgeon today still have teeth); and the gills, as necessary, became capable of both ingesting and expelling water for respiration whenever the mouth cavity was filled.

The fossil record so far is lacking in the intermediate forms that might demonstrate these changes, and the question of how any sort of intermediate form could be functional is one of those things that puzzle phylogeneticists. But the result for a sturgeon, once all the parts were in place, was the ability to vacuum-feed along the bottom for crustaceans, mollusks, and other invertebrates and advance into an ecological niche unexploited by other fish.

Sturgeons usually feed in both fresh and sea water, and so have never assumed the flattened body shape of marine bottom-feeders. Instead their form remains perfectly adapted to the special task of maintaining a position over variable bottoms in large, swift rivers—treading water, as it were. They achieve this partly with size, partly with brute strength, and also some morphological tricks: The hypochordal lobe of the tail, its bottom half, has been reduced in length to allow it to sweep back and forth directly over substrate; and the pectoral fins have become broad and lobe-like, like the diving planes on a submarine, allowing exact modulation of depth while swimming, or staying still in a strong current.

Taxonomists have coined the phrase "benthic cruising" to describe this feeding specialization, and its only practitioners remain sturgeons and their first cousins, the paddlefish. As specializations go, it covers a lot of ground. Sturgeon are indiscriminate bottom-feeders, relishing most everything they suck up: crabs, clams, crayfish, shrimp, starfish, snails, worms, insect larvae, sand hoppers, water sow bugs, water fleas, and so on down to microscopic diatoms. They crush these morsels, large and small and tiny, between the collagenous pads that have grown from the palate. Their snouts are sensory marvels of taste and touch and electroreception. They are also blunt instruments, useful for rooting through mud. In 1888, observers for the U.S. Fish Commission reported seeing a school of gulf sturgeons work like hogs through the muddy bottom of Tampa Bay.

But since sturgeons are strong swimmers, they continue to feed on fast-moving pelagic fish as well. The beluga feeds exclusively on these. Other large sturgeons, such as the Atlantic and the white, and to a lesser degree the gulf, become more piscivorous as adults. Serge Doroshov, a University of California biologist, asked a Columbia River fisherman to capture a live white sturgeon for him in the early 1980s and was surprised to be presented with a 400-pound specimen that had been caught with a 10-pound steelhead as bait. Fishermen report that sturgeons, like catfish, are delicate in their feeding, that they take bait so gently that it's sometimes hard to tell that a gigantic fish has struck your line.

Some prey items are unusual: Waterfowl and seal pups have been found in sturgeon stomachs, and also the infrequent cat or squirrel. A horse's head was once found in a beluga. White sturgeon will also gorge on the remains of spawned-out salmon. Gulf sturgeon come into the Suwannee in the spring with their stomachs full of brachiopods, shelled invertebrates now nearly extinct but common 300 million years ago.

Over all that time, benthic cruising has been good for sturgeons, at least until these final few ticks of Vulf Sternin's geologic year. Sturgeons and paddlefish are the last surviving representatives of the Chondrosteidae, the family of fish that gave rise subsequently to the Teleosteidae, the ray-finned and round-scaled fish that make up 95 percent of today's species. If sturgeons are indeed living fossils, the last living remnant of an earlier idea of fishiness, it is only because the blueprint defined 100 million years ago by Acipenseriformes was so spectacularly successful.

Whether the means was more peramorphosis or paedomorphosis, the result in the Cretaceous was not an evolutionary dead end, but the perfect gated cul-de-sac.

iii.

Fifty-nine sturgeons in two weeks is a good haul in the Suwannee these days, some of them leaking eggs that catch on your kneepads, and when the fish hit the net in clumps, it's actually too much of a good thing. But most of the time, it's a matter of hurry up and wait, especially now that the spawning run was beginning to thin out. There were no hits at Dead Boy Eddy that afternoon. Frank Chapman, after a couple of runs to the net, went back to his lab in Gainesville, and Daryl took off his pads and started to work on dinner.

The navy and gray houseboat was anchored at a kink in the Suwannee opposite an osprey nest in the crown of a bald cypress, a few hundred yards downstream from a net tied to the river's east bank. The 150-foot net was strung laterally across the current, its width just a fraction of the channel. The afternoon air was light as silk and eerily quiet, except for the occasional rattle of an outboard from somewhere else on the river. The water, rich in tannin and organic matter, looked as it must have in 1867, when a young John Muir had passed through this region at the end of a thousand-mile hike he undertook from Wisconsin to Florida's Gulf Coast: "black as ink," he wrote, "perfectly opaque, and glossy on the surface as if varnished."

Daryl, a Canadian, the plain-spoken and unpretentious son of a chef, had taken charge of the night's meal of grilled pork chops, rice, and beans. Also aboard were Jamie Holloway, another University of Florida biologist, and an undergraduate student known to the scientists only as Rory. Rory was an English major who had arrived at the houseboat just a few hours ahead of me. He had taken a work-study job in the Department of Fisheries and Aquatic Sciences to help pay off his federal loans, and he was amazed to find himself way down upon the Suwannee in search of a gigantic fish he had never heard of before.

Jamie had hung a tattered, old-fashioned twine net, with big 10-inch mesh, between the stanchions of the foredeck roof. While Daryl worked the grill, Jamie gave Rory a lesson in net-mending. Jamie's voice was molasses smooth and just faintly sweetened with the music of Dixie. He knotted two loose ends and said, "Glad no 'gators have gotten tangled in this so far. But if we get a manatee, that's the end of the program."

"Why's that?" asked Rory.

"Endangered species. You can't touch 'em. The feds'll boot us off the river."

"A manatee is an endangered species?"

"Yep—so's a gulf sturgeon, for that matter."

The Gulf of Mexico sturgeon and the smaller, short-nosed sturgeon of the East Coast, *Acipenser brevirostrum*, are the only two sturgeon species listed under the Endangered Species Act (ESA) of 1973. The short-nosed was listed at the act's inception, the gulf in 1991. Globally, there is no telling how many species of sturgeon have gone extinct in the past hundred years. Nor is there any certainty, exactly, as to how many species remain. Sturgeons are animals with a great many chromosomes. Where a human makes do with 23, sturgeons employ 120, 240, or even 500. This makes for slow rates of DNA mutation and species evolution, a general readiness for species to hybridize, and awkward difficulty in telling certain species apart. Even molecular analysis of DNA sometimes yields you-pick-'em results, but current estimates range from twenty-four to twenty-six species.

Those that remain, wherever they are found, are often on the brink of extinction or within swimming distance of it. Estimates for the number of gulf sturgeon in the Suwannee range from 2,500 to 7,650. There are others in rivers west of here, between the Suwannee and the Mississippi, but the combined aggregate of these would be no more than a few thousand, and gulf sturgeon live nowhere else. The gulf is at least in better shape than the Alabama sturgeon, *Scaphirhynchus suttkusi*: Only thirty-six specimens are known from museum records or photographs, and only nine live specimens were reported between 1993 and 1999.

This lent urgency to the activities conducted out of the houseboat that spring. Daryl Parkyn was working on the relationship between water temperature and a sturgeon's metabolic rate. He told me gulf sturgeon probably branched from Atlantic sturgeon 10,000 years ago, when Florida rose from the sea bottom and the Gulf Stream imposed a warm-water barrier between populations on either side of the peninsula. The gulfs became the world's most southerly sturgeons, lingering in rivers near cool artesian springs—known as "thermal refuges"—throughout the summer.

"It's amazing that they survive here at all," Daryl said. "No doubt they couldn't if it wasn't for those springs in the Suwannee and other rivers. We know they can handle water temperatures up to 95 degrees in captivity, if they're being fed, which is incredible. But we don't know what their real tolerances are in the wild."

This spring he and Jamie were attaching temperature loggers to all the fish they netted. These computerized sensors would keep a five-year record of the water temperatures through which a sturgeon moved. Also, they were pumping stomachs and analyzing their contents so that researchers could develop a better artificial feed recipe for farm-raised sturgeon, then attaching pingers—ultrasonic telemetry transmitters—to help track the fish as they marked out foraging areas. Other scientists would come to the houseboat during the spring for other studies.

Frank Chapman's special project was the same as last year's: the capture of several egg-bearing females and mature males for the artificial spawning of gulf sturgeon. There was no chance, however, that any fry that Frank produced would be released into the Suwannee or anywhere else. That was one of the points of conflict, in fact, in a new sort of civil war between Florida and the federal government, and a wellspring of bitterness for Frank.

"He and Jim Clugston, a federal Fish and Wildlife biologist, took a few hundred sturgeons that Frank had propagated, and they released them into the river in '92, and we still catch a lot of those fish out here," Daryl said over dinner. "There is criticism of the genetic effects of restocking, but it's my own theory that sturgeons are naturally inbred, and those issues aren't so critical in this case. For an organism tied so closely to a special environment, to one particular river system, they must have some sort of mechanism to deal with that."

"But Fish and Wildlife won't let you put fish in here anymore?" Rory asked.

"They are vehemently opposed to restocking, and that's a pity," said Daryl. "I mean, I understand why they want to be cautious, and yes, there's more research to be done, and sure, you've got to do that. But if the population trend is downward—well, I think some small-scale introductions might avert a disaster."

"They don't even like us out here doing what we're doing now," Jamie added. "They'd like to boot us off the river, period—manatees or no manatees."

After dinner Daryl set about testing a hydrophone, a Rube Goldberg device for homing in on a tagged sturgeon's telemetry signal. Sonar pings echoed around the cabin while Jamie scrounged up a Clint Eastwood film to pop into the houseboat's VCR.

The dusk deepened, and then night settled in, the riverbanks receding chromatically into the varnished black of the river and the varnished black of the sky. On our drive down the valley that morning, Frank had described this area as a drop-off point for drugs coming in from the south on small planes. Jamie confirmed that. He said the planes leave bales of marijuana known among fishermen as "square groupers." These were reeled in by Suwannee Swifties—fast boats traveling in the dark with no running lights. A fast boat swept by us as we cleaned the dinner plates, but too early for a Swifty. Then the silence resumed.

We got in the skiff and checked the net at 8 P.M., and again at 10. Nothing so far. We meant to continue through the night.

At 10:30 I climbed up onto the roof and found Rory there ahead of me, smoking a cigarette. There was no moon, but the stars were spread like headlamps across the sky. We were startled by a splash like a medium-sized boulder being dropped into the river, or maybe dynamite going off underwater, a sound from somewhere in the middle of the channel.

"You hear that?" Daryl called up. "That's a sturgeon jumping."

iv.

It was its meat that recommended the sturgeon to Native Americans throughout North America, and also—at one time—to Europeans.

There is puzzlingly scant evidence of sturgeon fishing by Florida Indians, maybe because sturgeons were never very numerous this far south. But the fish looms large in the economies and folklore of tribes on river systems throughout the northern reaches of the continent.

Meanwhile, in the urbanizing western Europe of the Middle Ages and the Renaissance, sturgeons were being slowly fished into oblivion, the meat avidly consumed, the roe discarded or fed to livestock. There was once so much sturgeon meat in Germany that certain room-and-board employment contracts stipulated sturgeon be served no more than twice a week. When at last the numbers of European sturgeon, *Acipenser sturio*, began to dwindle, Europeans themselves forgot they had ever liked the fish. And they continued to shun it in the New World. "There are plenty of sturgeon," wrote Henry Hudson in a 1609 report to the East India Company, "which the Christians do not make use of, but the Indians eat them greedily."

In fact, sturgeon joined salmon and lobster in a triumvirate of seafoods beloved by Indians but judged unfit for the consumption of Christians. In 1607, Captain John Smith's Jamestown settlers had to be pushed to the brink of starvation before they armed themselves with swords and frying pans and managed to corner several Atlantic sturgeons in shallow waters. Wrote Smith: "We had more sturgeon than could be devoured by dog or man; of which the industrious by drying and pounding mingled with caviar, sorrel and other wholesome hearbs would make bread and good meat." Nonetheless, some so gorged themselves, added Smith, "as it cost many their lives."

In Europe caviar was just becoming a minor item of trade with the Mongols around the Black and Caspian seas. The London Company, which was financing the Jamestown settlement, prompted Smith's men in 1609 to ship a few barrels of caviar to London for reexport to the Baltics. But the caviar arrived spoiled, and the settlers abandoned sturgeon as soon as their famine eased.

For the next two centuries sturgeons had little to fear from either swords or frying pans in Christian America. There was a limited trade in pickled sturgeon with Europe, most of it from New England's Kennebec and Merrimack rivers. A good deal more pickled meat went to the Caribbean to feed slaves on sugar plantations. Otherwise, sturgeons were ignored, unless they tangled themselves in shad or herring nets, tearing the mesh with their sharp scutes. Then they were clubbed to death by enraged fishermen.

Sometimes they boarded a boat on their own initiative. Sturgeons are unique among bottom-feeders in their tendency, dolphin-like, to occasionally leap clear of the water and go airborne. "In June, on the Suwannee, people even complain of being kept awake by the noise of their splashing at night," wrote Archie Carr. In daylight this behavior sometimes delivered them into the laps of startled fishermen or boaters. The 1888 Bulletin of the U.S. Fish Commission reported that once in Delaware Bay, "a large individual had actually jumped from the water high enough to go through one of the dead-lights . . . in the hull of a passing passenger side-wheel steamer, and thus found itself an unexpected prisoner in the hold of the vessel."

Sturgeon oil had some use as lamp fuel, the rest of the fish, perhaps, as fertilizer. The roe might be useful as bait for eels or perch. In 1820, the price of a 200-pound sturgeon in New York was twenty cents. Fifty years later, in Oregon, a 1,250-pound white sturgeon sold for a quarter.

On the other side of the ocean, however, Russian aristocrats—flushed from their defeat of Napoleon's Grand Army—were cutting a wide swath through the salons of western Europe. They brought with them not only an enthusiasm for caviar, but also the means of getting it fresh from the Caspian, even in Hamburg or Paris. For centuries caviar had been all too perishable, an item either inedible or just slightly better than that by the time it arrived anywhere that wasn't local. But with the spread of railroad lines and steamship routes, and the advent of ice from steam-driven compressors, well-heeled Russian travelers could enjoy fresh caviar wherever they went, and also share it with their hosts, who finally learned what caviar was really supposed to taste like.

The first result was a reappraisal of the once despised European sturgeon. But already depleted populations of that fish swooned quickly. In 1876, the German fish-curing and caviar firm of Dieckmann & Hansen dispatched the sons of its founders to America. Their purpose was to see what might be obtained from the great pods of Atlantic sturgeon that crowded Delaware Bay.

By then American fishermen were already catching sturgeon, at least in the Northeast. New European immigrants bought sturgeon meat because it was cheap, and those from eastern Europe remembered it as a delicacy. In 1857, a smokehouse opened in New York City, followed by another in Philadelphia. Street peddlers sold the smoked meat door to door in New York's ethnic neighborhoods, and Hudson River fishermen nicknamed it "Albany beef."

Eventually immigrant fishermen from Russia and Germany began to experiment with making and selling caviar. "Mr. Benedict Blohm of Penns Grove, N.J. . . . was the first to put up caviar, which he did about the year 1853," noted the federal Fish Commission's 1899 report. "For a number of years the business struggled along, owing to the low price received for the caviar and the prejudice prevailing against the use of the flesh."

But it was Blohm's caviar, exported to Germany, that caught the notice of Dieckmann & Hansen. The firm began paying for sturgeon in Delaware Bay, which were almost impossible not to catch, and soon fishermen began laying aside their shad gear. A small city—Caviar, New Jersey—sprang up almost overnight on the north side of the inlet. In 1880, Albany Beef became the trade name of a sturgeon packing plant's product, and soon after that the town of Caviar was sending fifteen train cars of its namesake commodity to New York City every day.

The bonanza lasted twenty years and spread throughout the country to other species: the short-nosed that swam alongside the Atlantic sturgeon; the lake sturgeon, *Acipenser fulvescens*, of the Great Lakes and the Mississippi watershed, said to yield the best American caviar; the Alabama sturgeon and other sturgeons and paddlefish of the lower Mississippi; the white sturgeon in the Northwest, whose caviar was too distant from European markets, but whose meat was prized; and finally the Gulf of Mexico sturgeon, first hunted on the Suwannee in 1895.

On Delaware Bay the fishermen lived in long houseboats called "lay boats," and the butchering and caviar-making were carried out on board. The best caviar went to Europe, where some of it was labeled as premium "Astrakhan Caviar" from Russia. Some of that faux Russian caviar was reimported to the United States and sold at the breathtaking price of six cents per ounce. But there was always enough saltier, and sometimes unripe, lower-grade caviar to provide a domestic glut, at least for a while. Bars in New York City offered free caviar, in bowls or in sandwiches, in the same manner that salted peanuts are offered today to keep their patrons drinking.

Conservation laws were on the way, but they politely waited until the sturgeons—and the profits—were gone. By 1897, the harvest in Delaware Bay was less than half the 5 million pounds taken in 1890. What fisheries analysts call "catch per unit of effort" was declining as well. In 1890, fishermen found an average of sixty sturgeons in their nets every time they hauled back; in 1896, this dropped to twenty-seven, and two years later to eight. But effort was unabated since prices were skyrocketing. The same 135-pound keg of caviar worth $9 to $12 to a fisherman in 1885 sold for $40 in 1894, and $105 in 1899. There were still a thousand watermen on the bay, catching only a fraction of what the bay once produced, but making as much money as ever.

Florida's fishery was a much more modest affair, but as effectively destructive. It began in Tampa Bay in 1887 and moved north. In 1900, 44,000 pounds of sturgeon came out of the Suwannee. That was the year, however, of a catastrophic crash in Delaware Bay, the Chesapeake, the Great Lakes, and the Columbia and Fraser rivers as sturgeons that would have then been spawning for the first time then failed to appear. The Florida harvest peaked in 1902, but the Suwannee was already in decline, and fishermen had begun to clean out the Ochlockonee and Apalachicola and other rivers to the west. The 1914 Fish Commission report surveyed the national scene in disgust: "Even in the present generation we have seen the shores of the Potomac River in the vicinity of Mount Vernon lined with the decomposing carcasses of these magnificent fishes, witnesses to the cruelty, stupidity, and profligacy of man, and the same thing has been observed everywhere in our country."

The fishing never stopped so much as it faded quietly away. Initiatives by industry members to rein in the harvest during the boom years had been ignored by state legislatures. After the crash, various minimum size laws were enacted by various states, but the sturgeons never came back. The Europeans contented themselves again with Russian caviar, though that disappeared as well with the outbreak of World War I. In America the numbers of fishermen and processors and shippers dwindled, and Caviar, New Jersey, became first a ghost town, then a salt marsh, and finally an oxymoron.

Elsewhere the fisheries became so vestigial as to be invisible, to the extent that Americans in Florida, on Delaware Bay, on the Great

Lakes, and on the Columbia forgot that there had even been numbers of sturgeon in their waters, that caviar had ever been at one time a famed American delicacy. Atlantics or gulfs are like most other sturgeons in not reaching sexual maturity until seven to twelve years of age, or even older. Then they spawn intermittently: the males perhaps annually, the females only every three to four years, or less frequently than that. "If there can be a single generalization about sturgeons," wrote David Secor of the Chesapeake Biological Laboratory in 2002, "it is that they tend to be poky at life: their heart beats slowly; they move deliberately, mature slowly, reproduce infrequently, and are slow to die." These characteristics also make them quick to succumb to heavy fishing pressure, and then painfully poky about recovering.

In a little more than two decades, the eternal sturgeon had gone the way of the buffalo, the passenger pigeon, and the Atlantic salmon. But since caviar itself had never become part of the mainstream American diet, remaining instead a food largely for immigrants or foreigners or bigwigs, the sturgeon disappeared with none of those other animals' tragic fanfare. When the great fish stopped coming up occasionally in the nets of shad fishermen, and as overfishing and dams and pollution caused those nets in turn to disappear from American rivers, the sturgeon simply faded from the American mind, as it had from the European.

In 1962, a pair of sport fishermen noticed frustrated gulf sturgeons congregating against a new dam across the Apalachicola River in the Florida Panhandle. The next year an article in *Outdoor Life* magazine by Robert Burgess celebrated "Florida's Sturgeon Spree." Fishermen came from as far as Canada to set out baited hooks on 20-pound test line and saltwater tackle, then take a Nantucket sleigh ride behind hooked sturgeon, getting towed around the river in an inner tube inflated around a washtub. The spree lasted a few seasons, then history repeated itself and the sturgeons were gone. "The bad thing was, nobody really knew what to do with the fish," said the owner of a local tackle shop. "It was such a strange, bizarre fish. I heard stories of people finding them on the riverbanks dead from people catching them and just leaving them."

In March 2001, only a week before I went to Florida, the corpse of a strange, bizarre fish, 5 feet long, washed up on a beach in Cape Cod. At first it was thought to be something like the coelacanth, a primitive creature new to science or else known only through fossils. But finally it was revealed to be an Atlantic sturgeon. The event was remarkable enough for a photo and an article in the *Cape Codder* newspaper, which called the fish a sea sturgeon.

v.

John Muir found the Gainesville of 1867 rather attractive: "an oasis in the desert, compared with other villages. It gets its life from the few plantations located about it on dry ground that rises islandlike a few feet above the swamps."

The day before our trip to the Suwannee, Frank showed me around his own sort of plantation at the Department of Fisheries and Aquatic Sciences. It was the place from which he had once hoped to launch a new paradigm for sturgeon management in Florida and restore the gulf sturgeon. Lately, however, it had begun to feel more like a Seminole hideout.

The department offices and Frank's fish farm were on the outskirts of the oasis, several miles from the university's main campus, at the end of a back road just at the point where the malls and the commercial strips, then the lawns and gardens, yield to tall grass, scrub, and swamp. The mid-morning sunlight was hard and brittle, the high-flying clouds floating thin and pale over the low buildings and open-sided, tin-roofed sheds.

We walked through rows of ponds, 30 to 40 yards across, that were murky, round-edged squares nicked cookie-cutter fashion into the ground. A black cylindrical shape, several feet long, neared the surface of one and then veered away, fading back into the murk. A number of circular fish tanks were housed in a white, one-story building, open at one end, with several larger tanks in the open air beyond that. Chulhong Park, Frank's fresh-faced Korean graduate student, had gone there ahead of us to check the pumps and filters and clean the tanks. Chulhong joined us at a small blue tank, washtub-sized, its crystalline water peppered with clouds of wriggling black flecks. "Rick, take a look at that," Frank said. "There are more gulf sturgeon in that tank than there are in the whole Suwannee River."

To be precise, there were 5,000 gulf larvae in that and three other tanks, almost twice the number Frank believes the Suwannee to support. Only four days old, these were spawned from four males and a 130-pound female that Daryl and Jamie had caught the previous week. Ultimately, only a few of these flecks would be kept to become part of Frank's captive population of gulfs. And the rest? "Well, I can't put them into the river—that's because their mother must be genetically inferior to have let herself be netted," Frank complained. "So I'll just dump them into the ponds. I got bluegills in there to handle whatever the big sturgeons don't eat. I'll let the bluegills eat 'em."

"We look at them under microscopes, and we see the hearts beating," Chulhong added gravely.

"I love life. I hate to kill these," Frank said. He nodded toward rows of other small tanks that made up this corner of the facility, all swarming with larvae and fingerlings, though not all gulf sturgeon. "There are about 100,000 fish in those tanks, man, and that's probably more sturgeons than there are in North America."

Apart from his jaybird feistiness and owl-like glasses, Frank Chapman is otherwise a great blue heron of a man: tall, long-limbed, fine-boned, with inquisitive eyes, a brilliant white smile, a heron's enchantment with fish, and a blue heron's tragic sensibility. Born and raised in Colombia, he speaks rapidly and passionately, at a bird's metabolic rate, in slangy, Spanish-inflected English. He gets his European color and his lankiness from his Dutch heritage; he gets his Anglo-Saxon surname from his grandfather, who had a weakness for piracy, Frank says. He fled the Netherlands, and then England, changing his name along the way.

In Colombia Frank and his father had to go into the jungle, to very remote areas, to catch any fish at all. But as a graduate student in fisheries biology at the University of California–Davis in 1981, Frank was part of a fishing expedition to San Francisco Bay. Opposite Sausalito and the Golden Gate Bridge they caught a white sturgeon, and Frank was thunderstruck to find something at once so great, so monstrous, and so beautiful there in the midst of those urban waters. At that moment, he said, he was "imprinted" and knew what he wanted to do with his life.

By then UC-Davis had become ground zero for sturgeon research in the United States. An émigré scientist from the Soviet Union, Serge

Doroshov, had arrived with some grasp of the techniques of artificial propagation and aquaculture that the Soviets were using to support their Caspian Sea populations of sturgeon. The university hoped those same techniques might help reverse a decline in the numbers of white sturgeon in California, and in 1979 Doroshov achieved the first successful artificial propagation of that species.

Frank became one of Doroshov's students, and for his master's thesis he took the next step in white sturgeon aquaculture by obtaining viable sperm from one of the males spawned by Doroshov. The male was only four years old, demonstrating that white sturgeon, like the species of the Caspian, grew and matured more quickly under hatchery conditions. The first of the females spawned in 1979 reached sexual maturity ten years later, and she in turn yielded eggs for successful artificial propagation. That closed the circle, setting in motion the development of an advanced sturgeon aquaculture industry in California.

It's an industry built around a native species, which is what Frank had originally hoped to achieve in Florida. In March 1989, when two fishermen working on a tagging project caught a gravid female in the Suwannee, Frank traveled hastily to a makeshift facility at the mouth of the river. There, in a campground on the side of a canal, he took a small portion of eggs from the female via cesarean section, stitched her belly, and returned her to the river. Milt from several captured males was mixed with the eggs in a plastic K-Mart bowl on a picnic table. The result in a week or so was 5,000 gulf sturgeon larvae, each little more than a mouth, a spinal cord, and a yolk sac. U.S. Fish and Wildlife gave Frank a plaque gratefully commemorating the feat, and the University of Florida gave him a job.

Here we go, Frank thought. Undammed and undeveloped, the Suwannee was as pristine an environment as could be found in America for the study of sturgeon in the wild. "And I'm enamored with Fish and Wildlife," Frank had told me earlier in his office. "We'll work together to restock the wild populations, and we'll also start an aquaculture industry in Florida. This was gonna be great, man."

In 1992, a very small number of Frank's hatchery-reared fingerlings were put into the river: 400 by Frank himself, another 800 by USF&W's Jim Clugston. It was the start of a seven-year joint study, and by 1999 the hatchery fish were found to have had a high survival rate. They made up almost 20 percent of the seven-year-old sturgeons netted in the Suwannee.

Those results, however, proved a Rorschach test limning the conflict between two warring philosophies of fisheries conservation. Frank was delighted: The experiment proved that hatchery-reared gulfs could survive in the wild and augment a wild population very quickly. But Clugston and other federal scientists were disturbed. Noting that the stocked fish were the offspring of one female and three males, they saw their success as proof positive of the threat of genetic swamping—that is, the displacement of wild fish by a hatchery population with only a fraction of their diversity. Clugston and his colleagues wrote in a 1993 paper on the experiment that the whole procedure had been "ill advised."

Frank thinks he offered excellent advice. No one disputes that sturgeon populations that are too small cannot sustain themselves, that they are doomed—if not by overfishing or habitat degradation—by routine mortality, the ordinary pratfalls and failures of spawning, or the long-term effects of reduced genetic diversity. No one disputes that some level of stock enhancement may be necessary. The ticklish part is where to fix that level.

Just counting the fish is ticklish. Frank believes there are about 3,000 sturgeons in the Suwannee; USF&W estimates nearly 8,000. Both numbers are bad enough, but the real argument is about population trend. Frank says there aren't enough breeding females and that, although population numbers may cycle up or down in the short term, the long-term involves a vortex of extinction, a process that could accelerate disastrously with any environmental disturbance. Ken Sulak of the U.S. Geological Survey counters that the population is stable and that the fish is only just now showing the benefits of the Florida ban on sturgeon fishing imposed in 1984. Jim Clugston agrees.

When Frank considers the consequences of Clugston and Sulak being wrong about that, he yields the sort of impolitic statements favored by that altar ego he calls Bad Boy Frank. "Fish and Wildlife, man, they are saving the sturgeon to extinction," he complained as we looked at the clouds of gulf larvae.

The Apalachicola has only a few hundred fish, but genetic differences between those and Suwannee sturgeons dictate that neither will any of these larvae end up there. A reminder of this from Chulhong provoked another explosion from Bad Boy Frank: "If you have 100,000 fish, then good, they will recover. If you have just 200, then show me where they are, and I'll shoot 'em. They are impeding the recovery process."

Chulhong looked at him with raised eyebrows, and Frank relented. "This is how I get in trouble," he sighed. "It's a personal issue. People don't like the way I say things sometimes. Okay, I understand, but that shouldn't be an impediment. My allegiance is to the sturgeon."

It was an argument Frank had no chance of winning anyway. The gulf's listing under the Endangered Species Act meant that the feds were calling the shots, and Bad Boy Frank couldn't help but think that the listing really had more to do with politics than science. "What a coincidence, all this hoopla," he said. "We develop this technology to do some stocking, and right at that moment there is this proposal to list the fish, and everybody starts backpedaling." A stream of expletives followed that exhausted his imagination. "I wish I had a bigger vocabulary of bad words," he sputtered.

Chulhong was satisfied. "That's big enough."

"But this fish lives a long time, man, and I'm gonna be here a long time too. I'm gonna live to a hundred."

Neither is there any use for these larvae in commercial aquaculture, though not for lack of trying by the Florida legislature. In 1999, the lawmakers decided to test the market for meat, authorizing the delivery of 700 of Frank's juvenile gulf sturgeons to a Miami cooking school, six fish wholesalers, and a Miami restaurant. USF&W objected and then alerted the *St. Petersburg Times*, which wrote on February 21, 2000, "The state has come up with a novel proposal to deal with one of Florida's rarest fish species: Gut it, clean it, cook it, and eat it."

The delivery was canceled, and later that year Florida governor Jeb Bush made it clear to the state wildlife commission that he preferred to hear not a word about any doings with gulf sturgeons. George W. Bush's presidential campaign was just gathering steam, and Jeb had no wish to get mired in an environmental controversy that might tar his brother as well.

But Frank never liked that meat trade idea anyway and sees limited commercial potential in the gulf sturgeon. Unlike California, however, Florida allows the importation and culture of exotic species, and Frank believes these to be the key to a local farmed sturgeon industry.

We left the tanks of gulf larvae and negotiated our way through knots and parapets of pipes, hoses, vase-like incubator jars, and larger fish tanks. The lime-scented whiff of water direct from the Florida aquifer moistened the air, as did, somehow, the heartbeat gurgle of its motion. We stopped at a fiberglass tank about 6 feet across, its water clouded green with algae and diatoms. Shapes the length and form of carving knives arced near the surface and dissolved.

"These are short-nosed sturgeons," Frank said. "There are fish of different ages in here, but most of 'em, the smallest ones, are about eight weeks old. Rick, do you want to hold one?"

Chulhong caught one of the juveniles with a net and placed it in my hands. It was about 18 inches long, its head much shorter in proportion to its body than other sturgeons'. The pewter-gray skin, lightening to olive along the flanks, was dry and gritty, with no scales or slime to it, as was the pearly belly. The fish was as easy to handle as a billy club. Its tooth-like scutes—two rows on either side of the belly, two on the upper flanks, and one down the spine—were white and sharp and serrated. In cross section the fish would become ovoid, and then round, as it grew, but now it was crisply pentagonal. It seemed like a fish that had been designed—after a lot of work with focus groups—for both distinctive styling and ease of handling. The sturgeon twisted twice in my hands, strenuously, and then lay still.

These short-nosed sturgeons are much smaller at maturity than gulfs or Atlantics, topping out at 4 to 5 feet, 50 to 60 pounds. They are also just as native to Florida, actually, once sharing river systems with the Atlantic sturgeon the whole length of the eastern seaboard. Today, wild short-noses in Florida may be found, perhaps, only in the St. John's River in the northeast part of the state. Fishermen during the caviar boom preferred the bigger Atlantic sturgeon but would take the short-nosed variety when it turned up in their nets, often believing it to be the juvenile form of the Atlantic. In 1973, nothing was known of its numbers, either historically or currently, and as a precaution the species was listed immediately under the ESA.

With help from UC-Davis scientists, short-nosed sturgeons were first artificially spawned in South Carolina in 1985. The mature fish in one of the tanks here were products of that spawning. "But officially they're dead," Frank said. "On paper they don't exist."

The ESA criminalizes trade or commerce in any animal on its list. Therefore, if they can't go into the rivers, the imminent fate of all hatchery-reared gulf or short-nosed sturgeons is either death or limbo. But Frank believes that there may be no better candidate in the world for commercial aquaculture than the short-nosed.

"This is a fish that matures in only five years, and so can produce caviar quicker than any other species," he explained. "With the right diet and water temperature, they will spawn twice a year. You can probably harvest short-noses for meat in only eighteen months. And because its head is shorter, you could get a higher percentage of meat from each fish. I have proposed that we de-list one population of short-nosed sturgeon—this population—for purposes of commercial aquaculture. Just one population. They did it for alligator and bison. With this fish we could kick butt, man, we could *bury* the white sturgeon. But they're not doing that for this so far. What a surprise."

Stonewalled on both native species, Frank reserves his most serious work in commercial aquaculture for the exotics. We went from under the roof to an array of larger tanks outside, 30 to 50 feet across and covered with chicken wire to contain any leaping. We stopped at the edge of the largest tank, where dark shapes swimming in circles beneath the surface were more or less the length of canoe paddles, though a couple looked on their way to becoming canoes. Most of the fish swam clockwise, their scutes flashing like chain links as they broke the surface. Occasionally one or two or three bucked the trend. One such effort led to a collision, and then a reverberating thump that we felt against our thighs as a startled fish smacked snout-first, like a pile-driver, into the side of the tank.

All but two of these fish, Frank said, were Russian sturgeons, *Acipenser gueldenstaedtii*, one of the three great caviar-producing species of the Caspian. They mature in the wild at fifteen to twenty years, reaching 6 feet and a sleek 130 pounds, though these juveniles were only half that size. The Russians were now the species of choice of three private aquaculture operations in the state—operations to which Frank provided consulting and cheerleading. "This is the real black caviar," he said. "This is the fish that produces the osetra caviar. They're saying in California now that their white sturgeon caviar is as good as osetra. Okay, that's great, but our caviar *is* osetra—or will be."

The two biggest fish in the tank were the most jealously guarded of the Caspian sturgeons: *Huso huso*, the great beluga, near the top of the World Wildlife Federation's list of the world's most endangered animals. Two of only four to be found anywhere in the United States (a third beluga is at the Tennessee Aquarium, a fourth at Chicago's Shedd Aquarium), these were juveniles themselves, six years old, but already close to 6 feet long. They moved like dreadnoughts among the slim, gray-streaked Russians: blacker, bulkier, more deliberate in their circuits about the tank.

"I don't know their sexes yet," Frank said. "If they're both females, and if Tennessee has a male, let's say, then we don't need any more." He smiled, his hands on the chicken wire as though holding it down, preventing a jailbreak. "I'm now in an aggressive conservation mode."

"Aquaculture is the best way to save sturgeon," Chulhong asserted. "People are going to have to acknowledge that."

"People are the weak point," Frank observed. "We're all saving the sturgeon to extinction. Look at the Caspian. We promoted democracy there, so in a way we're responsible for what's happening. But those stocks are all collapsed." He paused, then spoke more slowly: "And the sturgeon is doomed in this country, too, at least in the wild. Aquaculture is our only hope. I might be wrong—you never can tell what'll happen when money gets involved. But aquaculture might divert pressure from the wild populations, and I think it would reduce poaching, too. Anyway, what's certain is this: that what we do today will be reflected 100 years from now for all to see. We'd better do it right."

Behind us a great blue heron stalked the ponds, and overhead a turkey vulture rode a thermal and looked lengthily down on this oasis. Outside this tank, with its refrigerated water, there was no thermal refuge here for these fish from central Asia. Nonetheless, we gazed at the young belugas as though at the Adam and Eve of a new North American race of *Huso huso*.

Someone called Frank's name. He turned to see more visitors, a bearded man and two women, standing around the tanks where the gulf larvae wriggled and swarmed. He waved and smiled as he went to them, calling out, "Careful—you're within 500 feet of an endangered species. You're already in violation of federal law."

vi.

Midnight at Dead Boy Eddy. The four of us were in the motor skiff, in oilskins and headlamps, working our way, from float to float, down the length of a slack net. The tide was in, and the river breathed off a saltier scent. Jamie had a flashlight. When he swept it in the direction of the riverbank, downstream from the net, a pair of violet-red eyes stared back at us. "'Gator," said Jamie. "That one's about 2, 3 feet. We've seen 12-footers out here."

Daryl was surprised that we hadn't had a strike all afternoon or evening, but that was in keeping with the twilight feel of this whole enterprise, the suspicion in the minds of both Daryl and Jamie that this particular ride was coming to an end. When the state of Florida banned sturgeon fishing in 1984, it allowed its own wildlife agency to issue permits "to collect and possess sturgeon for experimental, scientific, and/or educational purposes." Frank had such a permit for the university's fieldwork on the river this spring, and also for the possession of some of his short-nosed sturgeons.

But the permits are good for only a year, and in recent years they have been reissued over the complaints of USF&W. This year Ken Sulak advised the Florida legislature that even though Frank's fish were returned live to the river, the aftereffects of the c-section could be fatal, and the eggs themselves couldn't be spared. In a letter to the Florida legislature dated February 23, 2000, he wrote that any commercial interest in gulf sturgeon would lead irresistibly to "the annual mining of the wild population for the needed broodstock."

At this point the whole dispute assumes a through-the-looking-glass character: The biologist who says the fish are on the verge of extinction maintains they can safely spare some eggs, while the one who says they're reasonably safe insists that they can't. In either event, Daryl and Jamie believed that this year's permit would likely be the last.

We saw only that alligator at midnight. When we rose for the 2 A.M. check, Daryl staggered as he worked his feet into his waders, then struggled to get their bulk up to his hips and the straps over his shoulders. Jamie tripped over the hydrophone, gave Rory a shake, and said, "This is when it gets harder to figure out why this is so much fun."

The cool evening had become a raw, clammy night. Jamie had rigged an electric lamp that hung from a mast stepped into the middle of the skiff, just in front of a holding tank that could be flooded with river water. A halo of yellow light, like Tinkerbelle on steroids, skimmed with us over the river as we moved away from the houseboat. Before we reached the net, we heard another motor running in counterpoint to ours, this one coming from upriver. Jamie killed our motor and told Rory to switch off the lamp on the mast. "That could be a legitimate fisherman," he said. "They'll come out here and gig all night for flounder or mullet. But we'll let him go by, whoever he is."

We drifted for a moment, the skiff swinging sideways to the mild current. The other boat had no lights either and was just a sound on the other side of the river. Before that had quite faded, Jamie started our motor again and we veered around the net's last float. He flicked the motor off once more. The skiff glided silently into the floats near the riverbank.

Our halo was on again, and the floats were pale and ghostly. The net dropped beneath them in spidery green tendrils trailing into tea-colored water. The stars had clouded over. The river beyond our light was cloaked in darkness. Daryl stretched headfirst over the squared-off bow and began pulling the boat up the length of the floats. He said he felt some tension in the line: "Could be we've got something this time."

Daryl hauled us 100 feet up the net, and then he found the fish. He called Rory, who stretched out beside him on the bow. Daryl had the sturgeon by the gill plate, and Rory got an arm around its midriff. Grunting, they drew it partly out of the water, then bent it over the gunwale in a tangle of netting and floats and slick reptilian skin. Once the scimitar tail arced out of the river and followed the rest of the beast into the bottom of the skiff, Rory sat back and stared.

A little less than 5 feet, and only a little more than 40 pounds, this one was small for what Daryl and Jamie had been pulling in. The scutes along its lower flank ran like hard pink blushes, like calcified hickeys, along the whiteness of its belly. The upper rows were strings of diamonds die-cut in pewter, darker than the aluminum tones of its dorsal skin. The fish lay placidly on its side, its left eye staring, its gills flaring, its mouth a gasping scroll-saw slash beneath its snout. Rory agreed with Linnaeus: "The thing looks just like a shark."

Daryl worked the last of the net free of its tail, and only then did the fish give a wrench that shook the skiff. Then it lay still again, resuming that calmness so striking to those meeting a sturgeon for the first time. A reporter for an 1892 edition of *Cosmopolitan,* writing when the slaughter was on in the Delaware and the Chesapeake, was unfavorably impressed. "And herein lies the degeneracy of the sturgeon, the hero descended," C.W. Coleman remarked. "With all its plated armor, all its gorgeous war paints, it possesses but a craven spirit, surrendering almost instantly in the toils of the net and offering little other opposition than its dead weight to the will of its captors."

Some captors would dispute that: those who were towed in their tubs by raging sturgeons on the Apalachicola in the 1960s, for example, or exhausted tackle fishermen today on the Columbia. But under certain circumstances—tangled in a net, trapped in shallow water, suspended in the air in somebody's arms—a sturgeon of whatever size displays not panic, not rage, but a sort of Gandhian forbearance that might be interpreted several ways: cravenness, resignation, pokiness, an out-of-body transcendence of alien abduction, or a simple faith that this, too, like meteor impacts and climate shifts, would pass. Biologists, including Frank, don't really understand this behavior. They sometimes speculatively relate it to the opossum's trance. Yet playing possum wouldn't seem to help young sturgeons escape capture by the animals around Florida that prey on them: barred owls, osprey, flathead catfish, alligator gar, alligator, possibly bull shark.

Archie Carr, for one, was enchanted. He took it for proof that a sturgeon is a peace-loving and agreeable animal. "No fish is so calm when brought into a boat," he wrote in *A Naturalist in Florida.* "If the sturgeon had the temperament of some other fish, our tagging project would have yielded less information and more injuries to personnel. Even a big bull sturgeon, with a hatchet-edged caudal peduncle more lethal-looking than a crocodile's tail, rarely thrashes about when brought into a boat but waits quietly and rolls his eyes. Sturgeon even remain calm when a dog licks them."

Carr had a research assistant who liked to bring his German shepherd whenever they were tagging fish, and if a sturgeon was pulled into the boat, the dog would regularly lick it "from head to toe, as it were." "This can't be reassuring to the sturgeon," Carr said, "but they never seem irritated; they only roll their eyes some more."

The day before, while cradling that juvenile short-nose plucked from Frank's tank, I couldn't help but be enchanted myself. Whether from patience or trust or more likely something different, the little fish with its nubbin barbels twitched and then seemed to settle into my hands the way a kitten might. After a long, serene moment, I laid it back in the water. It flicked its tail once and dove, the hero descending, this time into the dark to resume its benthic cruising.

Daryl lifted the captured gulf sturgeon like a railroad tie onto the deck of the houseboat. There it was placed in a tank of water laced with Tricaine, a mild anesthetic. Once its respiration had slowed, the fish was weighed and then turned belly up on a stretcher ranged between two sawhorses. It was measured, tagged, logged. Its stomach contents confirmed that sturgeons feed very little while in the Suwannee: a few worm casings, shell fragments, and a smattering of shrimp-like organisms, all saved in a plastic bag.

Finally Jamie donned a pair of sterile latex gloves and used a scalpel to cut a nearly bloodless two-inch incision in the belly just above the anus. He peeled back the skin and lining of the body cavity to reveal a pinkish-vanilla length of tissue, the surface of a ripe testis. "It's a male," Jamie said as Daryl wrote in the log. "Pretty well-developed, beginning to hydrate—I'd say stage three or four." In other words, this was a young but mature fish, ready to get lucky this year.

A glass-coated radio chip about the size of a grain of rice was inserted into the incision. This was the pinger that would communicate with Daryl's hydrophone. The fish seemed to awaken at this and gave a thrash that rattled the sawhorses. Jamie laid a hand on the incision, waited for the gills to slow again, and then began to sew the cut together with a needle and absorbable thread. He used a cruciate pattern of sutures, stitching three x's across the cut. Daryl urged one more suture. Jamie said, "This is the point where an *artiste* is always criticized."

At last he attached an electronic temperature logger, a device about the size of a button, to the base of the dorsal fin. Dabs of antiseptic ointment were applied to both wounds, and Jamie hosed the fish's gills clean of anesthetic. The fish was returned to the skiff and placed again in its smaller tank of river water.

The sturgeon had been out of the river a little less than twenty minutes. But there was no sure measure for the stress endured by the young male, or the danger of infection from the surgeries. Instead of going right back into the river, this fish would be brought to East Pass, to that cottage on the dock with the two fiberglass tanks beneath it. The sturgeon would be held there for two or three days to make sure that the wounds stayed clean and that his behavior was normal. Then he could resume his journey to the spawning grounds upriver.

Daryl stayed on the houseboat to complete the log and put equipment away. Jamie pointed the skiff downriver, with Rory and me aboard to help prepare the tank at East Pass. The stars were still blanketed over and the air smelled like rain. Rory confessed his amazement that he had grown up in Florida and never guessed that creatures like this were still swimming its rivers, or a few of them anyway.

I sat sleepily on a thwart in front of the tank with a song running through my head, one that starts on a trisyllable, stressed on the first syllable, that fits the meter of something the songwriter Dwight Fiske once wrote:

> *Caviar comes from the virgin sturgeon,*
> *Virgin sturgeon is one fine fish.*
> *Virgin sturgeon needs no urgin',*
> *That's why caviar is my dish.*

2

The World Is Not Enough

i.

Valley Stream is a town just outside Queens on the south side of Long Island. On the Sunrise Highway, Route 27, a glassy six-story office building rises from the street-level clutter of pizzerias, liquor stores, pawn shops, pharmacies, furniture discounters, credit agencies, and adult book and video stores.

The upper floors of the building are occupied by a health clinic and the New York headquarters of McDonald's, the lower by parking spaces. At the fourth floor, an elevator opens onto the offices of the U.S. Fish and Wildlife Service, a sort of Noah's Ark in reverse. Corridors and conference rooms decorated with the trophies of previous busts—a stuffed hyena nearly the size of a pony, a clamshell as big as a washbasin, an antelope head with impossibly tall horns, et cetera—lead eventually to that repository of evidence known as the Examination Room. There, several tall cabinets are crammed with dozens of raw furs suspended from shower-curtain rings: snow leopard, zebra, river otter, timber wolf, harp seal, and most everything in between. The furs, and also a few finished coats, hang in tawny, spotted, ragged-edged splendor, all stunningly anomalous in the plain gray cabinets. On a table in the middle of the room is spread the entire skin, complete with bottlebrush mane, of a rare Hartman's mountain zebra. The fur is dense and stiff, longer than a horse's, its stripes an op-art masterpiece. A door at the rear leads to a stand-up refrigerator, its racks piled with tins, jars, and 1-kilo containers of contraband caviar.

Special Agent Ed Grace told me that in recent years trade in endangered wildlife had gotten to be like the drug trade: similar methods and almost as much money. Elephant leg footstools and crocodile briefcases are—in the words of Marc Reisner, writing in *Game Wars: The Undercover Pursuit of Wildlife Poachers* (1991)—"the accoutrements of a wealthy and acquisitive urban society when it runs out of other things to have." When these accoutrements in turn begin to run out, they become objects of conspicuous consumption, that essential phrase coined in 1899 by Thorstein Veblen in *The Theory of the Leisure Class*. They become, that is, indulgences that trumpet wealth, acquisitiveness, and power precisely because of their exorbitant costs and their irrelevance to any concept of necessity. Waste is a sacramental virtue in this sort of consumption, and for certain iconic forms of wildlife the result is another sort of vortex of extinction, ramping up desire to whole new levels as the fur or the horn or the egg become ever more costly to obtain. What hope in this world, then, for the snow leopard, the black rhinoceros, and now the sturgeon?

In and around New York City, that would be Special Agent Grace and his few colleagues. Wearing a green tweed sport jacket, a blue button-down shirt, and a pair of blue jeans with a set of handcuffs dangling out of a back pocket, Ed Grace had a Davy-Crockett-as-played-by-Fess-Parker look to him: a 6-foot frame and straight black hair, a Midwestern drawl and probing brown eyes, a lawman's cool and laconic manner, a dash of frontier twinkle.

Grace grew up in Illinois but enjoyed his summers and falls in rural Iowa, where his grandfather took him fishing and duck hunting. He went to graduate school in fish and wildlife biology at the University of Illinois, and then went into wildlife law enforcement, taking a job with the State of Florida. He was posted to Reddick, a town 25 miles south of Gainesville. During the same time that Frank Chapman was beginning his ill-fated collaboration with federal scientists, Grace had begun hauling in alligator poachers.

He joined USF&W in 1996 and was posted to New York. In Florida he had spent most of his time outside, nosing around the woods, swamps, and rivers. Here in Valley Stream he divided his time largely between his office, the federal district courthouse in Brooklyn, and the nearby John F. Kennedy International Airport. He had worked on a variety of wildlife cases, making busts that involved Timorese pythons, smoked bats, bald eagle skulls, black bear gall bladders, and loot from Native American burial grounds.

Lately, tons of smuggled caviar coming through JFK had made him a near specialist in that area. Grace estimated that at least 70 percent of the U.S. trade in caviar was illegal. The walls of his small, windowless office were plastered with references—a list of airlines most popular with caviar smugglers (Aeroflot, Delta, Uzbekistan, LOT, Finn, Lufthansa, Sabena), photos of known couriers to be searched every time they traveled (all the names chunky and Slavic), and assorted memorabilia: magazine articles on USF&W successes; empty 500-gram tins of "Zukovsky Caviar," a fictitious brand stamped on the lids for *The World Is Not Enough*, a 1999 James Bond film; and a poster-sized photo of a burly, middle-aged man with close-cropped hair and a goatee.

The man in the photo, Eugeniusz Koczuk, a.k.a. Gino, was holding a briefcase up in a vain attempt to conceal his face. The photo had been taken at Koczuk's indictment after an investigation led by Grace. He would eventually be proven to be the most prolific caviar smuggler in U.S. history.

ii.

In January 1998, USF&W hosted a public meeting at St. John's University to describe new rules and procedures for importing caviar into the United States. Around fifty people came, and the sign-in sheet for that day reads like a *Who's Who* for the caviar business on this side of the Atlantic: Eve Vega, director of American operations for Petrossian Paris, the French company that dominated the U.S. retail market; Arkady Panchernikov of Caspian Star, which controlled the markets for the American airline and cruise ship industries, and which also supplied such storied restaurants as the Russian Tea Room, Le Cirque, and Panchernikov's own Caviar Russe; Arnold Hansen-Sturm, a descendant of the young scions dispatched to America in the previous century by the German firm Dieckmann & Hansen, and proprietor of Hansen

Caviar; Eric Sobol of Caviarteria, a company with bustling caviar bars in New York, Miami, and Las Vegas; Ann and Saul Zabar, father and daughter, of Zabar's, the Manhattan gourmet super-delicatessen; Alfred Yazbak of Connoisseur Brands, a general importer and retailer; and— among several other big players—Eugeniusz Koczuk of Gino International, since 1996 the biggest and most aggressive wholesaler in the U.S. market.

The meeting was necessary because of strict new regulations governing international trade in caviar. In 1975, the United States had been one of the original parties to a landmark conservation law: the Convention on International Trade in Endangered Species of Wild Fauna and Flora (CITES). The law defines the legal commercial status of various plants and animals, or their products, on the basis of three lists. Appendix I lists any species threatened with imminent extinction—for example, all the great apes, many big cats, various kinds of crocodiles, birds of prey, cacti, orchids, and so on—and bans all international trade in that species. Appendix II includes species that could become threatened with extinction if trade is not controlled. Commerce in these species requires proof that the specimen was legally acquired, and also an export permit. Appendix III lists species subject to regulation in their countries of origin, requiring only that member countries cooperate in controlling cross-border trade. Currently 146 countries are parties to CITES, and to various degrees the treaty protects some 30,000 species of plants and animals.

From a sturgeon's point of view, however, the lists are a bit eccentric. In 1998, there were two species of sturgeon listed in Appendix I: European sturgeon, fished out of its original range 150 years ago, and short-nosed sturgeon, which in 1973 was the only sturgeon listed under the U.S. Endangered Species Act. But a species rarer than the short-nosed and also now listed under the ESA—Florida's gulf sturgeon—is only listed in Appendix II. The same is true for the even rarer Alabama sturgeon.

It has only been since 1997, following a CITES conference in Zimbabwe, that any sturgeons have been in Appendix II. By then it had been six years since the breakup of the Soviet Union. Since the failure of the U.S. caviar industry a century ago, the Caspian Sea had become the source of more than 90 percent of the world's gourmet caviar. But in the post-Soviet era, the once tightly managed Caspian had become a caldron of crime, corruption, and unregulated sturgeon harvests. New exporters, importers, wholesalers, and retailers of caviar sprang up like fly-by-night used car dealers, and often their goods were just as dubious.

Alarmed by rapid declines in the numbers of the three major sturgeon species of the Caspian, and three other species also native to the sea, the United States and Germany cosponsored a proposal in Zimbabwe to place all six species in Appendix II. Some scientists and environmentalists at the conference urged Appendix I instead, an action that would have put an immediate end to legal international trade in Caspian caviar, but they were beaten back by the Caspian range countries and caviar industry interests.

Also alarming was evidence of burgeoning fraud in the marketplace. In 1996, two molecular geneticists from New York's American Museum of Natural History (AMNH)—Vadim Birstein and Rob DeSalle—had developed a test that could identify a caviar sample's species of origin. They performed a survey of New York retailers and found that nearly a third of the retailers' goods contained eggs different from the species claimed on the label. Some of the substituted species were of U.S. origin, which prompted the United States to successfully lobby for all sturgeon species (excepting the two already in Appendix I) being placed in Appendix II.

That meant a wholesale change in how business was done, which was what that St. John's meeting was about. Starting April 1, 1998, the feds warned, all caviar entering the United States would have to arrive with a CITES export permit from its country of origin or its country of re-export. The permit would certify that the eggs were of the appropriate species and that they had been obtained from legally harvested sturgeons. An exception would be made for caviar for personal use, but only up to 250 grams. The permits, meanwhile, would allow CITES to keep track of exports and enforce harvest quotas in the Caspian.

Between 1996 and 1998, no one had imported more caviar into the United States than Gino International: better than 11 tons, with a little more than half arriving in the first three months of 1998. In the seven months following April 1, however, the firm declared to U.S. Customs only 88 pounds, one shipment, of CITES-authorized caviar.

Grace said that he, or somebody else, should have noticed that. But USF&W's bare-bones level of staffing—only three special agents and eight inspectors for all of New York City—combined with the frenzy of implementing the new process, not to mention the routine flood of turtle oil and macaw feathers and cayman shoes into the city, some 20,000 wildlife-related shipments each year, effectively ensured that nobody had time to notice the apparent disappearance of Gino International.

iii.

One day in February 2001, I went with Grace and two uniformed USF&W inspectors—Rob Rothe and Roland Marquis—to Kennedy airport for an afternoon of routine inspections. After six years in New York, Grace had just been transferred to another duty station and would soon be packing up. "Ed's going over to JFK for one last look," suggested Rob on the ride from Valley Stream.

"Well, he's not going to see any caviar in Chicago," Roland said.

But Grace was ready for a change. He parked the Crown Victoria in a tunnel outside the Aeroflot baggage claim area. Then he took a deep breath of fuel-laden air as we left the car. "Love that air quality," he said. "Most Fish and Wildlife officers hunt poachers in places like Montana, you know."

"How many people do you want to sample here?" Rob asked. "Fifty percent?"

Grace said, "Less than that, but sample anybody who declares they have caviar."

Inside there was nothing but wide open spaces. We learned that the day's Aeroflot flight from Moscow had been delayed an hour. The area was empty except for a woman in the blue and white uniform of U.S. Customs. Low fluorescent lights threw a pale, milky sheen across the tile floor, the velvet ropes, the motionless aluminum baggage carts.

"What's on the Russian flight?" the customs inspector asked.

"Bound to be some caviar," Grace replied.

She smiled. "It must be inexpensive over there. I'd like to go to Russia someday just to eat caviar all the time."

Grace observed that it's not as cheap here as it used to be. He gazed down the terminal and told me that since CITES had gone into effect, the retail price on beluga caviar had doubled, from $50 an ounce to $100. But the system hadn't been foolproof. CITES permits could be counterfeited, some more easily than others, especially those from popular reexport points: Poland, Lithuania, Turkey, the United Arab Emirates. And a lot of caviar and other stuff was just smuggled in without permits. Grace said the wildlife market is directly proportional to the economy, that when the economy is hot, as it was then, the wildlife market heats up too. He himself was astonished by all the caviar he saw coming in now: "But hardly any beluga all of a sudden. They must be cracking down on that. Still, I don't give the beluga much chance of surviving."

The Aeroflot passengers, when they came in, did so in couples and small groups as the aluminum plates of the baggage carousel groaned and began to rotate. They talked and laughed quietly among themselves, carrying shopping bags that read "Moscow Duty Free," or else were printed in trellis-like Cyrillic figures.

"There's the beagle brigade." Grace pointed to a white-haired U.S. Department of Agriculture inspector walking a beagle on a leash. The dog paused variously at shopping bags, carry-on bags, and pant legs as it moved through the crowd. The dog approached an old woman with a shopping bag, and when the agent happened to touch her shoulder she leaped back, startled. "They're looking for fruits and vegetables," Grace said. "We need one of those for caviar."

By the time bags started coming down the carousel, there were about 150 people in the claim area. "You see why so many drugs come through here too. There's just so many people, and so little manpower to deal with them all."

Grace moved to an aluminum table next to the Customs booth as certain passengers and their baggage were intercepted. The first was a thirty-something American in a black leather jacket and already graying hair. He had declared no caviar but had been tabbed on a random basis. He said he made his living in metals commodities. Grace opened his bag, sifted through the shirts and sweaters and underwear, found nothing, and sent him through.

Also sent through was a petite Russian woman, a teacher, who said she had come here to help with some family problems. She had declared some caviar, and Grace found it: two 50-gram jars of red caviar, made from salmon roe instead of sturgeon. A few passengers later, a young Russian woman with olive skin, orange lips, tinted hair, and hoop earrings was found with two larger jars of undeclared red caviar. She was provided the opportunity to declare it. "Thank you very much," she said.

A middle-aged man in an ankle-length black wool coat, wearing a black T-shirt and blue jeans underneath, was also stopped on a random basis. He said he was an oil trader. His Russian was translated by his companion, a stunning young blonde in a jacket of lipstick red and slacks of cobalt blue. I thought she might be a stewardess, but Grace identified her later as an escort. When he opened the man's suitcase, a strong odor spilled out, a scent not of fish so much as of the sea and sky and driftwood.

Grace found a royal blue 500-gram tin of caviar labeled "Astrakhan Sevruga" wedged into one corner of the bag. That was a little more than a pound, twice as much as was allowed for personal consumption. "Sevruga" meant eggs of the stellate sturgeon, *Acipenser stellatus,* the smallest of the Caspian's caviar-producing species. The tin was barely held together by masking tape and had been crimped on one side. A clear oil and several dozen stray eggs oozed from beneath the lid. Grace opened the tin. Sevruga is usually black, but this tin revealed a goopy mass of cinnamon-gray globes, each more a grain than a globe, some of them elongated or collapsed. With the tin open, that marvelous sea-scent took on a faintly bitter, yeasty tone.

"It's spoiled," Grace said, and then called Rob to his side. "What kind is this? Is it sevruga?"

Rob peered at it through his wire-rimmed glasses. "It's sevruga."

"I've never seen it so light."

"It's been gray lately."

"The only way you can tell with absolute certainty is with DNA analysis," Roland said to me. "But Rob is right about 95 percent of the time."

Grace began working on the paperwork for government-seized property. The oil trader spoke to his companion, who asked, "Can he pay more money?"

"No," said Grace. "Bringing this much caviar into the country is a violation of U.S. law. But it's not so much that he'll pay a fine, or have a record. It's just being confiscated."

The girl looked at the open tin on the table and laughed. "Let's just try it. It's supposed to be delicious."

Grace gave the girl a withering look. The oil trader looked ruefully at the girl and then smiled at Grace, shrugging his shoulders. He said in English, "No hassle."

The suitcase was closed and the couple moved on. Grace struggled to reattach the tin's bent lid. A number of eggs spilled out the side. "I'm messing up your sevruga," he told Rob. "Well, we're just gonna destroy it anyway."

Dozens more passengers were searched, but there were no more seizures. The beagle brigade found nothing amiss. When the area was finally empty again, Grace pointed through doors that opened into a lobby leading to ground transportation. "Right out through there is where we made the Koczuk bust."

The customs agent got off the telephone and told Grace that they were "dumping the crew," meaning they were about to search or x-ray the baggage of the flight's crew members. "Good," said Grace. "Especially with Aeroflot."

Roland appeared from the other side of the carousel with a report that five unclaimed bags remained, all identical: black canvas affairs, zippered and padlocked, four of them wrapped in clear packing tape, each weighing about 50 pounds. "Maybe they belong to somebody still being processed somewhere?" he wondered.

"See if you can get Customs to move quickly on those," Grace said. "They're the ones to authorize opening unclaimed bags."

iv.

On the morning of October 28, 1998, Grace got a phone call from a Polish-speaking U.S. Customs agent. She had just heard from a customs attaché in Germany, who in turn had heard from a Warsaw airport employee, that there were sixteen suspicious suitcases in the belly of Finn Air Flight 003, originating in Warsaw and due that afternoon at JFK.

Grace and Rob Rothe and two other agents went to the airport prior to the arrival of that flight. They had the names and seat assignments of the seven men and women, all Polish nationals, who had checked those sixteen bags. They waited in Customs' secondary examination area as each of the seven claimed baggage and was brought in to be searched. Each of the bags was found to contain nothing but tins of undeclared and unrefrigerated caviar, wrapped in plastic bags or stacked in greasy cardboard boxes. About half of it was osetra, from the Russian sturgeon, and the other half beluga. All told, the bags held 901 tins of caviar, adding up to about half a ton and a street value of $1.2 million.

One of the couriers was Andrzej Lepkowski, a Warsaw deputy police chief, and another was a lower-ranking Warsaw policeman. Three others were stewardesses for Poland's LOT airlines and had been recruited by Lepkowski's wife, also a LOT flight attendant. Aside from a free round-trip ticket to the United States, they were each to be paid $500 for delivering their suitcases, which had been given to them, already packed, at the Warsaw airport.

With the couriers in hand, Grace went angling for their employer. He sent Lepkowski and two others out to the lobby with their suitcases. A woman and a man approached them, asking where the others were. Some conversation ensued, and as soon as the couriers accompanying Lepkowski were given envelopes of cash, Grace pounced, arresting Helena Koczuk, Gino's wife, and Wieslaw Rozbicki, Gino International's marketing director.

Rozbicki and Lepkowski both admitted to having done this several times before, but Rozbicki claimed that he understood the caviar to have CITES permits. Mrs. Koczuk said that her husband was in Poland, and that she had come here to conduct ordinary business at his behest. Grace let the six subordinate couriers go and took Lepkowski, Rozbicki, and Mrs. Koczuk to the Brooklyn Federal Courthouse for arraignment. The latter two posted bail, and Mrs. Koczuk went home to Connecticut to contact her husband.

It took Grace four days to obtain a search warrant for the Koczuks' home. Meanwhile, Gino Koczuk faxed a set of CITES permits from Poland to Kenneth Blum of Meridien Shipping, the company that had acted as a customs broker for Gino International's legal shipments prior to April that year. Koczuk asked Blum to intercede for his wife and Rozbicki, who had been arrested, he said, because they did not have these permits. He wrote that he would arrive the next day with the originals, suggesting, "Let's say it was Polish company mistake that the docs were not faxed to you."

Koczuk flew into New York the next day, but apparently he did not expect his home to be searched. Only Mrs. Koczuk was present when, on November 3, Grace and nine other state and federal agents knocked on the door of the modest ranch-style home in a Stamford suburb. They confiscated bank books, shipping records, caviar price lists, business cards, a Rolodex, boarding passes, taxi receipts, ledgers, a briefcase, and a computer. In the attached garage they found three refrigerators, their shelves crammed to bursting with 834 tins of caviar, 101 jars, and 10 cans of Budweiser beer. The caviar added up to another half ton.

Koczuk arrived during the course of the search in a blue old-model Mercedes driven by Rozbicki. He protested that there had simply been a mix-up in the paperwork and that his attorney, Walter Drobenko, had the necessary permits. He made a call to Drobenko, and then he and his wife sat calmly at their kitchen table while Grace and his agents walked out the door with everything but the beer. Not realizing that one of the Connecticut officers spoke Polish, the Koczuks made several incriminating statements during the course of the search. But the documents were proof enough. "When you run your own business," Grace told me, "I think sometimes you don't realize the full range of information you have stuffed into files and drawers." A search of Koczuk's Mercedes also yielded several books of receipts for sales of caviar.

When Grace saw Koczuk's CITES permits, he was unimpressed. The papers had not been validated by Polish authorities, and they pertained to a brand of Russian caviar not represented in that shipment. In fact, the same permits had been used a month earlier in sales of smuggled caviar to Urbani Truffles and Zabar's. Meanwhile, Koczuk and Rozbicki revisited an earlier gambit: They went to Meridien Shipping to persuade Blum to falsely inform USF&W that he had been expecting a legal shipment of declared caviar on the 28th. When Blum refused, Koczuk retrieved the fax he had sent him from Poland, unaware that a copy of the fax had been seized at his home.

At the same time Grace was learning that the 2,000 pounds of confiscated caviar represented just a spoonful of Koczuk's activity since April. His business records—with some invoices marked "sour"—indicated sales during that time of 19,000 pounds of undeclared caviar, worth more than $12.3 million, and much of it was sold to the same clients to whom he had sold legal caviar, among them Zabar's, Caviarteria, and Caspian Star. Most or all of it had arrived in the same way as the caviar Grace had just seized. Airport parking records and EZ-Pass highway tolls showed that although cars belonging to Koczuk had visited JFK only six times before April 1, they went back and forth thirty-six times in succeeding months.

Grace now believes that the Warsaw airport employee who provided the tip was someone disappointed not to have a stake in the action. Otherwise, as amateurish as it was, the operation could have gone on much longer. "Koczuk wasn't very sophisticated as a smuggler, but he was a shrewd businessman, very powerful, with a lot of pull in Poland," Grace said. "He was dealing in stuff that was smuggled out of Russia and walked past Polish Customs by Polish police officers. Then flight attendants got it onto planes to the United States. In fact, he went on smuggling even after he was arrested."

Koczuk's indictment in December 1998 was little noted in the newspapers, but it rocked the domestic caviar industry. And it attracted the attention of JFK's nephew, Robert F. Kennedy, Jr., senior attorney for both the National Resources Defense Council and Riverkeeper, the environmental organization that spearheaded the cleanup of the Hudson River in the 1970s. Kennedy was concerned that the Hudson's rare Atlantic sturgeon might already be a target again for poachers. He wrote in a petition to U.S. District Court Judge Frederic C. Block, who presided over the Gino Koczuk trial in the spring of 2000, that a tough sentence "will send a clear message to the caviar industry that laws designed to protect these extraordinary fishes will be strongly enforced and that such practices will no longer be tolerated."

Cynthia Monaco, assistant U.S. attorney for the Eastern District of New York, was also eager to make an example of Koczuk. Meanwhile, Grace was learning more and more from Koczuk's meticulous records about what else was going on in some of the darker corners of the caviar industry.

And Koczuk wanted his accounts settled. That winter, Walter Drobenko filed a complaint in Queens Supreme Court for $59,000 owed on a shipment of caviar delivered to Zabar's, a payment that was withheld after Koczuk's indictment. "The idea that you could sue a company for product that the government says is contraband is chutzpah," huffed William Wachtel, Zabar's attorney.

v.

Ed Grace believes in what he's doing, believes in CITES, believes in history, and believes in humanity's capacity to submit to the same temptations, make the same mistakes, commit the same crimes, over and over. "People wonder—well, Americans wonder—why they should worry about species of fish over in the Caspian Sea," he told me at the airport. "But with caviar, history is playing itself out again. We fished our own species of sturgeon to extinction, or near to it. Then Jay Gatsby came along to make caviar fashionable again. Now, when the Russian species are gone, the American ones will get hit all over again. It's happening already. We already see more and more caviar from domestic species showing up illegally in the marketplace."

In fact, that very thing was known to have happened in one high-volume instance as early as 1985. The story of Arnold Hansen-Sturm demonstrates the serendipity crucial to much wildlife law enforcement—the phoned-in tip, the unguarded CB radio announcement, or just a planetary alignment of unrelated events. If it wasn't for a little good luck, in other words, Grace and his friends might have no luck at all.

Arnold Hansen-Sturm is a fifth-generation descendant of Ferdinand Hansen, who was sent to America in 1886 to run Dieckmann & Hansen's New York office, and who appeared in 1904 before the state legislatures in New Jersey, Delaware, and Pennsylvania to argue in vain for a closed season on sturgeon. Even after the season never closed and the Delaware River was exhausted, Ferdinand stayed in America, eventually founding Romanoff Caviar. He imported most of his roe from Iran, as did his successors. Finally the family built Romanoff into the company that reigned throughout Jay Gatsby's Jazz Age and the postwar years as the most prestigious caviar house in the United States.

In 1969, Arnold Hansen-Sturm, then thirty, assumed the helm at Romanoff just as both that company and its progenitor, Dieckmann & Hansen in Germany, were being bought up by a Texas agribusiness concern. By the 1980s Romanoff was in bad shape. The company's ownership had changed several more times, its pipeline to the Caspian had been cut off by the U.S. State Department's trade embargo with Iran, and it had lost control of the U.S. market for premium caviar to Petrossian. Romanoff's ownership decided to change direction and focus on low-priced "affordable" caviars, that is, the salted roes of salmon, capelin, whitefish, lumpfish, and so on. In Europe, these products couldn't legally be called caviar, but they could in America so long as the fish species was identified on the label.

Hansen-Sturm, however, was determined to compete at the premium level, and he quit Romanoff to start his own company, Hansen Caviar. That was an uphill battle, since Petrossian had an arrangement with the Soviet government for the exclusive distribution of Russian caviar in North America. But somehow Hansen-Sturm prospered, landing lucrative accounts with the Waldorf-Astoria and the Rainbow Room in New York, and also United Airlines and Holland America Cruise Lines. Soon the man whose silver BMW sported license plates reading "BELUGA" became the most recognizable face in the industry, earning flattering profiles in *People Magazine* and *Playboy*. A good portion of his expensive caviar, however, wasn't really from the Caspian.

In 1990, a certain kind of luck intervened in the form of a bank robbery in Dollars Corner, a tiny town in southern Washington's Columbia River Valley. The thieves took cash laced with a vial of red dye that exploded as they escaped. Later, in nearby Vancouver, Washington, two men checked into a cheap motel, paid in advance for a month's stay with $900 in cash, and declined maid service. This aroused the suspicions of the motel manager. The next day, a Vancouver bank received a deposit from that motel containing cash stained with red dye. The motel manager told the FBI that only two rooms had been paid for in cash, and she had a strong feeling which one they should keep an eye on.

The FBI watched that room for several days, noting the comings and goings of two men whose ragged clothes, old pickup, and small trailered boat suggested they were fishing buddies. A bag of trash thrown into the motel Dumpster contained only one unusual item: an empty box of salt. One day the men drove to a Federal Express office in Portland, where they dropped off two packages. Without a search warrant, the agents couldn't open the packages, but they saw that both were sent to an address in Bergenfield, New Jersey.

Soon a smell emanating from the room at the motel convinced the manager that her guests were drug dealers as well as bank robbers. She let herself in one day expecting to find equipment for the manufacture of methamphetamines. Instead she found fishing gear, an outboard motor, a bucket of brine, and an unmistakable odor of fish. By then the other cash-paying tenants, the real bank robbers, had fled their own tidy room at the other end of the motel, and the disgusted FBI agents passed this room on to the National Marine Fisheries Service.

So began a two-year investigation that finally led to Arnold Hansen-Sturm, whose offices were in Bergenfield, and who may have emulated his forebears in personally teaching a Columbia River fisherman, Stephen Darnell, how to make caviar from the roe of poached white sturgeon. Between 1985 and 1990, Darnell and a friend shipped more than 3,000 pounds of caviar to New Jersey. Hansen-Sturm paid for the shipments in packets of cash mailed to various Washington post offices. Finally he packed and sold the caviar as osetra or beluga, which retailed then for $600 per pound, versus $130 per pound for white sturgeon caviar. One reason the scam worked as well as it did was that Darnell's caviar, it was generally agreed, tasted as good as the real osetra or beluga that Hansen-Sturm legitimately sold.

Hansen-Sturm was charged with obstruction of justice, lying to a grand jury, and felony violations of the Lacey Act of 1900, which makes it unlawful to traffic in protected wildlife. But these violations were reduced to misdemeanors in a pattern familiar to Grace and government prosecutors: U.S. courts tend to view wildlife violations as something of a victimless crime and are reluctant to deal out harsh penalties. Marc Reisner, whose book about the career of an undercover USF&W agent helped attract Grace to his current line of work, suspects that it goes deeper than that. He believes that Americans have an antipathy to game laws, that this nation of poor European immigrants has a bitter ancestral memory of the hunting and fishing preserves of that continent's leisure class. In America, therefore, legislatures wait too long to protect threatened wildlife, and the courts dispense slaps on the wrist.

In the end, Hansen-Sturm served eighteen months in jail, and that only because of his strenuous efforts to impede the investigation. Otherwise he would have served no jail time at all. He was also assessed $20,000 in fines, a small tax on the profit he derived from caviar that sold for nearly $1.8 million, and Hansen Caviar is still in business.

Stephen Darnell served eight months in jail and told a reporter that he was drawn into the scam by his love of fishing—and his disdain over the apparent waste that he had witnessed on the Columbia when fishermen had to throw away the eggs of legally caught sturgeon. "I saw a way to make money from garbage. I never did get rich off it," he said. "I was doing what I like to do. I like to fish."

The true cost of the five-year operation must be calculated in the waste that it wrought among the white sturgeon of the Lower Columbia, in the garbage that Darnell and Hansen-Sturm created there. Short of surgery, it's very difficult to tell a male from a female sturgeon, or often a female sturgeon with eggs from one without. Poachers, therefore, slaughter indiscriminately, cutting open every sturgeon they catch in the way that pearl divers work through oysters. Frank Chapman estimates that ten sturgeons are gutted and discarded for every one that has eggs. Federal investigators calculated that 2,000 adult sturgeons were killed to provide Hansen-Sturm his 3,000 pounds of faux Caspian caviar.

vi.

The Gino Koczuk trial was Judge Block's first case of caviar-related fraud, and he was having trouble defining who had been the victim in the affair. So far as he could tell, the victim was a fish, and the loss, if any, was "at best a loss to the Russian government of some conceptual nature," as he wrote at sentencing.

The penalty that Block finally pronounced—twenty months in jail and a $25,000 fine—was a little tougher than Hansen-Sturm's had been, but it fell far short of the guideline maximum in this instance of five years and $250,000. Cynthia Monaco was bitterly disappointed, as was, for that matter, Andrew Bowman, who had replaced Walter Drobenko as Koczuk's defense lawyer. Bowman felt that his client's special circumstances—his diabetes, his wife's depression—merited him a lighter sentence, and also that the search of his client's home had been illegal. When Bowman filed papers for an appeal, Monaco filed for a cross-appeal, anxious for another shot at a penalty that might mark out a heartland of tough sentencing standards for caviar smuggling.

Meanwhile, Grace was still sifting through Gino International's data trove. Even he was astonished by the length of Koczuk's client list. "With the exceptions of Petrossian and a couple others, it looks as though there wasn't a company in the country that wasn't receiving its caviar from Koczuk," he told me. Although caviar merchants deceived by Koczuk hadn't committed any crime, there were clues among Koczuk's records as to who wasn't deceived: retailers or other importers who knew they were buying smuggled goods, or who might be doing some smuggling of their own. Grace said, "All these companies started to fall with the investigation into Koczuk, sort of like dominoes."

The first domino was Maryland-based U.S. Caviar & Caviar. The firm had been founded in 1995 by a pair of Iranian-Americans, Hossein Lolavar and Ken Noroozi, who were determined to undersell Petrossian and other established dealers. Grace saw that U.S. Caviar & Caviar had bought great quantities of caviar from Koczuk, and a subsequent investigation by Maryland Fish and Wildlife revealed that Lolavar and Noroozi had also been mislabeling their goods, obtaining fraudulent CITES reexport certificates through bribing corrupt officials in the United Arab Emirates, printing counterfeit labels for their tins of caviar, and selling poached roe from such American species as the shovelnose sturgeon, *Scaphirhynchus platorynchus*, or the paddlefish, *Polyodon spathula*, both native to the Mississippi Basin. Grace learned that Koczuk, in fact, considered U.S. Caviar & Caviar a reliable dumping ground for any caviar too sour to sell in New York.

In July 2000, Lolavar and Noroozi pleaded guilty to twenty-two counts of conspiracy, mail fraud, and smuggling. The government calculated that in 1998 alone U.S. Caviar & Caviar had brought in 18 tons of caviar from the Caspian, which would have been slightly more than the entirety of Russia's CITES-approved quota that year. Finally,

Lolavar was sentenced to forty-one months in prison, Noroozi to fifteen, and the company was fined $10.4 million, the largest fine ever assessed in a federal wildlife case. Unfortunately U.S. Caviar & Caviar declared bankruptcy and never paid the fine. But the sentence was more like what Cynthia Monaco had had in mind for Koczuk, whose smuggling dwarfed even Lolavar and Noroozi's.

Meanwhile, Grace found that other leads from Koczuk's files led to the doorstep of Alfred Yazbak, and also to Arkady Panchernikov, who had grown to be a titan in the caviar industry. Yazbak was the owner of Connoisseur Brands, which had supplied the caviar for Dean & DeLuca's 1999 holiday catalog. The Christmas holidays are a time of high-volume sales in the caviar industry, and the 1999 season featured the additional sparkle of the millennium celebration. "New regulations made finding impeccable beluga caviar tantamount to seeking the Holy Grail this year," touted the catalog copy. "We got lucky."

Maybe not lucky, exactly, thought Grace. Maybe not impeccable.

But potentially the biggest domino was Panchernikov. He had come to the United States from the Ukraine in 1977, working days as an electrical engineer, moonlighting in caviar, and finally becoming the industry's own Horatio Alger. It had been Panchernikov's success in making Caspian Star the major supplier to leading airlines and cruise ships that had driven Dieckmann & Hansen, the world's oldest caviar house, out of business in 2000. Panchernikov also ran a thriving retail trade, a pricey little restaurant on Madison Avenue, and enjoyed a virtual lock on caviar from Kazakhstan's Ural River. "CITES has been a very positive influence," Panchernikov told me over the telephone in 2001. "Of course there have been some bumps in the road, but now everything has settled down, has stabilized. I think the CITES process is doing a good job for sturgeon."

In 1999, Grace led a team of federal agents in a raid on Caspian Star's offices at Kennedy Airport. No caviar was seized, but Grace claimed two computers and data for 125,000 pages of business transactions. Panchernikov paid a small fine for the unregistered Beretta handgun that Grace also found, then returned to business with all his customary panache.

Part of that business has involved a legal counterattack by a portion of the caviar industry against USF&W. Dealers such as Panchernikov are fighting back with lawsuits, the biggest of which had been filed by Caviarteria, which was not one of the shady start-ups that appeared after the collapse of the Soviet Union, but a reputable retailer operating in Manhattan since 1950. In the fall of 1998, Grace noticed that increasing portions of Caviarteria's stock were arriving with reexport permits from the United Arab Emirates and another suspicious source, Lithuania. DNA tests run on samples from a November shipment indicated the presence of beluga in Caviarteria's osetra caviar, and that its sevruga was roe from the very rare ship sturgeon, *Acipenser nudiventris*. That shipment was seized, as were two more shipments in January that also tested wrong.

Caviarteria was being run by Bruce and Eric Sobol, sons of the company's founder. Rob Rothe had been part of the federal team that had carried out a November raid on Caviarteria's warehouse, and he had feared for his life when an enraged Eric Sobol had put his leg up on a chair. It was then that Rob saw Sobol had a handgun strapped to his ankle. That episode ended in a standoff, with Sobol refusing to relinquish his caviar. Later the feds returned with a seizure warrant for close to $1 million worth of stock, and the Sobols filed suit.

Caviarteria's attorney, Walter Drobenko—also Koczuk's attorney at the time—sued for damages of $100 million, alleging that the government's testing procedure was illegal and inaccurate and that the delay occasioned by the testing process results in great quantities of caviar being spoiled. Regarding the test itself, Drobenko had a powerful expert witness: Vadim Birstein, the geneticist who had devised the first molecular test for caviar. Birstein had no confidence in the government's version of the test, and he believed that USF&W had stolen his and Rob DeSalle's data in developing that version.

Regarding the caviar, Caviarteria's impounded stock was indeed on its way to rotting under government seal. Many other retailers, meanwhile, complained of seeing their caviar spoil while waiting for the results of government testing. On one occasion, in the summer of 2000, the federal government authorized the auction of seized caviar, the proceeds to be held in escrow pending the outcome of the related suit. This was caviar from a small company called Russian Czar, and Arkady Panchernikov was a party to that company's suit against the government. The auction was held at USF&W's Valley Stream offices, and the government invited forty-five retailers with a letter that warned, "The United States of America makes no representation as to the quality, salability, usability, or accuracy of labeling and/or of weight measurement. . . . The caviar is being sold 'AS IS' and 'WITH ALL FAULTS.'"

Grace wasn't there, since he didn't want to become too recognizable among that crowd. But Panchernikov, conspicuous in a shiny, beige, double-breasted suit, was among those who came to bid. A reporter for the *New York Observer*, Jen McCaffery, described the scene in an article published August 2, 2000:

Mr. Panchernikov . . . opened a red plastic cooler sitting on a metal fold-ing table at the auction, pulled out a 500-gram tin, and twisted the top until it came off with a slight slurp. Glistening caviar pearls trapped in black goop slid down the side of the tin onto Mr. Panchernikov's hands as he peered at the eggs, then sniffed them.

"Can I taste it?" Mr. Panchernikov asked the federal agents who were looking on. No, against the rules, he was told.

"We don't want to see you licking your fingers either," joked Paul Cerniglia, a supervisory wildlife inspector.

Mr. Panchernikov looked back at Inspector Cerniglia, opened his mouth, stuck his fingers in, then languorously slid them out.

vii.

The five unclaimed bags were piled on the counter of a U.S. Customs of-fice adjoining the baggage claim area. When the lead customs inspector arrived, he asked Grace if he had had any luck on the Aeroflot flight. "We got one," Grace said. "There were a lot of people who declared what they had."

"Word's getting out," said the inspector, who nodded as Rob began to cut the locks off the first of the bags.

All five bags contained only household effects: clothes, linens, cook-ing utensils, dishes, silverware, and so on. By then, Grace had learned that the Aeroflot crew was clean. Rob zippered the bags closed again. Grace said it was time to hit the air freight warehouses.

We went out to the Crown Victoria, which wore a fresh patina of dust and grit. "I just washed this car," Grace remarked. "I guess it's just the air in here."

Then he moved across three lanes of traffic in a manner routine for drivers in New York. A smile creased Roland's lean, aquiline face. "Ed's gonna get a lot of middle fingers in Chicago."

Outside the tunnel the February afternoon light also had a patina of dust and grit. That light stopped at the door of the Air France warehouse, where the ceiling lights glowed like distant stars and the concrete floor was dark and oily. Grace led us to the back of the warehouse, to the airline's refrigerated storage area. The scent of smoked meat floated through the pallets and shelves. "I smell that African smell," Grace said. "Bush meat."

The door was unlocked, the room stacked to the ceiling with cardboard boxes. Grace said that Air France carries a lot of freight out of Africa. Since refrigeration isn't an option through much of the continent, most of the meat that comes in is smoked. Sometimes the meat is from animals on the CITES lists from Appendix I or II. Rob cut into a box at random, spilling a white shower of millet. A second box in another corner of the room yielded fresh green limes. A third revealed the source of that scent: dried fish. Each cut box was repaired with tape reading, "Opened and resealed for USF&W inspection."

In the front of the warehouse Rob came across a box from INDWIZ Trading & Taxidermy labeled "Carved Wooden Products." That raised a flag, since ivory sometimes arrives so labeled. Rob cut the box, not wide enough to tell exactly what the products were, but wide enough to satisfy him that they were wooden.

Meanwhile, Roland found a box of ostrich eggs, each with images of elephants etched like scrimshaw into its shell. The box said, "Made in Zimbabwe."

Grace decided to hold on to these. "Only the South Saharan ostrich is on Appendix II, so these probably don't require CITES permits," he explained. "But I don't know if they've been declared, and if there are more than eight of them, that's a commercial quantity, and the buyer would have to be a licensed dealer."

At the Evergreen Eagle warehouse, Rob took his knife to another pile of strong-smelling boxes. "You learn to cut in the middle and bottom," Roland told me, "because that's where stuff is always hidden."

We had stopped there because Evergreen Eagle handles freight for Aeroflot out of Russia. The boxes held more dried fish, the flesh brown and bony. The species? "Alien," was the best Rob could do.

Swallows chirped in the rafters of the warehouse as Grace examined a shipment of hand-crafted bows twined to leather quivers stuffed with arrows. The quivers were adorned with tufts of fur that Grace examined closely: "I hope that's not monkey."

Our last stop was at a warehouse Northwest Airlines operated, a converted airplane hangar. In its refrigeration room Roland homed in on two neat blue-and-white boxes marked "Aquatic Product Supply & Marketing" in English and Chinese letters. Both boxes held eight golden 1.8-kilogram tins of caviar, with "CITES/Kaluga Sturgeon" embossed in a hologram design on their lids. Styrofoam pads separated each two-tin stack. There was a care and cleanliness in the packaging of these eggs at the opposite end of the spectrum from photos I had been shown of Gino International's product line. Grace told me earlier that he had seen so much abused and sour caviar over the years that he could never stand to eat the stuff.

Roland donned latex gloves to open one of the tins, as did Rob with a second. Kaluga sturgeon, *Huso dauricus*, is found only in the Amur River, which defines the borders of Russia and China. It's a cousin to the beluga of the Caspian Sea, and nearly equal to the beluga in size.

The eggs seemed almost to expand as the lid of the first tin was drawn away, as several slid down the side, as the same stunning scent that had come from the Russian's suitcase earlier, but sweeter, spilled forth. The eggs lay as if planted in a honeycomb, round and large and golden-gray. Roland probed into their midst with a wooden tongue depressor, checking to see that the eggs on top matched those on the bottom. They seemed to, but they didn't exactly match the eggs in Rob's tin, which were equally large but more golden. He asked, "Are these the same species?"

Rob peered from one tin to the other. "Yeah, I think so."

"This stuff is very new on the market, but we don't usually have trouble with it," Grace said. "China's like Russia was years ago, and Iran is now—if you're caught poaching sturgeon, you're jailed, and possibly killed."

The caviar was new to Rob as well. He had heard that kaluga sturgeon eggs sometimes come mixed with those of the smaller Amur sturgeon, *Acipenser schrenckii*. "I've never seen this species close up," he said. "I'd say that for coloration, size, and consistency, everything here matches up. But it's hard to tell the difference visually between kaluga and Amur, and I'd like to compare this with that seized shipment of kaluga we have in our cooler."

The spilled eggs that hung to the tins were herded with the tongue depressors back into their honeycombs, one at a time and gently. Then Roland put the first tin on a table and crouched, working at eye level in order to be as precise as humanly possible in easing the lid back on. Grace, who didn't plan on being back here again, allowed Roland all the time he needed.

~ 3 ~

FLAVORS OF THE
DIVINE HORIZON

i.

"The City of Light had everything to offer after World War I," lamented
Eve Vega, "—except caviar."

A smile flitted in sequence across the faces of the four men and five
women seated at a long table in the rear of the Petrossian Restaurant on
the corner of 58th Street and Seventh Avenue in Manhattan, only a
block from Central Park. The restaurant occupied a portion of the first
floor of the Alwyn Court Building, in June 2001 webbed in scaffolding
thanks to a snail's-pace renovation process that had been vexing Eve
for the past four years. A blue wooden sign hanging from one corner of
the scaffolding promised that the Petrossian Restaurant & Boutique lay
sequestered, snail-like, somewhere beneath that particular length of
aluminum and canvas geometry.

Outside, the mid-afternoon traffic squalled and beeped and parried
its way past camera stores, barber shops, delis, and kiosks. Inside the
restaurant, in dim crystalline stillness, the serene geometry of Art Deco
reigned. Well-spoken waiters and elegant busboys stood guard among
linened tables, Lalique crystal wall sconces, and rose-colored granite.
Ours was the only party in the restaurant this mid-afternoon, and Eve's
low, melodious voice had just a serrated edge of a New York accent, but

it hardly stirred the quiet. Our smiles were alloyed with pity to think of Paris without caviar.

"So in 1920 the Petrossian brothers, Melkoum and Mouchegh—now remember, they had just arrived in Paris, fleeing the Bolshevik Revolution—placed a telephone call to the Soviet Union's newly formed Ministry of Trade," Eve said. "They wondered if they might buy some caviar for resale in Paris. After some delay they were finally told to get all their available cash, put it into a bag, and just leave the bag—I kid you not—on the steps of the Soviet Embassy. This is a true story, though it sounds like something out of Dorothy Parker."

"Trusting souls," judged a reed-thin elderly man in a pink shirt and black bow tie. His companions were middle-aged or older, their dress ranging from casual to semiformal.

"Well, they thought it was worth the gamble. One month goes by—no caviar. Two months go by—no caviar." Eve smiled ruefully and paused amid tittering laughter. "Then, three months later, after much anxiety, apprehension, angst, you name it, the first caviar shipment arrives. With that Petrossian Paris was born on the Left Bank—just in time for the Roaring '20s, a time when anything that was new, that was hip, that was happening, was embraced."

Our pity evaporated. Paris was saved. Eve Vega's job title at Petrossian Paris was executive director of America, which sounds Napoleonic, but it was a job that she sometimes found more pedagogical than executive. This afternoon was all pedagogy. She was presiding over the third in a series of twelve events hosted by The New School University's culinary arts program: "Behind the Scenes at the Great Restaurants of New York." For $85 a head per event, people could enjoy a private cooking demonstration, and/or a tour of the facility, and/or a special tasting of the restaurant's marquee items, here and at other locations. The proceeds went to a scholarship fund for aspiring chefs.

The woman whose very names suggest twilight and temptation stood slim in a black pantsuit at one end of the table. Her short black hair and the bright inkdrops of her eyes lent her face a gypsy aspect, a roguish look that defied easy chronology. She could be thirty, forty, or fifty. She liked a good story, and she had one in the founding of Petrossian Paris: the Armenian family with the two young heirs who fled when civil war broke out, journeying overland to Persia in order to finally rejoin their family in Paris. But how to live in Paris? And where to find good caviar? That bag of cash left like a gypsy foundling on the steps of the new embassy proposed an answer to both questions.

One food historian describes a more ordinary bureaucratic process— overtures, refusals, proposals, negotiations, and then the briefcase full of money—but one no less fraught with cash-up-front suspense. Another holds with Eve, that it was all done quickly and mysteriously over the telephone. In either event, there is no question that the Soviets in 1920 were wracked by inflation, bereft of industrial production, short on wheat, and desperate for hard currency. The Petrossian brothers' bag of francs marked one of the Lenin government's first economic relationships with the West. The brothers arranged as well to be the exclusive distributors of Russian caviar, though in time they came to share that privilege with Dieckmann & Hansen. So in Paris, after several angst-ridden months, their gamble was rewarded with 2 tons of malossol caviar—this is to say, lightly salted, the good stuff—packed into barrels whose staves were made from linden trees, since only the wood of the linden didn't taint the taste of the eggs.

But wait—Paris wasn't saved just yet. "Believe it or not," Eve said, "the French turned up their noses at caviar. The Petrossians offered free samples at the hotel run by Cesar Ritz at the Place Vendôme, but only with spittoons nearby, since so many people would spit the caviar out." Laughter from the table. "Ironically," Eve continued, "it was Americans like F. Scott and Zelda Fitzgerald, Ernest Hemingway, and Josephine Baker who helped cultivate a taste for caviar in France, and make this food, this food of the gods, as available as it is today."

All this was true, so far as it went. One of Ritz's spittoons would have been handy three centuries earlier when a young Louis XV took a gift of caviar from Russia's Peter the Great and spat it out on the carpet of Versailles, offending the Russian ambassador. The memory of that sin prompted Tsar Alexander III to keep his caviar to himself when he visited Paris in the early 1900s. But in fact the French had begun liking caviar after the Russian defeat of Napoleon. Bon vivants enjoyed it delivered by rail from the Caspian, or else made from the eggs of their own European sturgeon. When France's rivers were fished empty, they turned entirely to Russian, Persian, or American caviars. The trade from America trailed off around 1910, and the Caspian trade stopped with World War I.

The task of the Petrossians in 1920 was not so much to create a market as to rekindle it. The high-living Americans helped, but so did Cesar Ritz and a long-standing French fascination for Russian culture and cuisine. That fascination ran at high tide in the Roaring '20s, with Paris's large community of expatriate Russians, the hip and happening new music of Stravinsky and Prokofiev, and the presence of Diaghilev's Ballet Russe. The Petrossian brothers might have taken a big chance in trusting the Bolsheviks, but not in betting on a market for caviar in Paris.

Sixty years later, it was on to the New World. "Petrossian arrived in the U.S. in 1980," Eve went on, explaining that after opening up a small distribution center, Petrossian grew quickly. The restaurant opened in 1984, and Petrossian continues to cater to many of the hotels and restaurants in the United States. The firm has opened boutiques in New York, Miami, Dallas, Los Angeles, San Francisco, and Hawaii and supplies airlines and cruise lines. By its own estimate, Petrossian controls 70 percent of the North American retail market in caviar.

As big as this share is, it actually represents a decline from the near monopoly the firm enjoyed in the 1980s and early 1990s. Both Petrossian and its rival, Dieckmann & Hansen, have suffered from the likes of Gino International over the past decade, but Dieckmann & Hansen more so. That firm had always concentrated on the travel sector of the market, never establishing the branded retail line and name recognition that Petrossian did. When cost-cutting corporate buyers turned to Gino and other fly-by-nights, the venerable German firm had to close its doors. Since then, Petrossian had made its own inroads into the travel sector, though not so great as those of Arkady Panchernikov, whose Caspian Star line undersold Petrossian.

But Armen Petrossian, a son of Mouchegh who took over the firm in 1991, was proving a bit of a gambler himself. Petrossian Paris was one of the very few companies not on Koczuk's client list, a company so far unstained by the activities that had kept Ed Grace so busy. Armen didn't back down on his high prices through the 1990s, had never been embarrassed by any of his suppliers, and could still credibly cite the high reputation of his product. Still, the firm's recent expansions into Miami and various western cities was a bold move. Eve had told me earlier that times were hard, that Petrossian continued to be bedeviled by those peddling—she had trouble even pronouncing this phrase, to her the ultimate in oxymorons—"bargain caviar."

"There are twenty-four different species of sturgeon found across the world, but there are only three that are appreciated for their caviar," she told her diners. In a booklet she handed out to the group, Armen Petrossian appeared in some photos, all probably taken in Baku, the capital of present-day Azerbaijan. In these, he wore a white lab coat and cap and a somber aspect as he inspected the gaping belly of a 1,800-pound beluga; pressed heaps of black roe through a sieve to separate the eggs from bits of membrane; or stood among a group of other white coats and a pile of tins bulging with caviar as he sampled a finished batch. The beluga in the first photo lay on its flank on a factory floor, its trunk open from throat to anus. A man in oilskins pulled on the upper flap, revealing a gut that held a pool of blood and 200 pounds of glistening roe. A fourth photo was of a "master," an expert in applying just the right amount of salt to the eggs at hand. "Salt is absolutely necessary to caviar," the text read. "It facilitates its preservation, but moreover, it is the element that brings out the exalting flavor."

"Does he have to taste from all those tins?" wondered the man in the bow tie.

Eve smiled and said that one taste was enough, since the quality would be consistent throughout that lot. "It's a twenty-minute operation, from the sturgeon's belly to the airtight tin. And it's an important fact that the sturgeon has to die peacefully, cannot feel threatened," she added. "If it does, it will secrete a chemical that will ruin the entire batch of roe. So the fishermen have to take it out of the Caspian very gently, and that's a job in itself, with such a big fish. Then it's placed on a barge and taken to the factory, where it is anesthetized with a blow to the back of the head, and then the belly is opened up as you see in the photo there."

Uneasy murmurs moved through the place settings as people regarded this photo.

"I know, I know," Eve consoled. "But one thing you should realize is that nothing is wasted. The skin is saved, the meat is smoked. And the only thing stopping us from providing cesarean sections for each female sturgeon is that chemical I mentioned. But we're not that far away from solving that problem. I have a feeling that with the way things are going in the Caspian, in time a c-section will be the only way to go. That would help to stabilize the prices and allow each sturgeon to keep reproducing."

A woman with a British accent raised her hand. "You mentioned eggs. So this is the reproduction of the sturgeon?"

"Yes—so the roe that's not used for caviar will become baby sturgeons. And the fishermen are so good at knowing if a female sturgeon is ready or not. They just feel her belly and they know. But some of the roe obviously is used for reproduction."

I knew that in fact the Soviet sturgeon fishermen, and maybe those who fished for Petrossian's current suppliers, were wonderfully practiced in identifying egg-bearing females. And the secretion of that hormone, adrenaline, will cause eggs to start being reabsorbed into the ovaries, and will also spoil their taste. Sturgeons must be "anesthetized" quickly.

But I also knew there was no imminent prospect of the fish being saved by c-section, and that the problem was more fundamental than adrenaline. If the operation is done after a female sturgeon has ovulated, the same openings that develop in the egg membrane to admit sperm will also admit salt. The result the next morning is jelly, not caviar. If the operation is done before ovulation, the ovaries must be removed with the eggs, which renders the fish sterile. C-sections of ovulated eggs are fine for making baby sturgeons, as Frank Chapman has done, but not for making caviar. Although there are rumors of a secret Russian process for producing caviar from such eggs, there is no item like that on the market, and those same rumors report that the taste is very different, and not pleasant.

But these were ticklish subjects for the supper table. Throughout the industrialized West, people commonly buy their meat or fish at the supermarket, where it's already sectioned in packages that bear no trace of blood, fur, or feathers. This guarantees not only cleanliness and convenience, but also a willful innocence, allowing us to forget the mortal origins of our meals. Eve was putting her best gloss on the origins of this meal: a peaceful death in the present, sustainable use through technology in the future. The Petrossian booklet was more unrepentantly frank about how caviar was made, about the costs aside from money that it entailed. It wasn't easy to look at, but it was the best thing we learned that day.

When at last the booklets were laid aside, Eve said, "What you have in front of you are bowls containing three types of caviar. For centuries, only three species of sturgeon have been recognized for their caviar, and those caviars are known as beluga, osetra, and sevruga."

She indicated two silver presentoirs gleaming at opposite ends of the table. On each a lattice of leaping sturgeons supported three covered saucers of crushed ice, which in turn supported three glass dishes heaped with caviar. The eggs of the beluga were largest, each nearly the size of a raindrop, and several of the charcoal gray beads had slid off the mountain and traced an oily path down the side of the dish. The osetra was smaller, more golden in tone, almost amber. The eggs seemed transparent, nearly generating their own light under the dim luster of the wall sconces. The sevruga—the roe of the stellate sturgeon, *Acipenser stellatus*—was the darkest and most fine-grained. The presentoirs provided a sort of spiritualized sensuality, like the chalices and grails of the Eastern Orthodox Church.

Each place setting included a spoon-sized, silver-handled palette. The blades of the palettes were plated in 18-karat gold. Among metals only gold, said Eve, was neutral enough not to impart its own taste to the eggs. At her urging all palettes were taken up in concert. Just as it had been in Genesis, we were about to taste the food of the gods and grow wise.

ii.

Petrossian sells more than caviar: also smoked fish, foie gras, gourmet chocolates and teas, and the paraphernalia for properly serving caviar. This would include presentoirs, toast point trays, mother-of-pearl spoons (as taste-neutral as gold), these same golden palettes, and scallop-shaped, silver-plated rests for parking your palette.

Of course, polystyrene plastic is as taste-neutral as either mother-of-pearl or gold, but that's not the point. Thorstein Veblen knew what a golden palette is for. *The Theory of the Leisure Class* is a satire of both the nouveau riche and academic jargon, but beneath its puffed-up rhetoric lie some durable truths. "The consumption of expensive goods is meritorious, and the goods which contain an appreciable element of cost in excess of what goes to give them serviceability for their ostensible mechanical purpose are honorific," Veblen wrote of costly feasts and gaudy place settings.

In the West, among both the Greeks and Romans, sturgeon meat was a meritorious item, to say it in Veblenese. There is no incontrovertible evidence, however, that either people ate sturgeon roe, whether salted or not.

But sturgeon meat remained meritorious for a millennium after the fall of Rome. In the fourteenth century, King Edward II claimed by royal edict any sturgeon caught in English waters, unless it was the Thames, in which event the fish belonged to the Lord Mayor of London. By then Europe's aristocracy was growing curious about the small amounts of caviar that Venetian merchants were buying from the Mongols who then ruled the Caspian Sea, the Black Sea, and the Sea of Azov. This roe had to be heavily salted to survive its journey, and it often arrived spoiled anyway. Nonetheless, thanks to what food historian Felipe Fernández-Armesto has called the "stranger effect"—that is, the charm of the exotic, that taste of what he described in 2000 as "the flavors of the divine horizon"—a tentative demand began to grow.

The Mongols had controlled the Caspian and most of southern Russia since the thirteenth-century campaigns of Batu Khan, the grandson of Genghis. According to Vulf Sternin, it was this king who provided the first recorded use of the word "caviar" in his description of a meal he ate in 1240 at a monastery on the Volga north of Moscow. Three hundred years later, in 1556, Ivan the Terrible drove the Mongols from their capital at Astrakhan and seized control of the Caspian for the Russian Empire. Among the Russians, by then even the poor and the cloistered had been eating caviar for several centuries. The upper reaches of the Volga were full of sturgeon, and the Russian Orthodox Church—with its 200 days of fasting, including seven weeks of Lent—was an even better friend to fishermen than the Catholic Church. Though sturgeon meat was generally expensive, the roe was not, and caviar was enjoyed at all levels of Russian society.

Around the Caspian, the Mongols were replaced by a Russian mix of runaway serfs and religious dissidents, many of these fundamentalist Old Believers, a people who grew into the unruly Cossacks. In the 1660s these raised a rebellion against Tsar Alexis that nearly stormed Moscow. When finally it was crushed, the defeated Cossacks conveyed their submission to the tsar with the gift of a bowl of caviar. Alexis, in turn, assessed a tax on the sale of caviar and eventually claimed a government monopoly on all marketing of the food, granting the first contract for such in 1675 to a pair of merchants from Hamburg.

Peter the Great succeeded Alexis in 1682 and resolved to use trade in caviar as a means of broadening Russia's ties to the West. By then the Cossacks had grown as skilled as the Mongols in catching sturgeon with baited hooks anchored to a tree, or sometimes tied to an ox. They produced plenty of caviar, but it still had to be shipped up the Volga to Volgagrad, hauled overland to the Don River, and then floated to the Black Sea in order to reach merchant ships. European aristocrats remained ambivalent about a food that they knew to be more and more celebrated in Russia and the Levant, but which in Paris was still liable to be spat out on the carpet by an unprepared young sovereign.

Caviar's reputation in the West began to rise, finally, during the reign of Catherine the Great in the late eighteenth century. By then, roe was being packed in barrels made of linden wood. In Russia itself caviar had been transformed from something to be eaten on fast days by the poor to a central item of Masylanitsa, or Butter Week, the Mardi Gras–like celebration that precedes Lent. Though popular with the well-to-do, caviar was so plentiful in Russia at this time that it cost no more than butter and other staples, and in fact was used as a substitute for butter in sauces during Lent.

This began to change with the completion in 1856 of a railroad line linking the Volga to the Don. Once in the Black Sea, the linden barrels were taken up by fast steamships that could manufacture their own ice. The Caspian city of Astrakhan shipped a quarter of its production to Europe that year, and in Russia caviar began to disappear from the tables of the poor.

In Germany, the ambitious Johannes Dieckmann began to diversify his Hamburg barrel-making business. With his son-in-law Johannes C.F. Hansen, he began selling cheap salted herring and sturgeon meat from the Elbe River. He also began to notice the high prices that Russian caviar was fetching, while roe from the Elbe's *Acipenser sturio* was still being fed to pigs. By the 1880s, the firm of Dieckmann & Hansen was making its own premium caviar, fishing the Elbe dry, importing caviar from the Caspian, and looking for new sources of supply—such as the eastern United States.

Cesar Ritz opened his hotel in Paris in 1898. The Industrial Revolution had created a new and very wealthy leisure class, the one satirized by Veblen, and the City of Light was the capital of the Belle Epoque, drawing artists and aristocrats from both the other side of the Atlantic and the Eurasian heartland. Caviar arrived as well from both directions, washed down by either vodka or champagne. The flow of caviar from America would trickle down to nothing within a few years, and the flow from Russia would stop with the Austrian declaration of war on Serbia in 1914.

At that time, Melkoum and Mouchegh Petrossian were in Moscow studying law and architecture, and Vladimir Ilyich Lenin was in exile in Switzerland. Wheels were turning that would eventually prompt Monsieur Ritz to set out spittoons for those who didn't learn about caviar during its first go-round in France, and eventually—one June afternoon in New York City eight decades later, among etched Erté mirrors and Limoges china—put a golden palette into my hand.

iii.

Eve Vega encouraged me to go easy on Arnold Hansen-Sturm. "I feel bad for the man," she said during a conversation we had in the restaurant before the beginning of her class. "With all these black-market traders coming in during the eighties, it was a time when people in the industry had to make up their minds. You could either join them or say no, and it wasn't easy to say no. He had his livelihood to defend, a lot of people depending on him. What he did was wrong, but it's easy for me to pontificate—I wasn't in his position."

In fact, it was someone else failing to say no that had made Eve's previous position in the industry untenable. It was on a lark earlier in her career that the former real estate agent decided to try managing the New York office of a Los Angeles–based caviar firm. There she learned enough about the industry to be hired away by Aquamar Gourmet, a firm based in the Bronx that sold much of its Caspian caviar to Pan American Airlines.

Once inside, however, she found that Aquamar was dodging customs duties and substituting American paddlefish roe for the sevruga it sold to Pan Am. She quit in 1986 just ahead of the federal investigation that brought down Aquamar. She then interviewed at several other firms, among them Romanoff. She wanted to be more careful this time, and she was delighted to be snapped up by Petrossian, a company that wasn't engaging in price-wars with the new start-ups, banking instead that its reputation for quality would see it through.

But trying to sell the planet's most expensive caviar in what had become a buyer's market taught Eve compassion for Arnold Hansen-Sturm. "It was just a horror, believe me, trying to increase sales when many of your competitors are selling beluga for $300 less than you are," she said. "But we knew that if it began, it had to have an end, and when we heard about Vadim, we saw that as a light at the end of the tunnel."

Vadim Birstein and Rob DeSalle's 1996 DNA sampling of the caviar for sale around town, and the *Wall Street Journal* article that trumpeted the results, were sweet vindication for Petrossian, since its goods stood up well to the test. The implementation of the CITES process added considerably to the cost of doing business, but Eve and Armen Petrossian cheered lustily for it, and they had continued to cheer, especially as such dark-side competitors as Gino International and U.S. Caviar & Caviar were eliminated. But in terms of profits, the light at the end of the tunnel seemed as far away as ever, at least in Petrossian's U.S. markets, where people continued to shop for bargains.

"In France people still have knowledge of what good caviar is, and French law protects the use of the term," Eve said. "For a time Arkady Panchernikov at Caspian Star, for example, was shipping paddlefish roe to France and labeling it caviar, and they stopped him. It's like champagne from the Champagne region: The French will never look at ours, though it may be just as good, and I respect that. It's a matter of style, of their *joie de vivre*. A Frenchman doesn't need five different suits; . . . he'll have one good one that he uses every day. It's the same thing with caviar: They may not be able to buy caviar every day, but when they buy it, they buy good stuff. They leave the junkfish to the Americans."

Nor had the dark side been quite eclipsed, as events at Caviarteria seemed to suggest. The firm had been founded in 1950 as what has been described as the "anti-Petrossian." Louis Sobol's flagship East 59th Street restaurant was an unpretentious cross between a bistro and a deli, a place where the countermen wore baseball caps. Sobol's idea was to demystify caviar, making it more accessible—and more desirable—to the ordinary middle-class consumer. Maybe that's just what appealed to Greta Garbo, who regularly frequented that 59th Street Caviarteria until the *New York Post* caught her there.

That target customer, however, made Caviarteria more vulnerable to competition from those who were selling what-the-hell but calling it beluga and offering a very accessible price. Nonetheless, Louis Sobol's sons Bruce and Eric were countering Petrossian's expansion into Florida and the western United States with their own new caviar bars in Miami and Las Vegas. The verdict was still out on whether they were also cutting corners along the way and selling a little what-the-hell of their own; their civil suit against the government was still in progress then. In any event, Eric Sobol—the brother who had made Rob Rothe so nervous during USF&W's raid on Caviarteria's warehouse in 2000—wouldn't be there to hear it.

On April 15, 2001, Eric Sobol's body was found in his blood-spattered Mercedes. The car was parked in a Friendly's Restaurant lot off I–80 in Danville, Pennsylvania, just before the highway climbs into the Appalachians. Sobol held a gun in each hand and had died of two gunshot wounds to the head.

The death was ruled a suicide by Pennsylvania's Montour County coroner, and Ed Grace told me that he would have to believe the coroner on that count. The coroner also found evidence of heroin use—and a recently acquired tattoo: "Death Before Dishonor." Acquaintances of Sobol who accepted the coroner's verdict speculated that either he had been driven over the edge by the caviar seizure and the civil suit, or else had killed himself so his insurance policies could cover the debts incurred by Caviarteria's new locations, which were losing money.

Others said there was nothing in Sobol's personality or his mood in early April to suggest any such action. Certainly he was quarrelsome—and litigious, having previously filed suit against Petrossian for an alleged theft of Caviarteria's mailing list (the suit was dismissed)—and certainly he was falling deeper into debt. Vadim Birstein, for one, a 1991 immigrant to the United States from Russia, strongly suspected that Sobol had become involved with Russian organized crime and that his suicide was staged.

But there is little debate as to the grip that the *mafiya*, the Russian mob, currently holds over the industry's breadbasket, the fish camps of the northern Caspian. In 1996, a bomb planted in an apartment building in the Caspian city of Kaspiysk killed sixty-eight people, mostly Russian border guards and their families, in what is believed to be a mafiya operation. And only three days after Sobol's death, a mob of 100 sturgeon poachers stormed a Russian coast guard station in the town of Izberbash to reclaim confiscated motorboats and fishing nets. According to the *Moscow Times*, the poachers used their own wives and children as human shields and beat several policemen.

Poaching in the Caspian was estimated by Russian authorities to be worth $2 billion to $4 billion per year. Eve told me that Petrossian has always bought its roe from licensed fishing operations, and I've found no one to dispute that. But in Russia, harking all the way back to Ivan the Terrible, the operations of organized crime have blended imperceptibly into those of the government. Today they blend also into the affairs of the Russian émigré community in New York's Brighton Beach, and into the seams and crannies of the U.S. caviar market. Ed Grace didn't believe that Gino International had any links to the Russian mob, and he wouldn't speculate about Eric Sobol, but he thought certain firms under investigation did.

Eve regretted the end of the Soviet Union, which at least had been a good partner to a legitimate caviar dealer. "We brought Russian caviar to a level no one expected it could reach," she observed. "We took something good, that was full of mystery, and made it more available to everyone. The Soviet Union awarded us many medals of honor, and at their end they policed the Caspian very well. If someone was found dipping their finger into water near sturgeon, it was off to Siberia."

She described the current situation in the Caspian as similar to the Wild West, and she knew the numbers as well as I did. Combined harvests of the three great sturgeon species declined to roughly 1,000 tons a year in the late 1990s, down from catches that ranged from 20,000 to 30,000 tons two decades before. But those numbers reflected only the legal harvest. Estimates for the black-market catch ran from ten to fifteen times the legal limit, which still just lifted harvest levels to less than half what they were in the 1970s, only now the catch included anything with scutes, and not just a portion of the ripe females, as formerly.

In 1997, Armen Petrossian became a founding member and president of the International Caviar Importers Association (ICIA), which included Petrossian, Dieckmann & Hansen, and five other European houses. The ICIA was formed to defend the interests of both the caviar industry and the sturgeon, particularly in regard to CITES goals of a regulated harvest and trade. But since then, some other environmental organizations have taken a more aggressive stance than CITES in the Caspian, putting the caviar industry in an awkward position.

The most prominent of these was a coalition of three organizations— the Natural Resources Defense Council, the Wildlife Conservation Society, and SeaWeb—that had mounted a publicity and lobbying effort called Caviar Emptor. The main goals of that effort were for beluga to be listed under the U.S. Endangered Species Act and for CITES to elevate beluga to its Appendix I list. Of course, an ESA listing would lock beluga caviar out of the U.S. market (the world's second largest, consuming 28,000 pounds per year), and an Appendix I listing would lock it out of everywhere else, at least in any legal form.

Armen Petrossian and the ICIA didn't like being forced to speak out against increased protection for the beluga, but they had. "A ban on the caviar trade would do nothing but increase illegal fishing and smuggling," Petrossian asserted. He preferred quota reductions that allowed some level of legal commerce. CITES preferred that as well, but the four north Caspian nations—Russia, Azerbaijan, Kazakhstan, and Turkmenistan—had resisted additional reductions. At a meeting in Baku in May 2001, CITES had rolled out the bomb, imposing an immediate one-month suspension of all caviar exports from those countries. The moratorium would be extended indefinitely unless the four nations could quickly provide persuasive proposals for protecting sturgeon stocks in their waters.

Those proposals were due in Geneva next month, and Eve was on tenterhooks. The Iranians were still free to export, and in Europe, Iranian caviar was gaining a reputation for high quality and cutting into Petrossian's profits. Now that the United States had lifted its trade embargo against Iran, a couple of European firms with connections there were gearing up to challenge Petrossian in North America. And Caspian Star was attacking on the other flank. The whole U.S. industry, in fact, had been rocked just days before I spoke with Eve when the *Wall Street Journal* reported that Arkady Panchernikov had arranged to buy Kazakhstan's entire 2001 quota of exported caviar—33 tons, including the region's largest portion of beluga.

So far, because of the CITES moratorium, he had received only a fifth of what Kazakhstan had ready to ship. The rest sat in coolers in the city of Atyrau, at the mouth of the Ural River. The *Wall Street Journal* went to look at it there, but apparently the reporter mistook a thermometer's Celsius reading as Fahrenheit and wrote that the caviar was being kept in freezers. Freezing destroys the membranes of sturgeon eggs, and when the article appeared, describing all his inventory as frozen, Panchernikov was furious.

Eve sighed and sipped vaguely at her wine. She said CITES needed to involve not just the Caspian governments and fishermen in managing the sturgeons, but also the honest caviar buyers, who could stake out a middle ground between the hopeless extremes of either unregulated commerce or no legal commerce at all.

"Because we sell caviar and promote it the way we do," Eve said, leaning forward and underlining her words, "we're the sturgeon's best friend. We have a respect for the fish that exists at a level no one else can understand. That's because we realize that caviar is not just fish eggs. It's oh, so much more than that."

iv.

We started with beluga.

"Most people think that beluga is the be-all and end-all for caviar," Eve said. "I think that's because, (a) beluga is the most expensive, and therefore it has to be the best, though that's not necessarily true, and (b) it's the easiest to pronounce." Laughter danced around the table. "So to seem like we know what we're talking about, we say, 'Give me beluga,' which is fine, but it can be costly."

The reason we were starting with beluga, Eve explained, was that its flavor was the most subtle of our three caviars. "You see large-sized beads, a color variance from light gray to dark, and you'll find that beluga has the butteriest taste. I've had beluga so buttery it has almost a cheesy taste. So if I may, I'll take this palette, and . . . voilà, voilà."

Nine golden palettes followed Eve's into the bowls of beluga on the presentoirs, which presented no scent that I could detect. One man gasped as several eggs slid off his palette onto the table linen. Glancing about sheepishly, he used his index finger to roll them like Lilliputian marbles back into the clump on his palette.

Eve swallowed her portion and said, "The idea is to keep the beads in perfect condition as they go into your mouth. The master at the fishery took such great pains to bring them to you whole and perfect. And you're tasting it now just as you should. You see we have no condiments on the table—no eggs, no onions, nothing—to mask the true taste of fine caviar."

In my mouth the eggs slid like ball bearings into an even layer between tongue and palate. They crimped slightly as the tongue rose. Then they burst, several at a time, like an arpeggio of notes in a musical chord. The flavor was marine, irrefutably sea-like, but not at all fishy. The salt was an undertone—not a cymbal crash, as it had been with some Romanoff whitefish roe I had tried once—and so there was a buttery sort of sweetness. The eggs slipped down the throat almost by themselves, leaving not an aftertaste, but an echo consistent with that first sensation. The taste was pleasant enough, and unusual. Happy sighs rose from both sides of the table. The man in the bow tie nodded and smiled.

"You've tasted the beluga, and I think you found it very clean and true, and very light on the salt, right?"

"What sort of salt is it?" asked the man who had spilled his beluga.

"It's a sea salt, added not just for flavor, as you know, but also to extend its freshness. In Europe they add a small amount of borax as an additional preservative, but that's not allowed in caviar imported into the United States."

I remembered that in the 1700s caviar prepared for export from Russia was rolled in cloth and then buried in the ground. No one knew why that helped to preserve the roe, as well as improve its taste, until a high concentration of borax was found in the soils around the Caspian.

"Now the osetra is the blonde of the family, and that's simply because of its special color variance. The eggs of osetra caviar are usually a golden yellow, sometimes taking on brownish or even greenish hues. The beads are smaller than with beluga, and that's because the fish that produces these eggs—and forgive me, I have to do this, but with Fish and Wildlife and CITES and everybody else involved, we have to use the Latin name to prevent confusion—is *Acipenser gueldenstaedtii* on the Russian side . . . "

"Is there going to be a quiz?" asked the man in the bow tie.

"—or *Acipenser persicus* on the Iranian side. Those fishes are much smaller than the beluga and mature earlier. The longer or older the fish, the bigger the bead in the caviar. Now try the osetra, and compare it to the beluga, and when we finish with this, I'll tell you what my own favorite is."

These eggs were the prettiest, the most jewel-like, but I could tell no difference in taste from the beluga, unless the osetra had a slightly more iodine flavor. Others were more discriminating.

Eve asked, "Have you tasted the osetra? . . . Wouldn't you say it's a little bit nuttier in taste than the beluga? This is like a wine tasting, so whatever comes to mind, I want to hear it. The beads are firmer? Good, I didn't know if you'd recognize that—very good. Osetra is by far the firmest of the three."

A woman in close-cropped red hair asked where else sturgeons were found. "There used to be sturgeon in the Hudson River, and there are sturgeon in the Mississippi, and in the Amur River between Russia and China," Eve replied. "But the Caspian Sea—which is the same size as France—has the elements that we need for the finest caviar: just the right amount of salinity, the best sort of food supply for the fish, and the most favorable water temperatures. This makes the Caspian, and especially the Volga Delta, what we might call the Champagne region of the caviar world. Unfortunately, the Mississippi doesn't have those elements, so we're still a long ways off, many years I think, from producing fine caviar in the U.S."

The same woman asked if there was a difference between Russian and Iranian caviar. Eve observed that Islamic law forbids the consumption of fish without scales, and that the sturgeon was counted as such. So the Russians had been doing it longer, she said, and experience counts. "But it's true that I've tasted some very good Iranian caviar, and side by side, it's probably hard to tell the difference. Since the embargo has been lifted, the prices on Iranian caviar have been quite high, which probably endows it with some element of forbidden fruit— people may flock to it simply because it's been unavailable for so long."

Eve smiled, paused, clasped her hands in front of her. "That being said, let's dig into the sevruga."

Only motes of caviar and oil remained in the dishes that had contained beluga and osetra. The sevruga eggs were the darkest, varying from charcoal gray to black, the beads slightly bigger than pinheads, less than half the size of the beluga roe. Eve extended the first palette into this roe, as she had with the beluga, and the rest followed. The British woman asked how best to keep caviar.

"We keep our caviar at a constant 26 degrees Fahrenheit . . . "

"Doesn't it freeze?" the woman asked.

"It won't in its own natural oil. But it doesn't stop there. We still have to turn our tins over at regular intervals to make sure the oil is evenly distributed, and we keep them secure. Air is caviar's worst enemy. Once the air gets in, that's what ages caviar, and you can recognize old caviar by the way it looks and tastes."

The man in the bow tie wondered what old caviar looked like.

"The salt starts to surface, and you see white spots," Eve answered. "Also the oil has a tendency to take over, and you'll see the beads just swimming in oil. I can only speak for Petrossian caviar, but once we repackage the caviar for you, you can take it home to your refrigerator and keep it four to six weeks. But I don't know how many times you open your refrigerator. And I don't know how you could let it sit there for four weeks, either. I would think the temptation would be too great."

"More like four hours," suggested the bow tie.

Contented murmurs circulated about the table as the sevruga went down. These eggs had a more pronounced taste than either the beluga or the osetra—again, nothing fishy, but more oceanic, maybe more robust. I couldn't say which I liked the best, but the sevruga would be most identifiable to me in a blind taste test. The eggs broke in tiny bursts of flavor against the tongue, more a hammered chord than an arpeggio.

Eve asked people to name their favorite of the three, but as a group we were noncommittal. Eve said each caviar had celebrity endorsers. "You should know that Pablo Picasso would exchange his prints for Petrossian sevruga. Ian Fleming would only buy Petrossian osetra. And Madonna, because she has the budget and the means, buys Petrossian beluga."

"But what's your favorite?" demanded the bow tie. "You promised us."

Earlier Eve had described to me her first tastes of caviar as she prepared for work in the industry. She said she had heard that caviar was something you had to get used to, but she believed now that this principle applied only to bad caviar or "junkfish" roes. Her theory was this: that when you try caviar for the first time, you search your memory for something to compare it to, and this fails, because in fact there's nothing there for comparison—the caviar exists in a world of its own. It's not until the second taste, and the third, and so on, that you have any basis for comparison, and you become the sort of connoisseur of the meritorious that Petrossian craves.

"My favorite," said Eve, after a drum-roll sort of pause, "is sevruga. In my job, of course, the price is meaningless. I can have beluga, osetra, whatever I want. But I like the intensity, the richness of taste that you get with sevruga. It's a caviar that provides you with a wallop, and I like that wallop." She laughed. "I'm very simple—in terms of liking sevruga, I'm a cheap date. What can I say?"

A glance through the booklets handed out earlier confirmed that sevruga, as an honorific consumable, packed the most wallop per dollar: a 50-gram (or 2-ounce) jar of Petrossian beluga cost $139 at the time; the same amount of osetra, $98; and sevruga, $72.

A blue-blazered waiter served fillets of smoked Atlantic salmon, as pink as dawn and soft as butter, while Eve detailed the hoops she had to jump through to get Petrossian caviar into New York: They included delivering the CITES documents to USF&W and getting the eggs'

DNA sampled; taking the shipment to U.S. Customs for inspection and the payment of duty fees; then going to the Food and Drug Administration for the caviar to be tested for borax. Caviar for cruise lines sailing outside U.S. waters could legally contain borax, she said, and the trick was to keep those batches separate.

"So one part of my job is very glamorous, traveling all over the world and teaching people about fine caviar," she said, "and there's another part, dealing with all these government agencies, which is just intense, and wears you out sometimes. But I personally think this is one of the most exciting industries there is. I love it—love it dearly."

She smiled again, her face bracing into a gypsy's promise of delight. "The best part, of course, is that caviar is literally the food of the gods. I think of it that way, and really it is. It's low in calories, it contains—like olive oil—only good cholesterol . . . "

"It's expensive," the British woman interjected approvingly.

"—it's high in protein . . . "

"We're in a health food store," offered the bow tie.

"—and it quadruples as an aphrodisiac. Need I say more? That aphrodisiac role may be subject to question, really, but then again, you don't eat caviar sitting in front of the TV."

We polished off the salmon, scooped up the last remaining eggs in the presentoirs, left tips for the staff, and moved as a group past other gleaming tables and then out the front entrance. This was a shock. The scaffolding shaded us in part from the late afternoon sun, but not from the exhaust of the taxis racing past, or the heat radiating up from the pavement. No matter: Our destination, a short walk down Seventh Avenue, was the Petrossian Café & Boutique, where we had been promised a 20 percent consideration on any purchase of honorific goods.

We strolled beneath the scaffolding like a company of gods, fresh-minted Fitzgeralds and Hemingways and Bakers, newly versed in good and evil, revenants from the divine horizon.

～4～

THE PEOPLE OF THE STURGEON

i.

Brenda Archambo, from Michigan, sipped her coffee and wanted to know what she was going to learn at this affair. "Are we going to learn why sturgeons jump?"

Bill Casper didn't know why sturgeons jump. He said he heard it was to shake lampreys loose. "But we don't have many lampreys in Lake Winnebago, and the sturgeons are still jumping."

Casper was a retired machinist, a Wisconsin native, and strong as a leg-hold trap. We sat at one of the two dozen tables set up for breakfast in the big Regatta Room of the Park Plaza International Hotel and Convention Center in Oshkosh, where the Fourth International Symposium on Sturgeon, the first to be held on American soil, was about to unfold.

Casper picked at his bacon and told me that the Fox River once was used to run logs from Green Bay on Lake Michigan to Fond du Lac at the southern end of Winnebago. But the Fox drops 170 feet between Winnebago and Lake Michigan, and so the logging operation required the construction of seventeen locks on that stretch of the river, which was a lucky thing for Winnebago. Casper said, "Ships from Europe and the rest of the world used to flush their bilges in the Great Lakes, and that's how the sea lampreys got in there."

Not just the sea lampreys, which attach themselves as parasites to larger fish, but a host of other introduced exotics have transformed the ecology of the Great Lakes, scouring the water column of planktonic organisms and devastating native stocks. But the lake sturgeon, *Acipenser fulvescens*, was already fished out of the Great Lakes by the time the sea lampreys arrived in the 1930s.

"A few years ago that lock system on the Fox was in the process of being abandoned," Casper continued. "But Sturgeon for Tomorrow and the DNR—that's the Wisconsin Department of Natural Resources— fought to have one of those locks sealed to protect the sturgeon. And it worked. But now they're talking about reopening it for pleasure boats."

Brenda shook her head, and Casper's own settled into his shoulders, as if preparing for a fight, which he was, if that talk went on. Bill Casper played by the rules, but he was relentless within their boundaries. He had grown up on the east side of Winnebago, a boy who went fishing with his uncle at a time in the 1940s when you had the whole winter to catch your limit of five sturgeons. Winnebago is Wisconsin's largest inland lake, and a fisherman's dream, rich in walleye, white bass, yellow perch, and trout perch. But nothing got Casper's blood racing like the spearfishing he did each winter for Winnebago's biggest fish, using a method white settlers adopted in the early 1800s from Wisconsin's various Ojibwa tribes.

In the 1930s, he said, there was hardly anyone else out there. Wisconsin had prohibited sturgeon harvest of any sort in the Winnebago watershed in 1915, and then in 1931 the state opened up a spearfishing season with that five-fish limit. As more and more shanties appeared over the years, bag limits were reduced and the minimum size was increased. The sturgeons did fine: The 5,000 fish that the Winnebago system supported in 1955 increased fivefold by the 1970s. But by then there were so many shanties on the lake that the minimum size was up to 45 inches, the bag limit down to two, and the season reduced to the last two weeks in February.

Casper knew he was lucky to have one of the few legal sport-fisheries for sturgeon in the world right out his back door. But he didn't like the way the numbers were going for fishermen, and one night in 1977 he circulated a bulletin that drew 150 other sturgeon fishermen to the town hall in Taycheedah, near Fond du Lac. Their purpose was to pressure the Department of Natural Resources into establishing the sort of hatchery program for sturgeons that was used to supplement game-fish populations of salmon or trout. The DNR replied that nobody in the United States knew how to spawn sturgeon, which was true—Serge Doroshov wouldn't arrive at the University of California for another two years. But it could be done, Casper countered. He found a biologist at Dartmouth College who had just returned from a visit to the sturgeon hatcheries of the Soviet Union. Casper raised the money to fly the scientist out to Wisconsin and tell the DNR what he had seen.

So began a slow dance, involving some stepping on toes, between the DNR and Casper's activist fishermen. The results were several. In 1980, only a year after Doroshov had succeeded in spawning white sturgeon, a Wisconsin biologist, Fred Binkowski, did the same with lake sturgeon. Now hatchery-raised fingerlings were being spawned from wild stock drawn from river systems outside the Winnebago watershed and returned to those same systems. Plans were afoot to start stocking the Fox River, and also to devise a plan for restoring sturgeons to Lake Michigan.

Meanwhile, Casper's original pod of rabble-rousers had grown into Sturgeon for Tomorrow (SFT), at 3,000-strong the world's largest citizen advocacy group for the protection of sturgeon. Aside from raising lots of money at their winter fund-raising banquets, Sturgeon for Tomorrow provided volunteers for the construction of nursery sites, and then for guarding those sites on a round-the-clock basis during the spawning season. Casper was still president, and SFT's four separate chapters included a new one on Michigan's northeast peninsula. Brenda Archambo, wife of a third-generation sturgeon fisherman, was president of that chapter.

Yet things hadn't worked out entirely according to plan. Casper wanted more sturgeons, and even without any stocking in the lake, there were now some 52,000 fish there. That made Winnebago home to the continent's largest population of lakers. But Casper also wanted a longer season, and spiraling numbers of fishermen had made it shorter than ever. The bag limit was down to one, and the harvest capped at 5 percent of the adult population. That meant that last winter's season lasted all of two days. But that was all right with Casper, who contented himself with more sturgeons and enough public enthusiasm for the fish to make this part of Wisconsin famous in the sturgeon universe.

The *Fond-du-Lac Reporter* said that hundreds were expected at the symposium that July 2001: a potpourri of scientists, caviar retailers, agency bureaucrats, aquaculturalists, and environmentalists. Previous symposia had been held in France (Bordeaux, 1989), Russia (Moscow, 1993), and Italy (Piacenza, 1997). After breakfast with Casper, I went out to the registration desk, where a map of the world had been stuck full of colored pins, each designating the home of a symposium attendee. Pins grew in forests in North America, Europe, Russia, and the Caspian range states, including Iran. Scattered stands sprouted in China and Eastern Europe. Solitary pins staked out the unexpected: Paraguay, Israel, Ghana, Zambia, and Greenland. The Park Plaza billed itself as an international hotel, but I was sure that never before had Oshkosh hosted so many introduced exotics.

People were still arriving after breakfast, one of whom was Frank Chapman, with Chulhong Park trailing like a dinghy in his wake. Chulhong had his name tag on his own breast pocket and was trying to get Frank's pinned to his, but Frank moved too fast for him, careening from one networking opportunity to another as acquaintances and colleagues passed in and out the door.

From me he bounced to Chris Coco of the Tennessee Aquarium. Chris was caretaker of one of the continent's four live belugas, a fish personally brought from Russia by Serge Doroshov. Coco told Frank that he still didn't know the sex of his fish, which was twenty years old. Frank said that he could settle the issue for him with a biopsy of some fin tissue. "It's safe," he said. "I've done it lots of times."

Coco replied that it wasn't up to him, that he'd ask about it, and inquired after the gender of Frank's two belugas. Frank laughed and made as if to tango with Coco. He said, "I'm not telling that to anybody just yet. I'm hedging my bets, man."

I had met Casper the day before, when he had told me that he was to be one of the speakers at Sunday night's get-acquainted buffet dinner. He said he didn't really know what to expect from a crowd like this, but he was ready to give it a try. The hotel stood at the junction of the Fox River and the lake, and that night the sky rose in pastel shades of blue and pink above its tower. The Americans showed up in T-shirts and shorts and sandals, the Europeans and Russians in neat slacks and sport jackets, the Asians in one or the other or both. To walk listening from one end of the terrace to the other was like turning the dial of a short-wave radio, hearing in succession the whirring consonants and lilting vowels of one language after another.

One of the buffet offerings was grilled sturgeon: thick, pearly fillets of white sturgeon from California. It looked like something between turkey and cod but had a nice gloss to it. Alexandre Dumas, in his 1873 *Grand Dictionnaire de Cuisine,* wrote that "the flesh of the caviar [sic] has a delicate flavor, rare among cartilaginous fish. It can easily be mistaken for veal." Off the grill it was dense and fine-grained, also cool and melting, less complicated in its sensations than caviar. I went back for seconds, thought about thirds.

At the end of the buffet line, Mats Engstrom, the owner of Tsar Nicoulai Caviar in San Francisco, was doing some taste-test marketing. He moved like a ballroom dancer, tangoing with successive diners as he offered free samples of his American caviars, either white sturgeon (Engstrom called it "California farmed osetra") or paddlefish. He used a mother-of-pearl spoon to place dabs of one caviar or the other on the flesh between the thumb and first finger of each willing subject. In the July heat his graying temples were wet with sweat.

A blonde woman in a snug summer dress, an American, wondered what to do next. "How do you taste wine?" Engstrom instructed in seductive, Swedish-inflected English. "You look at it, you smell it, you use your eyes and your mind, and then you taste it, swirling it in your mouth, holding it on your tongue. You see that the paddlefish is lighter, more olive-gray than the osetra. Perhaps a stronger taste? A little bit nutty? What do you think?"

Several authorities in the historical record hold that lake sturgeons produced the best American caviar, but the laker was represented by neither meat nor caviar in the buffet line that night. Wisconsin, like Florida with its gulf sturgeon, was opposed to any commercial use of the fish. That was okay with Sturgeon for Tomorrow, which found there were more than enough people chasing the laker as it was.

Bill Casper declined his sample of California osetra. As we ate our grilled sturgeon, he told me he had never tried caviar himself until just last year, at a Sturgeon for Tomorrow fund-raiser. It was a walleye fry, but one of the local fishermen brought some lake sturgeon caviar that he had made himself, which was legal enough. Casper smiled and said it was true what they say: "You have to develop a taste for that stuff."

"It was better than I thought it would be," said Brenda Archambo. "I expected lard with some gravel in it."

After dinner the DNR's chief sturgeon biologist, Ron Bruch, played master-of-ceremonies to the welcoming speeches of the mayor and the congressman and the director of the DNR. Bill Casper was scheduled next, but inexplicably Bruch skipped directly to the chancellor of the University of Wisconsin, who claimed pride of place for Oshkosh: "The symposium in Bordeaux drew about 50 people," the chancellor cheered, "and the one in Moscow about 100. We have more than 400 in Oshkosh tonight. There must be something special in the water here."

By the time the applause died down and Bruch got to thanking everybody and shutting down the podium, Casper was seething. He rushed up front, where the embarrassed MC reactivated the public address system and apologized for forgetting about Sturgeon for Tomorrow: "If you folks wouldn't mind listening to just a few more words, this time from a man who has had as much to do as anybody with the turnaround with the numbers of sturgeon in this lake . . . "

But the speeches were to be followed by a mixer, and the mixing had already begun. The polite hush enjoyed by the previous speakers was beyond recovery. Nonetheless, Casper assumed the podium with a defiant air. "The value of this sturgeon and her eggs continue to increase as the numbers all over the world decrease," he read. "No matter what part of the world you are from, you'll have an almost impossible task on your hands if you do not have the support of the people—the fishermen. If you cannot instill in the minds of the general public the need to preserve, the need to assist in watching over this resource, your job will be most difficult."

He advised going into the schools, and always being mindful that some members of this generation were teaching the young only how to take sturgeons, and not how to be stewards of them. Casper paused, and then had to shout above the din, "Remember—while you are looking through your microscopes, others are looking for ways to remove this sturgeon from the waters."

ii.

After breakfast on Monday—and just before the symposium's plenary session, a time devoted to general presentations from various speakers in academia or the aquaculture industry—I ran into Frank again. Chul-hong was tugging at his sleeve, but Frank couldn't be pried away from the group he was talking with. It included Mats Engstrom, whose Tsar Nicoulai company traded in Caspian, Amur River, and American cav-iars; Peter Struffenegger, manager of the biggest white sturgeon aqua-culture and caviar operation in California, a subsidiary of Norway's Stolt Sea Farm; and Vulf Sternin, the Russian émigré coauthor of what might be described as the standard textbook on its subject, *Caviar: The Resource Book*, published in 1993.

That Gang of Four, I reflected, including Frank, represented a rain-bow of commercial interests in the sturgeon, and it reminded me that in the annals of wildlife conservation the state of Wisconsin boasted two near-native sons who were either leery of such interests (Aldo Leopold) or else outspokenly hostile (John Muir).

John Muir was born in Scotland, but in 1849 his family moved to a hardscrabble farm near Portage, about 50 miles southwest of Oshkosh, where he grew up enchanted by the teeming wildlife of the New World. Later he became the driving force behind the National Park Bill of 1890, establishing the Yosemite and Sequoia national parks, and was also the founder of the Sierra Club. To Muir the parks, and the wildlife they sheltered, were guideposts to an essential sense of self. "There is a love of wild nature in everybody, an ancient mother-love showing itself whether recognized or no, and however covered by cares and duties," he wrote.

No one was better versed in that love than Aldo Leopold. Born in Iowa in 1887, Leopold studied forestry at Yale, worked eighteen years in the Southwest for the U.S. Forest Service, and in 1933 joined the faculty of the University of Wisconsin at Madison. The classic textbook he published that same year, *Game Management*, established the young science of ecology—with its grasp of the web of interrelationships unit-ing all plants and animals in a given region—as the dominant paradigm for managing and restoring wildlife populations. His most popular book, *A Sand County Almanac*, was published after his death in 1949. A diary of the seasons on a piece of tired river-bottom land, the book also describes the spiritual satisfactions of the author's struggle to restore that land to health. "It is here," wrote Leopold, "that we seek—and still find—our meat from God."

Each, in his own manner, was a strident opponent of the commodification of nature and its parts. But even to the Romans, sturgeon, this other meat from God, had been a commodity, and—except in such blessed enclaves as Lake Winnebago—there was no separating it now from what Muir vilified as "the Almighty Dollar."

In fact, CITES was discovering, rather to its chagrin, that there was no more commercially prominent fish under its aegis than the sturgeon. Mats Engstrom's Tsar Nicoulai "California farmed osetra" had played to good reviews from the diners at the symposium, a number of whom were skilled at telling the honorific from the less so. The glass-half-full interpretation of the rise of a commercial aquaculture industry in sturgeon was that it might represent a way to ease economic pressure on wild stocks. The glass-half-empty take saw it as just another escalation in the species' commodification. Frank Chapman saw it both ways and believed that it was precisely because the sturgeon was worth money that we had at last gotten around to being careful with it.

CITES had gotten more careful, and the caviar retailers at the conference were all on edge because of it. Last month, under pressure from CITES, Russia, Azerbaijan, and Kazakhstan had all agreed to suspend sturgeon fishing for the rest of the year. The nations had also agreed to survey existing stocks before next January and develop a cooperative plan to thwart poaching. Turkmenistan still hadn't signed on as a party to CITES and had no representative at the meeting in Geneva—nonetheless, that country had to join the rest in this or face an embargo on its caviar exports. Iran was still free to fish and export.

The moratorium in the north end of the sea wasn't quite so tough as it sounded, since all four nations had already harvested 70 to 80 percent of their legal quota for the year. But supply would be down for the dealers during the holiday rush at the end of the year, when they typically did half their business. And no one could guarantee after New Year's that the trans-Caspian nations would hold up their end and that the moratorium would be lifted. At least exports of caviar that had already been produced and packed were moving once more, including Arkady Panchernikov's chilled, not frozen, windfall from Kazakhstan.

But many scientists were unimpressed by the whole thing, fearing that when push came to shove between CITES and the caviar industry, the Almighty Dollar would win. One such was the father of the American aquaculture industry in sturgeon, Serge Doroshov. The courtly, white-haired professor received perhaps the loudest welcome of any of the plenary session speakers as he moved to the podium. Talking quietly, with only a trace of a Slavic accent, Doroshov observed that the scientific study of sturgeon had begun only a century ago, and there were many aspects of sturgeon biology and life history, he said, "that remain enigmatic." A note of resignation crept into his voice when he added, "I guess it will always be true that people enjoy caviar and smoked sturgeon, and for that reason we will have to go ahead with aquaculture and the commercial development of these products."

iii.

There was no one at the symposium representing sturgeon poachers, at least so far as we knew, but the profiteering of that particular interest group cast its shadow over the whole week of the symposium. On Tuesday, a panel-presentation, "CITES and Sturgeon Law Enforcement," tackled that problem directly.

Peter Struffenegger, tall enough to dwarf the podium and good-humored enough to keep fights from breaking out, was the moderator. "Welcome to the room where science meets environmental policy, and environmental policy meets marketing," he said as people settled in. "There are a lot of different interests represented in this room today, and they're not often in agreement. The environmentalists say that we're facing the imminent demise of the sturgeon. The retail dealers say there are plenty of sturgeons left. The regulators say we don't have good data, we don't really know how many are left right now. And a fish farmer like me says, 'How did I get involved? I had nothing to do with it.'"

Struffenegger's panel included Caroline Raymakers, a Belgian representing Trade Records Analysis of Flora and Fauna (TRAFFIC), the research arm of CITES; Liz Lauk, from the Wildlife Conservation Society and its Caviar Emptor campaign; and Armen Petrossian, who had flown into Oshkosh the previous night with Eve Vega.

The presentations went exactly as Struffenegger had predicted. Caroline Raymakers reported that, taken as a whole, actual exports of caviar had exceeded export quotas by 15 percent in 2000—so not even the legal trade was quite under control. Liz Lauk passed out information packets on the beluga's decline, and also copies of an editorial published in the *New York Times* by celebrity chef Jacques Pépin on July 3, 2001. "The international trade in beluga caviar ought to be halted until the fish that produce it are no longer threatened with extinction," Pépin wrote. "During this time, caviar lovers might try the roe of United States farm-grown sturgeon, which has improved tremendously in the last few years and is more affordable than Caspian caviar."

When Armen Petrossian rose to speak—with his silvery hair, waxed handlebar mustache, and wire-rimmed glasses—he reiterated his conviction that any reduction in legal trade not only enlarged the illegal, but deprived hatcheries of needed revenues. Nor was the black market much inconvenienced by export bans. What couldn't be smuggled out could be sold domestically, he reminded us, in settings where CITES had no jurisdiction.

The debate joined in earnest during the questions from the audience that followed. Someone said that CITES's ban on international trade in elephant ivory had been helpful to the numbers of African elephants. Wouldn't the same be true for sturgeon? "The difference is that there is no inside market for elephant ivory," replied Petrossian, "while of course there is a very big one for caviar."

A young woman wondered why CITES didn't do more to promote aquaculture. "Aquaculture is great, but commercial fish farms won't save the sturgeon in the wild," said Raymakers. Mats Engstrom, who had joined the panel for the question-and-answer session, nodded his assent. "And in production terms," Raymakers added, "it's nowhere near ready to replace the volume of the wild harvest."

"Also you should remember that caviar from wild sturgeon and caviar from farmed sturgeon are two entirely different products," sniffed Petrossian.

Steve Fain, the director of USF&W's DNA testing program and the author of the test the agency uses, rose from the audience with a question for the environmentalists. If the beluga were to be listed under the Endangered Species Act, would they support an exclusion for the export and sale of the fish for purposes of aquaculture? "I'm asking because once it's put on CITES's Appendix I," he added, "there will be no money to be made off it in the Caspian, and therefore no incentive to protect it there."

Lisa Speer, the director of the Caviar Emptor program, rose from the audience to say they certainly wouldn't support that exclusion. "If the beluga is going to be farmed for profit or any other purpose, that should be done in the Caspian, where the scientific expertise already exists," she pronounced. "There would still be incentive to protect and rebuild wild stocks, because the goal is to get the fish de-listed as soon as possible. There is a time, though, when an animal belongs on Appendix I, and it looks like the beluga is there."

"The caviar industry would be completely against such a listing," objected Petrossian. "Such a measure would not only destroy the image of caviar—if you destroy one part of it, then you destroy all of it—but it would be premature and inefficient and based on inadequate information. All these numbers about the decline of the beluga come from the Volga, not the Ural River in Kazakhstan. But historically two-thirds of the harvest comes from the Ural, where conditions are much different. I believe that if, instead of working against each other, all parties involved in this issue—the producers, the importers, the regulators, the police, and so forth—if we all joined together in one common effort, that way we will make progress in the Caspian."

These were stirring words to many of the fifty or so who packed the room, and applause rang out. Then the questions resumed, and people started working against each other again, and we were back to making shift with the way things were.

Through the windows at the back of the room, the noise of traffic and the rich, midsummer scent of the Fox River wafted in. The lake sturgeon that swam in and about its mouth were troubled by neither the traffic nor our blustering. "Every living thing represents an equation of give and take," wrote Aldo Leopold in "Ecology and Politics," a 1941 essay. "Man or mouse, oak or orchid, we take a livelihood from our land and our fellows. . . . Ultimately we give ourselves. That this collective account between the earth and its creatures ultimately balances is implicit in the fact that both continue to live."

"No one wants to cut the tree they are sitting on," Armen Petrossian said. "We're all against this poaching, which is killing the industry. We are doing everything we can to help with that, and so is every other member of the Importers' Association."

Mats Engstrom thought about the April assault by poachers on a Russian Coast Guard station, and also the rebellion in neighboring Chechnya. These suggested such cares and duties as to exceed even John Muir's reckoning. "How can we expect the Russians to guard the fish in Dagestan when they can't even handle Chechnya, just 50 miles away?" he asked. "Do we think the Russians are going to put a battalion into Dagestan? Just ponder that, please."

iv.

After the first day of the symposium I didn't see Brenda Archambo, who was curious about why sturgeons jump, or else I would have directed her to one of the many poster-papers on display in the Park Plaza's LaSalle Ballroom. Its author was Ken Sulak, the U.S. Geological Survey biologist who played point-counterpoint to Frank Chapman in Florida.

I talked about this paper with John Waldman, a biologist with the Hudson River Foundation who would go on to write a column about it in the *New York Times* on October 21, 2001. Despite Eve Vega's statement to the contrary, there were still sturgeons in the Hudson, and Waldman noted that for many years the Hudson River Fishermen's Association had offered a cash prize, still unclaimed, to anyone who could provide a photograph of the fish in mid-leap. He himself had never seen a sturgeon jump until an outing that week on Lake Winnebago, where at last he witnessed what he described as "a visual epiphany." He wrote in his column that several other fish species make spectacular leaps, but these were all fast pelagic fish—tuna, sailfish, tarpon—and why a whiskered bottom-dweller like the sturgeon should imitate these, said Waldman, "is one of the great mysteries of the fish world."

In his poster-paper, Sulak proposed a new solution to the mystery. He mentioned all the folk and scientific explanations proposed thus far, including what Bill Casper had heard about sturgeons shaking parasites loose. But, wrote Sulak, "few well-adapted parasites, tenaciously attached to their hosts by special hooks and suction devices, would be dislodged or even mildly disturbed just because the host leaves the water momentarily." Other suggestions: to escape predators; to capture flying insects as prey; to help shed eggs during spawning; as a part of nuptial behavior; as a startle-fright response; because it feels good; or simply as a random activity pattern, which would be the technical way of saying there was no explanation. Waldman chipped in another: A fishing guide once told him that sturgeon eat crayfish, whose claws then nip the fish's intestines, and the fish leap to loosen their grip.

None of these, wrote Sulak, passed muster, especially regarding the thousands of jumps he had seen in fifteen years of studying gulf sturgeons. Escape or startle responses are unlikely for the biggest fish in a river, though conceivably the behavior could survive as a vestige of those times when even bigger predators were to be found. Nuptial or spawning behavior is more unlikely, since jumping occurs very rarely during connubial times, and at all times immature fish are as likely to jump as mature. Airborne feeding would be impossible: Besides being poorly adapted to compete with bats and swallows, sturgeons in the Suwannee feed hardly at all during the summer, which was when jumping occurred most frequently.

A different idea was suggested to Sulak by a passage in a 1731 natural history of Carolina and Florida, one that described the behavior of Atlantic sturgeons: "In May, June, and July the rivers abound with them, at which time it is very surprising, though very common to see such large fish elated in the air, by their leaping some yards out of the water; this they do in an erect posture, and fall on their sides, which repeated percussions are loudly heard some miles distance."

Sulak was intrigued to be reminded how loud those percussions were, which prompted him to take a closer look at precisely when and how often sturgeons jump. During several days on the Suwannee the previous summer, he and other observers counted sturgeon jumps per thirty-minute interval, timing their observations so that they covered all twenty-four hours of the diurnal cycle. The sound of the jumps was

recorded by hydrophone, and their distances calibrated by means of anchored reference buoys.

"Jumping activity is not random in time," Sulak wrote. Instead sturgeon jump most often in a two-hour period beginning thirty minutes
before dawn, with a much smaller peak in activity at dusk. Jumping
then occurs sporadically at low frequencies throughout the rest of the
day and night, amounting to several hundred jumps per day in certain
areas. The jumps themselves had a distinctive acoustic signal that could
be heard more than half a mile away, and probably a good deal farther
underwater. But why so often during the summer? Jumping is expensive
in terms of energy, and on the Suwannee, sturgeon tend to group near
the river's cool springs, moving little, living in what Sulak described as
a state of "trophic dormancy and energy conservation."

The peaks of jumping activity suggested to Sulak that the behavior
wasn't random, and the occurrence of jumping during a period of dormancy suggested also that it was important. A Russian biologist at the
symposium, Larissa Tolstaganova, had written that Atlantic sturgeon
and the various Caspian species produced far-ranging whistle-like sig-
nals during spawning, apparently for purposes of communication over
murky distances. Sulak hypothesized that jumping was another form of
acoustic communication, "serving to maintain group cohesion on the
summer holding grounds, much as lowing sounds are used by herd animals to maintain group cohesion within a given area."

So sturgeons jump, in other words, to remain in conference with
each other, rather in the way scientists use e-mail. But Frank Chapman
disagreed. When I talked with him about Sulak's idea, he said that his
own sturgeons jump even in the small ponds and tanks of his aquaculture operation, and the frequency was unchanged whether there was
one, five, or a hundred fish in a pond. He believed instead it had something to do with feeding habits, since it correlated by the clock with
periods of peak feeding activity, even if the fish feed little during the
summer. Nor had he found evidence of Tolstaganova's whistling in his
Russian sturgeons in the spring, though it was possible the hatchery environment simply didn't elicit that behavior.

John Waldman, whose own work focused on the genetic structure of
Atlantic, short-nosed, and gulf sturgeon populations, was piqued by

Sulak's idea but not persuaded that the mystery had been solved. On a visceral level, he was still attracted by another hypothesis, an idea discounted by Sulak, but one, as he wrote in the *New York Times*, that "gets closer to the soul of the fish: it simply feels good."

v.

On Friday, the last day of the symposium, I stood next to Frank Chapman on a bridge that spanned the Wolf River. This was Shawano County, where pastures and crop lands rolled to the horizons. Frank pointed to a ripple in the river, the wake of a large swimming object that had appeared in front of a DNR motor skiff. A leathery tail broke the surface at the side of a companion skiff, and the boat veered in pursuit. "Look, they got some," he said.

The bridge was lined end to end by multinationals, with many more spilling onto the road and riverbank. That morning the whole symposium had packed itself into six tour buses and headed north from Oshkosh through Appleton and onto Route 47. We stopped along the way at rock-strewn areas of the Wolf, where sturgeons once again were spawning in the spring, guarded by Sturgeon for Tomorrow volunteers as they did so. Restoring lake sturgeons to the Wolf was a joint project, we were told, of the DNR and the Menominee Native American tribe.

John Muir wrote in his autobiography that the Menominee sometimes came to his father's farm to barter for bread or matches, or else to sharpen their knives against his grindstone. In the fall he noticed small groups of them tracking deer through the woods. Formerly they roamed throughout central Wisconsin and Michigan's Upper Peninsula, but since 1854 they had been confined to a reservation about 45 miles north of Oshkosh. That was our destination, where we were to be the guests of the Menominee for a traditional feast and dance.

At the bridge, county sheriff's deputies herded passing cars and trucks through the crowd, their drivers staring about in mystification. A collective murmur rose from the throng as three DNR boats, each aluminum flat-bottomed skiffs with a crew of three and a big outboard motor, rounded the nearest bend in the river. The boats carried electric boom-shockers, which were metal hoops extending from the boat on long poles and trailing copper wires in the water. From a distance the devices looked like the empty frames of shot-out headlights.

Frank Chapman stood next to me and explained that the wires gave off an electric field that attracted sturgeons. Once they rose and swam close enough, the operator spiked the current just enough to stun them. "It's a standard fisheries sampling technique," Frank added. "We use it a lot in Florida. But timing it right is an art, man. If you aren't just right in how you do it, you can kill the fish."

A crewman on the middle skiff swished a large dip net through the water, then required the help of a mate to lift the green, writhing form of a lake sturgeon clear of the river. Another murmur ran through the crowd as the fish was borne dripping into the skiff. Within less than a minute, four had been captured, and the skiffs had raced to the southern bank of the river. There, on a square of canvas spread on the grass, the fish were prepared to be weighed, measured, and tagged. The crowd abandoned the bridge and surrounded the tarpaulins and the DNR agents.

Lake sturgeons can get as big as 8 feet and 300 pounds, but these were all much smaller than that. They ranged from 40 to 60 pounds, their snouts more rounded and conical than a gulf sturgeon's, their dorsal greens less vivid now than in the water, fading to gray against the grass surrounding the canvas. The gray-green was peppered with black flecks, and their bellies were honey golden. Fred Binkowski, the first to artificially spawn these fish, gripped the head and tail of the smallest as it was stretched along a board marked into inches and feet. Another biologist made entries onto a clipboard. Cameras came out of pockets and shutters scissored cricket-like in near unison. It occurred to me that many among the gallery had never before seen a wild sturgeon.

The Wolf spills down Keshana Falls in the midst of the forested Menominee reservation. Great numbers of sturgeons still spawned at the foot of those falls when the tribe assembled there to sign its peace treaty with the federal government in 1854. Then the Wolf was dammed, and no sturgeons had been speared at the falls since 1859. But the Menominee had obtained some lakers from elsewhere for this occasion, and within listening distance of the falls, on high ground above a natural amphitheater in the woods columned and curtained by towering pines, the tribe's vice-chairman welcomed us to a feast of bear, venison, hulled corn, fried bread, and quantities of fresh and smoked sturgeon. "You are the people of the sturgeon, just as we are," he said. "So I know the spirit of the sturgeon is honored that you are here, and that your presence will help us in our efforts to bring the sturgeon back again to Keshana Falls."

Men, women, and children walked in clumps past our tables as we ate in the open air, then disappeared down the trail that led into the Woodland Bowl. Many wore feathers, shawls, beads, and headdresses, all in riotous colors, their faces beautified by the same high cheekbones, the same grave and distant look to the eyes, that I saw in the faces of the Siberians, whether scientists or translators, who had come as part of the Russian delegation. The smoked lake sturgeon, the Menominee's meat from God, was no less sweet than Tsar Nicoulai's white sturgeon meat had been.

After the meal we filled wooden benches in the side of the bowl. There the oratory of the tribal leaders outlasted the daylight, until finally a group of men, both elders and young adults, assembled in the center. The first drumbeats rose in tremors through the ground, throbbing through the soles of our shoes and sandals, running in faint electroshock pulses through our bones. The dancers in their colors surrounded the drummers, each performing a personalized series of steps and motions as the group moved clockwise, like a galactic wheel, like sturgeons running in a circular tank, about the drummers.

After the Snake Dance and the Swan Dance and several others, spectators were invited to join in the Fish Dance. There ensued a long, nervous moment, a collective catch in the throat for an assembly of non-Natives that, as a group, had little dance experience. At last Vulf Sternin, the Russian caviar expert who now lived in British Columbia, strode decisively into the midst of the Menominee dancers.

Tall, skeletal, pale, and quite bald, in white pants and shirt, the elderly Sternin looked like a puff of chalk in the center of a burst of fireworks. When the drums started up, he raised his elbows and began a series of movements that were either satirical or exemplary of that very best sort of dancing, the kind you do when nobody's looking. The Menominee weren't looking. They were all in motion again, their feathers and fringed shawls cutting filets of brightness out of the gathering dark. Other visitors looked on and then came down, several dozens of them, Russians and Italians and Eastern Europeans, Chinese and Kazakhstanis, one or two or three from Zambia, Paraguay, and Greenland, falling into the beat and pounding the grass and helping to call the sturgeons back.

I sat halfway up the bowl, swimming in the music and letting events from the previous week run like flash cards through my mind. I remembered sitting at breakfast one morning while another industry advocacy group besides Armen Petrossian's importers' association took shape around me. Peter Struffenegger of Stolt Sea Farm presided over a table occupied by Mats Engstrom and several other sturgeon farmers, both European and American. "Okay," said Struffenegger. "We're here today to set up a sturgeon growers' association."

"Against CITES," snapped Engstrom. I knew from talking with these men that CITES had complicated the lives of growers as much as it had the lives of scientists and importers, adding time and cost and paperwork to their own international marketing, and making it difficult for growers working with nonnative species to obtain broodstock.

Struffenegger smiled. "No, not against CITES, but to represent the growers' point of view within the CITES process, which we remember is something that got going in the late seventies, or early eighties. . . ."

"Earlier than that," said Engstrom. "1963."

Struffenegger sighed. "Well, for the sake of argument, we'll say 1963 [CITES was founded in 1975]. Now this is an organization that has met, what, eleven times since its founding? And by now they have something like 30,000 species listed. So do the math—that's close to 3,000 species listed per meeting. What does that tell you about the review and assessment process? You can almost see those guys, saying, 'Hey, we gotta catch a plane, but wait, we can list twelve more species before then.'"

In a Park Plaza conference room, I remembered seeing Vladimir P. Ivanov, the director of Russia's Caspian Fisheries Research Institute (KaspNIRKh), standing at the podium in his white suit and gray hair, his charts lit on the screen behind him, his grim translator at his side. The institute had a reputation for erring on the side of optimism when talking about sturgeon numbers in the Caspian, but Ivanov's charts provided much to be grim about: No less than 98 percent of the belugas now caught had been artificially reared at hatcheries, and twenty to thirty large, mature belugas, especially females of 200 to 400 pounds, were needed each year from the wild to provide broodstock for the hatcheries, but it was becoming impossible to find fish that size.

More shocking—electroshocking—was a statement slipped almost as an aside in response to a question from the audience. How does one tell the difference between a beluga spawned in the wild and one reared at a hatchery? The matter was irrelevant, Ivanov said, because the beluga had ceased to reproduce naturally in the wild. The Russians used to mark the fingerlings they released from the hatcheries, but there was no point to that anymore.

There was a moment of audible hush, of the rapid sucking in of breath. Ivanov could speak with authority only of the Volga, but what had recently been seen as a dark eventuality was suddenly heard to arrive with a thud. That the bearer of evil tidings was the director of always-on-the-sunny-side KaspNIRKH, and that the news came so casually as this, made the thud all the more awful.

A forest of hands came up. When, exactly, did natural reproduction cease for the beluga? "We cannot say with certainty as yet." What about the 2 percent of the catch not reared at hatcheries? "They are older fish. All the young fish have been artificially spawned." What will be the impact of the fall moratorium on fishing? "If there is a moratorium, all trans-Caspian countries should participate, including Iran. We hope all five will sign an agreement to that effect."

The questions went on, Ivanov's words finally blurring into those of Caroline Raymakers, who sat next to me on the bus on our way to the reservation. The Belgian said that she had visited Azerbaijan in 1997. She went to the Kura River, a three-hour drive south of the capital city of Baku, where the Soviets had built the first of their sturgeon hatcheries. At one time there was also a caviar-processing factory on the Kura that employed a thousand people. But now that most caviar in Azerbaijan was processed on the black market, that factory had closed.

"So when people tell me that it is normal to poach, that they have to eat, well, there is a contradiction there," Raymakers said. "People have lost their jobs because of the poaching. Maybe some of them found other jobs in the black market, but I think very few. The others, well, when I arrived at the hatchery, people came from everywhere to crowd around my car. They were hoping that I had come to invest in the hatchery, to provide money to get it working again. It was very sad."

Then I fell into something like sleep, as the song that accompanied the Fish Dance rose into the dry Wisconsin sky, above the Woodland Bowl, and Keshana Falls, and the pastures of Shawano County, and then Lake Winnebago, where the sturgeons swam, and finally over the streets and darkened storefronts of Oshkosh. Its syllables sailed away like balloons, elated in the air, and then trailed into silence beneath a dim quarter-moon.

~5~

SITUATION UNPLEASANT

i.

Things were bad. Then they got a little bit worse. When Eve Vega finally had a chance to sit down, she said that four cases of Petrossian pressed caviar—about 190 pounds—had just been bounced back to Paris by a young USF&W agent at Kennedy Airport.

This was the Monday after Thanksgiving, ten weeks after the 9/11 incineration of the World Trade Center and the attack on the Pentagon. Petrossian and other importers were working with some new personnel at the Valley Stream office. Ed Grace was in Chicago, though at the moment he was up in the air somewhere, serving as a sky marshal. Rob Rothe was still around, but Roland Marquis had been reassigned to Boston. Why wasn't the caviar allowed entry by the new guy at Kennedy? "Because," said Eve, her black eyes flashing, "the DNA test revealed that there were eggs from four different species in the caviar."

Which is exactly the point with pressed caviar. It's a lemonade made from the mixed lemons—eggs that are soft, broken, or overly mature—rejected from various first-grade *malossol* caviars. These second-grade eggs weren't dry salted, like first-grade, but instead shaken (not stirred) in a warm, salty brine. Then they were drained, packed into cheesecloth or linen bags, and then—while still warm—put under a press, where the eggs were reduced to a quarter of their original volume.

Eventually the caviar was cooled, gently mixed to even out the salt content, and finally packed into airtight kegs or tins. The result is not unlike Spam, if Spam were served to the hoi polloi: cakey, spreadable, thick enough to slice with a knife. I've never had pressed caviar, but I'm told that it has a stronger flavor than the malossol varieties, and for that reason it's popular among Russians, who also use it in many recipes. Cossack soldiers are said to have brought kegs of it with them as they marched on Paris in 1812, and it may actually have been that version of Russian caviar that first seduced the French.

Pressed caviar is virtually unknown in the United States, but Petrossian—like everybody else in the caviar business—was looking for a way to get some momentum again. The events of 9/11 had staggered the whole U.S. economy, but this corner of it had been knocked off its feet. "Double whammy," Eve told me in October. "We're hit both ways. People in the city are afraid to go out, so they're not eating at the restaurants anymore. And if they do happen to go out, it seems thoughtless and uncaring to spend money at an opulent place like Petrossian's. At least the café is doing pretty well, better than the restaurant."

New Yorkers were staying home, and so was everybody else. "Obviously the world is very different now," said a gloomy Mats Engstrom over the telephone from San Francisco, where the malls and stores were empty, the streets quiet. "I don't know who wants to buy caviar today."

Eve and I were meeting not at the restaurant, but at Eve's office in the building that Petrossian uses as a warehouse, packing, and shipping facility on West 13th Street, at the northern fringe of Greenwich Village. Eve's third-floor office overlooked the street, but her black window-shades were drawn almost to the sills. She said she was glad at least that the pressed caviar wasn't confiscated. "There is a CITES notification on the label if the product is a mixture of different caviars," she explained. "It's almost impossible to say exactly how much might be this species or that species, but that doesn't matter. I told the agent that every egg in that caviar had already been counted against the right species quota at the time of harvest, and the CITES Secretariat in Geneva said we could bring this in. But this guy's a young pit bull, and he said that nobody had spoken to him about it, so send it back."

She called the agent in charge at Valley Stream, who listened sympathetically but replied that 60 percent of his agents were sky-marshaling, and that now more than ever he left judgments like these to his agents in the field. "A lot of people seem to feel that if you're in the caviar business these days, that's close to being a terrorist," Eve sighed. "And at Fish and Wildlife now, you're guilty until proven innocent. Well, there are so few people coming through Customs these days, maybe they've got nothing better to do."

Earlier Eve had described to me in quesy detail her eye-witness perspective on the events of 9/11. She understood that beyond its human consequences, the attack had economic consequences as well. Like a meteor impact, the destruction of the World Trade Center signaled a precipitous change in the commercial environment, and the proximity of a certain number of extinctions. Some entities that were well-suited to conditions before 9/11 found themselves struggling in its aftermath. Some that were struggling in the first place found themselves further down the slippery slope.

Eve was more afraid than ever that the caviar industry was on that slope. A part of her anger that day about the pressed caviar had to do with all the black-market stuff that was still getting in, despite the young pit bulls. Nor was she pleased to hear from me that Ed Grace had been transferred to Chicago. "Then I don't see this situation repairing itself," she offered. "The government isn't any closer to closing the loopholes, and these new inspectors don't know what's going on. The bad guys are just going to fester in a climate like this. And if the bad guys can't work the way they want to, then they're just going to ruin the industry. That's their attitude."

She didn't name names, but she knew that Arkady Panchernikov was still under investigation. Yet, Caspian Star was working the way it wanted to, and the industry was still buzzing from the news of Panchernikov's high-volume coup in Kazakhstan. The rumor mill cited figures from 13 to 30 tons for the amount he was bringing in. Panchernikov told me that he had 28 tons, and that he was dealing in such volumes not only for his own good, but the good of the market. "Don't get me wrong," he said over the telephone. "This is capitalism, and we have our markup. But our competitors—I won't name names—are talking about how little caviar is available, and so that is why prices are skyrocketing. But we don't do that sort of thing. We don't rip off our clients. We have a good amount of inventory, and that allows our prices to be normal."

Mats Engstrom believed there was no way that Panchernikov could sell that much caviar in this economic climate, that he would indeed end up having to freeze much of it. He believed as well that Arkady had the caviar on consignment through a deal worked out with the son-in-law of the president of Kazakhstan. "You think there is a fishery department in Kazakhstan?" Engstrom said. "It's a tribal fiefdom. And Arkady has lost all his airline and cruise ship markets. So he's trying to overwhelm ours on sheer volume. Everybody else is selling beluga now for at least $80 an ounce. That's the minimum required price to make any money on that. But Arkady is dumping his for $50. That's well below our purchase price, and we're going to have a tough time moving our stock. He's going to destroy a lot of business, I think, for a lot of people."

That left Eve trying to figure out some ways that didn't necessarily involve beluga to prime the market pump. Pressed caviar might prove popular, if only it could get past the gate at Kennedy. Some fresh sturgeon meat, intended here for smoking, was on its way from the Caspian as a complement to the restaurant's noted salmon. Eve reported proudly that breakfast on British Airways' supersonic Concorde now relied on Petrossian baked goods—croissants, rolls, and muffins—and there were negotiations in progress to put the Petrossian logo on the Concorde's tail. Then, please God, there was the Christmas rush, presuming that people were out on the streets and spending money again by then.

Eve took me on a tour of the rest of Petrossian's space there: the packing room, where two women in latex aprons and gloves spooned caviar from big 1.8 kilogram containers with Cyrillic lettering into glass jars and gold-plated tins, weighing it as they went; the refrigerator room, with its stacks of wooden boxes of 1.8 kilo containers, each with its CITES permit number; the telecommunications center, with its desks of wire-braided computers and telephones; the fourth floor and its shelves of catalog sales items, the pearl spoons and champagne coolers and Fabergé crystal presentoirs and all the rest, stacked like booty looted from palaces and penthouses; the fifth floor and its main refrigerator room, able to hold 10 tons of caviar, but containing that day just a few boxes of beluga from Kazakhstan, hustled out before Arkady shut the gate there.

Eve mentioned that during the holiday rush she girds for a workday that stretches—at least in the past—from seven in the morning to midnight. "You know that Dunkin' Donuts commercial, the guy waking up in the dark, telling himself, 'Time to make the doughnuts'? That's the way I wake up in December." She took a quarter-turn in her chair, with a sleepy sort of smile, and held up crossed fingers.

ii.

It was all supposed to be easier than this, and cleaner. Certainly no one was more disappointed with the way things had turned out than a man who worked halfway up a tall building only a few blocks from the Petrossian Restaurant.

The offices of the Sturgeon Society on the Upper West Side were also those of Birstein Computer Services. My meeting in those offices with Vadim Birstein happened before the world had changed—in June 2001. But things had already changed radically for Birstein, and in his offices there was work only for his computer services business. The Sturgeon Society, founded with such high hopes in 1994, existed in name only and was, for all practical purposes, extinct.

"I created this whole disaster," he volunteered, almost before we had finished our introductions. "If I knew what would happen, would I do it again? I don't know. The whole situation is unpleasant, all results disturbing."

The sobriquet "Sturgeon General" devolves inevitably to whoever might be in charge of whatever project involving sturgeon. Only one such general, however briefly, held sway over the entire world with a vision that promised the elimination of the black market, a fair chance of survival for each sturgeon species, and the scientific resources to rapidly fill in the gaps in our knowledge of the fish's biology and behavior. Birstein was a geneticist, intrigued by what the sturgeon's ancient family tree might reveal about the family itself and the course of vertebrate evolution through the ages. But he found that a snippet of sturgeon DNA, theoretically, could accomplish even more than that.

Arguably it was Birstein, a U.S. citizen since 1996, who discovered the black market in caviar, or at least drew attention to it. Then it was he and Rob DeSalle of the American Museum of Natural History who devised a cheap, elegant, and accurate molecular test for distinguishing the eggs of one species from those of another. The test, Birstein believed, would provide for foolproof law enforcement and also help fund his further research into the sturgeon family tree. The Sturgeon Society, which was founded, essentially, on the promise of that test, was to be the worldwide interface coordinating the activities of scientists, conservationists, and international police on the sturgeon's behalf. The outcome, alas, had been more complicated.

But the story should begin with Jacob Birstein, Vadim's father, the coauthor of a 1934 paper noting a widespread die-off of benthic organisms on the floor of the Caspian Sea. This was an event that threatened the sea's food chain, particularly its sturgeon populations, and the paper suggested that a small burrowing worm, *Nereis succinea*, be transplanted from the Sea of Azov to the Caspian. The Nereis project was deemed such a success that in 1948 Jacob Birstein and the paper's other authors were nominated for a Stalin Prize.

By then, however, Stalin's chief state scientist was Trofim Lysenko, who rejected the science of genetics and preached the inheritability of acquired characteristics—therefore a man who trained as a distance runner, according to Lysenko, would have children born with the lung capacities of distance runners. That was nonsense to Jacob Birstein. As soon as he said so, however, he was attacked by a jealous Lysenkoist, denied the Stalin Prize, and fired from his position at Moscow University. Vadim spent his childhood expecting his father's arrest by the KGB, though that never happened.

Vadim Birstein entered that same university in 1962 to study molecular biology in tacit defiance of the dogma that had ruined his father's career. He became an environmental activist as well, going with friends to the Volga Delta to cut the nets of poachers and then call the fisheries police. Later, after Khrushchev had fallen and Lysenkoism had been repudiated, he did postgraduate work on fruit fly genetics and got a job at Moscow's prestigious Koltsov Institute of Developmental Biology.

When I ventured a complimentary remark about the achievements of Soviet science during the Cold War years, Birstein fixed me with a smoldering glare. Now in his late fifties, Birstein was short and barrel-chested, at once bear-like and gnomish. The flash on my camera wasn't working that day, apparently, and the photos I took of him in his own office in the three-room suite failed to come out. But one provided a telling image: Birstein sitting against his window, a New York skyscraper looming in the white June sunlight behind him, all else in black silhouette except for his eyes—due partly to the red-eye effect, partly to glare from his glasses—glowing as red as two hot coals at the bottom of the sea.

Glaring just that way, Birstein reminded me of the murderous brutality of Soviet science, to say nothing of its ruinous biases. "That's why the idea of someone like Andrei Sakharov was so absolutely incredible," he concluded. "The system was so controlled, and so evil, but here was somebody who actually dared to say, 'Fuck you.'"

In the 1970s, Birstein became a dissident as well, working clandestinely in the human rights movement. He joined Amnesty International, hid people being sought by the KGB, helped the families of those already in labor camps, and came under suspicion himself. In 1984, his contract at the Koltsov Institute went unrenewed, and he found himself blacklisted, unable to find a job in Moscow and liable to arrest as a parasite. He fled to the Arctic, finding work at a small institute on the Barents Sea, where authorities were unaware of his reputation as a *neudobnyi chelovek*, a troublesome person. Four years later, in the thaw of Mikhail Gorbachev's *glasnost,* he regained his position at the Koltsov Institute and also found work with Memorial, a Russian human rights group concerned with unearthing the crimes of the Stalin era.

In 1991, Birstein gave a talk on genome research at a conference in Washington, D.C., and agreed while there to do some research for the New York–based Wallenberg Committee. He also met—and subsequently married—Kathryn Buraczynski, a volunteer for the committee. Birstein told me that he was "not technically an émigré. That is other process." In fact, until 1998, he was officially considered on leave of absence from the Koltsov Institute, even after he became a U.S. citizen.

He visited Russia once with Kathryn. Anticipating that he might not do so again, he returned to New York with a small collection of blood, fin, and tissue samples from various species of sturgeon.

iii.

What had come to fascinate Vadim Birstein about sturgeon was their phylogeny—that is, the history of their evolutionary relationships.

"The fish, yes, has great impact in terms of social issues," he told me. "But it also is of great interest in terms of science."

First, of course, the sturgeon is a living fossil, a complex vertebrate whose DNA is like starlight from the edge of the universe, providing a clear glimpse across eons not of time and space, but rather time and biology. Second, the sturgeon—unlike such other living fossils as the coelacanth—is exceptionally speciose, existing in twenty-something different forms. To those two simple dimensions of time and biology, therefore, we may add a third: evolutionary relationships.

From the time of Linnaeus to Vadim Birstein's arrival in New York, sturgeons were distinguished and classified on the basis of their behavior and morphological characteristics: size, color, the shape of the snout, the length of the head, and so on. But sturgeon behavior has been hard to observe in the wild, and morphological characteristics not only vary between individuals, but can change dramatically as a fish grows older, an inconvenient property biologists call "extreme polymorphism." Single sturgeon species as well are sometimes divided into races according to what time of year they enter rivers to spawn. A further complication lies in the fact that certain species will hybridize, and some hybrids—such as those of beluga and sterlet, *Acipenser ruthenus*, a small 3-foot sturgeon of the Caspian—are fertile, at least in the laboratory. Therefore, deciphering sturgeon taxonomy has always been something like predicting the weather, coming around at last to a worrisome amount of guesswork.

In the nineteenth century, some forty species of Eurasian sturgeon were described and accepted by scientists. In 1905, however, the Russian ichthyologist Leo Berg reduced the number of Eurasian species to a much more nearly accurate ten. It was also Berg who established from fossil forms that sturgeon were not related to sharks, as Linnaeus had supposed, and who first described the phenomenon of separate races within species.

Not even Berg, however, could always and with certainty assign an individual sturgeon to one species or another. That simple mystery concealed others in turn: the nature of the evolutionary relationship between Old and New World forms of sturgeon, and the when and where and how of sturgeons' dispersal and diversification into the species that exist today. These are questions relevant to any organism that is both speciose and widely distributed. With sturgeon, however, their answers pertained to the greater part of the history of vertebrates on earth, and therefore also to the deepest mysteries of evolution. The fish is one of very few organisms to offer such a long and continuous thread back into the heart of the maze. In 1991, Birstein, with his knowledge of genetics, and—as modest as it was—the best collection of sturgeon tissue samples to be found in the West, believed that he might at least have the means to pick up the end of the thread and begin the journey.

Rob DeSalle says that Birstein just came knocking on his door one day at the American Museum of Natural History. Birstein went to the AMNH because it was the biggest biological research institute in the city, and he sought out DeSalle because the youthful and informal midwesterner was codirector of the museum's molecular laboratory. Like Birstein, DeSalle had begun with fruit flies but then moved into molecular biology. He had abandoned an assistant professor's post at Yale, however, and come to the museum only a year before in order to do less molecular biology and more work with organisms. Yet he knew next to nothing about sturgeons until his meeting with this odd Russian who had dropped out of the sky, who demanded an appointment that DeSalle granted only as a professional courtesy. But then Birstein—carrying himself in a manner that was not at all deferential—arrived with both his remarkable curriculum vitae and an irresistible idea.

"I did a little research into sturgeons and realized they really were a very neat group," DeSalle would tell me later. "There are twenty-four, twenty-five, maybe twenty-six species, with a few subspecies hanging out there, and all spread over a few broad families. It makes for a really nice, tight, cool system, and with that number of species, there are interesting systematic questions that could be asked and probably answered, if only you had good specimens. . . . When Vadim told me that through his contacts he could probably get good specimens of every single species, including the paddlefishes, I was floored, because you very rarely have that with a living group of animals."

Finally DeSalle was able to offer Birstein an unsalaried position at the museum and the opportunity to scrounge for grants. Birstein began corresponding with other sturgeon specialists throughout the world, getting samples from some of them to augment his tissue collection. By 1993, however, the presence of more and more increasingly cheap caviar in New York City shops and restaurants told him that he was racing against time, that for some of these heretofore eternal species, the thread was fraying or already broken. That year he published a landmark article in the journal *Conservation Biology* that raised the alarm of the suddenly perilous situation in the Caspian. In 1994, Birstein, the Hudson River Foundation's John Waldman, and New York environmental activist Bob Boyle organized a conference on sturgeon at the museum that—like the Oshkosh symposium—dealt as much with issues of sturgeon conservation as biology.

The conference drew some 200 scientists from all over the world, including Frank Chapman. That was twice the number that had attended the 1993 International Sturgeon Symposium in Moscow, and the event established the AMNH as a world center for sturgeon research. Chapman cultivated contacts in the Russian delegation that helped in obtaining his belugas and Russian sturgeons, and Western scientists, as a community, were alerted to the dangers that confronted the Caspian species. The Hudson River Foundation underwrote the conference to the tune of $65,000, though a more conspicuous donation was made by the comedian Bill Murray, whose keynote address at the conference was a fiery mix of comedy and environmental passion. At the end of his speech, Murray signed a blank check, crumpled it, and threw it into the hands of a startled Kathryn Birstein.

The blank was later filled in for $10,000, and the money was used to set up an advocacy group, the Sturgeon Society (with Vadim Birstein as president), and finance a newsletter for scientists, the *Sturgeon Quarterly* (with Birstein as editor). Two years later, Armen Petrossian donated the same amount to the Sturgeon Society on behalf of the molecular research that Birstein and DeSalle were pursuing at the AMNH lab.

In the wake of that conference, Birstein found himself the leading light of what some already described as "the sturgeon movement." He was hired by the German government to organize a second meeting on sturgeon and the caviar trade. He was invited by the World Conservation Union to be the chair of its new Sturgeon Specialists Group. He was tabbed to write a draft proposal for a CITES listing of all sturgeon species, the core of the proposal that the United States and Germany presented to CITES's 1997 meeting in Zimbabwe. And he was funded by

TRAFFIC to travel to the Volga Delta in 1995, and then to the Danube River in 1996, to evaluate the status of stocks in those places. Birstein's reports were incorporated into materials that TRAFFIC's in-house researchers—including Caroline Raymakers—later presented to CITES.

During this time, he was also obtaining additional tissue samples from scientists all over the world. By the end of 1996, he had a collection that encompassed every known species of sturgeon and paddlefish, including samples from China that had eluded all previous collectors. He and DeSalle, as more samples continued to come in, were ready to pick up the thread and see where it might lead them.

iv.

Birstein needed multiple samples of every species of sturgeon in order to apprehend the extent of genetic diversity that exists within and between them. He did not, however, need to obtain large quantities of DNA. Thanks to the PCR method, only a snippet would do.

In the early 1980s, the molecular biologist Kary Mullis, who was awarded the Nobel Prize in Chemistry in 1993, used an enzyme present in a microorganism taken from the geysers of Yellowstone Park to act as a sort of molecular copy machine. Mullis found that applying this enzyme to a very small amount of organic material in vitro would set off a polymerase chain reaction (PCR), which is to say that sequences of that material's DNA would be copied over and over, up to a billion times. This method provides plenty of DNA for purposes that have since ranged from the O.J. Simpson trial to the human genome project. By the early 1990s, PCR machines were both cheap and portable, and they had been coupled with another machine, a DNA sequencer, that uses computer and laser technology to swiftly read the exact sequences of nucleotides that make up each strand of DNA.

Birstein had known for years that technologies like these could be used to compare the DNA of one sturgeon to another. Not only could this method provide a means of species identification much more exact than comparing physical characteristics, but it could also be used to reconstruct the sturgeon family tree, revealing when and to what extent the species diverged. Working on a grant from the museum, he and De-Salle identified portions of mitochondrial DNA that were unique to each species. Then they prepared chemical primers that, like poles on a gate, would restrict the PCR copying process to only that distinctive portion of a DNA strand. This process, in turn, would start only with the correct sort of DNA. "For instance," Birstein told me, "if you mix primers developed for beluga with a beluga egg, the PCR reaction starts and you can identify the product of the reaction—the amplified DNA fragments. If you mix the same primers for beluga with an osetra or sevruga caviar egg, the reaction does not start and there are no ampli-fied DNA sequences. You have a clear 'yes' or 'no' answer, and you do not need to continue."

DeSalle was beguiled by the beauty and simplicity of it. "It was like looking at a population of finches and seeing that they all have a huge beak," DeSalle said. "Then you go to the next population, and you real-ize these finches all have thin, narrow beaks. Only you're doing this now at the level of DNA sequences. And that was fun. Every time I went into the lab I was able to generate a new sequence for Vadim, and everything we saw about the relationships between these fishes, even with Vadim's vast knowledge of fish biology, was new and surprising. We collaborated on over a dozen papers on sturgeon systematics, and had a great time doing it."

Even with a PCR machine and a DNA sequencer, the task of gener-ating a complete set of sequences for all species was huge. Once they had those sequences, however, Birstein and DeSalle were able to zero in on sites that were uniquely characteristic of each of the three main Caspian species. They also collaborated on an attention-getting letter to the scientific journal *Nature* in 1996. The letter cited U.S. Depart-ment of Commerce statistics revealing that U.S. imports of caviar had risen by 100 percent since 1991. It mentioned that species of sturgeon inhabiting the Volga River were particularly vulnerable to "unregulated overfishing" because of demand for their roe. And it noted that caviar dealers have traditionally relied on such crude factors as egg size, smell, texture, taste, and color to identify a caviar's source species.

The authors, however, had developed a molecular test, using only mitochondrial DNA, that was easily administered and allowed an accu-rate and inexpensive identification of samples as small as a single egg.

They also mentioned that they had used this test to survey "twenty-three commercially available lots of caviar purchased in reputable Manhattan gourmet food shops and two brought from Russia. We identified five misrepresentations among the New York samples." They were particularly disturbed by the eggs they found instead: roe from the Siberian sturgeon, *Acipenser baerii,* which seemingly had just caught the attention of poachers; from the Amur sturgeon, *Acipenser schrenckii,* which was on the World Conservation Union's Red List; and from the ship sturgeon, *Acipenser nudiventris,* already extinct in the Aral Sea, and very rare in the Caspian.

That survey had begun as a lark, something DeSalle thought might be fun to try. DeSalle doesn't care for caviar himself, though sometimes he organized sample tastings in his lab to pique his students' interest. Birstein is fond of caviar, though he remarked that moving to the United States had blunted his taste for it. "There is a can of caviar in my refrigerator," he said. "The Russian colleagues gave me it as a gift at a conference in 1998. It is still untouched. It does not mean that I despise caviar. No, of course not. When Armen Petrossian invited me to his restaurants in Paris and here, I tried it. Simply I cannot get used to American hype that surrounds caviar. When I was a kid, it was not a big deal. In Moscow of my childhood, it was available and not overpriced."

The discovery, however, that in Manhattan caviar was available, overpriced, and sometimes fraudulently labeled got Birstein thinking about the application of their test to the enforcement of conservation laws. The letter to *Nature* was noticed by the *Wall Street Journal,* and the ensuing May 17, 1996, article on the test and its results in the local neighborhood caused something of a sensation. The authors didn't reveal to *Nature* from whom they had bought their caviar, and neither did they tell the *Wall Street Journal.* DeSalle was quoted as saying that there was no way the stores could have known that the caviar was different from what their Russian suppliers had claimed it to be.

Saul Zabar, president of Zabar's, the supermarket-sized Manhattan deli, agreed. "This is the first I've heard about it," he told the *Journal.* "As far as I know, we buy Russian product from acceptable wholesalers. At my level, I have no idea what goes on behind the scenes."

The authors didn't remain so indulgent with the dealers. They repeated the test in December of that year, finding that the substitution rate had climbed to 32 percent. In an article that appeared to rather less fanfare in the *Journal of Applied Ichthyology* in 1999, they named names. The dealers whose wares failed the molecular test included Zabar's, Connoisseur, Dean & DeLuca, Citarella, Marky's, Caviar Direct, Balducci, Vinegar Factory, Grace's Marketplace, and Caviar Aristoff. At Caviar Aristoff, the substitution was higher-priced beluga in place of sevruga—perhaps, surmised the authors, because the beluga was in too poor condition to pass for itself. Included as well, for several different samples, was Arnold Hansen-Sturm's Hansen Caviar. "Surprisingly," they wrote, "we found out that the same dealer continued replacements after he had been accused in frauds and served his time in prison."

Nonetheless, one of Birstein's hopes for their test was that small businesses in America and Europe might be protected from the unscrupulous wholesalers, the small-time poachers, and the Russian mafiya operations that would otherwise rob them blind. Birstein himself knew of an operation that had managed to avoid customs duties by working in collusion with Russia's Ministry of Fisheries to smuggle caviar into a packaging plant in Brighton Beach, the heart of New York's Russian émigré community. Meanwhile, the World Conservation Union had found little comfort in TRAFFIC's report from the Caspian, and international news organizations mined it for doomsday headlines. It was then that the World Conservation Union asked Birstein, as chairman of its Sturgeon Specialists Group, to write a proposal for listing certain sturgeon species under CITES.

It had been during the 1995 sturgeon conference in Germany, Birstein said, that Russian scientists talked openly for the first time about the plight of the sturgeon. A debate was carried on there that had begun at the New York conference: whether a CITES listing for at least the three main Caspian species should be on Appendix I or Appendix II.

Birstein said that the Germans just wanted to put everything on Appendix I, but his conversations with caviar dealers had led him to doubt the wisdom of that. "Of course small businessmen would suffer greater impact," he said. "And knowing what was going on in Russia, I decided there was no sense in putting sturgeon on Appendix I. Because you really cannot say, suddenly, no trade. So what do you do next? You cannot just destroy this complicated international network by simply saying it's bad. . . . You would only create an indestructible underground black market. Of course, either way you cannot control what happens inside Russia. But with an Appendix II listing you can at least create some regulation at the borders that might be helpful."

The debate was continued at a meeting of the CITES Animals Committee in the Czech Republic in 1996. Representatives of Boris Yeltsin's government agreed with Birstein about an Appendix I listing and asserted that even Appendix II would be pointless, since there was no method that would hold up in Western courts to reliably discriminate between different kinds of caviar. Birstein countered that indeed there was such a method, then being peer-reviewed, patented, and soon to be published. And it relied on science already accepted in Western courts.

With this, the ground crumbled under Russian objections to at least Appendix II for Caspian sturgeon. Birstein's position had the support of TRAFFIC, the U.S. government, and much of the scientific community, all of whom believed that some degree of international trade would provide money and incentive for conservation in the Caspian. In 1997, at the tenth meeting of the Conference of the Parties to CITES in Zimbabwe, the Germans, and eventually the Americans as well, sponsored a resolution to place all species of sturgeon and paddlefish on Appendix II. The only exceptions were the European and short-nosed sturgeons, which were already on Appendix I, and a pair of Siberian subspecies confined entirely to Russia. The resolution passed unanimously.

Only six years after his anonymous arrival in New York City, Vadim Birstein had not only opened up a new frontier of genetic research, but he had also made the world care about a strange fish of which it had previously known nothing, and found a way, it seemed, to once again cut poachers' nets on the Volga, this time on a scale unimagined in his youth.

v.

It remains a matter of conjecture why things went wrong. Some observers blame Birstein's flinty idealism, the chronic unwillingness of a *neudobnyi chelovek* to compromise or just play along. Others believe he suffers from a typically Russian sort of paranoia and shot himself in the foot during a gunfight that never needed to be fought. Others blame only the Western institutions he dealt with during his brief reign as Sturgeon General. But another question has to do with when things started going wrong. Maybe as early as that blank check from Bill Murray, which indeed inspired the troops, but also proclaimed that there could be money to be made in the business of sturgeon conservation.

Birstein's first disappointment with the CITES process, however, had nothing to do with money and everything to do with haste. Bureaucracies are rarely accused of moving too fast, but at CITES, only ten months intervened between the Zimbabwe resolution and the first demands for all the right paperwork from merchants. Just in scientific terms, this was too soon to answer certain questions about sturgeon taxonomy important to making CITES work—questions that Birstein and DeSalle's genetic research showed every promise of answering.

One important question addressed an old debate: Were the Russian sturgeon, *Acipenser gueldenstaedtii*, and the Persian sturgeon, *Acipenser persicus*, really different species? Birstein and DeSalle's preliminary findings indicated that these were just northern and southern stocks of the same fish. But all sorts of interesting things were turning up in the sturgeon family tree that they were building with their DNA sequences.

Of little surprise was the fact that the tree divided into three main branches, or clades, each derived from a different ancestor: those species ranging along either side of the North Atlantic; those along either side of the North Pacific; and in between, the various Eurasian species. But the DNA suggested certain mysterious affiliations within and across those branches. It may be, for example, that the short-nosed sturgeon of the eastern United States actually descended from the Eurasian branch, and the lake sturgeon of the North American Midwest from the Pacific branch. Beluga, which for morphological reasons occupies a whole different genus from other sturgeons (*Huso*, not *Acipenser*), was revealed with certainty to be a central offshoot of the Eurasian branch, and very closely related to the sterlet, the smallest sturgeon in the Caspian—thus the ability of those two very different-sized fish, the Great Dane and the dachshund of the Volga, to hybridize and produce fertile offspring.

Siblings they might be, yet the molecular test had no trouble telling a beluga egg, or piece of tissue, from a sterlet's. Things started to get foggy, however, with Russian or Persian sturgeons: They were the same fish, they believed, even though the mitochondrial DNA—in certain individuals—was similar to that of either Siberian sturgeons or the nearly extinct Italian sturgeon of the Adriatic. Some have suggested this is the result of hybridization between the species, but Birstein noted that their ranges do not overlap, and in any event natural hybrids are rarely fertile. He believes instead that these individuals are cryptics: that is, fish morphologically similar to Russian/Persian sturgeon, but actually related to ancestral forms of the Siberian and Italian sturgeons that existed when glacial lakes connected Siberian rivers to the Caspian Basin and the Adriatic Sea. He asserts that in the Caspian about 30 percent of Russian sturgeon carry Siberian-like DNA—that is, their eggs and tissue cannot presently be identified as Russian by his and De-Salle's molecular test.

It's an odd situation, and more work needs to be done there, but with CITES all such work had effectively come to a halt because scientists could no longer easily exchange the eggs or tissues of different species. "The CITES listing only includes a personal effects exemption, allowing traffic in 250 g of caviar by an individual without special permission," Birstein wrote in a 2001 paper. "Scientific samples, however, are not exempted, creating complications in international exchange of even a single alcohol-fixed egg."

This was a topic of gloomy discussion during the meeting of the Sturgeon Specialists Committee at the Oshkosh symposium. Though CITES's protections for sturgeon were implemented in almost a nanosecond of bureaucratic time, working the bugs out of those protections had proceeded at a conventionally glacial pace, or none at all. As it stood, each country was allowed to work out its own protocols for the exchange of scientific samples. And in the Caspian-range countries, a tradition of obstreperous, venal bureaucracy had combined with a native reluctance to share their sturgeons abroad. The result had been a crippling dearth of such samples.

Birstein's last attempt to collect samples was during a 1999 trip to Turkmenistan with two University of Alabama biologists. He meant to help fetch specimens of a Central Asian shovelnose sturgeon, *Pseudoscaphirhynchus kaufmanni*. What he got instead was a Kafkaesque nightmare of implausible document requirements, bizarre fees, and lengthy delays. Birstein and his companions came home empty-handed and much poorer.

But there were other surprises. The first, and most bitter to Birstein, was administered in January 1998, when CITES chose to let each member country also develop its own protocols—and methods—for testing caviar. The molecular test that had been essential to getting sturgeon listed with CITES in the first place ended up being ignored in the implementation process. When I asked Birstein in his office how this had happened, he suggested that I abandon my search for idealists at this level of wildlife conservation. "Follow the money," he said simply.

vi.

For all his fame and stature in 1997, at least within that thin intersection of the worlds of caviar, wildlife conservation, and molecular genetics, Vadim Birstein was a long way from Easy Street. His position at the American Museum of Natural History remained that of an unsalaried assistant to Rob DeSalle, someone scrounging for grants on a project-by-project basis. His work for the Sturgeon Society, the *Sturgeon Quarterly*, and the Sturgeon Specialists Group was also unsalaried.

Birstein was not only a scientist, however, but an inventor, working at a time and in a field—biotechnology—where there was less and less free exchange of information between scientists and more and more filing of patents. Birstein's critics accused him of spurning this free exchange and cloaking his molecular test in a patent in order to get rich from it. He replied, with naked contempt, that the critics must have no sense of the complexity and expense of the patenting process. "Rob and I had an agreement to assign our rights to the museum from day zero," he said. "De facto, the method belonged to the museum because they paid for writing the proposal, submitting the proposal, and so on. They spent a hell of a lot of money we simply did not have."

The only personal benefit that he and DeSalle hoped to incur, he emphasized, was the licensing fees that might help them continue their studies of sturgeon phylogeny. The patent application itself was the first to be filed by the AMNH in its history, and it was only for North American rights to the test. The AMNH agreed to leave the European rights to Birstein's discretion, and these he signed over to a nonprofit German environmental law firm headed by Dr. Wolfgang Burhanne: a friend, an anti-Hitler dissident, a concentration camp survivor, and the chairman of the World Conservation Union Environmental Law Group.

On that day in June 2001, the European patent was still pending, though its value had been obviated by the 1998 CITES decision to declare open season on DNA tests. "Nobody was interested in hearing about one standard method for testing caviar," Birstein complained. "In Germany, France, Switzerland, Russia, Bulgaria, and so on, government-affiliated scientists profited from the listing, received money from their governments for the development of their own molecular methods of caviar identification. In practice, all these efforts failed, but the laboratories got their money. Now it doesn't even make sense to patent our test."

Neither is the patent worth much in the United States, and there are two versions of what happened about that. Both versions agree that in 1997 Birstein and DeSalle were approached by Steve Fain, the USF&W biologist who had just been put in charge of the federal government's forensic testing program. Fain said that the government was interested in licensing their test, which he had read about in *Nature*. He also wanted access to two things that were still confidential: their database of DNA sequences for the three main Caspian species, and the chemical composition of the primers they used.

I met Fain briefly at the Oshkosh event, and we spoke later over the telephone. He was guarded in his comments on the Birstein case, but he was explicit on one point. "I don't know exactly what Vadim is saying, but I have heard him say that we stole his database, and that's just plain wrong," he said. "We were never given the database. And if I did have it, it wouldn't be because I stole it." By then the Birstein/DeSalle database had been published, and Fain said it contained many inaccuracies anyway. He claimed that Birstein had insisted on so many conditions and so much control over the use of the test that he had no choice but to throw up his hands and invent his own version.

Birstein countered that he was powerless to impose conditions, since the patent was the museum's. He recommended that Fain talk to the museum's lawyers about the database, and it was at that point, in Birstein's account, that USF&W morphed into something more like the KGB. Both DeSalle and Birstein were subjected to separate meetings with agency executives, who demanded—"in an ugly form," said Birstein—that the agency be provided the database and the makeup of the primers without licensing or any other conditions. "'Because you must be good American patriots,' they said," asserted Birstein. "I'm not joking. These were the exact words of the Fish and Wildlife's deputy head. Those guys were furious."

Finally DeSalle—at the behest of the AMNH, in this account—was compelled to surrender the database of sequences to USF&W without Birstein's knowledge. Several months later, the agency announced in a newsletter that it had developed its own method of identifying the species of sturgeon eggs and tissue, and not just for Caspian sturgeons, but for all species. "Some mysterious way this happened without having tissue samples," Birstein said.

The enraged Birstein was present when Jamie Rappaport Clark, the director of USF&W, announced the new method at a press conference at the New York Aquarium in March 1998. He rose from the press corps to ask how the test had been developed without tissue samples, and why hadn't it been peer-reviewed and published, and why was taxpayer money spent to develop it when a proven, cheaper test already existed. Birstein was referred to the director's deputy, whom of course he had already met, and who could provide no clear answers after the press conference.

That was because it was a straightforward case of piracy, said Birstein, followed by smoke and mirrors. "The issue with Fain is very simple," Birstein growled. "In layman's terms, he stole our data. Also, he has never proven scientifically that his so-called method exists. I can only guess what they are doing according to materials presented and speeches they give in court. What they presented is absolutely senseless. There is no way how it can work. It's voodoo, not science."

As near as Birstein could tell, Fain's method involved running amplified DNA through a DNA sequencer, an expensive contraption not needed for Birstein's method, and then comparing genetic sequences to a database through an as yet undescribed procedure. Fain told me that his test was on the USF&W website, but I couldn't find it. Neither could Birstein. Fain also said that he expected it to be accepted for publication soon in an independent journal, though that hadn't happened as of 2004. Thumbnail descriptions of both tests existed on the TRAFFIC website. Birstein and DeSalle's was described as costing $5 per sample, reporting in twenty-four hours, and requiring no special equipment. USF&W's costs $10 per sample, reports in ten hours, and requires "considerable" special equipment.

An article that appeared in *USA Today* on the day before the CITES regulations went into effect in 1998 described Fain "performing like a gourmet chef who is preparing a finicky dish" as he carried out his test. Down the lab's hall was a cardboard cutout of Clint Eastwood as Dirty Harry saying, "Go ahead—make my DNA."

Rob DeSalle knows exactly what happened between the museum and USF&W regarding the transfer of information, if any, but at the insistence of the museum lawyer, he will not comment. When Alex Shoumatoff requested permission from the museum to interview DeSalle for the *New Yorker*, he was denied—"KGB-style," Birstein would say. I contacted DeSalle directly, and we met quietly in the basement of the AMNH, in a small cubicle with an interior window opening into what DeSalle said was their Frozen Tissue Room: a half-dozen silvery vats, each filled with liquid nitrogen and thousands of stored biological specimens. Above us, pods of weekenders moved through the museum's exhibits on that November weekend in 2001, though admissions had plummeted some 90 percent, DeSalle said, since 9/11.

DeSalle looks somewhat like Sancho Panza to Birstein's Don Quixote. Broad-shouldered, easygoing, and bespectacled, he spoke with undimmed delight about the excitement of his work with Birstein, and particularly the fateful day that the Russian brought a tin of caviar to the lab: "That was one of the neatest things about the whole project, just taking some caviar out of the can, and squashing it, and taking DNA from it, and amplifying it, and seeing that our test really worked on it."

He bristled at Fain's criticism of their DNA sequences, and at his claims that USF&W had somehow assembled its own collection of tissue samples. He found it "irksome" that someone who had never seen their own tissue samples would question their science, which had been stringently peer-reviewed and validated, and coauthored by someone with 150 publications and several books to his credit. He dared Fain to challenge their sequences in print, and then dared him to improve on their tissue collection: "Just for example, we've got seventy to eighty tissue samples of Siberian sturgeon in our database. If he's got that many, then bring it on. That's how science is done." Regarding Birstein himself, DeSalle granted that his former colleague could be irascible and uncompromising, but he took pains to point out that he was a scientist not just of great skill, but of the highest integrity. "I only wish he weren't so misunderstood," DeSalle added sadly.

Birstein emphasized that his grievance wasn't with Fain, per se, but with the federal government. As Ed Grace and Rob Rothe and others made seizures and filed charges according to the results of Fain's test, Birstein's anger was fanned not just by his doubts about the USF&W test, but also by its effects on the lives of small business men and women on this side of the Atlantic. They were being unfairly penalized, he felt, for mistakes or crimes or acceptable practices, whichever, that were being committed on the other side, in a place where the terms "beluga," "osetra," and "sevruga" sometimes have meant roe from specific species of fish, and sometimes have referred simply to grades of caviar, in which roes may legitimately—according to custom, if not the new law—be mixed or substituted. Which is to say nothing about Petrossian's pressed caviar, which is by definition mixed.

It was in November 1998 that Rob Rothe and another agent raided the Queens warehouse of Caviarteria, seizing nearly $1 million worth of caviar from a gun-toting Eric Sobol. Part of that shipment was sevruga that tested out as beluga, and part was osetra that tested out as ship sturgeon. In January 1999, USF&W seized two more shipments from Caviarteria, these of Russian sturgeon osetra that tested out as Siberian.

Birstein knew all too well how likely it was that Russian sturgeon DNA could look like Siberian to an unwary analyst. When Sobol's attorney, Walter Drobenko, who was also the attorney for Gino Koczuk at the time, called and asked Birstein if he might serve as an expert witness in Caviarteria's $100 million suit against the government—well, there was no chance that Quixote would pass up a tilt at that gigantic windmill, even if it meant professional suicide.

vii.

The suicide part didn't take long at all. Through Drobenko, Birstein obtained samples of the Russian sturgeon osetra that had been confiscated in January. Rob DeSalle ran them through their molecular test at the AMNH lab and reported different results from Fain's. The AMNH, however, had just received $30 million in federal funding for a new planetarium and had no desire to get mixed up in a lawsuit against the government. The museum's lawyer put a lid on DeSalle's findings, and then the AMNH severed its relationship with Birstein. He was no longer welcome in its lab or on its grounds.

Complications had already ensued elsewhere. In 1996, the new chief of CITES's Species Survival Commission ordered Birstein and his Sturgeon Specialists Group to work under the supervision of a Russian scientist with ties to the FSB, the Russian secret service. This, Birstein said, was simply the KGB with a new nameplate on the door. He refused that arrangement, then refused to resign his position. Finally the new commissioner fired him—"Possibly the only case of a chairman being fired during the history of the World Conservation Union," Birstein said with just a touch of pride.

He remained the president of the Sturgeon Society, and editor of *The Sturgeon Quarterly*, but as those unsalaried responsibilities grew, he laid them aside. In keeping with the job description of a *neudobnyi chelovek*, he refused the request of the society's trustees that he resign. "Big scandal," said Birstein. That situation cooled to a stalemate, and both the Sturgeon Society and the *Quarterly* have faded away.

The *chelovek* himself was unrepentant, by and large. When he had told me that he had created this whole disaster, he meant that in devising his caviar test, he had unwittingly delivered his precious sturgeon into the bosom of an international bureaucracy that—to his thinking—had bartered away first the test, and now its subjects. Meanwhile, the CITES process demonstrated an immediate need for just his sort of expertise and research, and at the same time it erected insuperable obstacles to him or anyone else accomplishing that research. The word Birstein used to describe the situation was "Orwellian." But no such obstacles existed between Caspian sturgeon and those who would fish it to extinction, because the law, in its clumsy and limited fashion, addresses only trade, and not overfishing. Birstein applauded the arrest of authentic criminals such as Gino Koczuk, but he noted that by the time such arrests were made, too many female sturgeons had already been killed and gutted. In a 2001 paper, Birstein said that only 8 percent of the sturgeon harvested on the Volga in the spring of 2000 were females.

Now the onetime Sturgeon General of the World surveys what his "movement" has wrought and sees only ruin: situation unpleasant, results disturbing. He was glad of the American scientists who had enlisted their talents—about some of them, at least—but found them all naive about the Caspian: "They do not understand that in the extremely rough economic conditions of those countries, it's not enough to simply inform the local population and fishermen about the necessity to stop poaching."

For the rest, he had stronger feelings, particularly in regard to the Caviar Emptor campaign to ban the sale of beluga caviar: "I'm disgusted by the numerous opportunistic American and international environmentalists and conservationists who suddenly started to 'care' about sturgeons when it appeared that grants and salaries could be received, or political games can be played around the issue. This campaign to save beluga is a typical example. The people who started it had no professional knowledge about beluga, did not want to take into consideration local economic and political problems the issue included, but they used it as an opportunity to fight against the current administration in Washington."

Birstein's problem was that he cares about the people of the Caspian as well as its legendary fish. Their problem, alas, is that so many of them are Russian. He predicted that many fine things would be promised by Western companies about oil development in the Caspian, but in the end things in Russia would be done the Russian way, which meant oil spills in the water and no money for the fishermen. He said his wife Kathryn now worked for an investment firm on Wall Street, one that had bought heavily into Russia. "They have no understanding of Russian history," he continued. "Nobody in Russia wants to invest money there. They know that Russia is Russia."

Here in America, the thread that Birstein hoped to follow back into the ground floor of vertebrate evolution lay discarded and largely ignored.

Only he had the sort of collection to renew that quest, but he had no lab in which to do that. Rob DeSalle had a lab full of postdoctoral students, but no time: He described his current duties running the lab as those of a "silly administrator," someone who shuffles papers instead of unraveling DNA.

Vadim Birstein remains a proud scientist, if one who had yet to realize any return on his investment in America, and who could not expect a recommendation from the AMNH. He was hardly idle. He had recently completed the manuscript of an unsavory history: *The Perversion of Knowledge: The True Story of Soviet Science,* which was due to be published in 2001 by Westview Press, and was poised to start on another book, a history of the Cold War. He was still publishing papers based on his work at the museum. And he was preparing reports for Walter Drobenko on behalf of suits against the government involving not just Caviarteria, but also Russian Czar. It was Russian Czar's caviar that USF&W had seized and auctioned off at its Valley Stream office the previous summer.

Steve Fain told me the suits would not be a battle of genetic tests but would come down simply to the interpretation of data. Birstein professed to be indifferent about the tests, since the molecular version didn't belong to him. Developing it with Rob had indeed been fun, but now that was all in the past. The great matter to him was as it had been in the Soviet Union: government power and the appropriate use of science. "American citizens," he reiterated, "must not be tried on the basis of scientifically unsupported, not-peer-reviewed voodoo science of the government. Criminals must be caught and punished, but American government must not use lousy science for catching them."

It was unfortunate, from that perspective as well, that the progress of the Caviateria case had been thrown into confusion by that other complication, the death of Eric Sobol. Birstein was convinced the death had more to do with crime than despair. "Contrary to the press, I still think that Eric's death was very suspicious," he muttered, "and that the mafiya was involved some way in it."

We finished the interview in the last room of the suite, his own office, where the walls were ramparts of books with niches for photographs of Gorbachev-era unrest in Moscow, the desks banked with computers and monitors, these the tools of the data management and programming work that make up his day job now. Uneasy that I intended to visit Astrakhan in the spring, alone and with only the most nominal Russian-language skills, he produced telephone numbers and e-mail addresses for people who might help me there. A window was open, and the clamor of the midday traffic around Columbus Circle rose over the sill. I thought I caught a whiff of the Hudson River, but on second scent I could not find it again.

I asked if we could talk some more at the International Sturgeon Symposium in Oshkosh, which then was only a few weeks away. He said that the symposium was given over mostly to technical issues, and not the basic science that interested him. "Also," he added, Vulf Sternin "wrote to the organizing committee that they should invite me personally to discuss the problem of U.S. Fish and Wildlife testing. They have not done that. So I do not expect to go."

He sat obligingly in front of the window for a picture, this exile from his native land, now an exile as well from his life's work, blacklisted even in America, where so many universities and labs rely on federal funding. I set my flash to balance the natural light, but the flash failed, blanketing him in darkness, except for that double-paned glow of an internal fire.

～6～

A City of Water

i.

Joseph Mitchell, who for many years chronicled the New York City waterfront for the *New Yorker*, remembered the eerie thrill of his first glimpse of an Atlantic sturgeon, what he called a sea sturgeon, in the Hudson River in 1950. "I was on the New Jersey side of the river that morning, sitting in the sun on an Erie Railroad coal dock," he wrote in *The Bottom of the Harbor* (1994). "I knew that every spring a few sturgeon still come in from the sea and go up the river to spawn, as hundreds of thousands of them once did, and I had heard tugboatmen talk about them, but this was the first one I had ever seen. It was six or seven feet long, a big, full-grown sturgeon. It rose twice, and cleared the water both times, and I plainly saw its bristly snout and its shiny little eyes and its white belly and its glistening, greenish-yellow, bony-plated, crocodilian back and sides, and it was a spooky sight."

Mitchell was surprised to see a creature like that within the city precincts, but he shouldn't have been. "New York is a city of water," John Waldman told me. "People don't realize that, but it's apparent if you look at a map. Four of its boroughs are islands, or else parts of them are islands. The Bronx is bounded with water on three sides. The city has 578 miles of shoreline. Water is everywhere."

That's how Waldman, born and raised in the Bronx, became a waterman himself. As a youngster he often went with an uncle in a small cabin cruiser past City Island and into Long Island Sound, opposite Manhasset Bay, where the fictional Jay Gatsby once stared across the water at the green light of Daisy Buchanan's house. Otherwise he fished with friends at Pelham Bay Park, catching buckets of snapper blues using bloodworms and sandworms for bait. Later he built his own 10-foot johnboat.

Now Waldman prowled these shores professionally as chief biologist for the Hudson River Foundation (HRF). The foundation's sunlit offices occupied the ninth floor of a Chelsea high-rise on 20th Street. One floor below lay the headquarters of the Natural Resources Defense Council (NRDC), one of the sponsors of the Caviar Emptor campaign. The Hudson River Foundation was leasing offices from the NRDC, but the HRF was a different organization, created in 1981 as part of a government-brokered cease-fire between environmental groups and utility companies running power plants on the river. Its purpose is to provide independent, nonpartisan science on behalf of the public stewardship of the Hudson. That stewardship, in fact, had produced one of the great success stories of the American environmental movement. But the outcome of that story had been complicated for both its protagonists and the river's sturgeons.

The Hudson is a classic sturgeon river in the sense that it supports two sympatric species of the fish, which is to say, species that occupy the same area without interbreeding. Usually, one species is anadromous, migrating into the river from the sea in order to spawn, like salmon or shad, while the other is potamodromous, living its entire life in the river system. In the Hudson the wanderer is the Atlantic sturgeon that Joseph Mitchell saw leaping in the harbor, while the homebody is the short-nosed sturgeon, a juvenile of which Frank Chapman had let me hold.

Among North American Acipenseriformes, the Atlantic is second in size only to the white sturgeon, and it's easily the most seafaring. Little is known about the behavior in the wild of newly hatched sturgeons, but it's believed that Atlantic sturgeon fingerlings move slowly downriver from their spawning sites and remain in brackish water at the river's mouth for somewhere between two to five years. Finally they move into the sea and may undertake long journeys up or down the coast. Atlantic sturgeons tagged in the Hudson have been found north of Cape Cod and south of Cape Hatteras. The greenish-yellow, bony-plated, crocodilian fish that caused such a commotion when it washed up on a Cape Cod beach was almost certainly from the Hudson.

Sometimes they strike out overseas. Atlantic sturgeons of unknown origin have been found off the coasts of Venezuela and Bermuda. A recent examination of the DNA of specimens of European sturgeons taken from the Baltic Sea in the 1800s revealed they were actually Atlantics. Scientists concluded that the fish had crossed the ocean and colonized the Baltic 1,200 years ago, coexisting with the European species *Acipenser sturio* for some four centuries. Then the European sturgeon disappeared from the Baltic, maybe owing to cooling water temperatures during a time known as the Little Ice Age. Finally that far-flung population of Atlantics disappeared as well, fished and dammed to extinction.

In North America, the Atlantic sturgeon flourished in larger rivers from the St. Lawrence to the east coast of Florida. It was during his 1609 exploration of the river named for him that Henry Hudson saw that Indians relished the sturgeons they caught there, while Christians didn't. The storyteller Washington Irving, in "Knickerbocker's History of New York," related the occurrence of a religious conversion on the day that a drunk leaned over a ship's rail on the Hudson. The drunk's shiny nose so concentrated a beam of sunlight that it shot hissing into the water and killed a sturgeon. "This huge monster being with infinite labour hoisted on board," wrote Irving, "furnished a luxurious repast to all the crew, being accounted of excellent flavour, excepting about the wound, where it smacked a little of brimstone—and this, on my veracity, was the first time that ever sturgeon was eaten in these parts by Christian people."

Two centuries later, the refulgent nose was succeeded by the gillnet and the grappling hook. In New York, hundreds of thousands of sturgeon carcasses were stacked for windbreaks and burned for cordwood. The vast populations in the Delaware River and Chesapeake Bay were extirpated during the years of the domestic caviar industry, and then the triple screws of fishing pressure, damming, and water pollution harried the sturgeons out of nearly every other river in the East.

On the Hudson, however, there was no dam built south of Troy, which allowed surviving Atlantic sturgeons access to their spawning grounds near Hyde Park, 80 miles up. For the first eight decades of the twentieth century, total landings of Atlantic sturgeon along the East Coast were only 1 percent of their peak levels during the 1890s, but landings off New York and New Jersey suggested a small but persistent spawning population in the Hudson. Landings elsewhere revealed the errant nature of these fish, that they would enter freshwater again not only to spawn in the Hudson, but sometimes to mosey about other river systems, such as the Merrimack, the Connecticut, and the Delaware.

During most of that time, the Hudson was little better than a vast sewer, a dark stew through which no sunbeams could pierce. From the very beginning, of course, New York City had been dumping its raw sewage into the river. In the nineteenth century, factories, oil refineries, and railroads multiplied up its length and added their own wastes to the broth. Later, such corporate giants as General Electric dispensed tons of polychlorinated biphenyls (PCBs) into the water. Joseph Mitchell had no illusions about the purity of the Hudson and New York Harbor in the 1950s. He wrote that you could bottle the water and sell it for poison, that the smell from Brooklyn's Gowanus Canal would make a flag on a mast hang limp.

It took men like Bill Casper to turn things around. On the Hudson, actually, that meant men like Fred Danback and Bob Boyle. In the 1960s, Danback was a janitor at the Anaconda Wire & Cable plant at Hastings-on-Hudson. He was also a friend to shad fishermen who had seen their catches decline and their fish become unfit to eat. Danback didn't think it helpful that Anaconda dumped waste oil, copper filings, and sulfuric acid into the river, but his complaints to management went unheeded.

Bob Boyle was a writer for *Sports Illustrated* and an avid sport fisherman. Born in Brooklyn and raised in Manhattan, he came late to exploring the Hudson. But he loved its striped bass, even if they were in no condition to be eaten, and also its sturgeons, confessing himself awed by the fact that something so ancient and mysterious could still be found there. Boyle complained to the environmental group Scenic Hudson about the river's filth, but the group was unwilling to challenge the business interests purveying most of it. In 1965, Boyle found himself on the river near Croton Point in the midst of an oil slick, 3 to 4 miles long and 1 or 2 miles wide, discharged by the Penn Central Railroad's diesel and electric shops at Harmon. In his book *The Hudson River: A Natural and Unnatural History* (1969), Boyle wrote, "I was afraid to smoke; the river appeared to be a fire hazard."

Later in 1965, Boyle and a Manhattan College biologist organized the Hudson River Fishermen's Association (HRFA). They tried to goad federal agencies into enforcing clean-water regulations, but in vain. In 1969, Danback quit his job at Anaconda and joined the HRFA. Together he and Boyle discovered a stone for their slingshot in the battle against GE and the other goliaths of the river: the 1899 Federal Refuse Act, on the books for seventy years but never enforced, stating in part that no "deleterious or poisonous substance shall be thrown or allowed to run into any waters, either private or public, in quantities injurious to fish life inhabiting those waters or injurious to the propagation of fish therein."

The HRFA dusted off that law and took it into court, exacting fines first from Penn Central, then Anaconda, and then a host of other corporate tenants of the valley, including GE, which even now was in the midst of a decades-long cleanup of PCBs off the bottom of the upper Hudson. HRFA's effort led most famously to an epic battle against Consolidated Edison, which intended to build a 2-million-kilowatt hydroelectric plant, the largest in the world, at the foot of Storm King Mountain. The plant would sit opposite the river's major spawning ground for striped bass and suck in 6 billion gallons of river water during a single daily operating cycle. In a 1980 court decision that marked the coming-of-age of U.S. environmental law, not only did the HRFA defeat this proposal, but it exacted from Con Ed a $12 million endowment for establishing the Hudson River Foundation.

In the aftermath of that victory, Boyle fathered another organization, Riverkeeper, that was inspired by the riverkeepers of Britain, men who once guarded private stocks of trout and salmon from poachers. Boyle envisioned citizen patrols on all the country's rivers to safeguard their waters against the abuses once visited on the Hudson. In 1983, he hired a young enthusiast from Yonkers, John Cronin, to do just that for $50 a week. Cronin went out on the river, noticed Exxon tankers dumping oil, and nailed his first fine. By 1999, Riverkeeper had twenty-three chapters across America. In Wisconsin, Bill Casper's Sturgeon for To-morrow organization, with its vigilance of sturgeon spawning grounds, was an elaboration of Boyle's idea.

What was good for striped bass was also good for Atlantic sturgeon, which were still spawning in small numbers in the Hudson, and which had two circumstances working in their favor during the decades in which the river was poisoned. The first was the river's geology. "This is a very dynamic river system," Boyle told me over the telephone. "Its channel is very deep, very narrow, and it has a greater flushing capacity, for example, than the Chesapeake Bay. Also, since its bottom is deep and rocky, with very strong tides in its lower reaches, it's not easily fished. The Hudson River, in fact, is the only major estuary on the At-lantic Coast of the United States that still retains spawning populations of all its original fish species."

"Not entirely true," John Waldman advised me later. "Smelt appear to have gone extinct in the Hudson. But otherwise Bob is correct."

The second was the Atlantic sturgeon's prolonged life cycle, includ-ing its long intervals between spawning. While these are the very char-acteristics that make sturgeon populations vulnerable to fishing pressure and slow to recover, they also make the fish unusually resistant to spawning failures or long periods of environmental distress. Up to a de-gree, they can outlive all that.

Throughout the twentieth century, the filthy Hudson, in fact, har-bored the largest remaining population of Atlantic sturgeons in Ameri-can waters. That also meant that a legal fishery persisted in New York and New Jersey waters throughout those decades. From 14,000 to 30,000 pounds of sturgeon were landed annually, almost entirely as by-catch by fishermen looking for other species. The meat could be sold, and so could the roe, at least locally. "Once my director came in with a Chinese food container full of rich black caviar, and that was my first exposure to caviar," Waldman told me. "We ate it in obscene quantities. It was delicious. It was locally prepared, but it wasn't marketed. In those days fishermen were fishing for other things. They were still catching shad, and there was a good blue crab fishery as well."

In the 1980s, sturgeon landings shot up tenfold, and suddenly there was a targeted commercial fishery for the fish, one centered in the New

York Bight, those waters off coastal New Jersey and the southern shores of Long Island. Maybe it was because the river was cleaner and the sturgeons were coming back, or maybe it was reawakened demand, or maybe a little of both. "From what I heard anecdotally," Waldman recalled, "someone learned how to process caviar just the right way, and also how to ship it. Then all of a sudden fishermen went from taking the occasional sturgeon for a few extra bucks and a little fun to really focusing on sturgeon for serious money."

And yet again and once more, greed outran stewardship. By 1990, meat was going for $40 a pound, roe for $50, and fishermen were working the river as well as the bight. Waldman heard of one Hudson fisherman who, when the season shrank to only a month, stayed on his boat day and night to work each tide of those thirty days. When a quota system went into effect, some would tether smaller fish in hidden locations in hopes of finding bigger fish to sell. Waldman heard in the early 1990s that a big female was worth $3,000 to a Hudson fisherman. Much of the roe was bought by Arnold Hansen-Sturm, who packaged and sold it legitimately as "American Sturgeon Caviar."

New York dragged its heels in protecting the sturgeons, and New Jersey's heels hardly budged. "The New Jersey fishermen became the Bosnian Serbs of the East Coast," Boyle fulminated. "These people just slaughtered sturgeon to meet demand, whatever it took. They probably took 500,000 pounds before it was over."

John Waldman wondered how many of the fish caught in the New York Bight were from the Hudson, and he was shocked to learn from DNA analysis that no less than 99 percent of the catch was of local origin. He was dismayed as well to see that many of the fish taken were juveniles, which apparently migrate in and out of the river as they grow. "As it was," he said, "we were the only game in town. There was no fishable population spawning anywhere else from Maine to Florida. And in the mid-'90s that last fishable population on the East Coast crashed. The Atlantic should be the endangered species in this river, not the short-nosed."

Waldman gazed from the HRF's conference room across a vista spiked with skyscrapers and water towers. He smiled and described the Atlantic sturgeon as a creature "about as cryptic as a big beast can be.

To exist in and around one of the world's biggest cities, to be 6 to 8 feet long, and to not generally be noticed," he said, "is remarkable." But lurking as they do among the Hudson's deep channels and sunken logs, the beast evaded even the notice of biologists. Bob Boyle got interested in sturgeons in the early 1960s when he met some fishermen who went out from Verplanck for the short-nosed variety, and who occasionally found themselves wrestling with big Atlantics. Eventually Boyle got a scientific collector's license from the state of New York and began bringing specimens of odd fish of all species, but mostly sturgeons, to the American Museum of Natural History.

Biologists, for the most part, couldn't get money for sturgeon research and stayed away. It took an alignment of stars for that to change: publicity about Vadim Birstein's work; bad news about sturgeon stocks in the Caspian; the surge in coastal landings; and the rebirth of a local caviar industry, however small. In 1993, the Hudson River Foundation sent out a special call for proposals on sturgeon research, finally committing to a range of projects suggested by Cornell biologist Mark Bain. Then Waldman, Boyle, and Birstein joined forces in organizing that seminal 1994 conference on sturgeons at the AMNH.

One of Bain's projects concerned population trends of the Atlantic sturgeon in the Hudson. The great fish once again were scarce as hen's teeth, and Bain's scrupulous data made it impossible to blame anything but excessive fishing pressure. By 1998, the Atlantic States Marine Fisheries Commission had grown tired of waiting for the states to rein that in and imposed an emergency closure and a forty-year fishing moratorium.

Waldman was still exultant about that victory. "In the world of fisheries management, that's just an extraordinary success," he said. "Usually it's a bloody battle to get a one- or two-year moratorium on fishing a particular species. Forty years? That's just unheard of."

He hoped the Atlantic sturgeon might have a future, after all, in the Hudson, but he wasn't so sure about other rivers. He knew from his own work on gulf sturgeons in Florida that those fish were divided into four distinct populations among eight rivers, and that the gene flow rate between the populations—in other words, the frequency with which gulfs from one group swam boldly into another group's river to spawn—

varied, but was always very low, less than one female per generation. Waldman conceded that the wandering Atlantics were a little more forward that way. "But I think, overall, sturgeons find their home rivers very well to begin with," he said. "Every sturgeon species we've looked at shows almost as low a rate of gene flow as the gulf. These fish know where their homes are, and they go back to them."

The good news is this: Being both cryptic and curious, the Atlantic sturgeon still exists, at least on a seasonal basis, in a surprising number of East Coast rivers. Besides the Hudson, these include the Kennebec, Androgscoggin, Penobscot, Merrimack, Connecticut, Delaware, Roanoke, Pamlico, Neuse, Cape Fear, Santee, Ashepoo, Savannah, Ogeechee, Altamaha, Satilla, St. Mary's, and St. John's. In some of these rivers reproduction is occurring. But the fact that Atlantic sturgeons are so finely tuned to their natal environments is also the bad news. They may be happy enough to visit other rivers, but they are slow to recolonize them.

Waldman remembered that a few years back a mature Atlantic female had been found dead on the banks of the Delaware River during the spring, which suggested that sturgeons were at least trying to spawn there again. He said, "The Hudson was never entirely clear-cut of Atlantic sturgeon in the 1890s the way that the Delaware was. I don't know why."

There were other things he didn't know; nor did anyone else. Do Atlantic males spawn every year, or only at intervals, like females? What's the ratio between the sexes when they gather to spawn? How do the larvae behave in the wild? When do juveniles first venture out of the river? Where do the fish go in the winter? A few years ago these sturgeons were the most intensively studied population in the United States. Now even the vague size of that population was uncertain, and in 1997—the last year in which Atlantics were netted by scientists on the Hudson—only males were captured. That's a bad sign, but the fish had fallen into that funding trough between population extremes: so many fish that important fisheries exist, or so few that the species is in danger of extinction. Either extreme generates dollars for research; any point in between leaves even an 8-foot animal in a prolonged state, once again, of being cryptic.

The river itself is less so, clean enough now for groups of competitive swimmers during the summer to race nearly the length of Manhattan, from Washington Heights down to Chelsea. They report no oil slicks, raw sewage, or floating corpses. Neither do they see any sea sturgeons. Greenish-yellow, bony-plated, and crocodilian, the beast had disappeared once again, retiring into the depths and keeping its own counsel.

ii.

In the 1960s, long before his battles against Penn Central and Con Edison took place, before he founded the Hudson River Fishermen's Association, the Hudson River Foundation, and Riverkeeper, Bob Boyle tried his hand at making caviar.

He got his roe from short-nosed sturgeons caught by the Verplanck fishermen he had befriended, and his know-how from *McClane's Standard Fishing Encyclopedia and International Angling Guide* (1965), in an article written by Malcolm Beyer, the president of a gourmet foods subsidiary to the restaurant "21," and then the largest U.S. importer of caviar from the Soviet Union. Boyle and a friend rubbed the eggs across a minnow seine stretched over a bowl and held in place by a rubber band. The eggs separated and fell into a bowl, where they were stirred, rinsed, and drained. Then they added 3 percent salt by volume to the roe, mixing that in with a cake spatula. Finally they ladled the eggs into sterilized jars, refrigerated them for a week, and brought a sample of the finished caviar to Beyer, who judged it equal to the best sevruga and offered to buy all he could get.

That prompted Boyle to lay out a plan to a pair of skeptical Verplanck fishermen for an entity he called the Greater Verplanck Caviar Company: a big boat, some large-mesh netting, and the annual harvest of 1,000 to 5,000 Atlantic sturgeons, which were more numerous than the short-nosed, to produce a golden-brown caviar comparable to the Soviet Union's osetra. Boyle projected conservative wholesale prices of $10 a pound for the roe and 50 cents for the meat. He figured they could gross $1.5 million in three months. At that point, the doubting fishermen fell silent, and there was an exchange of glances around the table.

Boyle's fishermen came aboard, as did a friend and fellow journalist with connections on Wall Street and access to investors. Beyer was already unhappy about the way things were going in the Caspian and entirely enthusiastic about serving local caviar. But Boyle's friend died suddenly, and the seed money never materialized.

So Boyle abandoned his dream of a caviar company and later came to regret whatever role his writings might have played in drawing attention to the Atlantic sturgeon in the 1980s. But he was still fascinated by the fish, and certainly his gifts were better used as an organizer and gadfly than as a caviar master. He met Serge Doroshov during a trip to California for *Sports Illustrated* and prevailed upon him to come to the Hudson on a grant from the Hudson River Foundation. Later—"after four or five years of kicking them in the ass," he told me—he persuaded the HRF to sponsor the 1994 conference on sturgeons that he helped organize. Then he became a member of the board of trustees of the Sturgeon Society headed by Birstein.

Those were good times for Boyle's American Dream style of optimism, one that recalled John Muir and Aldo Leopold in its preference for clean water and abundant wildlife over money and the trappings of material comfort. "There was this wonderful faith in what we were doing," Boyle said, remembering, in particular, his work with Riverkeeper. "It was all very clean and aesthetic. Now I feel like—what do you call them? a stylite?—one of those monks sitting on a pillar in Syria in 300 A.D."

The problem, he found, was that clean water costs money. When Boyle hired Joe Cronin as the Hudson's first riverkeeper in the 1980s, he paid half of Cronin's pittance of a salary out of his own pocket. There was no money for a motor for Cronin's boat until a wealthy donor footed the bill. Then Boyle was amazed—and maybe a little seduced—by the celebrities who showed up for the boat's launch, a crowd that included newsman Tom Brokaw and boxing coach Cus D'Amato (with student Mike Tyson).

Celebrity, Boyle understood, was a way of evening the playing field against the corporate behemoths that Riverkeeper stalked, and also the legislators who protected them. Celebrity attracted not only money, but the cleansing light of media attention and public scrutiny. It could also provide the rocket fuel to take Riverkeeper beyond the Hudson.

So Boyle was delighted when in 1983 a bona fide celebrity, Robert F. Kennedy, Jr., came aboard as Riverkeeper's chief prosecuting attorney. Almost instantly, Boyle's bulldog tenacity and Kennedy's combination of legal smarts and star power set the threadbare little nonprofit on its way to becoming not only one of the nation's toughest environmental organizations, but its most glamorous. Glitterati such as Alec Baldwin, Glenn Close, and Lorraine Bracco flocked to the cause as Riverkeeper racked up successful suits and spawned other chapters. The organization's annual dinner dance became not only a high-octane fund-raiser, but one of the highlights of the city's social calendar.

Best of all for Boyle, at least early on, it was clean, aesthetic, and fun. New York's *Talk* magazine described Boyle, Kennedy, and Cronin as Riverkeeper's Father, Son, and Holy Ghost, presiding with style and élan over the comeback of the blue crab, the shad, and the sturgeon. A former board member said, "They were enchanting, these three spirited Irishmen, bantering with each other."

Through Kennedy, Boyle found the money to trumpet his message and win more courtroom battles. But Boyle was also adamant that nothing in the organization's fund-raising should taint either the purity of that message or the motive for those battles. For his own part, Kennedy wanted to do more than trade on his name when it came to making money, especially as the budget grew and fund-raising demands increased.

And so, inevitably, the Irishmen came to blows. In 1998, Kennedy proposed that Riverkeeper sponsor a bottled water company, the profits to be donated to environmental causes à la the Paul Newman model. Boyle, as president, said no, fearing that their legal suits could be viewed as vehicles for selling more water. Kennedy went over Boyle's head to the board of directors, where the idea was voted down by a narrow margin. Kennedy then submitted a letter of resignation that—much to his surprise—was accepted by an angry Boyle. In the end, Kennedy stayed on, finally founding his own bottled water company, Keeper Springs. But the bantering had stopped.

There ensued a series of disputes that polarized the Riverkeeper board into Kennedy versus Boyle camps. Low-level skirmishing escalated into a decisive firefight in 1999, when Kennedy hired William Wegner as one of Riverkeeper's staff scientists. Wegner was willing to work for less than the going rate, and Boyle discovered why: He had been the ringleader of a gang of smugglers that, from 1985 to 1993, had secretly brought cockatoo eggs from Australia into the United States.

Once hatched, the birds were sold for prices ranging from $1,000 to $16,000 each, depending on the species. Over the years the operation grossed some $1.5 million, and Wegner had just gotten out of jail.

In his own statements, Kennedy tended to minimize Wegner's crimes, claiming the smuggling had little impact on cockatoo numbers in Australia and emphasizing that Wegner had paid his debt and deserved a second chance—not unlike Kennedy himself, who had come to Riverkeeper from doing court-mandated volunteer work with the Natural Resources Defense Council for possession of heroin.

"Kennedy told me that his family had always defended people like this, just like they defended blacks and homosexuals," Boyle told me. "I said, 'Bobby, that's a bizarre analogy. This man is a convicted criminal, who pleaded guilty to wildlife smuggling. He's also a perjurer, and there is no way Riverkeeper can have someone like this as a staff scientist. Every argument we put forth in a court of law would be immediately impeached because of his record. He should not be with us. Let him teach school in Detroit, or fix tires in San Antonio.'"

Boyle promptly ordered Kennedy to dismiss Wegner. Kennedy refused, and the battle again was carried to the board. Cronin sided with Boyle, but then the Holy Ghost resigned. Moderates in the organization tried in vain to craft a compromise. Boyle's last best offer was this: He would step aside as president and take a seat on the board if Wegner were sent packing. Otherwise, like Cronin, he would resign outright. "I'm not going to hire a child molester to run a nursery school," he vowed. Kennedy was unyielding.

In June 2000, in the offices of a Manhattan law firm, the board cast its vote: thirteen for Kennedy, eight for Boyle. Boyle swiftly resigned, as did those eight directors and most of his supporters in Riverkeeper.

No one had ever described Bob Boyle as a diplomat. He had always been better at fighting a war than forging a peace, and even some moderates in Riverkeeper felt that, after nearly twenty years in command, it might be time for the old general to step aside. Those same moderates wondered why the chief prosecutor was so committed to Wegner. Some came to view the matter in Oedipal terms: that Kennedy had found a scientist whom he knew Boyle couldn't abide, and the Son had hired him expressly to drive the Father out of the organization.

The damage to Riverkeeper remained to be assessed. With no less than fifteen proposals for new power plants in the Hudson River Valley, the new leadership had important tests ahead of it. But Kennedy hadn't forgotten the sturgeons. His letter to Federal District Court Judge Frederic Block urged a tough sentence—and not a second chance—for Gino Koczuk.

Bob Boyle, however, was still stunned by the turn of events and dismayed by the changing character of the U.S. environmental movement. "When I was a kid at summer camp in New Hampshire, I spent all my time in the brooks fishing, catching frogs, turning over rocks to see what was underneath," he said from his home in Putnam County, overlooking the Hudson. "Then I traveled across the country for *Sports Illustrated*, still fishing, and I could see all the destruction that was being wrought on our rivers and wild places, though we were all told it was progress. That whole world seemed to be vanishing, and the chance to do something about it was disappearing as well." But now, he lamented, more and more people saw the environmental movement as an opportunity for "self-advancement, self-promotion, or a way of making money. It's a means to an end that's not the river itself, but personal power, public glory. And now it's commingled with a new set of attitudes: Don't rock the boat on this issue, got to get along with the governor on that issue. Don't do this or we'll lose that grant. I don't go for that."

Hence that feeling of sitting on a pillar in Syria. But the way this had all sneaked up on him put Boyle in mind of another metaphor. "Did you ever see the Charlie Chaplin movie *Modern Times*? In one scene Chaplin is walking down a side street and this lumber truck goes by. It's got a red flag on the end of a log, but the flag drops off. Chaplin picks it up and runs after the truck, trying to return the flag, but the truck swings out into a main boulevard. Chaplin keeps on running and waving this flag as he runs down the boulevard, and he doesn't see that there's a parade of anarchists marching right behind him. So he's leading this parade and waving a red flag, while right around the next corner are the Keystone Kops, slapping their billy clubs and ready to pounce. That's how I feel. I just wanted to protect the river, and now look what's happened."

In my mind's eye I saw Boyle sharing a pillar with an equally per-plexed Vadim Birstein. But that would be a brouhaha as well. Boyle was disappointed by Birstein's terminal neglect of the Sturgeon Society, and the two men had a personal falling out before then. "It was never a good idea putting Vadim and Bob Boyle together in the same room," Rob DeSalle once told me.

Fred Danback died in 2003. Instead of that pillar, I imagined Boyle gazing from a Hudson bluff at the blue water of the river that he and an Anaconda janitor had started to clean up when the world was much younger. At night, maybe, he dreams of sturgeons, waking up beguiled all over again by the enormity of their tenure, their existential tenacity: beyond mishap, beyond conspiracy, beyond the entropy of time itself. "I think of this thing that existed even before the dinosaurs," the exile said wonderingly. "It survived Nemesis, or whatever it was, that did in the dinosaurs, and my God, it's still with us."

iii.

The Brooklyn office of Assistant U.S. District Attorney Cynthia Mo-naco overlooks the East River and the skyline of southern Manhattan. It was a genial sort of Indian summer evening, only a month since the destruction of the World Trade Center. The lights in Manhattan were just coming on, while the skyline itself still had a bloody, gap-toothed aspect to it.

The office was booth-like, long and narrow, just slightly wider than its occupant's desk. The shelves were crammed with paperwork from the case at hand, the walls hung with her Harvard Law School diploma and an award from Attorney General John Ashcroft for her work on the Gino International case. That night, however, she found it galling that she had yet to conclude that particular case. Ed Grace, seated in front of her desk, was disappointed as well. "You know what?" Cynthia fumed. "I'm going to end up spending more time on this case than Koczuk will spend in jail."

I had flown into La Guardia early that afternoon, and Grace had met me there. He was spiffed up for his appearance in court that afternoon—

a black suit, a cobalt blue shirt, a glossy red tie—and he looked as neat and crisp as any young lion on the stock exchange. After all his years in New York City, though, and now Chicago, Grace still looked more like an outdoorsman than a broker. His square-jawed hunter's face floated above the necktie as though it had been inserted into a carnival costume cut-out board.

We went out the terminal doors and walked past a detachment of Secret Service agents awaiting the arrival of Hillary Clinton. October 2001 was still an edgy time in New York City, and Grace would begin his sky-marshal duties later that month. But he was still involved in some of his caviar cases. As he worked the car through traffic on I-495 through Queens, he mentioned Arkady Panchernikov, saying he believed Mats Engstrom was right, that Arkady's 28 tons were probably coming in on consignment, and he'd only have to pay for what he sold. Grace added that many caviar dealers claimed large up-front costs, when in fact they were doing business on consignment.

That was when we topped a rise and could suddenly see southern Manhattan. The thin film of haze that lingered visibly over the site of the Twin Towers was still unsettling. Grace was due in Brooklyn for a three o'clock meeting with Cynthia Monaco at the Federal District Courthouse. Then Koczuk's resentencing hearing—the result of the Second Circuit Court of Appeals' rejection of Judge Block's original sentence—was scheduled for four. But Grace bore east, heading for the Midtown Tunnel, judging that we had time to at least approach Ground Zero before his meeting.

We crawled down Fifth Avenue while Grace alerted me to some good theater to anticipate at the hearing. He said an attorney from Zabar's, the gourmet super-deli on the Upper West Side, would be bringing twenty cases of spoiled caviar into court that day, caviar that Zabar's had bought from Gino International in 1998 just before Koczuk's couriers were intercepted. Koczuk and attorney Walter Drobenko were still carrying on their suit against Zabar's for not paying for that caviar, and Zabar's wanted relief from the court on that suit. Grace yielded up a thin smile and shook his head. "Drobenko's got a lot of gall," he said.

We picked up Broadway in Greenwich Village and worked our way through clotted traffic to Soho and Little Italy. On Canal Street we were still more than a dozen blocks from Ground Zero, but traffic beyond that point was allowed only to trains or buses. Grace thought about continuing on foot or via subway, but decided there wasn't time. The haze to the southwest had thickened to a peculiarly orange vapor, and a faint scent of combustion still hung in the air.

Cadman Plaza in Brooklyn is a small park cum war memorial overlooking the East River. The federal courthouse there is a war-like block of concrete and glass on the other side of a leaf-strewn lane. Inside Courtroom 6, Judge Block, from his elevated bench, with slabbed marble panels and the great federal seal behind him, finished prepping the jury for a grand theft case. The actors for the next hearing were already present, seated in benches at the front of the room: several attorneys, including Cynthia Monaco; such potential witnesses as Ed Grace; an English-Polish interpreter; and the appellant, Eugeniusz Koczuk. Three women crept in from the hallway and slid into the rearmost seats. Fluorescent light shone from the 30-foot ceiling with the effect of sunlight through water: very bright above, sifting into dimness toward the floor.

"For some reason, all you folks look familiar to me," Block said after he had called Cynthia and defense attorney Andrew Bowman to the bench. "We meet again."

"Your Honor, I'd be happy to send you cards and to write, so that you didn't miss us," said Cynthia, "if you could just finish this case." Tall, in a dark skirt suit and shoulder-length brown hair, at once street-tough and feminine, she wanted to get on with things. Her gaze as she glanced about the room had the quality of small-arms fire.

Unfortunately, there was to be no getting on today, as Block had to leave in fifteen minutes on a personal matter. "But let me give you some things here to think about," he said, "for when we come back in the near future to complete this."

Grace stood behind and to the left of Cynthia, his hands clasped behind his back. His old quarry, Koczuk, stood between Bowman and the interpreter with head bowed, his short gray hair combed straight forward. He was a beefy man in a V-necked blue prison shirt and a white T-shirt underneath. His shoulders sagged abjectly. His arms hung like benched oars. I supposed that one of the women in back was his wife, Helena.

Block called Bowman forward, reminding him that health considerations in this case were among the reasons he had assigned a sentence of only twenty months: Koczuk's diabetes, his wife's posttraumatic stress disorder. But he had no update on Mrs. Koczuk's condition from her doctor.

Better get that soon, said Block, since the government's cross-appeal put Koczuk in jeopardy of a stiffer sentence this time. "I will say on the record, because I like to stick my neck in the noose," he added, "that I would not like to sentence him to eighty-seven months."

Bowman also needed to provide more evidence of rehabilitation on Mr. Koczuk's part, which currently extended only to his attempts to learn English. Cynthia fidgeted as she stood next to Grace, who by then was rocking back and forth on his toes.

"Your Honor, if you're done with the homework assignments," she said at last, "there is one matter I would like to take up in court. There is a victim here."

Heads turned to the third legal party in the courtroom. Eli Zabar occupied a front-row bench with his attorney, Bill Wachtel. Zabar was a tanned, craggy-faced man in a teal sweatshirt with sunglasses folded into its neck. The nodding, smiling, and bespectacled Wachtel was short and similarly tanned, in an attorney's sober suit and tie.

Cynthia reviewed the circumstances. After Koczuk's arrest, caviar that Zabar's had bought from Gino International was not turned over to USF&W. Nor did the agency seek its forfeiture on a search warrant. "It was very old by the time of the trial," she said, "so I don't think anyone anticipated that anyone would sell it or ask for it back."

Block wondered what had finally happened to the caviar. "Did Zabar sell any of it?"

"It's apparently outside in a car, and Zabar's wants to turn it over now to the Fish and Wildlife Service."

"Well, who do we have here from Zabar's? I just have a few minutes."

Wachtel rose and said that in fact $59,000 worth of ruined caviar was in that car. Walter Drobenko, he added, had asked for the return of the caviar after his client's arrest. But USF&W said that it couldn't be returned, since it was contraband. "We were in a Catch-22, and out of an abundance of caution, kept it."

"So what do you need me for?"

Wachtel wanted the restitution provided by the government to the innocent victims of criminal activity, specifically: "The restitution order we're seeking is that this civil case involving nonpayment for caviar, which is still ongoing in the Queens Supreme Court, be dropped." Wachtel nodded toward Koczuk. "That is certainly within this man's power."

Cynthia observed that the government, while not requiring forfeiture, had asked for the caviar to be turned over in the first place. Perhaps there had been a miscommunication.

"Excuse me, your Honor," Wachtel protested. "I did not believe there was miscommunication. There is no circumstance under which we chose to hold on to this product—that is, we, Zabar's."

Cynthia fixed Wachtel with a sharp glance, lasting little more than an eye-blink, and then wondered aloud what Bowman's position might be on his client's suit against Zabar's. "Your Honor, I don't think there's a loss," Bowman said. "I don't understand what the claim of loss is. They didn't pay for it."

Block replied that his only concern was an appropriate sentence for Koczuk's crime, and this matter seemed to lie outside that. Wachtel persisted: "Just so we're clear, your Honor, the lawsuit that is pending is for nonpayment in respect of contraband—just so you understand."

"It sounds odd to me, and I understand that it has a bizarre aspect to it, but let's deal with his criminal culpability. Anything else before we go?"

Cynthia pointed out that the Zabar's suit wasn't entirely a sideshow. "Mr. Koczuk, after being sentenced as a felon by this court for caviar smuggling," she said, "turned around and sued one of his victims. His victim is incurring substantial legal expenses in defending itself. Whether or not they turned over the caviar for destruction, they didn't profit from it."

This gave Block pause. "If there's a lawsuit and there's no basis to it, and if it's done just to harass or whatever, that may be something that I can consider that may warrant a more severe sentence," he conceded. "It may be that Mr. Koczuk might be well advised to reflect on that."

The final hearing was set for November 27, and Block hastened out of the room. The proceedings had been underlined by the low murmur of the translator as she whispered into Koczuk's ear. Other than an occasional nod of his head, Koczuk stood transfixed. The women in the back of the courtroom made no attempt to capture his attention as he was led away, and he made no sign that he knew they were there.

Thirty minutes later, Grace and I were in Cynthia's office in Brooklyn, where the assistant U.S. attorney was still decompressing. She said Zabar's had been a major customer of Gino International for quite some time, and that none of the permits that accompanied Koczuk's last shipment there had a USF&W stamp. That looked suspicious, but in exchange for Zabar's receipts and testimony, there would be no questions asked. She and Grace spoke to Wachtel, offering to take the contraband, but the boxes were never relinquished.

"Then Drobenko comes up with this wacky lawsuit, and Wachtel calls me up in a panic, asking, 'What do we do now?'" she said. "Well, by then it was too late for us to take it, though I reminded him he had his chance. So Wachtel comes out in front of the judge today and claims it was our fault the caviar didn't get turned over. Basically, they were calling us liars."

Cynthia liked to tease Grace to the effect that her successful prosecutions against caviar smugglers had made him famous, or at least as famous as a caviar cop could be. But now Grace was a former caviar cop, and in the afterhaze of 9/11, seizures of smuggled caviar and other wildlife items in New York had dropped off the chart. Meanwhile, the Koczuk case, their most famous collaboration, had become both her crown and her albatross.

"I can't believe I've got more briefs to file," she sighed. But file them she would. "Did you hear what Block said? 'I don't want to give him a severe sentence, even if it means sticking my head in a noose.' He's still convinced there's no victim here outside the Russian economy."

Somewhere, as we spoke, whether in Brooklyn or Queens or someplace else by now, a car nosed its way through traffic with $59,000 worth of malodorous caviar in freight. Judge Block had ruled correctly: It had a bizarre aspect to it.

iv.

John Muir visited New York once. In 1867, carrying only a comb, a brush, a bar of soap, a towel, a change of underwear, the New Testament, and some volumes of poetry, he walked from Kentucky to the

Florida Gulf Coast, studying plants along the way. From there he caught a schooner to Cuba. He wanted to go on to Brazil and the Amazon rain forest but was unable to get passage. Finally he rode with the same schooner and a cargo of oranges to its next destination, New York City.

He waited ten days for a ship to San Francisco and was eager to explore Central Park. But the young man who had just navigated 1,000 miles of back roads and woods without so much as a compass found himself afraid to venture more than a few blocks from his ship. "I can make my exhilarated way up an unknown ice-field or sure-footedly up a titanic gorge," he wrote later, "but in those terrible canyons of New York, I am a pitiful, unrelated atom that loses itself at once."

Neither he nor anyone else noticed the short-nosed sturgeons that swam about those canyons. At 4 feet and up to 50 pounds, the puppy-like fish was known as a "mammose" to fishermen in the 1880s and 1890s and presumed to be a juvenile Atlantic sturgeon. Taxonomists were still debating whether Atlantic and European sturgeons were different species, and they had only just noticed that the blunt-nosed mammose was something else entirely. Harvest numbers of these were unknown because catches of the fish were so frequently lumped in with those of the Atlantic. When populations of the latter collapsed around 1900, a fish that had been seen only in the shadow of the sea sturgeon anyway disappeared completely from view.

In succeeding decades, there were incidental landings of the short-nosed up and down the East Coast, but by 1967 even those landings had largely ceased. It was feared that the fish had gone extinct everywhere but in the Hudson, and there three-fourths of the short-nosed taken by Bob Boyle's Verplanck fishermen showed signs of fin rot and other afflictions. The fish was believed to be anadromous, moving back and forth between rivers and the ocean like the Atlantic sturgeon, and when it was placed on the Endangered Species List, jurisdiction for its recovery was assigned to the National Marine Fisheries Service.

The ESA listing provoked a little bit of scientific activity. The short-nosed was found not to be anadromous at all, and also still extant—albeit in low numbers—in twenty-five river systems from New Brunswick to Florida. The Connecticut River stock included a landlocked population, trapped above the Holyoke Dam in northern Massachusetts, that had gone undetected ever since the dam had been built in 1849.

But if the wandering Atlantic sturgeon is slow to recolonize rivers, then the stay-at-home short-nosed is positively glacial. On rare occasions, individuals are captured at sea in near-coastal waters, and it's possible that such free spirits are the means by which an otherwise poky fish expands its range. But as it is, the twenty-five river systems that the short-nosed occupies now are balkanized into nineteen distinct populations, each with its own genetic signature, and it's unlikely that there is any exchange of DNA at all between northern and southern stocks of the fish.

This makes for behavioral differences between the two. Southern fish feed throughout the year, for example, while northerners cease foraging when water temperature drops below 50 degrees Fahrenheit. Then the fish may eat only incidentally for six months, clustering in somnolent groups in slow, deep water over sand or cobble. Biologist Boyd Kynard of the University of Massachusetts has gone to the Connecticut River to make an underwater video of wintering mammose. It's not an action film: The video reveals hundreds of adult and juvenile fish that are virtually immobile, hanging suspended in the current, some with their pectoral fins partially buried in sand.

When Mark Bain of Cornell came to the river in 1994 to gauge the decline of the Atlantic sturgeon, he wasn't surprised to see short-nosed sturgeons turning up in his nets as well. But he was very surprised by how often that happened. He applied to the Hudson River Foundation for a grant to study that species and set about examining the mystery of how these two different versions of the same fish, which share so many life-history characteristics, manage to coexist in the same environment—rather like Christians and Muslims in New York City, maybe, or Jews and Arabs, or even Yankee and Met fans.

It had been presumed that the fish get along by staying to their own sides of the street: the short-nosed tending to stay upriver in fresh water, the Atlantics near the estuary in brackish, and each having different times and places for spawning, feeding, migration, and so on. But Kynard has found that certain short-nosed populations spend the majority of their lives in the estuary. Then Bain discovered that, in the

Hudson at least, juveniles of both species mingle seamlessly, year-round, sharing the same habitats and some of the same foods in the lower reaches of the river. This is at a stage, Bain noted, when both species are about the same size and growing at the same rate. Then the Atlantics customarily emigrate to ocean waters just as they reach the size of a small adult short-nosed. In a paper presented at an American Fisheries Society symposium in 2000, Bain and his colleagues wrote, "The conclusion that the two species are not spatially segregated for large parts of their life histories indicates that the Hudson River estuary may be unique within the joint ranges of the species."

Bain was even more impressed, however, by the sheer number of short-nosed sturgeons in the Hudson. In the symposium paper he provided context: "Biodiversity is being threatened and lost in aquatic environments at a much greater rate than in terrestrial systems. In the last one hundred years, three genera, twenty-seven species, and thirteen subspecies of fish have been extirpated from North America. The US government currently lists more fish species as threatened and endangered than any other major taxonomic group. Despite the broad legal protection, there is no evidence of recovery of any federally listed endangered fish. In the twenty-seven years since passage of the US Endangered Species Act, just four species have been removed from the endangered species list—all by extinction."

In the Hudson, though, this ESA-listed fish was quietly experiencing the opposite of extinction. Bain estimated that there were about 61,000 short-nosed in the river, which would represent a 450 percent increase from the 1980s. That number is also higher than the combined estimates of all other short-nosed populations in the United States and Canada. Better yet, the vast majority of those fish—57,000—are adults that participate in the spawning migrations and winter gatherings. It's a mature and healthy population, in other words, that seems not to suffer from fishing pressure, predation, or environmental stress. It also provides perhaps the only example in the world of a large, long-lived fish existing in an unexploited condition. Very few such fish populations, noted Bain, have ever been studied.

Bain's paper didn't attempt to explain this renaissance, but over the telephone he lauded the fish's early ESA listing and the improved water quality in the river. He mentioned that the Endangered Species Act applies to populations as well as species, and that certainly this Hudson stock was qualified for de-listing as the first ESA success story for fish. But there was no movement on that from the National Marine Fisheries Service, and though Bain's paper created something of a stir in the academic community, the news about these flourishing sturgeons was greeted with little fanfare in New York and elsewhere.

"I guess it's only bad news that grabs the headlines," Bain sighed.

~ 7 ~

Poor Man's Lobster

i.

An Ojibwa Indian tale tells of two young girls who slept outdoors in winter and talked of making love to the stars in the sky. They awoke one morning to find themselves in the sky world and married to stars in the shape of men much older than they wished. An old woman in that world showed the unhappy girls a hole in the sky, through which they could look down upon their former world.

There are different levels to earth and sky, suggest the Ojibwa, and one day in February 2002, Gary Ninneman and I shared a hole in the sky of Lake Winnebago. We sat on stools on either side of a rectangular piece of water, 3 feet by 4, edged by the frame of an open trapdoor upon the ice. The shanty that enclosed us provided a starless sort of darkness in which the only light came from below, a chilly fluorescence bouncing off the lake bottom 9 feet beneath us. We stared into water that was the color of pale green tea sweetened with honey. A crosswise assembly of white PVC pipes marked the bottom and was just barely visible through the tea and its drifting flecks of organic matter. Between the ice and the pipes hung a wooden fish, a 15-inch decoy carved in the shape of a long-snouted gar with metal fins. We shared between us two pronged spears, each as heavy as a deer gun and with five sharp tines at its business end. It was our intention to effect a miraculous and deadly ascension, to haul a legal-sized lake sturgeon through this hole in the dome of the lake.

"It's hard to judge the size of a fish down in the water," Gary told me. "The minimum size used to be 45 inches. One time back then Bill Casper was in his shanty with a film crew from one of the TV stations around here, and he speared a sturgeon that shrank quite a bit as it came up and out of the water. Later he was taking it to a registration station to have it measured, and the camera was still running, and Bill was there whispering out of the side of his mouth, 'Don't hold its nose up to the board, whatever you do.' We put the raspberries on him pretty good for that."

I'd met Gary the previous summer at the Oshkosh symposium, when we'd found ourselves next to each other on a bus to the boomshocking demonstration on the Wolf River, and then to the feast and dance on the Menominee reservation. Gary was tall and fair and rangy, wearing a camouflage jacket and West Shore Fishing Club baseball cap. He was a machinist like Bill Casper used to be, but one still punching his time clock as he put two kids through the University of Wisconsin. He also served as the shop steward for the local chapter of the machinists' union. He was an officer as well in Casper's Sturgeon for Tomorrow organization, and as full of the facts and numbers of the lake sturgeon harvest in Wisconsin as he was of the family lore—going back several generations—of hunting and fishing around the big lake.

His grandfather once ran a dairy farm on this southwest side of Winnebago. And this winter dose of spearfishing was a tradition in the Ninneman family, on both sides of the gender line. Eight years ago, Gary had been fishing with his grandmother at the northern end of Winnebago where the water is deeper, 20 feet or so, and it takes some time for a thrown spear to reach a fish. "She threw it at the head, but hit it near the tail," Gary said. "Now if you don't hit a sturgeon somewhere along the spine, then you've got a heck of a fight on your hands."

The spear's tines had detached from the handle, which had a rope running through it. Gary ended up outside the door of the shanty, hanging onto the handle with his boots dug into the ice, while his grandmother hauled on his belt loops. That laker came in at 55 inches and 50 pounds, which was modest next to the 90-pounder she'd speared thirty years ago. That time, she looped the rope around the door and hung on until a fisherman from a neighboring shanty came to help. "Later she got drunk and fell off her stool," Gary laughed. "We got a picture now of her and that fish and two big shiners for eyes."

More difficult than landing a sturgeon, perhaps, was the level of attention required just to get a chance at a strike. The fish glide silently beneath these waters, and if you don't see a sturgeon until it's in the middle of the hole, it's already too late. Gary said, "You've got to watch the frame, not the picture. You've got to see the fish the instant it breaks the border." He laughed again, shaking his head slightly. "I used to be a much more dedicated spearer. I never took my eyes off a hole, even to take a leak. I have a cousin who got up once to adjust the CB radio, and he sat down just in time to see the tail of a sturgeon go by. He told his father about it, my uncle, and my uncle booted him in the ass. That's how serious they are."

The biggest sturgeon Gary ever landed was a 78-pounder. He struck the fish in its flank just fifteen minutes before spearing was scheduled to stop for the day. The sturgeon went to the bottom and rolled, trying to scrape the tines out. Then it veered back and forth beneath the hole like a pendulum, lunging to the length of the rope and leaving cross-hatched grooves in the muddy bottom. When it rose from the bottom a second time, Gary hit it squarely in the spine with a second spear. "That took the fight out of him," he said.

In thirty-one years of spearfishing, Gary calculated that he had landed twelve to fifteen sturgeons. Lately, however, he had been in a slump. "The last time I got one was in '98," he noted. "And last year, they were throwing them out all around us."

Gary started forward in his seat. "Did you see that?" I saw only the same shimmering box of water, the slowly turning decoy, and the white pipes slipping in and out of sight. Maybe, though, I didn't have all quarters of the border under the same surveillance. Gary settled back, murmuring, "I saw something. Maybe just a big silvery carp."

His battery-run CB radio was kept as handy to the hole as the spears. He said that accidents happen, that last year a fisherman he knew, a big guy, fell into his hole and was too stocky to pull himself out. He was in there half an hour before he was found, just barely alive. Gary reached for the mike and called up Rowdy, the CB-handle for his brother Todd, who occupied the shanty next to us with a friend. Their shanty was half again as big as ours, big enough for two holes. "You see anything yet over there?" Gary wondered.

"A lot of shad went by one hole a minute ago," Todd said. "Hundreds of them."

"A shad's a silvery fish, too," Gary told me. "That's probably what I saw. If you see a sturgeon down there, on the other hand, it looks like it gives off a glow."

A sturgeon may have to give off fireworks to be seen in this water. The winter had been mild in Wisconsin so far, and snowfall very light. Sunlight through lake ice that was both thinner than usual and lacking in snowcover had brought about an algal bloom, making Winnebago as murky now as it usually was in summer. The Wisconsin Department of Natural Resources had set quotas for three categories of lake sturgeon—males, juvenile females, and adult females—and would close the season on the day that 80 percent of any one of those quotas was reached. The quota for both sorts of females was 400, or about 5 percent of the present numbers of each; that for males, 1,375. That conservative level of harvest, and a record number of shanties out on the ice last year, nearly 5,000, made for a 2001 season that had lasted only two days.

Bill Casper thought the season would go a lot longer this year. "It's ridiculous, it looks so bad," he told me when I had called him last week. "I could barely see a yellow decoy 2 feet under the ice, so how is anybody going to see a dark sturgeon? But a lot of people are going to be out just the same. I'll be out there, too. I'll be fishing the east shore."

Gary and I were on the west side, about a mile out, more or less in line with the family land, and his parents were fishing in a shanty somewhere near us. The lake is 10 miles wide, east to west, and 28 miles long. Some years on Winnebago the ice grows to 3 feet thick; we had a foot beneath us now—good enough here, but not good enough to make the entire lake safe. There were areas of open water, including one stretching in a charcoal line in front of two islands just to the north of us.

We had come out at six that morning on snow machines with Todd and his buddy and a married couple, Rob and Jen Noe, friends of Gary's. At one point we crossed a jagged split in the ice, less than a foot wide, across which someone had placed ramps for wheeled vehicles. The separate cakes of lake ice sagged perceptibly beneath our weight as we moved from one to the other. We arrived at the shanties—"The S(t)urgeon Is In" read a sign on the door of Gary's shanty—just as the morning light was brightening a bank of fog that lay to the south. A skyline of hundreds of peaked and flattened roofs jutted through the breadth of the fog bank, and I asked Gary if that was Fond du Lac I was seeing. "No, those are other shanties," he said.

It was now mid-morning. The only sounds, besides our voices, were the hiss of the propane heater, the rattle of snow machines outside, and the stream-of-consciousness murmur of the CB. A voice there said that someone had speared a 54-inch sturgeon up near Stockbridge, over on the east side. "The last six or seven years," Gary observed, "the water has been so clear you could drop a peanut on the bottom and see it."

At last we saw another silver fish, maybe a catfish, thought Gary, or else a burbot, that nuzzled a moment at our decoy. A lake sturgeon wasn't likely to eat even a small gar, but Gary knew that decoys like that will arouse a laker's lively curiosity. "Some people call them coaxers, and they don't necessarily have to be fish," he said. A couple of old automobile hubcaps in a corner of the shanty had served that purpose before. Other folks tended to use old washing-machine agitators, Gary told me, or even bowling balls wrapped in tin foil. Some brighten up their decoys with Green Bay Packer logos or snarling University of Wisconsin badgers. "My grandpa had a buddy who spread newspapers on the bottom. He said that when the sturgeons came to read them, he'd spear them."

Another voice on the CB wondered what the 10:30 report from the registration stations might be, and someone else replied that only forty-two fish had been registered across the lake so far. A third voice complained that he was about to quit, that he was butt-tired of sitting on a stool and staring into a hole for four hours. "Remember when we used to do this all day?" a fourth asked.

Fishing today closed at 12:30 P.M., a big reduction in time from last year's eighteen-hour fishing days. Then it would start again tomorrow morning at 6:30 for another six hours, for as many days after that as was necessary for one of the harvest caps to be triggered. The shorter daily hours were one way to lengthen the season, though fishermen traveling long distances to get here were unhappy about that. Some were unhappy as well about the low harvest caps. Gary said, "They think there are more sturgeon in the lake than the DNR says there are, and maybe they're right—it's not an exact science. At Sturgeon for Tomorrow, though, we like to err on the side of caution. This isn't like managing deer."

He shook his head, blinking, saying, "I'm getting transfixed looking into the middle of that." He shifted his stool to the left, stared from a different angle, and mentioned hearing about a girl at a gas station who couldn't decide between buying a spearing license or a lottery ticket. Finally she picked the license. "Last year DNR sold 36,000 licenses, and there were 1,590 sturgeons caught. We like to see people catch fish, but there are some folks out there who can never catch enough, or catch them often enough. I gave a speech a while ago for Sturgeon for Tomorrow, telling it just the way it is—I've been spearing a long time, and I know as much about that as anybody—and I actually got booed. Maybe we're doing too good a job."

The CB was the voice of the collective unconscious of this temporary city of fishermen, but the cell phone was making inroads. Gary used his phone to call Ron and Jen in their shanty and learned that they thought they had seen two sturgeons, but they couldn't be sure. "Can you see the bottom?" Gary asked. "Do you have pipes down there?" They didn't have any pipes, which help to fix the size and position of any fish passing above them, and Gary said he'd bring some over.

He scrounged in a corner of the shanty as the CB kicked in again. The registration station nearest us was at Wendt's On the Lake marina, a few miles up Route 45, and someone reported that only two fish had been registered there today. "Looks like this is one of those days when you just have to wait them out," another man said.

A little gizzard shad, as bright as chrome but not glowing, wriggled like a blown leaf across the length of our hole in the sky, and then the dark weather settled in again.

ii.

Before Gary and I went out on the ice that morning, Gary's friend Jen, a bright and pixie-faced woman who had taught special education for twenty-nine years, showed me the photo of a sturgeon she had speared during last year's season: 71 inches, 92 pounds. Later Gary told me that the fish was a ripe female and that her nearly 20 pounds of eggs had filled a 5-gallon bucket to the brim. "We tried to make caviar out of it," Gary said. "We put it through two screens of different mesh sizes, trying to separate out the membranes, and then we added salt. But you couldn't eat it, so we threw it all out. It's illegal to sell the eggs, but there should be some sort of window that allows that, just so you avoid the waste."

Avoid the waste. Ah, that's the whole trick.

Once upon a time the lake sturgeon—like the Atlantic, the short-nosed, and the white—couldn't be wasted fast enough. Lakers from Winnebago and the Great Lakes were plowed into the ground as fertilizer, fed to pigs, burned for cordwood, and thrust into the boilers of steamboats. They were also believed, mistakenly, to feed on the eggs of the valuable whitefish. "A sturgeon is like a hog in a hen roost," a Lake Erie fisherman said in 1894, according to Margaret Beattie Bogue, author of *Fishing the Great Lakes* (2000). "They go around and suck up all the spawn there is." Therefore, sturgeons netted in whitefish grounds were hacked in the neck and thrown back to deter the presence of other sturgeons.

These lakers weren't so big as the Atlantics of Delaware Bay, but still big, with documented landings of fish as long as 9 feet and weighing more than 300 pounds. In the 1700s, the Ojibwa sold isinglass to the Hudson's Bay Company. European traders in search of that gelatin—made from the air bladder of the sturgeon and useful as an adhesive or clarifying agent—were amazed to find themselves in danger of being capsized if they ventured by boat into a sturgeon spawning ground. Mishe-Nahma, King of Fishes in the poem by Henry Wadsworth Longfellow, was a lake sturgeon, big enough to swallow Hiawatha, his canoe, and his fishing-line of cedar. In August 1867, after three separate sightings, a 40-foot "lake serpent" in Lake Michigan was proposed to be some sort of giant newt or a trapped whale, but it was most likely an unusually big sturgeon. Photographs exist of boys mounted on the backs of lake sturgeons trapped in shallow waters, riding them like ponies.

An atavistic thrill in the power of these fish—and in a self-congratulatory fashion, the even greater power of *Homo sapiens*—is transparent in a 1906 Chicago newspaper account of the fate of a laker named Bismarck: "Instead of roaming, a conqueror up and down the long stretches of the feeding ground, the monarch of fishdom gasped today for life in a narrow cell of a boat on the beach in Rogers Park, his lease on life depending on a barefooted boy, who has the task of pumping water for his majesty. Bismarck is seven feet six and a half inches long and weighs 245 pounds. He was captured yesterday and for twenty minutes made a terrible fight to free himself from the meshes of a seine where five men fought to subdue him."

On the Great Lakes, as it had been on Delaware Bay, it was German immigrants who first figured out how to make money from sturgeons. The brothers Siemon and John Schact had fished together on the Delaware before moving to Sandusky, Ohio, and beginning a small caviar-processing operation on Lake Erie. They paid fishermen twelve and a half cents for each female sturgeon, and then they began buying males as well for the production of smoked meat, oil, and isinglass. At first the caviar went overseas to Germany, but gradually domestic markets developed. By 1871, the brothers were processing 10,000 to 18,000 fish per year, and a company in Chicago reported that it had more orders for smoked sturgeon than it could fill. The success of the Schacts pleased biologist James Milner, who was surveying the Great Lakes fisheries that year. "Out of a shameful waste of a large supply of food," wrote Milner, "they have established a large and profitable industry."

By 1885, sturgeons were being processed, and caviar being made, in lakeport cities from Buffalo to Green Bay, and the combined sturgeon harvest from all the lakes approached 9 million pounds. Sandusky became the largest freshwater fish market in the world, and an 1888 city publication bragged that its caviar was not only being sold for good prices in Russia and Europe, but gradually doing away with the import market for caviar in this country. Sturgeons also were still being used for fertilizer, conveyed to plants in long, freight car–like barges packed to overflowing. In the fishing camps, men dined each night on parboiled sturgeon in spiced vinegar. Meanwhile, the citizens of Sandusky could spend a nickel on a mixed drink of soda pop and wine and enjoy with that approximation of champagne a free lunch of smoked sturgeon or caviar.

And so the first shameful waste yielded to the second. The harvest in the Great Lakes was down by two-thirds in 1889, and ten years later down to only half of that. By then fishermen were leaving the lakes and moving up the rivers, trolling with three-pronged grappling hooks over spawning grounds in the spring, mutilating hundreds of sturgeons in a fishery that sickened federal biologist H.F. Moore, who described it as barbarous. In Sandusky, Siemon Schact was still in business (John had returned to Germany), but one of his competitors, Philip Neilson, knew that the end was near. "The great trouble in the United States," Neilson said in 1894, according to Bogue, "[is] when they go into a thing, they go in head over heels, and just get all there is in it and do not consider the future at all, and the next generation will have to take care of themselves."

The next generation saw Sandusky wither as other commercial species in the lakes collapsed as well, though none with the dispiriting finality of the lake sturgeon. In 1928, the total sturgeon harvest in all the Great Lakes was only 2,000 pounds, and in 1929 commercial fishing for sturgeon was banned in Lake Michigan, the only one of the lakes not shared with Canada. Newspaper reports into the 1940s repeated hopeful assurances from fishermen that the sturgeon were coming back, and in 1943 a 310-pounder was captured in Lake Michigan. The *Sandusky Register-Star* observed on September 19, 1949, that on Lake Erie, "the few sturgeons found in nets were quickly cleaned and whisked away to Detroit and other markets where almost prohibitive prices are made for steaks and caviar produced from the roe." The Lake Michigan population remains just 1 percent of its historical size today, and the only extant commercial fishery for sturgeon in the Great Lakes is on the Canadian side of Lake Huron.

Compared to Canada or other states, Wisconsin was far-sighted in its 1903 adoption of an 8-pound minimum weight limit in its sturgeon fisheries, even if that only protected very young juveniles. More helpful was its 1915 ban of any sturgeon fishing in the Lake Winnebago system. That was rescinded in 1931, but only in favor of brief and tightly regulated hook, set line, or spearing seasons. The achievement of Sturgeon for Tomorrow has been in its ability to link values of service, stewardship, and sustainability to the sturgeon harvest. The organization was also the driving force behind Wisconsin's $1,500 fine for poaching sturgeon, the biggest in the nation. Together with the state DNR, they have built the Winnebago stock into the largest self-sustaining population of lake sturgeons in the world.

The major problem now was an imbalance between males and females, a 6 to 1 ratio among adults. Female lakers mature much later than males, twenty-five years versus fifteen to seventeen, and in fact are among the pokiest sturgeons in the world to reach reproductive age. The females also live much longer, some one hundred years to a male's forty. For that reason the 45-inch minimum size limit adopted in 1974 led to many more females being taken than males. In 1997, the minimum size was set back to 36 inches, and very narrow quotas were imposed on adult and juvenile females.

However disproportionate their numbers, males and females have more places to entertain each other now. Stones placed in the bends of meandering rivers as riprap to retard erosion have provided many new spawning sites in the Winnebago system. Where naturally there might have been a dozen, there were now more than sixty. Gary had often been among the volunteers, not just from Sturgeon for Tomorrow, but other conservation and service groups as well, who stood guard in twelve-hour shifts over those sites from April to June.

A video presented by Ron Bruch and Fred Binkowski at the symposium the previous summer—a film immediately dubbed "fish porn"—showed what spawning looked like on the Wolf River. The fish congregate over hard, rocky bottom in water that's often shallow. There one or two males will swim at the side of a gravid female, quivering like tuning forks and beating their tails along her abdomen. The female eventually begins extruding clumps of eggs in bursts lasting several seconds each, with the quivering males giving up sperm at the same time. This attracts up to a dozen other males, who cluster about the original group and begin vibrating as well, sometimes with their backs and tails partially out of the river, sometimes leaping in sudden lunges, sometimes with their pounding caudal fins producing a low and audible pulse, a sound like the drumming of a grouse. If a river is shallow enough, its water boils with this activity. Canoes and small boats will overturn.

The female will typically rest a few minutes after a spawning episode and then begin again, over and over until her eggs are spent. This activity continues for over a day or more. Big females may produce as many as 3 million eggs, though loads of 50,000 to 700,000 are more typical. The eggs are delivered in a ritual unfathomable in its antiquity, and—among fishes—uniquely primal, orgiastic, and brazenly conspicuous. The immediate success rate, however, is no better than that of other fish who resort to broadcast spawning: less than 1 percent of fertilized eggs survive to maturity.

iii.

So the sturgeons that swam—or didn't—beneath Gary's shanty were members of an elite group, rare survivors against near-lottery odds in a genus of fish that, after eons of unparalleled success, was facing long odds all over the world. In an interview with the *New York Times* on July 2, 2002, the biologist Fred Binkowski described the laker as "an American treasure," and it's the sort of treasure that can't be easily mass-produced. Lake sturgeon fingerlings in hatcheries, Binkowski has found, won't feed on the salmonid commercial mixes that satisfy other species, but only on expensive bloodworms or brine shrimp.

Yet what Gary and I proposed to do, given the chance, was to kill one of these treasures, and in a manner not much more humane than the grappling hooks that fishermen once used. Special education teacher Jen Noe, I think, is good at reading the subtext of the things people do and say. She didn't have to know me long before asking, "If you see a sturgeon out there under Gary's shanty, are you going to be able to throw that spear?" She knew already what I'd known myself before buying a license and coming out there—knew that my feelings about that part of the job were, well, complicated.

John Muir had spent his boyhood hunting and fishing not far from here. In his maturity, during times in America that encompassed the Industrial Revolution, the growth of cities, massive immigration, the Indian wars, and a new generation of weapons and killing technologies, he laid those pursuits aside. Of course one reason that North American sturgeon species collapsed with so little fanfare is that they were just one more item in a vast catalog of wildlife suffering wholesale slaughter then, whether for food, money, or sport. Witness the fate of Bismarck, described in terms suggesting the captured king of an enemy empire.

The gunfire of the time was expended in what might be viewed as a war of independence from nature, though Muir saw that such independence was neither possible nor desirable. He was particularly repulsed by the killing wrought in the name of sport. Early laws regulating hunting and fishing drew only acerbic praise: "The murder business and sport by saint and sinner alike has been pushed ruthlessly, merrily on, until at last protective measures are being called for, partly, I suppose, because the pleasure of killing is in danger of being lost from there being little or nothing left to kill," he wrote in 1912, in *The Story of My Boyhood and Youth*.

Of course, those measures, combined with the flight of population from rural areas into the cities, also meant that ever fewer American youths had the opportunity to grow up hunting and fishing—and farming—as Muir had. One corollary of that, observed Muir, was a loss of depth in our understanding of death. In *A Thousand Mile Walk to the Gulf* (1916), he wrote, "On no subject are our ideas more warped and pitiable than on death. Instead of the sympathy, the friendly union of life and death so apparent in Nature, we are taught that death is an accident, a deplorable punishment for the oldest sin, that arch-enemy of life, etc. Town children, especially, are steeped in this death-orthodoxy, for the natural beauties of death are seldom seen or taught in towns."

As death became divorced from life in our popular understanding, so did it become divorced from food. A boneless chicken breast in its cellophane package has become a product entirely removed from its animal origins, and as infinitely reproducible, apparently, as any plastic widget or synthetic doodad. Aldo Leopold wrote that one of the spiritual dangers of not owning a farm was supposing that breakfast comes from the grocery store. One can just as easily suppose that caviar comes from tins, as did Eve Vega's guests at the New School University event the previous summer, at least until Eve's photographs disabused them of that notion.

But those early protective measures that Muir mocked, and that arrived too late for the sturgeons and some others, nonetheless marked the first legislative victories of the conservation movement to which Muir has since become such an avatar. They also defined a new sort of relationship to nature, one different from that in Europe, where for centuries the freedom to hunt and fish had been largely a matter of class or privilege. There, surviving populations of partridge or salmon were guarded from the poor by the gamekeepers and riverkeepers who would later inspire Bob Boyle in his assault on another sort of privilege. And as early as the fourteenth century, any sturgeon caught in English waters belonged either to the king of England or the mayor of London.

But in America, an armed and unfettered citizenry repaired to the woods and rivers first for their living, and then for their sport. By Muir's time, these citizens were numerous and well-equipped enough to effect wholesale slaughters, and in 1899 Thorstein Veblen could observe that while sportsmen profess a love of nature, "it is, indeed, the most noticeable effect of the sportsman's activity to keep nature in a state of chronic desolation by killing off all living things whose destruction he can encompass."

Yet at last it was the sportsmen themselves who were most effective in putting an end to those decades of chronic desolation. They did so by establishing in their game laws the revolutionary notions of sustainable harvest and limits to resource consumption. They neither paid their bills nor, necessarily, stocked their larders with the animals they took. Though this may have satisfied one definition of waste, it also removed the most important incentives for ignoring the laws and exceeding the limits, and so fostered conservation practices that had public support and a practical chance of working. It traded the privilege to cull individual animals from populations of a species for a promise to the long-term welfare of that species as a whole. It also prepared the way for the recognition—with help from Aldo Leopold—that habitat, no less than size limits and bag limits, was crucial to that welfare.

The ideas of habitat and ecosystem were the cornerstones of Leopold's new science of ecology, and on behalf of those ideas, protective measures have been extended to a myriad of species of no direct interest to hunters or anglers or spearfishermen. "All history shows this: that civilization is not the progressive elaboration of a single idea, but the successive dominance of a series of ideas," Leopold wrote in 1938. "Engineering is clearly the dominant idea of the industrial age. What I have here called ecology is perhaps one of the contenders for a new order."

Although the study of ecology has yet to put engineering schools out of business, Leopold's contender is now the triumphant paradigm of wildlife science, and in the developed world no engineering project is carried out without consideration of its ecological impact. Meanwhile, the conservation movement as a whole has grown far beyond the numbers of our sportsmen, enough so to foster constituencies hostile to the activities of hunters and fishermen under any circumstances, within the law or outside it.

I doubt, however, that John Muir would condemn this Wisconsin spearfishing season and other regulated hunts. He might regret that it's not more a subsistence activity, though in fact the newspapers that week in Oshkosh and Fond du Lac were full of recipes for lake sturgeon. "You can fry it, bake it, cream it, smoke it, basically like you'd do with any other fish," one fisherman told the *Fond-du-Lac Reporter* for its February 17, 2001, issue. "You can dice it and boil it in water with caraway seed, dip it in butter, and you've got a good poor man's lobster."

Nearly all the people out on the ice that day first came out here from the woods and farmlands as children, as had Gary Ninneman and Bill Casper. In sitting out there in the cold, in taking their chances on the shifting ice for a bit of poor man's lobster, in smearing themselves in blood and slime while enlisting in this ancient ecology of predator and prey relationships, they also challenged that urban orthodoxy of death as the enemy of life, or else a soulless industrial process. They learn something of the sympathy between the two, of their "friendly union," especially as the best of these hunters, in consideration of the future and the next generation, abandon their spears to stand guard at the spawning grounds in spring.

One of Leopold's essays, "The Land Ethic" (1947), concludes with a famous summary statement: "A thing is right when it tends to preserve the integrity, stability, and beauty of the biotic community. It is wrong when it tends otherwise."

Gary's second spear rests at my right hand. In a daytime dream I see the olive-green bulk of a big laker breaking the frame of the hole, obscuring the PVC pipe on the bottom, nuzzling at the coaxer. With my heart aching, I bless the sturgeon—this monarch of fishdom, this American treasure—for its charity. Then I take my shot.

iv.

Christmas hadn't saved the faltering post–9/11 U.S. economy. Eve Vega reported that the holidays had been difficult at Petrossian and that the company's overall revenues were down 15 percent from last year.

Nonetheless, in February 2002, Caviarteria's Bruce Sobol told an on-line business magazine, *inc.com*, that he was feeling optimistic.

Sobol, whose suit against USF&W was still being negotiated out of court, said that 80 percent of Caviarteria's business came from its catalog, as opposed to hotel chains or cruise lines (up from the 30 percent that Eric Sobol reported to a Florida business magazine before his death), and for that reason he thought the company would weather the downturn. "I've brought the entry-level price point down so that people seeing the catalogue for the first time see that they can afford this," he explained.

These days Caviarteria was targeting young consumers, particularly at its new cafés in Miami Beach and Las Vegas. "I love to see tables full of young, tentative couples who put the spoons in their mouths, smile, and say, 'This tastes great,'" Sobol said. "I want them to walk out of my place feeling like gold."

While young couples spooned in Miami, another domino fell in the aftermath of the Koczuk investigation. Alfred Yazbak, the owner of Connoisseur Brands, had worked in tandem with Gino Koczuk on a false invoicing system that understated the value of legitimate imports into the United States. He had also bought great quantities of the frozen or unrefrigerated black-market caviar that arrived in Koczuk's suitcases. That stuff was then subjected to a process called "caviar washing"—draining it of oil, washing it with salt water, adding either walnut or hazelnut oil to mask any spoilage, and then partially pasteurizing the eggs. Finally it was sold to Trader Joe's, Zabar's, Balducci's, Harry & David, and Dean & DeLuca. A covert USF&W operation also revealed that he was selling paddlefish roe from the Tennessee River Basin and labeling it Russian sevruga. In a case that, compared to Koczuk's, moved at the speed of light, Yazbak was arrested, convicted, and sentenced to two years in prison and fines and restitution of $160,000.

That happened in January 2002, and later that same month Cynthia Monaco finally filed the last of her briefs on the Koczuk case. The re-sentencing hearing postponed to November had been postponed again until after Christmas, but when the principals finally convened, Judge Block told Andrew Bowman that he was "somewhat impressed with Ms. Monaco's argument that some of Mr. Koczuk's postarrest activities have been troublesome, to say the least. We know what that Zabar's scenario was all about. I know you've advised the court that you have withdrawn that lawsuit. But there's a lot of postarrest activity here that really weighs against the notion of rehabilitation."

Koczuk, speaking through an interpreter, noted that the appeals process had dragged on so long that he only had a few more months to serve on his original sentence. If he were to receive a longer sentence now, he would fear for his wife's health and his chances of ever seeing his elderly mother again. "Your Honor," Koczuk added, "it is true that I disobeyed the law, but I didn't do such a harm to this country or anybody else. Because of my account, nobody was hurt and nobody was harmed."

For his part, Block continued to insist that the government was overstating the seriousness of the crime and to express disappointment that the circuit court had rejected his original sentence. But in the end, he resentenced Koczuk to four years, the longest prison term meted out thus far for a caviar-related offense in the United States.

"Your Honor, I think you have to advise him of his right to appeal," Bowman said at the end of the proceedings. "Not that I am recommending it, but I think it ought to be done."

"Thank you for pointing that out to me," Block said. "I don't do resentencing every day, fortunately."

I suspect Cynthia Monaco's heart stopped as she listened to that exchange. But as it turned out, Koczuk and Bowman were done exercising that right. USF&W's reports on wildlife-related court rulings are usually sober, understated documents, but in reporting this decision, the author indulged in an exclamation point: "The government won!"

v.

In Gary's shanty, a voice on the CB said that two snowmobilers had just gone through the ice. "That must be over on the other shore," Gary remarked. "Earlier this week a woman drowned on her snow-go. I heard she was trying to skip her way across open water."

The movements go both ways: fish up through the ice on the tines of a spear, men and women and their snow machines or pickups down through that ice when it shifts or gives way beneath them. No sturgeon had come up through the hole that we guarded, or even been sighted.

Already bad enough, visibility had worsened in the lemony soup beneath us as the morning wore on. The pipes on the bottom flickered in and out of sight. They looked like the "x" marking the spot where a treasure was buried, except that the spot disappeared the harder you stared at it, and the treasure wasn't there.

At eleven o'clock another voice on the CB inquired if anybody had a sturgeon yet. "Randy Krohn," somebody volunteered.

"That's it?"

"And Ron Goebel," someone else added.

Gary pricked up his ears. "Ron Goebel? His shanty's almost right next door." He allowed himself another long stare into the murk beneath us, inspecting each quarter of the frame, and then suggested that we go see what Ronnie found.

Outside, the wind was whistling through moist, raw air. The temperature had climbed into the mid-forties, and a vague, sourceless light washed in from the south. Ron Goebel's shanty was the one just past Todd's. His sturgeon was as long as his pickup truck was wide, or a few inches longer. The fish lay on its right flank on the lowered tailgate. The belly was the same gritty white as the snow on the ice, the fins broad and striated and spatulate, the four barbels segmented like worms. The lips were wide and fleshy, the lower with jowl-like lobes at each end. Lake sturgeon occasionally eat other fish, and this one had the tail of a small fish protruding from its jaws, as though the sturgeon had been snatched from one of those cartoon sequences showing the marine food chain, each fish consumed in turn by a larger. Gary said the little fish was what they called around there a sheepshead, a species of freshwater drum. "That's unusual," he remarked.

The sturgeon's upper surface was a slate-colored green, well suited to the hues of the lake, but had turned more slate in this chrome light. The wet skin glistened in the light but felt almost dry to the touch. The gills were high on its skull, flaring in fronds of such deep maroon that they were nearly purple, and the skull had the laminated texture of fiberglass. The small black eyes gazed sightlessly from beneath that sheathing. I turned the fish on its belly and saw that Ron's spear had hit it square on the spine, entering just below the skull. Braided rivulets of blood ran down its opposite flank and onto the tailgate. The blood was as red as holly berries. "You don't want to spear it any higher on the spine than that," said Gary. "If you hit it on the head, the spear just bounces off."

A green tag had been wired to its tail by Ron, and a wire tag would be attached later at the registration station. A short incision had been cut into the fish's abdomen. A black and globular jam of eggs, several spoonfuls, spilled from the cut.

Gary knew Ron Goebel primarily from having worked at the machine shop for a while with Ron's dad. Ron wore a short white beard topped by piercing dark eyes. He came out of his shanty with his twenty-something daughter and said that by his reckoning the fish was 67 inches long and weighed 90 pounds. Gary whistled and replied, "She must be just full of spawn. A fish that long will usually weigh only about 70 or so."

Ron nodded, sighing. "She's a female. She's not supposed to be. That's not what you want to take, but what are you gonna do?"

We went back to our shanty, and after ten or so uneventful minutes, Gary rang up Todd on the CB. "Hey, Rowdy, you see anything lately?"

"Nope," Todd said.

"Did you go over to look at Ronnie's fish?"

"No, but I heard about it."

"The thing's like a tree, it's so thick."

"Did he spine him or fight him?"

"He spined her."

Gary and I resumed our vigil. The pipes on the bottom were just a memory by then, and even the turning decoy was fading in and out of sight. Gary checked his watch as the last minutes of the fishing day ticked off to 12:30. Finally he got back on the CB. "Hey, Rowdy, you're down to exactly twelve minutes to dagger one."

"We're concentrating intently," Todd assured him. "We're not even eating."

Another voice broke in: "That's eleven minutes and thirteen seconds."

Gary laughed. "That's Dad."

Eleven minutes and thirteen seconds later, Gary rose with a shrug to close our hole in the sky. "Not today," he said. He pulled the pipes and the decoy up, then shut the trapdoor that covered the hole. The windowless shanty went dark as the light off the lake bottom was extinguished. He snuffed the propane heater and hung the spears on the wall. Then we stopped concentrating and began to eat.

First there was beer and bratwurst cooked over a portable grill outside Todd's shanty. Rob and Jen were there, along with some other friends, and also Gary's parents. His father, Glenn, had a muscular build and the same crisp edges to his features as Gary. Lois, the more avid spearfisherperson, was small and trim, with a face crinkled into smiles by years of the sun and wind. The sun had broken through, burning a hole in the clouds, and we threw shadows across the ice as vehicles on either side of us fled to the shorelines.

When the bratwurst was gone, we adjourned to Gary's uncle's house on the west shore, where turkey was being deep-fried, and after that to Wendt's On the Lake marina. Wendt's had a restaurant and bar, and some of the fish caught that morning were still being registered there. Four medium-sized sturgeons, ranging from 40 to 60 inches, hung from their gill plates on hooks dangling from a gallows frame in Wendt's parking lot. A small crowd milled around these, and camera shutters clicked as people took turns posing with them. Two young women stood side by side, each smiling and hugging one of the sturgeons to her breasts like a lover, Ojibwa maidens who had traded in their elderly celestial husbands. Three of the fish were males, and the fourth had some pink tissue and black roe extruding from the cut in her belly. A young man in a dirty sweatshirt knelt below this fish, his mouth open and tongue extended just below that cut. "Goddam caviar!" he shouted as the cameras snapped.

A snowstorm hit the next morning, and my drive back to the airport in Milwaukee was slow and difficult. The *Fond-du-Lac Reporter* said that poor ice conditions and murky waters on opening day contributed to a 79 percent drop from the number of sturgeon taken last year. "Official registration stations around the lake reported that 227 sturgeon had been taken by noon on the opening day of the 2002 season. That compares with a record 1,074 speared on opening day last year." The article added that the number of shanties on the ice, 4,368, was down by only a few hundred from 2001.

The *Reporter*'s outdoor columnist opined that there were too many people out hunting for sturgeon nowadays, and that just increasing the price of a license, as the DNR meant to do next year, wouldn't provide for a longer season when conditions were good. Instead, the time had come for a lottery system. Maybe everybody didn't need to go spearfishing every year. I read that on the airplane. Clouds blanketed Lakes Michigan and Erie, and all that former world beneath.

The warm weather persisted, and ice conditions got worse. Gary called me at home the day after I got back to report that only 454 fish had been taken by that evening, and that some shanties had fallen through the ice. "We got ours off the lake on Sunday," he said. "It looks like the season's gonna go on for a while."

∼ 8 ∼

RUSSIAN CALIFORNIA

i.

"If this place is the launching pad," said Joel Van Eenennaam, "then these seven fish are the original astronauts, and Serge Doroshov is our Wernher von Braun."

We stood at the side of a concrete tank 30 feet across. Its water was an opaque and milky sort of green, and a warm April breeze pricked and rippled its surface. A dorsal fin sliced clear on the far side of the tank, and then another near at hand. That fin disappeared, and a dark shadow coursed beneath our hands. The shadow was at once slender and enormous.

Joel said there were seven white sturgeons in the tank, six females and one male, all grown to about 250 pounds. "We keep them to show to school kids when they come visit," he told me. "These are the original artificially propagated broodstock for this facility, and so also for the whole California aquaculture industry, really."

So these very fish, then, were the ones that closed the circle. They were spawned right here, in 1980, at the University of California's Center for Aquatic Biology and Aquaculture, on Putah Creek on the eastern outskirts of Davis. Their parents were wild sturgeons that were returned to the Sacramento River. Ten years later—here and at an early commercial farm, Arrowhead Fisheries—these fish became parents themselves of a second generation of artificially propagated sturgeon.

By then, of course, the Soviets had been hatchery-spawning their Caspian species in huge numbers for three decades, but then releasing their fingerlings into the wild. Doroshov's feat in 1990 marked only the third time in history, and the first time in North America, that hatchery-spawned sturgeons had been raised to maturity and then successfully spawned themselves. It was a moon landing of sorts, one that had since been repeated hundreds of times here and at commercial aquaculture operations in out-of-the-way corners all over the world, many of them dedicated to white sturgeon. It remained, however, an uncertain and delicate sort of journey, one still fraught with mishap, an esoteric ritual and the central mystery of California's new religion of farmed sturgeon. That day at Putah Creek, it was Joel's intention to perform it twice more.

And if Frank Chapman's Florida operation looked like a jungle compound, this Putah Creek facility had the more ephemeral look of a moon base. The main office was half of a mobile home that occupied one corner of a precise geometry of circular water tanks and low-slung, squared-off corrugated sheds and Quonset huts. There were thirty-two tanks of various sizes, some harboring striped bass or carp, others white sturgeon. All were shaded by tall specimens of eucalyptus, valley oak, and Pacific willow. Beneath the sweep of this blue sky, however, and along the oceanic plain of California's Central Valley, even these big trees seemed shrubby.

Joel was already a little uneasy about the way the spawning process for the first of his fish was developing. We walked to a small tank covered by a black scrim, which Joel removed. Then he ran a pond strainer through its silty water. The strainer yielded a few seeds, bits of leaf, and the pepper-flecks of several single sturgeon eggs. "The weather got pretty cold last night," Joel observed. "The water temperature in this tank dropped a few degrees, and she's starting to ovulate a little later than expected." He rolled one egg between his thumb and index finger. "The eggs are still a little bit soft."

Somewhere in his forties, Joel wore a baseball cap that couldn't quite contain his brown hair, which escaped from beneath its brim in thumb-sized tufts. His rumpled jeans and fish-spangled sweatshirt made him look like a young grad student from a distance. Up close, the lines in an otherwise boyish face give him a vaguely elfin look.

He had grown up in Michigan, fishing for walleye and perch and bluegill in the Great Lakes. After college he joined the Peace Corps and went to Thailand, where for four years he helped spawn carp and tilapia at Thai government hatcheries. He finally came to Davis to learn more about aquaculture. There, he assisted Doroshov's doctoral students—one of whom was Frank Chapman—with various white sturgeon projects. By 1985, he had his master's and a job supervising Doroshov's labs as a research associate. These days, his skills in spawning sturgeons were considered second only to Doroshov's.

The fish in this tank was only about a third the size of Doroshov's astronauts, but she was a $1,000 fish, Joel said, sold to the university by Ken Beer, who ran The Fishery. Beer's operation was one of the two major aquaculture businesses in the area, and Beer himself was a former Doroshov student.

Joel said that thirty-six hours ago he had injected this fish with a pituitary hormone that stimulates ovulation. Yesterday morning, Thursday, she had gotten a second dose. That sort of chemical intervention was necessary because neither wild nor hatchery-raised sturgeons will spawn of their own accord in captivity. Instead, the eggs that a mature female develops end up being reabsorbed into the ovaries. Several males had been shot full of the same hormone on Wednesday and then put ventral side up on a stretcher and milked of their sperm. You do that by massaging the abdomen and sucking the milt through a plastic tube into a syringe. The fruit of such sturgo-eroticism could be kept under refrigeration for two to three days or treated to last a few weeks.

I wondered if $1,000 might be a lot for one farmed fish, but Joel said it was a bargain, actually, given that the sturgeon had cost Beer $2,000 to $3,000 to breed and raise. Now she was one of sixteen subjects in a study of the effects of a high-selenium diet on sturgeons. Selenium is a valuable nutrient, but above an as yet undefined level, it becomes toxic. Selenium also occurs in shale rock and petroleum, and it's a waste by-product of the oil-refining process. Northern California refineries had been dumping selenium into San Francisco Bay for years, and there were high levels of the substance in the tissues of the bay's harbor seals, waterfowl, and white sturgeons. Beer's population of hatchery-raised sturgeons was numerous enough now to be self-sustaining, but they still needed the occasional infusion of genetic diversity provided by wild broodstock. On Beer's part, then, the sale of the fish below cost to UC-Davis had been an investment in the long-term health of that broodstock, so long as it helped establish standards for selenium concentrations in the bay.

Joel took another turn with the strainer. There were more eggs than there were twenty minutes ago nestled like ink drops in its mesh, but they were still soft, which meant that the female hadn't really begun to ovulate. Cool temperatures are good for spawning sturgeons, Joel explained, but temperatures that spike too low, as the previous night's had done, could delay and endanger the whole process. "I told everybody to be here at ten this morning," he said. "I hope we have something to do."

ii.

Once this land was known as Russian California. In 1812, the Russian-American Company established Fort Ross on a seaside meadow 80 miles north of San Francisco. The Russians brought Aleut hunters from Alaska to pursue fur seals and sea otters, which they did with such skill that within eight years the seals and otters were gone. Finally, in 1841, the Russians sold Fort Ross, and also the territory of Russian California, to the Swiss speculator John Sutter on credit for $30,000.

Sutter had promised to pay that sum out of the wheat to be raised by the colony of Swiss émigrés he intended to found. Instead, he moved Fort Ross's cannons to a fort and trading post that he built in California's Central Valley, in Mexican territory, at the junction of the Sacramento and American rivers. There he did a flourishing business with American settlers filtering illegally into the region from across the Sierra Nevada Mountains. In 1848, only nine days before Mexico signed the Treaty of Guadalupe Hidalgo ceding California to the United States, one of Sutter's employees found gold on a fork of the American River.

The ensuing frenzy dispossessed Sutter. He declared bankruptcy in 1852 and spent the rest of his life suing in vain for recompense from the state and federal governments. The Gold Rush itself lasted only two years, but within that time forests were stripped away and hillsides scarred by erosion. The Sacramento River ran thick with dirt, clogging the gills and ruining the spawning grounds of both salmon and sturgeon. The oyster fisheries of San Francisco Bay were destroyed by the muck from the river, and for more than a century afterward fish in the bay betrayed traces of the mercury used in sluice boxes to amalgamate with gold.

And when the gold stopped coming, so did other forms of currency. California's overheated economy crashed, and a depression settled in that persisted until a more enduring source of wealth was found: the agricultural cornucopia of the vast Central Valley. Its rich alluvial fields ran so wide and so flat and so free of rocks that farmers there would invent the gang plow: multiple plowshares bolted to a single beam, working in echelons, up to thirty-five plowshares across, and 400 horses, stretching in a single line across the horizon.

But when John Muir arrived in California in 1868, great tracts of the valley were still unplowed. Traveling in steerage from New York in a ship jammed with other hopeful emigrants, Muir debarked in San Francisco at the end of March and asked of a passerby the swiftest route out of town. He was directed to the Oakland ferry. From there he walked east into the mountains of California's Coast Range. In *The Yosemite*, he wrote: "Looking eastward from the summit of the Pacheco Pass one shining morning, a landscape was displayed that after all my wanderings still appears as the most beautiful I have ever beheld. At my feet lay the Great Central Valley of California, level and flowery, like a lake of pure sunshine . . . one rich furred garden of yellow compositae."

He went to the Yosemite Valley, where he was even more dazzled. He stayed in California, marrying in 1880 and raising fruit in the Alhambra Valley, some 25 miles northeast of San Francisco. Through Scotch thrift and innovative management, Muir cleared $100,000 in ten years on his orchards and vineyards. Then he sold some of his land and leased the rest, the better to travel and study. During an early visit to Alaska, in 1880, he told a pair of prospectors about a gravelly creek bed he thought worth checking for gold. The prospectors' subsequent strike at just that place started the Alaskan Gold Rush that led to the founding of Juneau. But Muir had no regrets about not panning that creek himself. In 1899, he was back in Alaska as a member of an expedition sponsored by the railroad magnate E.H. Harriman. When someone remarked to him about Harriman's wealth, Muir replied, "Why, I am richer than Harriman. I have all the money I want, and he hasn't."

Meanwhile, a second, and much more modest, gold rush was being carried on in the Sacramento River at the end of the 1800s. At one time the Sacramento may have been the site of such sturgeon hunts as this, witnessed on the Fraser River by British Columbia's colonial secretary in 1864: "All the Indians now fishing and it is great fun to watch them spearing sturgeon which here run to the great size of 500 and 600 lbs.," the secretary wrote. "The Indians drift down with the stream perhaps 30 canoes abreast with their long poles with spear attached kept within a foot of the bottom of the river. When they feel a fish lying they raise the spear and thrust it at the fish seldom missing. The barb of the spear immediately disconnects from the pole but remains attached to a rope, and you see sometimes two or three canoes being carried off at the same time downriver at any pace by these huge fish."

It was an alluvial version of the gang plow, but the Sacramento's white sturgeons had been much reduced by the effects of the 1848 Gold Rush by the time of the American caviar boom. Also, even by rail and steamship, it was difficult to get white sturgeon caviar to European markets before it spoiled. But there were domestic and foreign markets for the meat I had tasted in Oshkosh. Most of the Sacramento's fish were caught in San Francisco Bay or the river's lower reaches, with the fishery peaking in 1885 at 1.66 million pounds, versus the almost 6 million pounds landed in Delaware Bay at that fishery's peak in 1888. The Sacramento dwindled to 300,000 pounds in 1895, and then was closed entirely in 1901.

The state reopened the commercial fishery in 1909 on the premise that the sturgeons had rebounded by then, but low harvest rates proved otherwise. Two more attempts were made to reopen the fishery before sturgeon fishing for any purpose was banned entirely in 1917. A sport fishery was opened in 1954 that continues to this day, but it's as tightly regulated as Wisconsin's.

iii.

Mats and Dafne Engstrom still remembered their first glimpse of white sturgeon roe in a trailer-house cooler some thirty years ago. "There were masses of roe, 30 pounds of eggs, at least," Dafne said over the telephone. "We'd never seen anything like that before."

Mats Engstrom had begun his career in Sweden as a chemical engineer in his father's pulp and paper company, a concern founded in 1578. He went on to the Harvard Business School and married the athletic and outdoors-minded Dafne Nicoul. In 1970, they moved to San Francisco, where Mats worked as an investment officer at the Bank of America, Dafne as a sales representative for lines of Swedish clothing. On weekends they caught crayfish in the lakes of Marin County and cooked them at home in remembrance of the crayfish banquets they had enjoyed as children in Sweden.

When a disease decimated Sweden's stocks of native crayfish, Dafne asked a friend in the food industry there if he wanted some American crayfish. He did, and he wanted a lot. The Engstroms suddenly found themselves going into the crayfish export business, cooking and spicing and shipping vast quantities of the crustaceans out of their own kitchen, but they were discouraged by the seasonal character of the market in Sweden. Mats had quit at the bank by then and was doing some consulting. One morning he was at work for a paper company when he was asked to attend a meeting with California's Department of Game and Fisheries. The game department distributed a pamphlet that mentioned—to Mats's surprise—the presence of white sturgeon in California waters.

Mats started talking to local fishermen and found some who took part in the sport fishery. They told him the females were sometimes full of black roe, which they put down the garbage disposal or else fed to their cats. Six months later, a fisherman called to say that he had some roe in his cooler and they could help themselves. Mats and Dafne drove out to his trailer house and were struck dumb by the possibilities.

They had no idea how to make caviar, however, and found information hard to come by. They were unaware of the *McClane's Standard Fishing Encyclopedia* entry that Bob Boyle found helpful. Descriptions in the American historical record were sketchy, and otherwise the process had been reclaimed as something of a trade secret in the Soviet Union. A chef in San Francisco provided some advice, but all they could produce from those 30 pounds of eggs was a gooey mess that Dafne characterized as borscht.

They kept on experimenting with other batches of eggs while taking note of the farmed salmon industry that was just beginning to emerge in Scandinavia. At the same time, other wheels were turning: UC-Davis biologist Wallis Clark was visiting the Soviet Union, observing the techniques of artificial propagation used there to support the Caspian species, and wondering if something like that might reinvigorate California's thin stocks of white sturgeon.

Meanwhile, Serge Doroshov was a successful ichthyologist studying the life histories of fish species in the Black Sea and the Sea of Azov, and later the aquaculture of America's striped bass. He supervised a lab working on the domestication of sturgeon hybrids, and he traveled frequently—though he wasn't a member of the Communist Party—to international conferences. His father had been a party member, an apparatchik in agricultural management, and finally a victim of Stalin's purges. Doroshov remembered that and bided his time, vowing that his own children would not come home one day to find their father arrested.

In 1978, he traveled with his family to Cuba to work on a project for the United Nations Food and Agriculture Organization. When their flight back to the Soviet Union landed in Rome, they took refuge in FAO headquarters. Doroshov's contacts in the U.S. scientific community gained him asylum in the United States, and he went to join friends at the University of Washington. There he taught a course on aquaculture, and in 1979 he applied for an opening at the department that Wallis Clark had taken over at UC-Davis.

Later, a friend of the Engstroms' noticed a small article in the newspaper: "Russian defector joins faculty at UC-Davis." The friend suggested that they share some of their homemade caviar with him.

"So he had some, and he said it was wonderful, just like the caviar from the Volga that he had as a child," Dafne told me. "Now he claims that he never said that, but it's burned into my brain, exactly those words. He looked at it, tasted it, and then said, 'Let me go get the dean.' So Wally Clark came and tasted it. 'You made this from the sturgeon here?' he asked. 'Could you make 20 pounds for me to take to Washington, D.C.?' Sure, we said, though we weren't really sure we could find that much roe."

They found it, Dafne said, and Clark took it to Washington, where California white sturgeon caviar was served to good reviews at two parties for members of Congress. Clark, however, was hoping for an appropriation that would provide funding for sturgeon aquaculture. When he requested caviar for a third party, a function hosted by Montana senator Mike Mansfield, the Engstroms insisted on invitations themselves. Both California senators were there as well. With the charismatic Swedes working the floor, Clark got his money, a $600,000 grant from USF&W to explore the potential of both wild-stock enhancement and local commercial enterprise in aquaculture.

It wasn't a gold rush, by any means. Just the same, Russian America was back in business.

iv.

Over that winter, public television ran a series of promotional spots that involved creative thinking of one sort or another, and in each instance the tagline was "Stay Curious." In one spot a little girl watches a lone goldfish swimming in a bowl, wishes that it had some companionship, and decides that aquaculture is the way to go. She gets a tin of caviar and empties it into the fishbowl.

But growing fish has never been quite that easy, and sturgeons are a special problem entirely. In the 1860s, a Rochester, New York, fish dealer named Seth Green began experimenting with growing his own fish, and he achieved such spectacular results with American shad that the U.S. Fish Commission hired him to restock rivers in the East with that fish, and then to introduce it into the Sacramento and other rivers in California, where it still flourishes. In 1869, a Russian scientist succeeded in fertilizing and hatching the eggs of the little sterlet, *Acipenser ruthenus*. Subsequently Green began experimenting with Atlantic sturgeon, achieving his first success at a hatchery on the Hudson River in 1875.

The 1888 *Bulletin of the Fish Commission* described a process for spawning sturgeon similar in some respects to that used today by Doroshov and Joel Van Eenennaam. "With close attention to the details of the work of propagation," wrote biologist John Ryder, "very important results might be obtained and the work of restocking the Delaware and other streams might be undertaken with a very fair prospect of success."

From 1875 to 1912, this work was duly undertaken using Green's methods, and eastern rivers were stocked with millions of fingerlings. But there was no success, fair or otherwise, in producing adult sturgeons. By 1920, the effort had been abandoned, and knowledge of the nuances of sturgeon propagation faded away in America as surely as had its know-how in making caviar.

Serge Doroshov wasn't even aware of that, however, when Wallis Clark proposed the propagation of white sturgeons. Doroshov met me in his lab at UC-Davis's Meyer Hall on the day before Joel meant to spawn that fish from Ken Beer. That was two months after Gary Ninneman had told me that the spearfishing season on Winnebago had gone on for sixteen days before one of the quotas was filled, and that neither he nor Bill Casper had gotten a sniff of a sturgeon. And it was a month after Eve Vega had reported that she had run into Arkady Panchernikov at a convention of airline in-flight caterers in Germany. She said a gloating Arkady had shown her pictures of his 28 tons of caviar being wheeled into his warehouse.

"Wally was the major initiator of this project. I was a little hesitant at first," Doroshov told me. He sat at his desk in a crisp, short-sleeved button-down shirt. White-haired and fine-boned, with an easy smile, he exuded a sage-like serenity. His eyes were often roaming somewhere else, in apparent shyness, but lit with a sort of humor by turns weary or optimistic.

"First of all," he continued, "because I didn't know sturgeon well enough. They are very different from other fish. Second, I knew they take a very long time to mature. They are very large fish as well, and it takes a lot of patience and money to work with them. I had my doubts. But finally I decided to go ahead."

Which is when Doroshov found that he would be starting virtually from scratch. He said, "There were some good scientists from the Department of Fish and Game here who had been monitoring the population for management purposes. But they had no experience in breeding or the reproduction of the fish, and there were many unanswered questions about its life history. The literature of the Caspian, however, was very helpful." He had made a trip to the Library of Congress in Washington to retrieve all the information he could, particularly from Russian sources. "The species from the Caspian are fairly similar to the white sturgeon in their reproductive biology, though there are differences as well," he said. "But it was good to know the historic background from the Russian scientists."

A process of trial and error ensued not unlike the Engstroms' experiments in making caviar. Doroshov and other Davis scientists conducted telemetry studies to link the several stages of the white's life history and to locate its spawning sites in the Sacramento. The fish's hormonal regulation of its reproductive cycle had to be understood with clockwork precision. So, too, the role of such x-factors as temperature variation in the water and the influence of stress. Then the food and water requirements of the spawned larvae, fingerlings, and juvenile fish had to be mapped out as rates of growth and maturation kicked in that were—happily enough—far more rapid than for fish in the wild. The threat of disease had to be reduced, and an answer had to be found for that question in capital letters at the bottom line of any business proposal: Can this be profitable?

Doroshov was coauthor with Samuel H. Logan and Warren E. Johnston of an influential 1995 paper on that question published in the journal *Aquaculture*. The estimated start-up costs were daunting: nearly $1 million for a small operation with five broodfish producing only sturgeon meat; nearly $3 million for one with fifteen broodfish producing both meat and caviar. But in the latter case, if caviar prices were low, fish could be profitably harvested for meat at just eighteen and a half months. A sturgeon's feed-to-weight conversion ratio—1.5 to 1.0 or better—was far better than for salmon or trout.

It was sort of like planting a tree to produce paper, but it was an enterprise to reward those with deep pockets and plenty of patience. "Given the necessary time to recoup the investment," wrote Doroshov and his collaborators, "there is little question that sturgeon and roe production offer a highly profitable venture in aquaculture. It is likely that continuing efforts in domestication and breeding of sturgeon will result in improved performance and management, and, therefore, in improved economic performance of the firm."

By 1995, of course, the Engstroms, Ken Beer, and several others had been working in partnership with Clark and Doroshov for a decade. It had taken Doroshov only a year to achieve his first success in spawning wild white sturgeon. Then 12,000 fingerlings from that spawning were placed in the Sacramento River in the spring of 1980, this to abet that first goal of the USF&W grant, the enhancement of the local wild stock. But that effort was abandoned, Doroshov said, after the discovery of sustainable natural reproduction in a stretch of the river just downstream of its first dam.

That left him free to concentrate on the fish's reproductive biology as it related to farming. For sturgeon farming to succeed, however, he knew that farmers in this valley must produce not just caviar, but delicious caviar. He regarded that task with a generalist's optimism. "When white sturgeon is cultured," he said, "it may be possible to enhance its taste through modifications in food, water temperature, other things related to husbandry. So theoretically it is possible to produce a very good quality caviar with this, as good as the very best. But even now I find no large difference in the taste. It was never something that I had when I was in the Soviet Union because so much of it was produced just for the export market. It was very rare that anyone had a chance to buy caviar in Soviet stores. So I did not develop a taste comparable to a connoisseur's, and I am still not particularly enthusiastic about caviar, I have to tell you."

The industry's Wernher von Braun noted that the white sturgeon had crossed the equator, fueling the launch of farming operations in Uruguay and Chile. "Commercial aquaculture, once it's established, will occupy the niche now taken by wild caviar, which will almost automatically be out of the game," he proposed. "This will be much easier for Petrossian and those others. This caviar will be predictable, consistent, well-regulated, and available in a constant supply."

And he believed the Central Valley to be the perfect place for sturgeon farming, California osetra's own Champagne region. The pieces were all in place: climate, water supply, the availability of wild broodstock, a state legislature that supported the use of a domestic species, and also levels of investment, expertise, and hands-on production that were a decade ahead of anywhere else in the world.

Doroshov himself was less interested in that, however, than in the original number one goal of that grant of some twenty years ago. "What we are doing here will add to our knowledge of the biology of the sturgeon," he suggested, smiling and enunciating his words with characteristic deliberation. "What we have learned about the genetics and biology of salmon and trout from aquaculture has been applied in turn to the management of wild stocks of those fish. In a similar manner, we will use what comes from the knowledge we acquire here to better manage and support wild stocks of sturgeon."

v.

Joel showed Javier Linares-Casenave a single egg, a singularity of darkness, perched on his index finger. He tapped it with his other index finger and concluded, "This is a good one."

Swarthy and cheerful and Valentino handsome, Javier had arrived to get some work done on California's other native sturgeon, the green sturgeon, *Acipenser medirostris*, one of the most mysterious and little-known species in the world. Ranging historically up and down the North Pacific Rim, from Mexico to China, the fish survives in spawning populations in only three rivers in North America. The Sacramento was one of them, but little was known about the green's numbers, life history, or habitat requirements because the fish had never been of any commercial interest. Its meat was once thought to be poisonous, though Joel said it tasted all right—"It has a stronger taste than a white's. It's got more red muscle"—and its roe still has few admirers.

Green sturgeons can grow to about the size of lake sturgeons, about 7 feet and 300 pounds, but with a sleeker, more stem-like build. The green sturgeon's egg, however, is bigger than a beluga's, nearly as large as a salmon's, and its larvae are twice the size of a white sturgeon's at birth. That got Joel and Doroshov to thinking—might it be possible to spawn hybrids of the white and green sturgeon, as the Soviets did with the beluga and the sterlet? If so, the result might be a very palatable, large-beaded caviar, and a fish with much of the meat potential of the white sturgeon. A little more than 100 two-year-old green sturgeon juveniles coursed in crescents of shadow in another tank at the facility.

Javier, a Spaniard, was a postdoctoral student in charge of the green sturgeon project, but he had just been drafted by Joel into this other activity. Javier agreed that the egg was firm, and Joel got on to the next step, sprinkling a measured amount of Tricaine, the same cocaine-based anesthetic that Daryl Parkyn and Jamie Holloway had used in Florida, into a holding tank next to the big tank in which the ripe female swam.

Inside the fish, the slender membranes that bind each individual egg to the ovary walls were beginning to rupture, the eggs to drop into the body cavity. This wasn't happening all at once but instead in a slow wave that moved from the back end of the ovaries to the front over a period of several hours. Eggs still enveloped in that membrane can't be fertilized; nor could those that stay in the body cavity too long. The trick was to surgically remove the eggs when half were entirely ovulated and the other half in the process of breaking free. Missing that stage by more than thirty minutes on either side would result in a vastly diminished spawn.

Joel's pool strainer was now picking up dozens of expelled eggs, all black and firm and bursting into flecks of white sap when crushed. We had been joined by William Wright, a first-year research assistant, and Regina Linville, the Ph.D. student who was heading up the selenium study. Javier and William donned waders and climbed into the tank. They carried a green canvas stretcher, which they tried to extend beneath the female, but the fish was swimming more rapidly now. "Missed her," said William.

This, too, took timing, and on the third try the fish was lifted from the water and into the light. The sturgeon was seven years old, sexually mature at an age eight to twenty years younger than what occurs in the wild. At about 5 feet long and some 70 pounds, though, she was only a fraction of the barge-like dimensions of a full-grown white. The fish lay with characteristic calm in the dripping stretcher, her gill plates flaring, her eye a copper disk stapled to an iron button. Her scutes were strings of rattlesnake diamonds down her spine and flanks, still with something of an edge to them.

Had she just been plucked from the bottom of the Columbia or Sacramento, her dorsal side would be a milk-and-pepper gray fading at mid-flank into the pearly hues of her belly. These hatchery fish, however, swam near the surface in shallow tanks, and their skins produced more melanin than that of their wild counterparts. This and the other white sturgeons at Putah Creek tended more to an umber-tinted charcoal gray.

Javier and William eased her into the tank with anesthetic and let the stretcher drop beneath her. She swam forward, bumped into fiberglass, and drifted back again. Then she threw herself several times at angles into the side of the tank. Javier grimaced, saying, "They fight the anesthesia sometimes. They don't like it and hold their breath."

When she was calm again, and breathing evenly, Joel put a hand on her dorsal scutes and turned her, exposing her belly and rubbing it briefly. Several eggs slipped from the tight fold of her vent. He released her and she righted herself, floating passively in the tank, occasionally lifting her snout to the surface, as if to sniff the wind. Her attendants were equally passive. "She's not quite into her roll yet," Joel noted. "We don't want her too lively."

After five minutes she rolled, flexing onto her side in the water, her vent spewing a black gusher of eggs. Joel nodded, and the stretcher enveloped her again. She thrashed several times as she was hustled like an accident victim into a nearby Quonset hut.

vi.

Inside the hut the fish was turned belly up and the stretcher pegged at operating-table height. Joel looked on as Javier began pressing her belly above the dorsal vent. Eggs and a crystalline liquid, coelomic fluid, spilled out, and he collected it with a plastic ladle and spooned it into a stainless steel basin.

Then he used a knife to make a half-inch cut, which overflowed immediately with blood, fluid, and eggs. These were passed into the basin, and then the cut was enlarged to nearly the length of the abdomen. Javier grabbed the skin on one side of the incision and opened the body cavity, so revealing gleaming parallel masses of dark eggs. One ovary settled as the sheltering skin was withdrawn. The eggs that were still attached shivered in that sort of rippling, continental motion seen in the twitch of a muscle on a horse's flank. Javier dipped his ladle into the plenitude. The eggs that were ovulated swirled to fill it. These too were passed in heaps into the steel basin.

Joel had timed this well. The ovaries to the rear were pink and striated masses of tissue, nearly bare of eggs, except for the tiny white pinpricks that Javier said would have been the next generation of eggs, already equipped with yolk. Elsewhere the eggs were just on the verge, falling like ripe fruit into the ladle. The contents of the basin had separated into three distinct layers: a small amount of blood, just an auroral blush; the coelomic fluid, so clear, apparently, as to have powers of magnification; and the eggs, whose velvet blackness had taken on more the richness of burgundy. There were enough for Javier to fill several basins.

When the cavity was clear, he took the first basin and swirled it like a goldpanner. The blood and fluid rotated to the rim, and these he poured off with infinite care into the gravel floor of the hut. An occasional clump of unseparated eggs was poured off as well. "That's all right," Javier said. "We've got so many."

A thin layer of adhesive jelly, a marvelous substance that would become sticky on contact with water, covered each remaining egg. If this were the Sacramento River, the eggs would sink to the bottom of the river, to the rocky surfaces that sturgeons universally prefer, and the adhesive jelly would secure them from being swept away by the current. In the hatchery environment, though, eggs that stick like barnacles to any hard, wet surface are, shall we say, inconvenient. This quality had confounded John Ryder during his open-air experiments in sturgeon propagation in 1888. He found himself with masses of cemented eggs as big as a man's head and discovered that the jelly diffuses throughout the water, "so that the whole becomes ropy," he wrote. "If a lot of the eggs is taken up in the hand from the water glairy filaments formed of the ropy solution will trickle down between the fingers, and if the wind is blowing these may be drawn out for the length of two feet or more."

But Joel had some tricks for dealing with this jelly, the first of which was to be sure that the basins used to receive the eggs were bone dry. After most of the blood and fluid had been tipped out, Joel set the first basin on a table and poured into it a mixture of milt and water. He swirled the eggs and milt solution together in a sort of wet batter with his hands, and after about two minutes—at the first hint of stickiness in the eggs—added an amount of fine clay silt, one to two times the volume of the eggs. The silt covered the sticky jelly as it formed, miraculously defeating the adhesiveness of the eggs. This magic also illustrated why sturgeons so prefer hard substrate for spawning, and why they did so poorly during the silty years of the Gold Rush. The mixture looked like creamed coffee, the eggs rising and sinking about Joel's hands like stirred-up coffee grounds.

A second basin was started with William doing the mixing. Javier took the corpse of the female outside to saw off the tail and drain the blood. Reggie Linville needed to examine the organs and tissues in order to see what effects the selenium had, and the sacrifice of Beer's $1,000 fish, and fifteen more like her, was the cruel necessity of the study. Her offspring would be monitored to see if the selenium had any effect on their survival rate, and then they would be euthanized so their tissues could be studied. But the offspring of the eight control fish, which had been fed a normal diet, would be given to Beer and other contributing sturgeon farmers.

Joel and William continued with the de-adhesion process, separating any clumps of eggs with their fingers and adding more silt. After a little more than thirty minutes, the first batch was judged ready for the incubation jars, where upwelling jets of water would keep them agitated enough to discourage the growth of fungi.

Over the next six to seven days, barring mishap, the vast majority of eggs would develop embryos curled like necklaces around their yolks. The embryos then hatch tail-first into tadpole-like larvae, carrying their egg yolks like auxiliary fuel tanks in their puffed-up chests. In rivers, the larvae disperse throughout the water column for their first few days and then become photophobic, hunkering down into the substrate. In incubating jars they swim immediately upward into pipes that conduct them from the jars into fry collection tanks.

Joel felt good about the outcome of the morning: nearly 5 liters of ovulated eggs, 90 percent of what the female carried. A second fish underwent the same procedure after lunch, but this time something was off kilter. Only 20 percent of that fish's eggs had ovulated when the body cavity was opened, and a disappointed Javier was compelled to cut out and discard ovaries that still had thousands of useless eggs attached to them.

Joel had to go over to Meyer Hall to report the day's happenings to Doroshov. We took Joel's car, and Joel told me that just as all the crazy-quilt variety of these Central Valley farms had been consolidated over the years into the ownership of a few giant agribusinesses, so have the dozen or so commercial aquaculture operations that sprung up here in the 1980s shrunk down to two major players: The Fishery, where Ken Beer so far produces only meat for the consumer market; and Stolt Sea Farm, which sells both meat and caviar, and which buys Beer's roe to help supply its caviar end. He said the Engstroms, after some reverses here and then some adventures in the Far East, were looking to get back into growing sturgeon again. "Mats calls me at all hours with questions about sturgeon biology," he said.

Doroshov was in his lab, where he received both the good news and the bad with equanimity. "Everything looked good with that second fish," Joel offered. "Her belly was soft, the eggs were firm, she was releasing a lot of eggs through her vent." He shook his head, adding, "A strange fish."

He and Doroshov reviewed all the variables of water temperature, water flow, and the timing of the various procedures of the past few days, but they could find no available explanation of why spawning largely failed with that second fish. I remembered a paper presented in Oshkosh by Blaine L. Parker, Kevin Kapperman, and John A.S. Holmes, members of a joint project between USF&W and Oregon Native American tribes in the midreaches of the Columbia. "After two years, five females and twenty males, no juvenile sturgeon were produced," the authors admitted in obvious exasperation. "Numerous discussions with state, tribal, and university researchers have demonstrated that spawning wild sturgeon is still more of an art than a science."

"Our work is difficult," concurred Doroshov. "There are so many things that are hard to control, and you see that spawning is a very sensitive sort of thing."

It was all a matter of staying curious. Doroshov asked if any of the green sturgeons were ready to go yet, and Joel replied, "It's too early to tell. Let's hope the weather stays cool."

~ 9 ~

A POETRY OF PLACE

i.

It took Mats and Dafne Engstrom only a few years to become very good at making caviar. In 1979, *New York Times* food critic Craig Claiborne tasted some Tsar Nicoulai caviar and wrote that it was "outstanding in texture and flavor. I would place it in competition with any imported caviar sold in this country, from no matter where." Claiborne asked the couple if they would sell their product to the general public, perhaps by air express, but the answer was no: "Quantities are too limited."

Trying to make quantities less limited would prove to be their task for the next two decades. It was also a quest of sorts, one whose dramatic high point—so far—might be a car-and-truck chase through the streets of San Francisco in pursuit of 6 tons of caviar that had been stolen from them. I'd overheard Peter Struffenegger telling the story in Oshkosh, but I'd missed a lot of it. In April I drove from Davis to San Francisco to get the rest.

The Engstroms met me at their warehouse and offices opposite Pacific Bell Park on the west side of town, close enough to the Pacific to hear its surf. We went through a hallway hung with press clippings and culinary awards, then up the stairs to their office. It was Saturday, and the Engstroms were casual—the gray-templed Mats in a hip-length cardigan, Dafne in a white satin blouse and olive sport jacket—but couldn't help being elegant at the same time.

Quantities were limited in 1979, I learned, because it was illegal for Sacramento sport fishermen to sell their sturgeon roe. Mats and Dafne received the occasional donation of what the cat or garbage disposal didn't get, but most of their roe—2,000 to 10,000 pounds each year— had to be bought from commercial sturgeon fishermen in Canada, Washington, and Oregon. That provided just enough caviar for a short network of regular customers. That also meant that the roe they got wasn't as fresh, cleanly processed, or predictably available as they would have liked. They branded it Tsar Nicoulai, a Russified elaboration of Dafne's maiden name, and sold it for a little more than $6 an ounce, or about a third the price of beluga caviar at the time.

During the early 1980s, they managed to ramp up to 15,000 pounds annually of "California osetra," which at that time wasn't farmed, and began getting some of it out to the public. There were even recipes that specified Tsar Nicoulai caviar appearing in cookbooks by Claiborne or James Beard. But good roe was still hard to find, and the Engstroms were among those most interested in the progress of Serge Doroshov's first generation of hatchery-bred sturgeon.

That year they joined several other investors in founding California Sunshine Fisheries. They established a partnership with UC-Davis and built a 20,000-square-foot aquaculture facility in downtown Sacra-mento, where they intended to raise fingerlings that had been spawned at the university. Then, using a model taken from the poultry industry, they would rent the juvenile fish out to local farmers, who would grow them to maturity. But in 1985, a short time after delivery of the first crop of one-inch fingerlings from Doroshov, the new facility burned to the ground. "All the fingerlings were cooked, and we had to do some re-thinking," Mats pronounced.

Food for thought was provided one morning at 4 A.M. by a telephone call from China. Apparently the Engstroms had come to the attention of the Chinese government as two of the few people outside the Soviet Union and Iran with expertise in making caviar. Would they be willing to come to China to improve the operations of caviar factories near the juncture of the Heilongjiang and Amur rivers? These plants processed the roe of the Amur sturgeon, *Acipenser schrenckii,* similar in size to the Russian sturgeon, and also that cousin to the beluga, the kaluga sturgeon, *Huso dauricus.*

Well, of course.

It was an outside-the-box sort of solution to the problem of supply, and all the more appealing because the ground floor of the aquaculture industry around Davis was already getting crowded. Dafne went first in order to assess the condition of the plants. Traveling on a military visa, she flew that winter into Beijing, then journeyed forty hours in an unheated train, through temperatures that dipped to twenty below zero, to meet a jeep that carried her to a ferry that dropped her at last in Fuyuan, a village in Manchuria not visited by westerners since the Russian Revolution. Tall, blonde, and pretty, she was followed by an amazed crowd wherever she went among houses built of mud and clay and roofed with straw.

Mats arrived a week later, and they stayed for five seasons. The Chinese plants lacked refrigeration, packing materials, and even running water. The Engstroms solved the water problem first, sort of, via water tanks built on the rooftops of the factories, filled by hand with ladders and buckets from the river. The water was drawn from locations not far from community outhouses, however, and the Engstroms struggled with unwholesome sanitation standards throughout their stay.

Work challenging enough on its own terms was ratcheted up to another level by military hostilities on the Amur. The border between the Soviet Union and China was defined by the shipping lane down the 1,800-mile river, but over time the lane had shifted to the north or south of certain islands in the channel. This provoked border disputes and occasional gunfire. "Fishing for sturgeon was an interesting exercise," Mats said dryly, "when rockets were flying and the Russians were ramming all your boats."

In 1989, a Japanese firm bribed its way into the Amur, taking over two of the refurbished caviar plants. Mats was still rankled by the turn of events: "One refrigerator and a color TV did the trick. That meant our contract was broken, and the Japanese took over. How do you prevent that? Do you sue? What does that mean, in a country where there is no court to receive it, no judicial system to speak of? So obviously it's an issue of the Golden Rule: People who have the gold, they make the rules. In this case the Chinese had the caviar, and that was the gold. We came away with nothing. It was a wonderful experience, but not really very profitable, I must say."

At least they had learned that Amur River fish produced very palatable caviars. The Soviets had no caviar production on their side, but just as many Amur and kaluga sturgeons. So another outside-the-box idea: Why not build their own caviar plants from scratch on the Soviet side? It seemed plausible, given that Caspian production was already in decline and that Gorbachev had initiated his business-friendly era of *perestroika*.

In San Francisco, Mats had become friendly with the Soviet consul-general, who suggested he send a letter outlining his plans to the Ministry of Fisheries in Moscow. Mats did so, and three months later received a reply informing him that he was mistaken, that there were no sturgeons in the Amur, and therefore there was no reason to have a caviar plant there. The consul-general responded with a shrug. "Moscow is Moscow," he said.

Characteristically undissuaded, Mats resolved to bypass Moscow. In 1990, he obtained one of the first tourist visas issued to Kharabovsk, the Soviet city located at that point on the Amur where the border abandons the river and turns south to the conjunction of Russia, China, and North Korea. By then he understood that Moscow's failure to find sturgeons in the Amur had a time-honored purpose, which was to protect the preeminence of the Caspian fisheries. In Kharabovsk, he met with bureaucrats and scientists, all of whom were unwilling to argue with Moscow about that. He carried in his briefcase, however, a file of papers on sturgeon biology given him by a doctoral student at UC-Davis. One of the scientists with whom Mats spoke had a name that rang a bell. "I'm very familiar with your work," Mats said as he reached into his case to retrieve a paper the scientist had authored.

For whatever reason, that seemed to be a turning point. Mats had a contract in his pocket within a week: the Engstroms to supply the capital and expertise, the Soviets to provide land and labor for a facility that would be both a caviar plant and a hatchery.

The Engstroms returned to the Amur in 1991, making only salmon caviar that first season. The next year, they came with Peter Struffeneg-

ger, who would help build the hatchery. Struff was already working for
Stolt Sea Farm, but work was slow there at that time, since their first-
year class of females had yet to mature, and Struff needed to learn something about the secrets of making caviar. The Engstroms, for their part,
found him helpful as both an engineer and a negotiator. "He's a big,
strong fellow, as you know, and there was one Russian there who was just
awful to us," Dafne said. "But Peter just took him by the shirt, poked his
nose into his face, and we had no more trouble from that direction."

Trouble enough came from other directions. The building to house
the facility turned out to be little more than an old foundation. Then
the plans produced by the Soviets for completing the building included
such perks for the labor force as a nursery, a dormitory, and a canteen,
all to be paid for by the Americans. Struff tossed these aside and decided to build the hatchery on a barge in the middle of the river, assem-
bling it out of shipping containers used as modular units. Running
water, as in China, would arrive via gravity feed from a tank on the
roof, but the Russians refused to fill the tank by hand. Instead, a water
pump was ordered from the Soviet military.

"The Russians have this expression, *zavtra*, 'tomorrow,'" Struff told
me later. "When will the pump arrive? 'Zavtra.' Always, it was 'zavtra.'
When the pump finally did arrive, there was a hole in it. The Russians
tried to whittle a plug of wood to fill it, but they never got it to work. So
here we were, floating in the middle of one of the biggest rivers on earth,
just as the spawning season was starting, and we couldn't get water."

Finally the barge was moved to the riverbank, and a line run from a
nearby well to the hatchery. But the well water was polluted with hydrogen sulfide, and the fish that had been caught for broodstock immediately died. Then Struff was called away to Norway for two weeks on
Stolt business. On his return, one of the Russians showed him a line of
floating, screened-in wooden boxes that trailed away from the hatchery
like a segmented tail. Inside the boxes a few hundred Amur sturgeon
fingerlings swam about, fish spawned in his absence by the Russians and
then confined in this new system. "You Americans with all your technology, you can't get anything done," scoffed the Russian. "You see how
easy it is?"

"If you just had had the pump in the first place," Struff exploded,
"you could have had *tens of thousands* of fish like that."

The Engstroms labored through similar layers of procrastination and reversal in getting electricity to the facility. At last they had to bring in their own generators after the season had already started. But they still managed to make 6 tons of very good caviar, Mats thought.

They only needed export permits from the provincial governor to get the caviar to the U.S. market. But those were not forthcoming. Instead the governor ruled that the Engstroms had failed to deliver the hatchery operation promised in the contract, and therefore the caviar properly belonged to the people of the Kharabovsk region—which was a comradely way of saying that it belonged to him. Mats subsequently learned that the governor had already sold the caviar by then to a man regarded as a regional crime-lord.

Mats tried hiding the caviar. He and Struff got up early one morning to move all 6 tons to another refrigeration facility in Kharabovsk. But the new location didn't remain a secret for long, and in the end it made no difference. Without an export permit or legal protection, Mats could play games, but not win. When a Russian friend advised him to leave, warning that his safety couldn't be guaranteed, he and Dafne bought tickets home to San Francisco.

That seemed to be the end of the story. The Engstroms were sitting in an Alaskan Airlines passenger jet on the runway in Kharabovsk. Mats was tallying up his losses and gloomily watching freight-handlers load luggage and commercial goods into the plane's cargo bay. Suddenly he started forward in his seat. Included in that freight, in boxes stamped "Royal Amur Caviar Company," was their own caviar.

This was both a spectacle and an occasion for more rethinking. Once they landed in San Francisco, Mats said, he hid in a bathroom aboard the airplane until the cargo started to come off. Then he stood watch outside the Alaska Airlines terminal as the caviar was loaded into an unmarked truck. Dafne arrived with their car, and they followed the truck into San Francisco. In Hollywood, this is where the stunt drivers would take over and the fruit stands would fly. Instead, they simply lost the truck in city traffic.

But Mats was still thinking. Once they got home, he began calling every airline in the telephone book. "Yes, did you receive my shipment of caviar from Kharabovsk today?" he asked. "I'm calling just to make sure that you put it in cold storage."

After several dry runs, he got an affirmative from American Airlines. "And you do know the destination?" Mats pursued.

"Oh, yes," he was told. "We'll ship it in two days to Chicago."

At last the chase ended with a San Francisco judge posting a restraining order on the shipment. But that had to be rescinded when representatives from this new caviar company produced documents from the Russian governor vouching for their title to it. The caviar had been bought, the Engstroms learned, by the Browne Trading Company of Portland, Maine, a reputable firm that had pioneered the reentry of Iranian caviar into the American market.

Mats attached a satisfying epilogue to the story. Weeks later, he was much surprised to find his own picture presented in Royal Amur's promotional literature as that of the "Russian master" who had made the product. "Then Browne entered this caviar at a competition here in San Francisco, where it got an award for best caviar," Mats said. "We actually showed up at the awards ceremony, where we served papers in a lawsuit against Royal Amur for misuse of my image."

That came to naught, as did their whole Russian adventure—or less than naught, since it cost them their entire investment. It also cost them their place at the table in the early growth of the farmed sturgeon industry here. For nearly a decade now they had been buying roe from Ken Beer while also working on a way to grow their own white sturgeon. A number of different arrangements had so far produced some fish and then failed, including a joint venture with a farm near Modesto and a relationship with another in Idaho's Snake River Basin. In Idaho, the Engstroms were the outright owners of 5,000 white sturgeons, but in the cold water of the Snake, those fish were growing much more slowly than California fish. "We have females there that are twelve years old but weigh only 50 pounds," Dafne sighed. "They will have to be moved."

Indeed, something would have to be done for what soon could be enormous demand for white sturgeon caviar. In 1998, Molly O'Neill of the *New York Times* assembled a panel of Manhattan chefs and caviar retailers, one of whom was Eve Vega. They sampled a variety of caviars, and the California version took the panel by surprise. "Domestic caviar has come into its own this year," O'Neill wrote in the December 23, 1998, issue. "Virtually all of it comes from Stolt Sea Farm in Sacramento, whose top grade is called Sterling caviar and is comparable to Kazakh-stan osetra in both quality and price."

That led to the appearance of both Sterling and Tsar Nicoulai caviar at such restaurants as Charlie Trotter's in Chicago, on the shelves at Zabar's and Balducci's, and at the counter of Caviarteria's flagship store in New York City. Since then, the additional endorsement of domestic caviar by the Caviar Emptor campaign has made media darlings of the two California firms.

Just that past February, while I was spearfishing with Gary Ninne-man, a blind caviar taste testing was hosted by the *Wall Street Journal*, whose panel was made up of four "caviar junkies," one neophyte, and Matthias Radits, the executive chef of a Palm Beach resort. An expen-sive Russian caviar was secretly included with a variety of domestic caviars. The "balanced, buttery flavor" of Tsar Nicoulai caviar was rated very highly, but it was edged out for Best Overall by Stolt's Sterling Pre-mium. That caviar's "greenish-gray eggs" were deemed "rich and com-plex, with a buttery, delicately salty flavor and an ample sense of chew."

"And that fancy imported Russian caviar that we slipped in as a trick?" wrote the *Journal's* Charles Passy on February 23, 2001. "Nobody noticed. In fact, our panel awarded it fourth place."

The Tsar Nicoulai caviar might well have taken Best Overall had not Radits criticized it for too many crushed eggs. "The company blames that on rough handling during shipping," explained Passy. Radits's per-sonal favorite, however, was neither the Stolt nor the Tsar Nicoulai, but rather a spoonful of plump, evenly gray-colored eggs that had in them what Radits described as "a little bit of ocean."

"Gotcha," wrote Passy. "That caviar may actually have been from the Tennessee River. It was $9.95 paddlefish roe from Kelly's Katch, a small producer from Savannah, Tennessee, that harvests wild fish in rivers throughout the south. When Mr. Radits found out about the cost, his handlebar moustache nearly came uncurled. 'For that price, you can buy 5 tons,' he said of the caviar from Elvis country."

Mats advised Elvis to be wary of that. Though he and his wife had struggled so long to produce caviar in quantity, there was such a thing as too much. "Why is caviar so expensive?" he asked, shrugging his shoulders. "Obviously it's a matter of image. It's not something that's price-driven, because there has always been only a finite market for this commodity, and obviously there is no sense trying to make it into some sort of fast food everybody can afford. You will not increase demand with lower prices or an oversupply. So my advice to Stolt is don't ever market more than 100 tons of caviar in the U.S. If they're smart, if they make more than that, they'll just flush it down the toilet."

ii.

This was the pivot point between the cat's breakfast that was unprocessed roe and the black gold that was caviar.

Rich Helfrich was the caviar processing manager for Stolt Sea Farm, and his clothes gave clues to what that involved: the neon-yellow, suspendered oilskin pants of a fisherman; the white cotton coat of a lab technician; and the crinkly latex shower cap and gloves of a food-service worker. He stood in a refrigerated room over a small white sturgeon, only 35 pounds or so. The fish had been laid on its back. Rich's hands held open a long, bloodless incision in the fish's belly. Anthony Knight, a Stolt technician, pulled a skein of eggs from the left side of its cavity. The eggs were as black as coal. They shone with a bituminous luster in the cool silvery light. "That's a very dark egg," Rich said. "That'll grade out as Royal Black. Only 2 or 3 percent of our eggs come like that."

It was an ordinary April morning at Stolt Sea Farm's processing plant in Elverta, a few miles north of Sacramento. Each week, from February through June, a certain number of adult female sturgeons were harvested here for their roe and meat. In a typical year, only a select few were kept for broodstock. This female's uniformly black eggs made for a prized attribute, though whether that made a difference in the taste was a matter for exquisitely tuned palates. In any event, there was no proof yet that egg color was genetic, and in fact the incidence of unusual colors is only one of several mysteries of nurture in sturgeon aquaculture. So the fish wasn't saved for broodstock. Instead, she provided this blackest of black caviars.

You control what you can, always happy to get lucky, as Stolt did with this fish, but choose your broodstock for those physical attributes that promise larger quantities of either roe or meat. That's how the week started yesterday, a morning on which I hitched a ride with Peter Struffenegger in a flatbed truck loaded with four 500-gallon water tanks. We drove into the foothills of the Sierra Nevada to a small trout farm where, at this time of year, sturgeons were boarded for the sake of the cool water, which helps their eggs to develop better. From a distance, the half-dozen 30-foot fish tanks shone like a painter's palette of blues and greens amid pasture-like stretches of grass, clumps of oaks stretching their limbs like sleepy arms, and then the flawless blue ether of another cloudless sky.

There we conducted a sort of beauty contest with mortal stakes. The tanks were full of eight-year-old females, all of whom were sexually mature and had ovaries full of eggs. Left to their own devices, the fish would start reabsorbing those eggs, but the great majority were due to be sacrificed for their caviar the next day. Struff came to pick out the favored few, whose body shapes were just right, or whose eggs were very large-beaded. These were to be set aside and then injected with Doroshov's pituitary hormone to yield the next generation of farmed white sturgeons.

Anthony Knight and Brendan Moore were there ahead of us, both powerfully built men well suited to sturgeon-wrangling. In the tanks, man-sized submarine shapes, dim and ghostly, stippled in pixilated patterns of chalk and slate and olive and gray, coursed about the edges, rising nearly to the surface. Struff and Anthony put on waders, rain jackets, and rubber gloves and went in to get the fish, many of them already over 200 pounds, maneuvering them one by one into a buoyant rectangular frame of PVC pipe strung with nylon fishnet. Struff held a surgical knife in one hand, and a straw-like length of plastic tubing dangled from his mouth.

Once captured, a fish was turned on its back in the frame, and Struff cut a brief incision, only an inch or so, into its belly. The plastic tube was swiftly inserted into the cut, a few eggs sucked into its length, and then the fish allowed to right itself. Struff blew the eggs back out onto his right glove, where they lay like gritty tar. He rolled several between his thumb and forefinger, then tasted them. Fish with firm eggs were ready to be sacrificed the next day for caviar. Those few with large-beaded eggs, or the right sort of body shape—short in the skull for more meat, or broad in girth for more eggs—were set aside as broodstock for the next generation. Beauty points for each fish were debated among the three men—"You want the babies or the money?" Anthony asked Struff of one sturgeon—and then the less comely were hoisted from their tanks in a hoop net hung from the boom of a front-end loader. From there they went into the tanks on the back of the flatbed truck.

Struff offered me several firm and very dark eggs direct from the belly of a sleek 100-pounder. They had none of the bitterness that I remembered from the raw salmon eggs I had tried once, but neither did they have any of the distinctive flavor of finished caviar. Instead they conveyed just the palest suggestion of that in a taste that was bland, watery, inoffensive.

It was Rich Helfrich's job to oversee the alchemy that would change that. The fish that yielded those royal black eggs had been the very first down the line that day, and tagged #772 in Stolt's roster of caviar producers this season. Anthony paused a moment, holding that first skein of eggs like an ingot of pure obsidian as Rich made notes on a form regarding tag number and weight. "That's not a big fish, only 35 kilos, but the ovaries are clean, almost no fat," Rich said approvingly. "There'll be about 5 kilos of eggs there."

Number 773 and subsequent fish provided roe of more ordinary hues of dark gray with highlights of black or gold. Eggs that were firm could be more purely cleaned of their shells and membrane and were then sold under Stolt's Sterling Premium label. Within that category, the eggs were classified and priced according to color. Most of it, 85 percent, Rich said, came out as Sterling Classic. One in ten fish would yield roe light enough in color to be Sterling Premium. Only 5 percent combined provided eggs either light enough for Sterling Imperial Blonde or dark enough for Sterling Royal Black. But Stolt's color charts defined as many as eight different colors in a white sturgeon's eggs, which might appear in forty-four different combinations, or else arrayed in agate patterns, lightning bolts, bull's-eyes, cat's-eye marbles, or even mottled into Rorschach abstractions.

The twin sacs of premium Royal Black were passed down to Joe Melendez, another technician, who rubbed them over a swath of screen positioned above a stainless steel basin in an aluminum sink. Melendez's hands moved in a gentle and circular pattern, as though he were stroking a kitten. Slowly the sacs lost their structure and flattened out against the mesh. Then they started to pass through it, in raindrops of darkness, to the basin beneath. Finally the basin was filled to half its volume with a slippery soup of tarry beads. The screen was left with a litter of membrane, broken eggs, bits of fat, and fragments of shells.

Melendez filtered the Royal Black just once more, pouring the contents of the basin through a fine-meshed colander that caught the eggs as the water drained away. The eggs were rinsed again, weighed, and dried. Finally he began kneading a precisely measured portion of salt into the eggs, working his gloved fingers through their mass in movements at once probing and caressing.

"It's just a matter of weight, how much salt we add," Rich said. "Sometimes we experiment with a slightly higher salt content, but our rule of thumb is .0425 percent. That's a nice sellable product. Petrossian wants us to have some guy like those Russian masters who decide on a different salt content for every batch of eggs, but we don't have anybody here who can do that. Instead we make up for that with consistency in our product, and we find that people appreciate consistency in the things they buy."

Petrossian?

"Yeah, they're thinking about carrying our caviar," he said. "They had some people here looking at our operation and making suggestions. They said we could produce more with an assembly line procedure, but we don't have enough staff to do that."

It had been only three years since Stolt's Sterling Caviar had first been marketed nationally, at a time when the company had only 3,000 pounds to sell, and there was a poor-man's stigma attached to American caviar. But ever since Charles Passy's article in the *Wall Street Journal*, Stolt's telephones had been ringing off the hook, Chuck Edwards had told me the day before. Edwards was Stolt's marketing director, and he said Stolt had produced 8,500 pounds of caviar the previous year. Struff and Edwards hoped to make 12,000 pounds this year, from 15,000 to 17,000 by 2003, and have production ramped up to 30,000 pounds annually by 2006. That would still be far below Mats Engstrom's ceiling. The market was safe.

Regarding their boost from the Caviar Emptor campaign, Edwards just smiled and said, "We'll take it." He mentioned that Stolt had supported the CITES process for the sake of the Caspian stocks, even though that meant that for a year Stolt couldn't sell its own caviar outside the United States. Not even U.S. representatives to CITES had guessed that there was such a thing as domestic American caviar, and there was no mechanism at first for the product to be exported. Now Stolt was selling Sterling in Europe and Asia as well, but Edwards refused to promote the product as a replacement for traditional beluga or osetra. "Our caviar has a slightly lower salt level than the Caspian stuff, has a little milder flavor, and is very smooth on the finish," he said. "But in a time when you really don't know what you're getting with Russian osetra, for example, we can guarantee a consistent sort of taste and consistently high quality. Aside from the sustainability of this product, that's our main selling point."

By the time Joe Melendez had finished salting the Royal Black roe of #772, other batches of eggs were at various points in the production line. Another technician was weighing out the salt for #773, which would be Classic, while Anthony and two others were screening or filtering the roe sacs of other fish. The light itself seemed a chilled, pale blue in this refrigerated room of sinks, counters, cabinets, scales, and fish eggs. Only the mildest, freshest scent of fish hung in the air, more a hint than a scent.

Rich Helfrich came over dabbing at his brow with the back side of a gloved hand. He gestured toward Joe's eggs. "We'll let that drain for fifteen minutes, and then pack it away. It's just salt and fish eggs at this stage. It takes two to three months for the flavor to mature into that real buttery quality."

Melendez stood to one side, like an artist whose handiwork had captured a couple of passersby. There looked to be enough eggs there to fill four 500-gram tins. They lay on a synthetic cutting board in a loosely molded heap of ebony stars and dew-struck berries. They absorbed the chill light, reflecting it back in pinpricks of rose and vermilion.

Rich had gone to high school with Struff, and they had worked for a time on an oyster farm together. Then for twelve years he had run his own business in smoked fish and poultry while Struff had worked on various salmon or catfish farms before being hired as the manager here.

Rich had sold his business three years ago to come work at Stolt. He thought for a moment about those other jobs, those other foods, and then considered all the history and mystique that had just assumed tangible form in this newborn batch of Sterling Royal Black.

"It's just salt and fish eggs," he repeated, a smile tugging at the corners of his mouth. "It's still amazing to me there's such a demand out there."

iii.

On Shattuck Avenue in Berkeley, on the other side of the Bay Bridge from Tsar Nicoulai, behind a honeysuckle hedge and a monkey puzzle tree, is a restaurant called Chez Panisse. In 1976, the young restaurant offered a dish that Herb Caen, a columnist for the *San Francisco Chronicle*, found laughable. Caen wrote, "Chez Panisse is doing a week of recipes from the immortal Chef Auguste Escoffier's *Guide Culinaire* (1902). The very first item on Panisse's menu being 'crêpe with sterlet caviar from Sacramento.' . . . Sacramento? Vassyou dere. Owgoost."

At that time, Chez Panisse was something of a contradiction in terms: As ambitious in its cuisine as the great French restaurants of New York, it was no less committed to the French tradition of *gourmandise* but drew inspiration also from the politics and values of Berkeley's student counterculture. No set of values could possibly have been more antithetical to the Old World–style snobbery of such shrines as Le Pavillon, but a way to tie it all together had been foreshadowed right in New York at the Four Seasons, the restaurant where the chef James Beard had prepared meals in the 1960s. Beard had grown up in Oregon, enjoying succotash and salmon cheeks, hunting and cooking the crayfish that the Engstroms so relished. At the Four Seasons, Beard dazzled Craig Claiborne and other food critics with menus that dared to stress homeliness, authenticity, and indigenous American ingredients.

In charge of the kitchen at Chez Panisse then was Richard Olney, who had moved to France in the 1950s to paint and had become a chef instead. He had published two classic cookbooks—*The French Menu Cookbook* and *Simple French Food*—that were as much statements of gastronomic aesthetics as they were collections of recipes. Stressing directness and simplicity, the beauty of local fruits and vegetables picked at the height of their ripeness, and the general use of the grill, the cookbooks essentially translated Beard into *gourmandise,* but with an emphasis that was less national and more regional. When Olney began his tenure at Chez Panisse, he faced the challenge of applying that aesthetic in the context of the foods available in northern California.

Another Olney principle was directness and simplicity in language, particularly in the writing of menus. He refused to gild his menu items with the sauce of French appellations, and that provided a larger opportunity for derision and pidgin French from Herb Caen. Because California food, alas, had no cachet. "Sterlet caviar from Sacramento?" That, in fact, was white sturgeon caviar that had been made by Mats and Dafne Engstrom. Maybe it was small-beaded enough to be called sterlet. No doubt it was tasty. The real problem lay in that phrase "from Sacramento." It was difficult for Caen to believe that any sort of decent caviar could possibly come from the vicinity of Sacramento. It was the perfect oxymoron, the stranger effect turned inside out and made ridiculous.

Food historian Patric Kuh sees it as a problem endemic to California foods. Kuh recommends a visit to Rockie's, a truck stop off Interstate 5 at the junction of the San Joaquin and Sacramento rivers. "It is indeed a cheerful place," he wrote in *The Last Days of Haute Cuisine* (2001), "and the steak and eggs are hearty, but to sit in a booth at Rockie's, and to look out at the flat asparagus fields that surround the restaurant knowing that there isn't a chance you'll be offered asparagus in any form, is to understand something about California, and that is that food here is devoid of any context, and for all the power of California agriculture, it has no relationship to food."

That's because all the power of California agriculture was turned outward. In the 1870s, a combination of drought and economic depression bankrupted many of the small farmers who had poured into the Central Valley after the Gold Rush. The farms were bought up in great tracts by urban speculators who kept their costs down with migrant farm labor and their profits up by shipping their wheat and asparagus elsewhere. These operations pioneered industrial-scale efficiencies in the production and distribution of food and reenergized old national myths of abundance and plenitude. But they also defeated any attempt to define a California cuisine, or to endow California foods with any special allure.

California wine, for example, was originally known as "tank car wine" for the way in which some of it was shipped east, and it was impossible to sell on the basis of quality. Instead, the more high-falutin' marketed themselves as sort of like this noted French vintage or another, but at an affordable price, and aimed to look good on the shelves behind glossy labels made to resemble gilded scrolls. Nomenclature was key and came to be a sensitive issue for the more ambitious. As early as 1941, wine critic Frank Schoonmaker wrote, "Already, intelligent wine-drinkers across the country are wondering why honest, American place names and grape variety names cannot be used for honest, American wines. To these persons (and there are more of them every day) Lake Erie Island Catawba has a better ring than 'Grand Duke Rhine Wine'; Napa Valley Zinfandel than 'Royal Charter Brand Claret.'"

It was also in 1941 that the first of New York's great French restaurants, Le Pavillon, opened its doors, serving on its opening night copious amounts of caviar and other "creditable viands" to guests including the Vanderbilts, the Cabots, the Rockefellers, and the Kennedys. But American place names were already on the way. The cookbook author M.F.K. Fisher, a native Californian, experienced an epiphany that same year on eating a bowl of bean soup in Mexico. It was a sort of religious conversion, one that precipitated a qualitative shift in her cooking away from external matters of style to internal matters of sustenance and spiritual value, from faux Old World sophistication to New World rusticity. Moreover, it stressed local ingredients, and—with help from James Beard—legitimized ethnic cuisines other than French, as well as American regional styles. Kuh admitted that this sort of approach has led to its own set of clichés and pretensions. "But at its best," he maintained, "it becomes truly innovative, a supranational style where culinary boundaries recede before the quality of restraint that all good food shares."

In March 1976, Chez Panisse's Richard Olney was attempting to marry that style to his beloved French cuisine via the Engstroms' "sterlet from Sacramento," and he took some punishment for it. It was only two months after that meal, however, that California wines stunned the world at a blind taste-testing in Paris. Hardly anyone had noticed Napa Valley's shift to grape varietals, or the steadily increasing skills of Robert Mondavi and the Gallo brothers and other winemakers. Very suddenly, California wine had cachet, and its elevated status was reflected, by and large, in the new character of its labels: simple, understated papers proudly citing their origins in the specific ridges, lanes, ranches, valleys, hills, and creeks of northern California—honest, American place names, in other words, on their way to suggesting on their own terms what Kuh described as "the European idea of the poetry of a place."

Olney finally succeeded in translating the food of Chez Panisse, including its Sacramento caviar, into this new sort of poetry. No less so than Le Pavillon, Chez Panisse has provided a model to many other restaurants in its bailiwick, and at one of these—the French Laundry in Napa Valley—the chef Thomas Keller has plumbed deeper into what might be described as the fundamental meaning of the food he serves.

Also a native Californian, Keller cooked at restaurants in the Hudson River Valley, Manhattan, and France before opening the French Laundry in 1994. At a tiny restaurant along the Hudson, Keller learned how to use local ingredients, how to flavor and cure his own meats, and decided that if he was going to cook and serve rabbits, he should know how to skin, gut, and butcher them as well. In *The Soul of a Chef: The Journey Toward Perfection* (2001), food writer Michael Ruhlman described the horror Keller felt in slaughtering live rabbits and learning how to break them down. "But he learned something more," said Ruhlman. "He had taught himself about respect for food and its opposite, waste. It had been hard to kill those rabbits because life, to Keller, wasn't meaningless. If their lives didn't mean anything, it would have been easy to kill them. He took that life, and so he wouldn't waste it. But how easy it is to forget about a piece of meat in the oven, throw it in the garbage, and fire a new one. He would not overcook this rabbit. He cared about it too much at this point. These were going to be the best rabbits ever. He was going to do everything possible, short of getting into that oven to cook with them, to make sure they were perfect."

It was at that point, perhaps, that Keller became a gastronomer. "The gastronomer is the highest development of the cooking animal," wrote Joseph Dommers Vehling, the German chef and Latin scholar who in 1936 published a translation of the cookbook attributed to the Roman bon vivant Apicius. "He—artist, philosopher, metaphysician, religionist—stands with his head bared before nature . . . eternally marveling at nature's inexhaustible resources and inventiveness, at her everlasting bounty born of everlasting fierce struggles."

Keller stands with his head bared, in fact, not only before a rabbit, but also a crouton, and the struggles implicit in that. "What was true of rabbits was true even of wheat," Ruhlman continued. "Thus to burn a crouton was a waste of life. Not the life of the wheat but the life of the person who grew the wheat, the life of the person who baked the bread, and the life of the cook who spent time cutting that bread and burning the croutons." The same truth exists in the reply, in the 1816 Sir Walter Scott novel *The Antiquary*, of a fish merchant to a complaint about high prices: "It's no fish ye're buying. It's men's lives."

Keller's respect for the most humble of his food items, then, extends also to those in other ways involved with those items: the Hudson Valley farmer who raises rabbits, the Central Valley migrants who pick strawberries. But the French Laundry counts no migrants among its clientele. Reservations are hard to get, and the prices very high-end. The menu, as it was at Chez Panisse, is in ordinary English, for the most part, but Keller works more squarely within the mainstream of *la grande cuisine* than Olney, relying more on the calf's brain and the foie gras and the other signature items of that cuisine, and making no special virtue of simplicity. It's more the sort of menu recognizable to the Vanderbilts and the Cabots, and Ruhlman's description of one of his meals at the French Laundry—nineteen courses lasting four and a half hours, four half-bottles of wine, a quenelle of sevruga caviar from the Caspian, and a double espresso—is more the sort of event recognizable to Apicius.

So has American haute cuisine come full circle at the French Laundry? Has Le Pavillon, where famed restaurateur Henri Soulé ladled out caviar to the Rockefellers, where *la grande cuisine* was sacrosanct, been reborn in Napa Valley? Hardly. Ruhlman singles out one item as definitive of the French Laundry, a dish that Keller calls "oysters and pearls," an assemblage of sabayon, pearl tapioca, caviar, and an oyster. "To serve caviar, one of the most expensive foods on earth, an item that connotes luxury, taste, refinement, elegance, class, on tapioca pudding, given that item's literal and sensual associations with infantile childhood," wrote Ruhlman, "was ironic."

So where M.F.K. Fisher, James Beard, and Richard Olney in their various ways stressed simplicity in adapting French cooking to the American landscape, Keller provides irony in the form of odd juxtapositions of the luxurious and the elegant with the foods—or at the very least, the concepts—of middle- and working-class America. You can get a grilled cheese sandwich at the French Laundry, or surf and turf, or several other items that you might find on the menu at Rockie's off I-5. But these foods are very different coming out of Keller's kitchen. Keller enjoys the irreverence, though, of providing hip versions of these warhorses of American mass consumption to the rarefied gourmands who flock to his restaurant.

It's all part of that continuing dialogue between two estranged cousins: the Old World, with its refinements of hierarchy and privilege and *gourmandise*, and the New World, with its egalitarianism and natural bounty and fast-food restaurants with so many millions served. In its grace notes of luxury, taste, refinement, and so forth, caviar is the opposite of grilled cheese. In 1976 the *San Francisco Chronicle* offered only ridicule to a chef who would serve—in all seriousness, without a breath of irony—"sterlet of Sacramento." That was because caviar was the quintessential Old World food, and yet it had certain New World characteristics that were irresistible to Olney. You want authenticity, simplicity, restraint, a certain rustic quality? As Rich Helfrich loves to remind himself now and then, caviar is just fish eggs and salt. It's usually a wild food as well, a direct product of "nature's inexhaustible resources and inventiveness, . . . her everlasting bounty born of fierce struggles." Once upon a time, America partook of this wild bounty, but the nation's greed was such that the bounty proved neither inexhaustible nor everlasting. The sturgeon was gone before any sort of poetry of place could take hold, and so, three-quarters of a century later, "sterlet of Sacramento" became an object of derision.

The New World's cornucopia, however, was defined only in part by its fisheries and its forests, the flowers of the Central Valley and the wheat and asparagus planted over them. In the twentieth century, as the sturgeons disappeared, the wheat steadily increased. A portion of that bounty continued to pour forth, thanks to what is familiarly known as the Green Revolution, which—in its reliance on fertilizers, pesticides, dams, and irrigation—was largely a chemical enhancement of the Industrial Revolution. In California, we look to technology once again—specifically, a Soviet technology adapted to an American species in an industry fueled by American and European capital—to bring the sturgeon back, if not to our rivers, at least to our supper plates. "California osetra" is a phrase now granted its poetry of place, one greeted not with mockery, but with deference, in the marketplace. Petrossian was thinking about selling Sterling caviar, and Mats Engstrom was only afraid that his competitors would make too much of the stuff.

Spring was on the move in the Northern Hemisphere, moving in its checkerboard pattern up through the microclimates of Europe, Asia, and North America. Remnant populations of wild white and green sturgeon were spawning in northern California. In a few weeks, in that one remarkable place in the Old World where multiple species and great numbers of wild sturgeons continue to swim, those species would be returning to the Volga, the Kura, and other rivers to spawn. There, where for caviar the poetry of place had been recited for centuries, the harvest would be gearing up to its annual peak, catching in its net not only millions of pounds of prized beluga, Russian, and stellate sturgeon, but also—for better or for worse—the shapes of men's lives.

"It is desire that creates the desirable," wrote Simone de Beauvoir in *The Ethics of Amgiguity* in 1947. And the desire to live prompts us not just to eat, but to eat the food of the gods, to aspire, like F. Scott Fitzgerald's Jay Gatsby, to suck on the pap of life, to gulp down the incomparable milk of wonder, even if it leads us into ambiguity.

It was time to visit the Caspian.

⌒ 10 ⌒

The Iron in the Garden

i.

I remember the birds: scores and scores of cormorants that nested in the willows that lined the narrowing Volga waterway. The slough was just a few yards wider than our motorboat and shrinking. The cormorants raised their black skulls and beaks in alarm as the boat approached, then rose complaining from their nests of knotted sticks. The wake of the boat opened in a funnel of foam through trunks that had been drowned in the river's spring flood, through trees that were bare and skeletal. The birds unfurled their wings against the white sky. We ran on, a noonday darkness gathering behind us.

We were en route to a *tonya*, one of the myriad fishing camps that line the banks of the Volga as it divides, and divides again, into nearly a thousand separate channels, toward its mouth on the Caspian Sea. From its source northwest of Moscow, the Volga winds 2,500 miles in all as it twists and turns through the populous heart of Russia. The river is Europe's longest, and its delta sprawls over Europe's biggest wetlands, some 7,400 square miles.

The Volga is a European river, but it marks nearly the eastern boundary of that concept. And if the Volga is a boundary, so the Caspian is a nexus, the Old World's omphalos, its historical meeting place of Europeans, Asians, and Arabs. It's a nexus as well of climatic zones and tectonic plates. As big as the combined surface area of North America's Great Lakes, the Caspian is temperate in Russia and Kazakhstan, where its water freezes in the winter, and subtropical in Iran. It was born 10 million years ago as the brackish remnant of the ancient Tethys Sea that once stretched across Eurasia. Shifts in global climate have made the Caspian as small as a great pool at the base of Iran's Elburz Mountains.

About 300 rivers drain into the Caspian today, but all are dwarfed by the Volga, whose waters provide 80 percent of its volume. By now the river has sifted 10 million years' worth of organic debris into a seabed that cooks over a seismic hot spot—a place where oceanic crust creeps northward from the Mediterranean, undercutting the continental crust that lies beneath the sea's upper basin. The region is wracked by earthquakes, peppered with boiling mud volcanoes, and laced by hydrocarbon seeps. Before the birth of Christ, Zoroastrians built temples at the jets of flaming gases that issued from the naptha-rich sands of Azerbaijan's Apsheron Peninsula. In the thirteenth century, an amazed Marco Polo witnessed natural fountains of oil.

By Marco Polo's time, control of the sea had passed from the Jewish Khazars, who were renowned merchants, to the Golden Horde of Batu Khan—the same Batu Khan, grandson of Genghis, who in 1240 provided the first written reference to caviar in his record of a meal at a Volga monastery. The Khazars believed the sturgeon to be without scales, and therefore unclean. But the Mongols built wooden weirs in the Volga to capture migrating sturgeons, structures that would be maintained into the nineteenth century. They fished in the Sea of Azov as well, and from there they provided Italian merchants with the very salty sort of caviar that was first introduced to the West.

Four hundred species of fauna are unique to the Caspian, but historically the sea has been more remarkable for the density of its wildlife. Its waters have boiled with vast numbers of fish: species of sturgeon, of course, but also herring, kilka, shad, salmon, carp, and more. There are birds as well: Almost all the waterfowl of Eastern Europe visit the Caspian along their migratory flyways, from the flamingo to the Siberian white crane, and hundreds of species besides cormorants nest in the Volga Delta. Meanwhile, the wilder parts of its wetlands—its outlying sloughs, creeks, and channels, its reed and cattail meadows and thickets of willow, ash, and mulberry, its floating plantations of lotus and white water lily—still support numbers of wild boar, bear, fox, raccoon, and beaver. It was enough to charm even a Bolshevik; in 1919 Lenin set aside a portion of the delta as one of the Soviet Union's first nature preserves.

There were four of us in the motorboat on the delta that morning: Anatoly Babrovsky and Nikolai Kodyakov, two off-duty members of the fisheries police; Katya Godunova, a university student; and the American writer who wished to see how sturgeon were caught. Anatoly and Katya had picked me up at my hotel in Astrakhan early that morning. Katya was the English-speaking daughter of Galina Godunova, a journalist and environmentalist, and the first source I had called in Astrakhan. Anatoly was in his late fifties—barrel-chested, white-haired, with round spectacles and big hands—and a friend to the Godunovas.

Skirting the flat western edge of the delta in Anatoly's Toyota SUV, we had driven through streets lined with simple farmhouses, through rural areas with free-ranging cattle and flocks of chickens, and past hills planted with the eight-pointed crosses of the Russian Orthodox Church's Old Believers. These hilltop crosses were monuments, said Katya, to Stenka Razin, the bandit-hero who in 1671 raised a rebellion from Astrakhan that stormed up the Volga and nearly toppled Tsar Alexis. Anatoly pointed out a railroad line under construction at a place where the German advance had reached its farthest point south in World War II. Hitler coveted the oil fields of Baku, and the Volga for carrying oil to Germany. But his Sixth Army was surrounded and destroyed at Stalingrad, and at last his war machine ran dry. By then, some 50 million Russians had died.

And we had driven through Ikranoye, the dusty village named after the word for "caviar" in Russian. There, sturgeons still swim by fishermen's doorsteps, and the village remains a center of legitimate and black-market fishing. Against the delta's wide horizons, the ramshackle houses suggested both the tenacity of their hold on this land and the frailty of all that supported them. It took no stretch of imagination to see Ikranoye, once the sturgeons were gone, as starved as that other Caviar, the one in New Jersey: the homes vacant, crumbling, and finally overcome by the slow insinuations of grass and wind.

Houses disappeared beyond Ikranoye. Eventually the road turned to dirt and we stopped near a grove of trees, wide stately willows with catkins lifting in the breeze, to wait for a ferry. Katya, a tall flowerstalk of a girl with blue Slavic eyes, climbed gratefully out of the Toyota and breathed in the springtime scents of the river. Anatoly got a bucket and sponge from behind the vehicle's rear seat and began rinsing the dust off its fenders with river water. A few minutes later we saw the ferry breasting its way across the mile-wide breadth of the water. The ferry was an old tug with a steel platform welded over its deck behind the wheelhouse, charging a fare of eighteen rubles, or about sixty cents.

Twenty minutes later we arrived at Nikolai Kodyakov's house, a sturdy brown clapboard affair hidden behind a chain-link fence and banks of lilac bushes blooming luxuriously in white and lavender. Nikolai had Tatar blood in his veins: Swarthy and powerful, he was, like Anatoly, dressed in rubber boots and military camouflage gear, but with an automatic pistol holstered at his side.

Nikolai's boat, a 16-foot skiff with camouflage paint and a powerful outboard, waited beneath a covered berth in a slough behind his house. "This is a working boat," Nikolai observed. "It's not for tourism."

By 10 A.M. we were speeding down the slough and then out into the Volga. The water in our wake boiled up brown and white then settled into sparkling expanses of blue. We raced by a fish processing plant with racks of fish drying like strings of pearls in the sun, a sunken ship with only its two rusty smokestacks showing, and an unfinished brick building with its windows like empty eye sockets against the horizon. Nikolai nodded in its direction. "Perestroika monument," he said. "We have many of them."

"What's a perestroika monument?"

"Gorbachev started building that factory during perestroika. Then the money ran out." He laughed harshly, easing the skiff past a drifting log. "Now it's another government monument."

ii.

It is not just desire that creates the desirable, but also freedom: the freedom to choose beluga or osetra, a conservative candidate or a reformer; the freedom to compare, to reject, to demand, and even to waste according to Veblen's orthodoxy of conspicuous consumption; the freedom to eat to fill your belly, or else simply to thrill your palate and impress your associates.

One of the external symptoms of this sort of freedom is the billboard. I had arrived in Russia on a Saturday afternoon, flying into Moscow's Sheremetyov Airport and being met there by a driver from the Hotel Moskva. The driver held a sign in Roman lettering that displayed the results of my scratchy Russian: "Harry Richard." We drove thirty minutes through low fields crisscrossed by power lines. The highway widened, but from there the Moscow skyline was blotted out by billboards: Bravo gin, Chesterfield cigarettes, Samsung computers, Clinique cosmetics, and other creditable foreign goods all the way into the city.

The Moskva lay in the heart of the city, opposite Red Square. A landmark specimen of the Soviet Imperialist style, the hotel was once the refuge of the Communist elite, and also of foreign visitors who could rely on being shadowed by the KGB when they went out, and being eavesdropped on when they stayed in. The Moskva's mismatched and ungainly shape has an explanation that lies somewhere between history and myth, which is like history, except more true: that Stalin signed off on two different sets of architectural plans during the hotel's construction in the 1930s. Uncertain of Stalin's preference and fearful of offending him, the builders carried out both and simply joined the two plans in the middle.

Opposite my window stretched the dark walls of the Kremlin and the cobblestones of the square where Stenka Razin had been executed. But beyond one corner of the Kremlin wall lay pretty Manezhnaya Square: a pastoral expanse of plazas, fountains, lawns, and kiosks selling hot dogs, potato chips, Coca-Cola, and Mors Wonder-Berry drink. On that mild and lucid spring night, it seemed that half the population of Moscow had come to stroll and be seen there. In one plaza a military brass band broke into a series of waltzes, and a dozen or so older women or mixed couples rose to dance. A woman in a floor-length lavender gown and a gray-haired man in a white shirt and black bow tie appeared to have been waiting for that moment, sweeping across the bricks with enough grace and brio to convert that tame Old World dance into a tango of erotic elegance.

No more than 20 yards away, a cadre of metal-pierced teenagers cranked up a boom-box and offered break-dance routines for small change. A marble tableau of three rearing horses, their hooves flailing, rose from the midst of a fountain in a plaza below the break-dancers. A pair of teenaged boys had gotten a girl in blue jeans and an Abercrombie & Fitch T-shirt up to the stone rim of the fountain, but they were having trouble throwing her all the way in, since she had sunk her teeth firmly into the shoulder of one boy's black leather jacket. Finally the other thought to pinch her nostrils. In a moment she released her grip and tumbled backward. Families and couples walked placidly by as the girl rose laughing and cursing from the waist-deep water.

Walking around the Hotel Moskva was like circling the Alps, but on its other side rose the gray office buildings and glassy storefronts of the Moscow business district. The streets there were quiet, the stores dark, though McDonald's was busy. In a little grocery store next door to the restaurant, I found a cooler with caviar for sale: 113-gram jars of osetra, branded Russkaya Ikra, "Russian Caviar," the official government brand produced by the caviar factory in Astrakhan that for decades had supplied Petrossian and Dieckmann & Hansen. I paid 178 rubles, or a little less than 6 dollars, for one of the jars, and ate some of it under the spray from that fountain near the Moskva. The eggs were flavorful, but mushy, with a number of them broken.

Once again, in a curious loop of history, Russians have the freedom to desire caviar, which was once as commonplace a food item up and down the Volga as fish soup. Over the centuries under the tsars, caviar grew in stature, passing from a palatable recourse on fast days, a staple of peasants and fishermen, to something revered—yet inexpensive—at all levels of Russian society, particularly during the feast days preceding Lent.

That it achieved such status here without being scarce or high-priced is testament enough, perhaps, to a grace independent of hype. During the 1800s, however, as methods of shipping and preservation improved, as global demand for caviar widened, and as ever greater portions of the Volga harvest were exported abroad, the food became pricey enough here to become what it always had been in the West: a signature dish of the economic elite. After the workers' revolution it became even harder to find, since the Communists made caviar an item exclusively either for export or for high-level state entertainment and manipulated its levels of scarcity to get the best price. The workers had lost not only a sensual indulgence but an important health food. Russians believe that caviar's arsenal of vitamins, lipids, and albumen enable it to fight cancer, lower blood pressure, cure anemia, lessen fatigue in pregnant women, and enhance virility.

Now this quintessence of Russian cuisine is available to the people again, or at least some of them: more so to city-dwellers, and very much so to Muscovites. When Gino Koczuk was doing business, Moscow was the distribution center for all the black-market caviar going to Europe and North America. Now there are other busy routes as well, but TRAFFIC estimates that tons of illegally harvested eggs still arrive in Moscow every day. A large portion of that still goes out in suitcases or other contrivances, while some of it stays home, but all of it—the good, the bad, and the mushy—taps into what the Russians call *azart*, that combination of wildness and charisma that brings a person power, wealth, sex; the ability to indulge either the whimsical or the forbidden, or the panache to throw your girlfriend into a fountain, or to dance the waltz as though it were foreplay. Caviar has been described as edible *azart*, and whether as a commodity or a metaphor, there is no item so expressive of Russia's new and troubled relationship to the West.

Which, except at the very beginning, has always been troubled. The kingdom of Kiev, where the seed of Russia was planted in the tenth and eleventh centuries, was an extension of eastern Europe, and the children of its princes married into the ruling houses of England, Germany, France, Sweden, Hungary, and Byzantium. Then came Genghis Khan and two centuries of brutal Mongol rule. When Russia emerged again, with Moscow the seat of a Eurasian empire built by Ivan the Terrible, the Moscow court was very different from Kiev's: insular, xenophobic, despotic, and tending in politics and war to do things as the Mongols had done them.

After the defeat of Napoleon, with Russia secure and powerful and expanding to the Pacific, the French traveler Alexis de Tocqueville predicted that both Russia and the United States were destined to eclipse Europe in strength and influence. But the costs of the Russian empire were paid by the unrequited labor of its poor, reduced to virtual slavery two centuries before by the institution of serfdom. While revolutionaries and reformers in the West were limiting central government, broadening education, and securing individual property rights, in heavily militarized Russia—observed Russian historian Vassily Klyuchevsky—"The state swelled up, the people grew lean." It was a state, moreover, that was rigidly hierarchical and still governed through the patterns of terror, violence, and deceit defined by the Mongol khans.

At the beginning of the twentieth century, defeats in the Russo-Japanese War and World War I spelled the end of tsarist rule. Then Lenin and the Communists promised to build an egalitarian system based on plenty. "Instead," noted historian Geoffrey Hosking, "they created a hierarchical one based on scarcity." One bad sign was the continued absence of caviar from the tables of the people of the People's Republics, even as harvests and exports of caviar grew through the decades and the heavily militarized Soviet state assumed superpower status. Another was the persistence of government terror, violence, and deceit.

At least the people were less lean than during tsarist days, and desire was kept in check not only through terror, but through propaganda, the control of information, and the opiates of guaranteed jobs and pensions. In the 1970s, however, new information technologies revealed to an ever more urban and educated Russia that westerners enjoyed both political freedom and superior access to consumer goods—including, curiously enough, Russian caviar. While Mikhail Gorbachev struggled in vain to graft free-market principles to a planned economy, Boris Yeltsin and other more radical reformers grew popular attacking the privileges of the Communist elite. "As long as no one can build or buy his own *dacha*," Yeltsin declared in 1990 in *Against the Grain*, "as long as we continue to live in such relative poverty, I refuse to eat caviar followed by sturgeon." By the time the Berlin Wall was down a year later, and the perestroika monuments frozen in place, the people were ready for free markets, a free press, free elections, and to eat caviar followed by sturgeon. A new culture of desire had been set in motion.

But thanks to mismanagement by Russian leaders and their Western creditors and consultants, and also to patterns of corruption with roots trailing back to the Mongols—thanks to Russia being Russia, Vadim Birstein would say—the onset of Western-style consumerism has proven more a train wreck than a magic carpet ride. The poverty line in Russia is as low as $20 a month, yet 38 percent of its people made less

than that in 2001. The Soviet safety net is gone, the villages are empty-
ing out, and marriage and birth rates are tumbling because men can't
afford to marry. Yet at the same time, Russian caviar is in the stores
at various levels of price and quality, along with Iranian and even a
little American. Sales of cars and durable goods are up and climbing.
One explanation might be that there is a lot of unreported income
out there.

Yeltsin, who succeeded Gorbachev at Russia's helm, was succeeded
in turn by the more authoritarian Vladimir Putin, a former KGB officer
who has set about reasserting the state control of information. But it's
possible that the spark of desire that Yeltsin struck is still smoldering. In
October 2001, on the day that U.S. troops invaded Afghanistan, stat-
ues of Ronald McDonald were under attack throughout the world: shot
at in Indonesia, set on fire in Ecuador, bombed in Turkey, vandalized in
Pakistan. But nothing of that sort in Russia, where the McDonald's I
visited was one of seventy-four in Moscow, St. Petersburg, and many
provincial cities as well.

McDonald's arrived with some other Western fast-food chains in the
early days of the Yeltsin era, when Russians visiting Moscow would fly
home with Quarter-Pounders in their luggage, carrying them as if they
were caviar, as if the cold, dry beef were charged with azart. The other
chains—such as Pizza Hut—came only for quick profit and bailed out
when the ruble plunged. But McDonald's stayed the course, buying
Russian produce with Russian rubles, indoctrinating its workers with a
sort of messianic cheerfulness not seen since Lenin's Young Pioneers,
and promoting from within to the extent that McDonald's in Russia
was now run entirely by Russians. It could be the beginning of something more like what the people had in mind, forged not from the top of
the haute cuisine food chain, but from the bottom. It raised the possibility that the Russian people, kept lean for all these centuries, would at
last grow fat, at least in a literal sense.

I knew that Moscow was a showcase city, the tip of the nation's economic iceberg, which presently floated on a favorable tide of oil prices
and something of a balancing act on the part of its enigmatic president.
I watched the dancer in the black tie and his partner in the lavender
dress waltz their way through a good part of the long, magenta dusk of

the evening. The horns of the military band caught fire as the sun set-tled into the horizon, and its light slanted into their bells.

I went back to my room in the Moskva, fielded a telephone call from a woman recommending a "sex massage," and finished my osetra. In the morning, as I packed for my flight to Astrakhan, I heard the sound of a loudspeaker outside my window. An old woman was declaiming from the steps of the history museum opposite the Kremlin. Behind her hung a poster of Lenin and a pair of red Soviet flags. Forty or fifty people were in attendance, all of them middle-aged or older. A squad car and a small detachment of blue-jacketed Moscow police stood off to one side. They chatted among themselves or else basked in the sun as the voice of the old Communist grew ever more strident and bitter.

iii.

My room in the Hotel Korvet in Astrakhan filled up rapidly during my first morning in the city. Katya arrived first, on foot. Her mother, Galina, had volunteered her the previous night as someone who could assist as a translator and guide. I tried to negotiate fair payment with Katya for this sort of help and found her unyielding: She was happy to practice her English and would not take so much as a dollar or a ruble for her trouble. Anatoly Babrovsky arrived shortly afterward, dispatched by Galina to introduce me to the situation in the Caspian, and then Galina herself. Finally, a professional translator from the Caspian Fish-eries Research Institute, Elena Zhuravleva, came to arrange my visit to the institute the next day.

The day before had been rainy. Aeroflot's small Tupelov airliner from Moscow had dropped out of the sun through banks of wet clouds to a tundra-like expanse of mud, grass, and water. Scores of narrow lakes, like great wheel-ruts filled with rain, ran north-south to the horizon, with the lazy weave of the Volga transecting some of these. Astrakhan, caviar's ancient city of gold, appeared on the horizon as a swath of low, dark buildings thrown like driftwood along the banks of the river's main channel. I had taken a taxi to the hotel, where the driver cheated me on the fare and the clerk was annoyed to have to check in a guest.

At one time, because of its summer heat and such former afflictions as fish odors, mosquitoes, and malaria, Astrakhan was an alternative destination to Siberia for Soviet exiles. Nonetheless, the city was always popular with the Communist elite's sportfishermen, and otherwise was closed to outsiders until 1992. *Sputnik* was launched from a Soviet rocket base near here, as were manned space missions. Military exercises were conducted under space-program levels of darkness, as was the manufacture of caviar. The records of the sturgeon harvest were sealed as state secrets, and only a small and carefully measured portion of the caviar made each year was passed on to Petrossian or Dieckmann & Hansen. As much as 90 percent was reserved for domestic use, though very little of that found its way into Soviet stores. Nowadays the city struggled to reinvent itself as a tourist destination and watched with great trepidation the decline of the fishing industry and the progress of oil development in the north Caspian.

The Hotel Korvet was small, clean, and quiet, set back from the street and on top of a restaurant amid a glade of trees in one of Astrakhan's outlying commercial districts. Across the street from the Korvet, an open-air market hosted booths run by men and women with knotty, sunburnt faces and sinewy hands. From dawn to dusk, seven days a week as the cars and vans and trolleys rolled past, they sold bread, milk, cheese, figs, nuts, chocolate, cigarettes, and quantities of fruits and vegetables.

Anatoly, when he arrived, spoke less as a member of the fisheries police than as the fisherman he used to be. He had been a fisherman since the cradle, he told me, as his grandfather had been. "My grandfather ran his own fishing company," he said. "They sold all the commercial species, including sturgeon. But then the Communists came in with their new economic policy. All rich men were deprived of their property, and so was my grandfather, who was beaten as well."

I supposed his grandfather had been lucky. Astrakhan was under Bolshevik control in 1919, but the country as a whole was still in the grip of its civil war. The city's paper mill workers and fishermen liked neither the Communists nor the food shortages that followed in their wake. They staged a general strike, which the Communists answered with wholesale executions, these visited upon not just striking workers but also upon "bourgeois elements." Group executions were carried out on the fish-processing barges, and the river ran red with blood. That also was the end of Astrakhan's *belle epoque* as a cosmopolitan city of theaters, hotels, and gourmet food stores.

Anatoly himself fished for sturgeon through perestroika and most of the 1990s, running lines of hooks along the bottoms of sloughs; these would catch the ground-hugging fish in the belly or tail as they passed, or in the mouth if they were feeding. But eventually the Yeltsin government divided the sturgeon quota into large shares that it then put up for auction. "There is no quota share smaller than 10,000 kilos," Anatoly explained. "Only the big industries can buy quota shares, and that put the small fishermen out of business."

This was described by Moscow as a move to exert greater control over the industry and reduce poaching. Instead, said Anatoly, the opposite had happened: "Now there is industrial-scale poaching. Professional militias or fish protection guards make deals with the poachers, who take the eggs and leave the rest of the fish to rot. Not all fishermen without quotas poach, but many do. It's too bad, because Putin considers small business fundamental, and he has discussed special laws to develop that sector. But out in the country the bureaucracy is out to destroy small business. Here they have monopolies, and small business is dying."

Also dying, he said, was the sterling reputation of Russian caviar, particularly in Russia. "Astrakhan is not a good place to buy caviar," he said. "In Moscow you see much more, but people who taste it say it is not up to the mark. Caviar produced for export is made the natural way, and quickly, but the caviar sold in Russia is made by poaching. The sturgeon is killed, and then because conditions are so poor on those boats, the eggs are allowed to dry out. Later the eggs are sprayed with seltzer water so they enlarge again, but the taste is disgusting. Sometimes you find hair or pieces of fingernail in the caviar. People prefer Iranian caviar now. People who taste the Russian receive a very bad opinion."

By then Galina Godunova had arrived. A reporter at the Astrakhan bureau of the Russian newspaper *Izvestia* and an officer in the city government, she was also a member of the Caspian Environmental Center (CEC), a nongovernmental advocacy organization, and founder of a CEC program protecting the endangered Caspian seal. Slender, but not as tall as her daughter, she wore a crisp gray sport coat, round glasses, and had a manner as grave as it was kindly. Her smiles, carefully hoarded, were radiant when released. She took a seat next to Katya and said that Putin had come to a conference in Astrakhan that spring and coined a word to describe sturgeon poaching that actually rather shocked her and other journalists: "bioterrorism."

Anatoly nodded and mentioned the two Russian provinces just to the east of Astrakhan. "The border guards say their work is much more dangerous now in Kalmykia and Dagestan. I saw on TV luxurious cottages along the shore in Dagestan that belong to lawyers and mafiya bosses. It is impossible to gain such money through legal industry."

"The most awful thing is the electroshock method many of them use now for sturgeon extraction," Galina added. Then she described the same technology I had seen the Wisconsin DNR using the previous summer for capturing live lake sturgeon, except that in Dagestan the voltage was cranked up. "The electricity is so powerful," Galina said, "that the eyes of the sturgeon explode. Of course all bioresources in the electrical field are destroyed as well: the plankton, the other fish, everything."

I asked Galina if fishermen in Dagestan and elsewhere had no choice but to poach. "That's an old-fashioned opinion," she said. "Nowadays everybody understands the danger that the sturgeon is in, and it's not true that you have to poach to feed your family."

Anatoly gently disagreed. "For the people who live along the shore, the choice has always been simple: You fish, or you die in poverty," he said slowly. "Years ago 90 percent of the villagers were busy fishing. Now only 10 percent can fish legally for the corporations. The other 90 percent, they have to survive somehow. Maybe from one side that's an old-fashioned opinion. From the other side, maybe not."

We talked for thirty minutes more, until Galina had to return to her office for an appointment. Anatoly and I had begun making arrangements for a visit to a tonya when Elena arrived from the Caspian Fisheries Research Institute, a.k.a. KaspNIRKh. Only a few years older than Katya, in a white muslin blouse and snug black slacks, she raised her sunglasses to the crown of her short blonde hair and agreed to wait, sitting on the bed, while I finished making plans with Anatoly. Then she interrupted several times, speaking only in Russian to Anatoly. From what I could understand of her remarks, she disapproved of what we proposed. Anatoly shrugged her off. We agreed on Thursday for our trip down the Volga. Then Anatoly invited me to join him and some friends for a sauna that night. "We had an American journalist join us several years ago," he said, "and by the time we were done, he was a good Communist." He nodded to Elena and left.

I asked Katya later about Elena's concerns about visiting a fishing camp. "She said that it could be dangerous," Katya told me, "and that it would not be proper for you to see such poverty."

I agreed to meet Katya later that afternoon for a walk around Astrakhan. Elena had a car and driver waiting for us outside, where there was no trace of yesterday's rain. We sped through a jumble of streets, then angled off into a leafy cul-de-sac. KaspNIRKh, the Jerusalem of sturgeon science, was a stolid box of a building, four or five stories high, housing 500 people and eighteen different laboratories and departments. The lobby inside its front door was floored in a swirling tile mosaic of lobsters, fish, and sturgeon. Across the opposite wall stretched a mural of a soldier kneeling to kiss the slack corner of a Soviet flag. The corridors beyond the lobby were wide and gloomy but at the same time so alive with the scents of brine and fish that it seemed a change in tide might bring water running down them.

The office of Svetlana Stepanyan, the institute's public information officer, was adorned in prints of French Impressionist paintings and a map of the Volga Delta detailed enough for its twining channels to look like capillaries running through lung tissue. She shared this office with Elena and another translator. Elena spoke with her briefly and disappeared to fetch some papers I needed to sign. Svetlana then turned to me with obvious concern. Who was the man with whom I had been speaking this morning? Who had given me his name? Where exactly had he proposed to take me?

Uncertain of her interest in this, I allowed myself more generous portions than usual of forgetfulness and confusion. Svetlana reminded me that my visa for travel to Astrakhan had been granted on the institute's recommendation. "We are responsible for your movements and safety," she explained, "and we will need a very accurate indication of your schedule."

The paperwork concerned the services of KaspNIRKh translators over the next three days. Elena returned to report that the accountant had forgotten to figure in the value-added tax, and that unfortunately the fee would be $100 more than originally specified. I negotiated that back to the original price by dismissing Elena for the balance of that day, though she still guided me through a tour of the institute's museum. In a diorama, a pair of stuffed sturgeons swam over a beach-like bottom of sand and shells: a stellate sturgeon, a little more than 4 feet long, with its needle-nose snout and pink freckles scattered in constellations along its flanks, and a Russian sturgeon, half again as large, with a blunt and rounded head and metallic gill plates.

Later Katya walked me through Astrakhan's central fort, the white-washed kremlin built by Ivan the Terrible with stones taken from the former capital of Batu Khan. Among the tribute required from the defeated Mongols was sturgeon delivered fresh to the tsar; the fish would be wrapped in straw, its snout in vodka-soaked rags, and then brought by boat the 800 miles to Moscow. We walked from the kremlin to the waterfront, where men fished for carp with hand-held lines from the gangplanks of moored barges, where Peter the Great once commanded that church bells be silent and oars muffled, the whole length of the Volga, during sturgeon spawning season. Centuries later, Konstantin Paustovsky, a writer of the early Soviet period, offered a vivid description of this waterfront in his book *The Black Gulf:* "Night and day sunburnt people on the fishing rafts, all covered in scales as with a coat of mail, hauled the mottled carcasses of the sturgeons from their fishing smacks with a boathook and flung them down with heavy thud on the planks. Endless files of blue-trousered girls bore carp to the refrigerators, holding the golden, stupid fish by their wet coral gills."

Along the way we met a statue of Lenin still standing atop its tall limestone pedestal. I asked Katya to stand before it to provide scale for my camera, but again she was unyielding. She refused to keep company in any way with an image of Lenin.

The next morning, after my steambath and on our way to a hatchery, Elena and I stopped at the city's historical museum to see Astrakhan's most famous stuffed fish. The immense beluga rested in mid-air atop a pair of steel stanchions: well over 2,000 pounds, nearly 14 feet long, and about the size of a Japanese minisub. The fish was caught as recently as 1989 in the river near Astrakhan. It was a male estimated to be seventy or seventy-five years old. Its skin was a pebbly and grass-tinted blue, fading to white about its gaping, rubbery lips, which opened forward, in the direction of its snout, like a basking shark's, rather than down like other sturgeons. Its eyes were glassy marbles, and as small as that, in the mountainous slope of its brow.

Elena claimed that even yet such monsters were to be found. "Only one or two months ago a fish nearly this size was caught by poachers," she said. "But the fish was too old and the eggs could not be used."

iv.

The Russian peasant poet Serge Esenin described Bolshevism as the last and most extreme product of the "steel fever" of the cities, an "electrical uprising" leading to an Armageddon contested not between Christ and the Antichrist, but between—in the phrase of another rural poet, Nicholas Kliuev—"the iron and the land."

The sturgeon hatchery Bios, located on the banks of a Volga channel about 25 miles southwest of Astrakhan, very near Ikranoye, was founded in 1994, after the demise of Bolshevism, communism, and perestroika. But Alexander Kitanov, the chief scientist at Bios, could not help but suggest that old Bolshevik dream of a harmony between iron and land, between industry and ecology, in discussing his work there.

"The decline of sturgeon populations in the Caspian is very well known," he said. "But with the establishment of Bios, it became possible to raise broodstock for the replenishment of those populations on an industrial scale."

I would pass by Bios again a few days later with Anatoly and Katya, but my journey there with Elena was my first visit to the Russian countryside. This was low country, full of marsh and reeds and willows, especially as we approached Ikranoye. Magpies squabbled in the trees, and a wandering herd of goats delayed us at one turn of the road. Amidst an electrical uprising of power lines, fishermen worked many of the creeks and sloughs with handlines and small nets, pursuing what Elena termed "ordinary fish." At a wider portion of the river, a group of a dozen or so prepared to wrestle a much larger net out into the current. "They're fishing for sturgeon," Elena said.

A pair of cows grazed heedlessly in the grass near Bios's gate, where a blue and white sign spelled out the mission of the hatchery in both Russian and English: "To save the relict Sturgeon broodstock on our planet for the present and future generations." The offices and labora- tories behind the gate were housed in neat, ground-hugging buildings of white stucco and tile roofs. Banks of gardens hugged the walkways, well-trimmed shrubbery the margins of the buildings. A pair of Bios staff members conducted Elena and me into the conference room of the hatchery's administrative building. Its windows were large, but shaded. We sat at a broad oaken table in cool and musty darkness. Dr. Kitanov, in a dark suit, did not so much arrive as materialize out of the shadows. He sat with his hands folded on the table, scarcely moving as he fielded my questions.

"Our work rests on the foundation built by the former hatcheries of the Volga," said Kitanov, an expert in sturgeon reproduction and the man de- scribed in Russia's *St. Petersburg Times* as Astrakhan's "fish-master." "We have about 10,000 tons of fish here now," he continued. "Our concern is with the reproduction of the commercial species of fish in the Caspian. We produce broodstock for the maintenance and enhancement of those species, and broodstock also for commercial aquaculture enterprises abroad."

I knew that in the late 1950s a series of hydroelectric dams had been built on the Volga, culminating in the closing of the massive Volgagrad Dam in 1959. That great parapet blocked the river's beluga sturgeons from 90 percent of their spawning grounds and eliminated large por- tions of the spawning grounds of other species as well. The Soviets im- mediately built sturgeon hatcheries, trusting that the iron hammers of science and industrial technology would produce what the Volga by then could not.

In 1965, a little more than 42 million fry were released into the Caspian basin. Two decades later, nearly 103 million—not fry, but fingerlings— were stocked in the sea. By then Soviet scientists had determined that they could triple the survival rate of the young sturgeon, from 1 percent to

3 percent, if they held them forty days at the hatchery and then released them over feeding grounds outside the river. The Soviets also instituted harsh penalties for poaching sturgeon—up to twelve years in prison—and in 1962 moved the location of their fisheries from the open sea, where sturgeon of all ages were caught, to the rivers that in the spring and fall drew mostly mature sturgeon, and that were also more easily policed. Other species were stocked as well: salmon, carp, bream, roach, inconnu, and even crayfish.

In effect, the Caspian Sea had become a gigantic fish farm, and for a time it was a very prosperous one. Sturgeon harvests swooned in the late 1950s and early 1960s, recovered, and then shot to nearly unprecedented heights between 1975 and 1985. More than 29,000 tons came out of the Caspian in 1980, which was nearly equal to the region's record harvest of 33,000 tons in 1900. Soviet scientists pioneered the commercial aquaculture of sturgeons and experimented with sturgeon hybrids, most notably the bester. They found that raising sturgeon in the warm effluent waters of thermal power stations accelerated their growth. They considered stocking reservoirs around the Volga with besters but wisely abandoned that idea out of fear of disturbing the gene pools of wild fish in the Caspian. Unwisely, they never tagged or marked the fingerlings they released, and for that reason the exact role that the hatcheries played in the increased harvests cannot be exactly quantified. But all outward signs indicated that the Soviets had done something entirely remarkable: They had successfully engineered the world's first wholesale recovery of sturgeon stocks to peak-harvest levels.

But there were other signs that were not so positive. The water flowing through the dams and into the Caspian was clearer, but not cleaner. The silt piling up at the feet of those dams once provided not only cover to young sturgeon but also nutrients to the plankton and mollusks they fed on. In place of that silt was a deadly elixir of dissolved chemicals spewed out by the new factories powered by the dams. These were similar to the potions then poisoning the Hudson River: pesticides, heavy metals, PCBs, and dioxins. Various hydrocarbons were thrown into the mix as well. For the sake of their fisheries, the Soviets had forsworn drilling for oil in the shallow north Caspian seafloor, but rising sea levels were engulfing leaky shoreside installations in Azerbaijan. Finally there was the radiation. Surface atomic bomb blasts that accompanied military exercises in the 1950s raised the Caspian's levels of tritium, an enriched radioactive element, by factors of 300 to 400. Then, over the next three decades, a series of underground nuclear explosions beneath the Caspian spread radioactive fluids as the resulting chambers filled and leaked.

The iron was working at cross-purposes with itself. In the 1980s, fish began appearing with deformed eggs, and then began displaying signs themselves of disease or deformity: missing eyes or nostrils or tails, twisted spines, degenerative muscles or organs, tumors. The sturgeon harvests fell again, down to 18,000 tons in 1990, and then the iron wheels fell off with the collapse of the Soviet Union. The hatcheries, by and large, went dark, the sea was divided into different national jurisdictions, and the poachers went to work. In 1995, the legal harvest of sturgeon in the Caspian basin was 3,000 tons, and four years later a paltry three-quarters of a ton. Even given a black-market take ten to twelve times those numbers, a harvest that would include great numbers of wasted males, juveniles, and fallow females, the final tally indicated a fish farm in free-fall to bankruptcy.

Eight hatcheries had been restarted in the Astrakhan region in hopes of arresting that fall, and of them Bios was the most notable. Its director, Lydya Vasilyeva, wasn't a scientist but a former Communist Party department secretary who had arranged through her party contacts to rent Bios in the early days of the Yeltsin era.

Unable to secure loans from any bank for modernizing the equipment at Bios, she had used her contacts again to arrange a visit to Bios by Yeltsin's minister of fisheries in 1994. That led to a sort of reverse privatization scheme in which the federal government provided capital for equipment and a degree of continued support. That support was in part for the resumption of the hatchery's stocking activities, and otherwise for Vasilyeva's ideas about making money, ideas that the Soviets would have considered heretical: She wanted to pursue not just the production of caviar from cultured fish, as Doroshov and his disciples were doing in California, but also the sale of fertilized eggs and Caspian broodstock to aquaculture operations elsewhere in the world.

"The caviar we have produced is sold in Russia under the Russkaya Ikra trademark," Kitanov told me. "And we have steadily expanding markets for our eggs and mature broodstock—markets, for example, in the United States, Germany, Greece, and China. We have a great deal of interest from China."

I knew Frank Chapman had obtained his beluga from a farm in Romania, his Russian sturgeon from elsewhere in Europe. Nonetheless, in the 1990s, scientists and aquaculturists in the United States and elsewhere were amazed to find eggs and broodstock for these legendary species were available for purchase directly from the Caspian, and Bios quickly became famous. Subsequent Russian fisheries ministers, however, had not been so sure about this scheme and had engaged in a tug-of-war with Vasilyeva about the extent of those sales. These days, the sale of beluga, Kitanov added, "is of course entirely prohibited."

Bios and its sister hatcheries had not been able to match the volume of the Soviet hatcheries in the release of fingerlings into the wild. This year a combined total of some 50 million would be released, 2 million of those from Bios. Nor had they matched the at least temporary success of the Soviet hatcheries in increasing sturgeon numbers. Money remained a problem. So did water quality, especially since the water in the hatchery came from the Volga. Some say that the hatcheries themselves were part of the problem, and always had been, diluting the strength and diversity of the gene pool to a degree that was now catching up to them. And then there were the poachers, who have had an effect on the biology of the sturgeon populations. With so many mature females fished out, younger females were starting to bear eggs before they were quite ready to do so.

"Even just five years ago, we could only take females who were in very good condition and let the rest go," Kitanov said. "But now 80 percent of the females that we see are not fully mature, and a much lower proportion of their eggs are able to hatch."

Mature beluga females had become hen's teeth and were never shunted into caviar production. In 1995, neither Bios nor any other hatchery was able to obtain any mature belugas; Birstein was convinced that natural reproduction had already ceased by then, that there was no reproduction of the species, either natural or artificial, that year. Since then, Bios has pioneered, at least in the scale of its application, another practice for which it is famous: cesarean section and the maintenance of broodstock over the years necessary for females to produce multiple generations of eggs.

v.

Maybe that sort of mercy accounted for some part of the cheerful and maternal demeanor of Tatyana Scherbatova, who took us across the road after our conversation with Kitanov to show us the day-to-day operations of the hatchery. In close-cropped brown hair and a black sport coat, she skipped ahead of us as we navigated our way through incubation machines with trays of eggs suspended in running water, through banks of stainless steel chutes and flues, though rows of plastic tanks and murky cement pools. The sound and loamy smell of running river water filled the air. In the trays of one incubator, American paddlefish eggs were spread in a purple sand. "That is a species with a very high rate of growth," Tatyana said. "We use it for its meat, its caviar, and also as broodstock. Our main customer for paddlefish broodstock is China."

The tiny fry swarming like flies in the plastic tanks were various forms of hybrids: bester, but also some newer experimental forms—Russian and stellate; Russian and the rare ship sturgeon; even a hybrid-hybrid in the form of a beluga-bester combination. Tatyana said that the hybrids were being developed in hopes of faster rates of growth and higher disease resistance.

Other tanks contained foot-long juveniles of thoroughbred Russian and beluga sturgeon. She caught one of each with a dipnet, cradling each fish calmly for a moment in her hands, taking obvious delight in their sculpted beauty. At that size, the two species were much alike in their short snouts, hard edges, and outsized tails. The beluga's frame showed only the promise of its native battleship bulk. Tatyana laughed and turned her face as the beluga spun itself out of her hands and splashed back into the tank.

The cement pools were 50-foot circular vats that receded nearly out of sight beneath an architecture of reinforced roofing, fluorescent lights, and elevated pipes. There were also a few recessed pools in a sort of open-air pagoda enclosed by chain-link fence. All these, in Tatyana's delicious phrase, were part of "the Department of Prolonged Keeping," where the hatchery's broodstock was housed. Several technicians in orange and black rain gear were in the process of moving some fish from the vats to the several pools in the pagoda: full-grown Russian sturgeon, gravid females, which they carried by pairs in fine-mesh stretchers like those used in California. Inside the pagoda the fish were lifted by the gill plates and then dropped into the pools.

The fish were between 4 and 6 feet long, and the men could just barely lift the largest. They were carried, twisting and curling, with their bellies facing out, as white as the overhead lights in the pagoda's gloom. Tatyana said these fish were due to have their roe surgically removed in an operation that took about twenty minutes per fish. "They will not be killed," she emphasized. "We have more humanity here."

Humanity could come at the expense of diversity, especially with the beluga, as a very few queen-bee females were called upon, over and over, to provide the same sets of genes to fingerlings in the Caspian. Also, Russian scientists had noticed that, for whatever reason, hatchery-bred beluga were smaller than those born in the wild, or that once were born in the wild.

Birstein approved of the caution of American conservationists and scientists regarding restocking. Yet he wrote, no doubt sadly, in 2000, "Despite the questions it raises, restocking may be the only opportunity to maintain and/or restore the main wild populations of Eurasian and American sturgeons and paddlefishes." To him that was such a slim opportunity, however, as to almost be discounted. That left commercial aquaculture. "Ironically," he continued, "it seems that business interests, not international conservation effort, are providing the only ray of hope for sturgeon survival."

I watched the egg-heavy Russian sturgeons begin to circle around their new pools and recalled an earlier exchange with Alexander Kitanov. I had mentioned that American consumers bought 80 percent of the world's beluga caviar, and that some American conservation groups were urging the U.S. government to put the beluga on its endangered species list, and so ban the importation of its caviar. Would that be helpful to Bios in its mission to "save the relict Sturgeon broodstock"?

Kitanov brooded, his eyes narrowing. He said finally, "I do not think that it is the place of the American government to decide policy in addressing problems in Russia."

And the eventual fate of sturgeon in the Caspian? "There are so few healthy and mature fish being caught now," he volunteered, "that I am certain they will continue to disappear."

∽ 11 ∽

THIEVES WORLD

i.

Wednesday, May 8, was my third day in Astrakhan and a holiday in Russia: Victory Day, the anniversary of the Third Reich's surrender to the Allies. The television screen in my room at the Hotel Korvet was filled with patriotic music and film clips from the war or movies about the war. In one clip a group of sailors aboard a submarine applauded one sailor's skillful Charlie Chaplin imitation, then laughed and hissed after the Little Tramp turned, adjusted his makeup, and then turned back as a brutish, knuckle-walking Adolf Hitler. That was followed by archival footage of soldiers on a train, returning from the sack of Berlin, Hitler dead and their faces young and radiant with hope.

I bought my breakfast of yogurt, fruit, and fresh bread at the market across the street. There were fish for sale that day, carp and herring and bundles of dried roach, or *vobla*, but neither sturgeon nor caviar. On other days there was sturgeon meat, I was told. It was illegal to sell caviar there, but I learned that I could find some if I wanted to put in the time. In a grocery store I saw beluga meat for sale, palm-sized slices vacuum-packed like slices of turkey breast in plastic. The label said it was Astrakhan beluga packed in Azerbaijan. There were also various sorts of pike and salmon caviars, and two sturgeon: a 113-gram jar of Russkaya Ikra sevruga for the equivalent of $33, and 90 grams of

Naturalnaya beluga caviar (allegedly), in an inappropriate aluminum can, for only a dollar.

Elena arrived at mid-morning with another driver from KaspNIRKh. We drove back to the institute through streets dotted with shuffling old men in military uniforms, the surviving veterans of the Fatherland War, their faces the same as those of the boys on that train, but fallen, I thought, with more than the weight of fifty-seven years.

KaspNIRKh was busy on the holiday. The institute was founded in 1897, during Astrakhan's biggest sturgeon harvests, and was the first of its sort in Russia. Since then it had provided the science for managing sturgeon and other species, building the hatcheries, and overseeing the introduction of alien species into the Caspian and other waters. Some of these introductions had worked out fine: in the 1930s, the *Nereis succinea* worm, brought from the Sea of Azov at the recommendation of Jacob Birstein, Vadim's father, to fill out the bottom of the sea's food chain, and, during the same decade, two species of Black Sea mullet. Now both are important commercial fish in the Caspian. Others failed: In the 1920s, for example, stellate sturgeon were introduced from the Caspian into the Aral Sea, but they carried a parasite that devastated formerly abundant stocks of ship sturgeon there.

In the 1990s, KaspNIRKh had been the first to ring the alarm about the declining sturgeon harvests. With Vadim Birstein pointing the way, papers published by institute scientists got the attention of Western scientists, and statements made to Russian and international media by institute director Vladimir P. Ivanov got the attention of environmentalists. This was the same Ivanov who reported at Oshkosh that natural reproduction of the beluga had ceased. It was also Ivanov who, in 1995—at the request of Vadim Birstein—saw to it that historical data on the Soviet harvests were declassified. Ivanov and other KaspNIRKh scientists were instrumental in persuading the Yeltsin government to sign the 1998 CITES accord and to vastly reduce Russia's legal harvest and export quotas. Since then, Ivanov had been publicly lobbying against both oil development in the sea and unilateral approaches to solving the poaching problem. "If we can't get an agreement with the other Caspian states that stops poaching," he told *National Geographic* magazine in May 1999, "we may have to ban fishing completely for several years."

I had spoken briefly with Ivanov in Oshkosh and looked forward to interviewing him in his office at the institute. In the fall, however, he had been dismissed from his post by the newly appointed head of the Russian Fisheries Committee, replaced—as reported by Birstein—by "a 'new Russian,' a former banker with good local and Moscow 'business' connections. If this is true, forget about sturgeons in the Russian part of the Caspian Sea."

Entirely by chance, Elena and I met Ivanov in the lobby that morning at the institute, going out as we were going in. It was an exchange of pleasantries. He nodded his swept-back mane of white hair, regretted that he wasn't available for interviews, and wished me good luck.

We went upstairs to the office of Ivanov's longtime deputy director, Alla Mazhnik, a genial woman arrayed very formally that day, whether for us or Victory Day or some other reason, in a pearl necklace and double-breasted blue satin suit. We were joined moments after our arrival by Anatoly Vlasenko, head of the institute's lab for sturgeon stock assessment, and the top-ranking KaspNIRKh scientist to attend the 1994 sturgeon conference in New York City.

Dr. Vlasenko had played a leading role in a high-profile task: the north Caspian sturgeon count required by CITES as a condition for the resumption of legal exports this spring. He had had to coordinate that assessment with scientists from Azerbaijan, Kazakhstan, and Turkmenistan. Now exports were moving and the numbers were being crunched, a process that would require, I learned, several more months' work. I knew Vlasenko was well-advised to count carefully, that the numbers his team produced would have to be credible to other scientists, to CITES, to government-sponsored fishing interests, and to international environmentalists—particularly, it was hoped, to those working to shut down the beluga caviar trade to the United States.

"The future of the sturgeon depends on many factors," Vlasenko observed. He was a lean and Lincolnesque man with thick eyebrows and windblown black hair, in his black coat a somber contrast to Alla Mazhnik. "The different political jurisdictions make the managed use of bioresources a difficult matter," he continued. "Agreements will have to be reached and documents signed before it is too late. Also difficult is protecting the ecology of the Caspian. All the littoral states have accelerated their exploration and development of oil fields. Much depends on our use of gas and petroleum resources, and the incidence of pollution."

Mazhnik, smiling, raised her hand to interrupt. "The Russian company Lukoil will be extracting petroleum in the Russian sector, and they adhere to zero-tolerance for waste and pollution in their methods," she said. "The costs are great, but in this instance well worth it. The other states do not use such methods. When President Putin visited Astrakhan recently, he made this point—he wants all the states to use zero-tolerance methods. Also, the situation in general is much better regarding pollution now. Industrial effluents have been reduced, the Volga is cleaner, and water quality has stabilized for the better."

Vlasenko said that another variable was the degree of support that could be provided to sturgeon reproduction. "The Russian Federation has measures—Bios and its other hatcheries—to sustain sturgeon stocks, but we struggle to provide for natural reproduction, and we are uncertain of the commitment of other nations to funding artificial propagation."

"But the other littoral states are helping," countered Mazhnik. "Iran is building hatcheries and releasing juveniles, Kazakhstan has built two new hatcheries, and Azerbaijan has just secured funding from the World Bank for hatcheries. It is true that the greatest scale of propagation lies in Russia, but these are positive developments."

The deputy director disagreed with Ivanov's assertion that the beluga no longer spawned in the wild, but to her that was not the point. "Ninety percent of the beluga caught now are artificially propagated, 50 percent of the Russian, 40 percent of the stellate," she said. "The efficiency of artificial propagation has been proven, its results published. Sturgeon populations have stabilized since 1998. There are a great many juveniles now, and in time there will be a great many adults."

Money was always a limiting factor—money for the hatcheries, money for KaspNIRKh, money for its fleet of twenty research vessels—though in every instance, Mazhnik said, the government was supportive and doing its best. Vlasenko eventually fell silent, and Mazhnik took over, acknowledging the difficulty of accomplishing what was expensive, and also of forging coalitions with suspicious neighbors, but it was happening nonetheless, and this conversation today was an opportunity to redress a wrong.

"There is a great deal of negative information being published about poaching in the Caspian," she declared. "But now all the littoral states are taking measures to counter that, and poaching has stabilized at a level much lower than ten years ago. Now there is no such sharp decline in our stocks as people read about. And it is false to say that the poor people on the coast will eat the last fish. The government has increased its financial support. Salaries are up, the fisheries police have new boats, and the border guards offer protection as well. Though this is all very expensive, we do our best and we have seen positive results. These results signify quite firmly that there were, are, and will be sturgeon in the Caspian Sea."

ii.

The Russian Federation's customs declaration requires travelers to disclose any dangerous items that they might have in their possession—weapons, ammunition, explosives, drugs, psychotropic substances, radioactive materials, or printed informational media—and also any cash or valuables. The previous Saturday, as my flight had approached Moscow, I'd confessed to having some books and magazines on my person, and also several thousand dollars in cash.

At the customs booth in Sheremetyov Airport, the young officer there asked to see my cash. I opened my wallet and displayed what I had changed into rubles. Where was the rest? I explained it was in a money-belt around my waist. The officer said he would regret subjecting me to a strip-search. I had a feeling that my next line, according to the script, was to ask what sort of honorarium might save us both that trouble, but I tried passive resistance instead. I became perplexed and hard to communicate with. It was a public setting, there were no other officers to assist at the time, and other passengers were waiting and watching. At last the stupid American was waved on through.

Later, stupidity would have proven more expensive, had it not been for Galina Godunova. I had hoped to visit Iran after Russia, but my visa had still not arrived when I left Boston. Repeated visits to the Iranian consulate in Astrakhan proved fruitless. Finally I gave up and went to an Aeroflot office to change my next destination from Tehran to Baku, Azerbaijan, a change my travel agent had told me could be made without penalty in Russia. The agent at Aeroflot assured me there was no penalty but said there would be an $80 processing fee. Since I was used to being robbed this way by American air carriers, I paid without complaint.

Galina, however, was among those Russians infuriated by the routine graft of daily life in their country. When I happened to mention that fee to her and Katya, I could see Galina's eyes light up in anger behind her glasses. There were neither penalties nor processing fees, she said, but more than enough corruption. The next day Katya and I had to jog to keep up with her as she marched in her wrath to that Aeroflot office. She identified herself to the agent who had handled my ticketing as an interested party, an *Izvestia* reporter, and head of the city's Bureau of Foreign Relations. The agent reviewed her guidelines and was embarrassed and apologetic to find herself mistaken about the processing fee. My money was cheerfully refunded. "Russians are afraid of reporters and bureaucrats," Katya whispered to me as we left the office. "My mother is both."

Galina, however, was still angry about the whole episode, and ashamed. On our way to visit an art museum, we took a shortcut through an alleyway that included a two-seater outhouse, its door loose on its hinges and hanging open, its odor coloring the morning air. "Look in there," Galina said, her eyes still flashing, "and you will find the heart of Russia."

If Galina meant that this sort of poaching—$80 here, an available sturgeon there—was so ingrained as to be more a biological process than a moral reckoning, her point could be well taken. For 700 years, whether at the hands of the Mongols, the tsars, or the Communist Party, the Russian people have had their labor, their property, and their lives stolen by their rulers. In such an environment a pirate and warlord such as Stenka Razin becomes a folk hero. So do many lesser dissidents—even petty thieves.

It goes back to resistance to serfdom and the outlaw peasant bands of the early seventeenth century, many of which were swept up into Razin's army. In a world where both the land and those who worked it belonged to the tsar, political resistance and ordinary criminal activity inevitably blended into each other. Over time these bands evolved into the beggars' guilds and thieves' societies of the nineteenth century, organizations that built an underground culture and society called *vorovskoi mir*, Thieves World. Its members neither paid taxes, held regular jobs, nor served in the army. Profits were shared equally out of a communal fund.

Not only did *vorovskoi mir* persist into the Communist era, it in some ways helped define that era. The Bolsheviks modeled the secrecy and discipline of their revolutionary cells after the criminal gangs, sometimes raising money by working in partnership with them. Later, Stalin completed a process set in motion by Lenin: the development of a model of leadership in the Communist Party that paralleled that of a criminal syndicate.

The original thieves and brigands, meanwhile, were swiftly disillusioned by the workers revolution and became as defiant of the Communists as they had been of the tsars. But a sort of détente was achieved: The Communists excused the activities of a small criminal elite at the top of *vorovskoi mir* so long as its members squashed other syndicates and allowed the government some leverage.

During and after World War II, however, Thieves World fractured in two as some of its rank and file set aside their scruples to enlist in the army or work in munitions plants. Those who did not join up branded the patriots as traitors. In the prisons and gulags after the war, a series of brutal reprisals and counter-reprisals were carried out that came to be known as the Scabs' War. The scabs who survived came out of the prisons with the same larcenous instincts, but no loyalty to the old disciplines of *vorovskoi mir*. Over the next few decades, they put on neckties and forged alliances with the party's bureaucrats and businessmen. They went into drug trafficking and bank fraud. They became the financiers of the black market.

According to Soviet dissident Lev Timofeyev, the term "shadow economy" was a misnomer for the Soviet black market. A better term would be "universal." In his book *Russia's Secret Rulers* (1992), he wrote, "In the last decades of the USSR, not a single product has been manufactured and not a single paid service has been performed outside the confines of the black market. [It was] the living blood circulating in a dead organism."

This sort of life support was a testament not only to the initiative of these new brigands, the Red mafiya, but also to the design of the Soviet legal system, in which it was impossible not to break the law, in which ordinary matters of daily life could be carried on only through payoffs of one sort or another. Therefore, dealing with the mafiya became part of the cost of doing business for any enterprise, however innocent, and yet the brigands, by and large, remained folk heroes and role models. Perhaps they worked only for themselves now, but at least they worked in opposition to a Soviet ideology that—through hypocrisy and mass murder—had revealed itself to be even more corrupt.

Gorbachev's perestroika was, in part, a crusade against corruption, a vain attempt to clean up the Soviet economy through ties with Western businesses and corporations. In the 1990s, Yeltsin's Western advisers tragically underestimated the institutionalization of corruption in Russia. And with their chief competitor, the Communist Party, marginalized, the syndicates blossomed and fought, building security forces that outgunned the police, conducting bloody gangland wars in the streets of Moscow. Their bosses strutted into exclusive nightclubs, drove armored Mercedes-Benzes and BMWs with sirens and flashing lights that forced other traffic off the road, and—eating conspicuous amounts of caviar—modeled the most vertiginous heights of the capitalist consumer lifestyle.

They also discovered that with the Communists out of the way, caviar could be bought for next to nothing in the Caspian and sold for a markup of 7,000 or 8,000 percent in the West. That made the sturgeon—in terms of its numbers and the ease with which its eggs could be converted to cash—the single most valuable wildlife resource in the world. The black gold rush was on.

To the east of Astrakhan lie the barren steppes and grasslands of Kalmykia and Dagestan, two of the poorest republics in Russia. As peoples, the Kalmyks and Dagestanis suffered terribly under Stalin, and their farms and pasturelands were ruined by Soviet agricultural policy. When the USSR collapsed, the republics' factories, canneries, and fish hatcheries shut down. Unemployment skyrocketed. Even the lucky ones—

a man, say, who might earn the equivalent of $9 a month driving a trac-
tor on a collective farm—could make twenty times that by selling the roe
of a single sturgeon on the black market. The mafiya syndicates boosted
productivity with the provision of fast boats, satellite navigation systems,
automatic rifles, deck-mounted heavy machine guns, and various degrees
of legal immunity. This was the genesis of a new sort of brigand: the
brakanieri, or buccaneers—professional sturgeon poachers organized into
an estimated 500 armed gangs along the coastline and in the Volga Delta.

Russian law enforcement agencies—fisheries inspectors, police, the
coast guard, and the border guards—have tried to stem the *brakanieri's*
activities, but at great risk. Vladimir Ivanov reported to a Canadian
newspaper that sixteen inspectors were murdered over eighteen months
in 1993 and 1994. In 1995, a trawler-load of contraband sturgeon confiscated by the fisheries police was taken back at gunpoint by Dagestani
police and restored to the poachers. In 1996, there was that apartment
house bombing in Dagestan's coastal city of Kaspiysk, where sixty-eight
died, all border guards or their wives or children. Then in April 2001,
there was that incident in Izberbash, a town south of Kaspiysk, in which
a mob of poachers, using their own wives and children as human shields,
stormed a coast guard station to reclaim confiscated boats and nets. If
poachers are arrested and brought to court, they currently face a maximum of two years in prison, or fines per fish ranging from $44 (sterlet) to
$511 (beluga). Often the cases are dismissed by friendly local judges.

Russian law enforcement has made its own accommodations with the
brakanieri. As Anatoly Babrovsky admitted, they make deals. Salaries in
law enforcement range from $60 to $100 per month, and policemen can
often be persuaded to take bribes in fish, roe, or cash. Also, by law,
agents are required to confiscate any contraband that they find, and
caviar is supposed to be taken to a dealer designated by the government
as a buyer of *konfiskat,* or confiscated caviar. The government sets the
price for that transaction, but the dealer provides a bonus to the officer
for his business and then sells the caviar to a retailer at a 500 percent
markup. The retailer marks it up at least another 100 percent to sell it in
Astrakhan or Moscow. This arrangement ensures that the police and the
government, even when obeying the letter of the law, profit from the il-
licit trade and are thus complicit in it.

In Mats Engstrom's old stomping grounds of Kharabovsk this winter, for the first time in several centuries caviar was fed to pigs. Five and a half tons, to be exact, were publicly fed to swine at a local farm to counter allegations that police were illegally trafficking in *konfiskat*. Reporters could not help noting, though, that it was less valuable red caviar, from salmon, and had spoiled anyway.

In the Caspian or Kharabovsk or anywhere else, profit is maximized if the government is cut out of the transaction, but of course the government itself has a long tradition of shady caviar dealings. The Soviet Union's Ministry of Fisheries was famously corrupt, conducting a number of gigantic scams, and Russia's present ministry is regarded with equal suspicion. Even the academy, allegedly, is not immune: A scientist at KaspNIRKh once told Vadim Birstein that the institute, which since 1991 had fought so hard to bring money and attention to the plight of the sturgeon, had hidden a small caviar-processing plant among its laboratories.

The Chechens are part of the malaise now, too. Groups that formed to protect Chechen businesses from mafiya control soon became mafiya-like themselves, and Chechnya—a mountainous geographic wedge between Kalmykia and Dagestan—has become as important a transit route as Moscow for contraband caviar on its way out of the country. If the Muslim republic wins its independence, it will also control a portion of the oil pipeline that runs from the Caspian to the Russian port of Novorossiysk on the Black Sea.

In places such as Ikranoye, Kaspiysk, and Izberbash, fishermen never had an opportunity to make much money off the sturgeon: First the fish belonged to the tsar, and then they belonged to the Communist elite. They knew as well as scientists at KaspNIRKh and Bios that the fish were being taken too fast and too young. But in a world of thieves, they saw themselves as powerless to stop that from happening, and as having their only chance now, a brief one, to derive any profit from the sturgeon. And in the republics outside Astrakhan, there is little love for the uniformed Russians who were saying—once again—that a fisherman had better hand over that fish.

Scarcity will be no defense. The last beluga will be the most valuable, a tragic and iconic nexus of history, perversity, and desire. I may have seen it already, or a premonition of it, in "Black Gold," one of *LIFE* magazine's last photo essays, which appeared in February 2000: a gutted, bloody carcass, floating on its side and left to rot in water that draws peacefully away to the wooded horizon of the Volga Delta, and from there to the heart of Russia.

iii.

The channel grew even closer, so that the nodding heads of more low-lying reeds whipped against our faces, and the cormorants in even greater numbers swarmed into the sky. The slough seemed to be a cul-de-sac, ending in a drowned tangle of brush, but at the last second Nikolai heeled the boat to starboard and we broke free again into a much larger and wider portion of the river. The clamor of the birds faded behind us as Nikolai bore toward the farther bank of this water.

We passed a fisheries police post, a low gray building nestled among trees, a 20-foot motorboat tied to a dock. Then a series of tonyas, one after another, but widely spaced along the riverbank. "Fishing collectives," Nikolai shouted over the motor. "They pool their equipment and their labor and fish for one of the licensed quota holders, if they take sturgeon." He gestured back to the police post, adding, "It's easy to observe crime in this area. Everybody's boat is well known."

The tonyas were cleared areas of the riverbank, some with trucks or cars, others accessible only by boat, all fringed at the shoreline by skiffs, motorboats, barges, or houseboats. At one a group of eight men uniformed in yellow oilskins waded in the Volga, drawing a circular net tighter and tighter, raising a silvery swarm of small fish, maybe Caspian shad, to the surface. At another, a diesel-powered net reel puffed and strained from the stern of a barge to retrieve a much larger net from the river.

We passed a collection of low-slung roofs that Nikolai said was a sturgeon farm, like Bios, and then, steaming in the opposite direction up the river, one of KaspNIRKh's research vessels: white, well-scrubbed, and jaunty, about the size of a small tug, with the crisp white, blue, and red bars of the Russian Federation flag snapping in the breeze.

The river broadened, so wide at this point that the other bank was just a fringe of green across the horizon. Anatoly said that we would be seeing banks of lotuses in some places were it not for the high water. We swept by a nesting pair of mute swans at the mouth of one slough and then watched a ragged skein of gray geese pass overhead, bearing north. But Nikolai headed west, turning suddenly into a narrow slough that shrank down almost as tightly as the previous reed-fringed bottleneck. Again we burst into open water, into a parallel strand of the river that was wide, but only a fraction of the width of that other channel. Along its western bank stretched chain-links of soft low hills, partially wooded; along its eastern side, a mile-long swath of open grass and sandy beach, part of which was populated by the largest of the tonyas I had seen that day. Nikolai slowed, allowing the motorboat to drift muttering into the midst of the camp, killing the motor as its keel struck sand.

We splashed in our rubber boots to the shore, joining a group of twenty men as they watched another motorboat move in a slow arc three-fourths of a mile or so out in the river. Scores of white plastic floats curved in a row from the shoreline to the stern of the motorboat. Beyond these an aging fish tender, its wheelhouse spiked by radar and communications antennas, lay at anchor against the opposite hills.

These were all men well-known to Nikolai and Anatoly. They ranged in age from twenty to seventy, and there was nothing uniform in their dress: woolen watch caps, cotton baseball caps, tweed hats, oil-skins of various shades and states of repair, patched-up sweaters, grease-stained jerseys. Their faces were as creased and brown as wallets, their palms as hard as Formica. They laughed and shook hands with the off-duty policemen, and then with me. They preferred not to give their names, preferred also not to be visible in any pictures that I took with my camera, though they said there were surveillance cameras anyway in the tender offshore, which bought their fish from them. Why, then, were they shy of photographs as they hauled their net? "There might be red fish," an old man said simply.

"Red fish" is the generic term, in Russian, for sturgeon, though there is nothing literally red about any of the Caspian species. I think it has more to do with all the meaning bundled with *krasnaya* (red) in Russian. The color is thought to bring good luck, and *krasnaya* also means "beautiful." So to be lovely, as a sturgeon is to a Volga fisherman, is also to be red. I wondered if, in murky water, the fish might also give off that ruddy glow described by Gary Ninneman in Winnebago's lake sturgeon. One sees it sometimes, said another fisherman.

This water was murky, the color of wet sand, darkening to a shade of scrubbed denim blue near the tender. A series of double-ended wooden skiffs, long and gracefully narrow, were tied end to end along the beach. These served as fish bins, and their bottoms were layered in the fish taken from previous sets of the net. There were perhaps 2,000 pounds of bream: broad, silvery, hump-backed fish, 12 to 18 inches long, 3 or 4 pounds each, the little staring heads attached like an afterthought to the fleshy lumps of the bodies. Littered across these, or piled heavily at one end of a skiff or another, were several dozen big carp, 25 to 50 pounds. Anatoly stood in one skiff and grunted to lift one in each hand by the gill plate. The scales on the biggest fish were the size and shape and, on the upper body, even the color of tortoise shell guitar picks, one overlaying two others in a chain-mail pattern from the gills to the tail, lightening to pearl on the belly. The dorsal fin was low but long, lending one touch of aerodynamic elegance to an otherwise fat and stocky fish.

There were no sturgeons so far. The old man who told me there might be red fish surveyed the catch with obvious disappointment and said that these were the worst of times. "I have been fishing since I was twelve years old," he said. "I am seventy-one now. The fish are fewer now, and fewer than there were in the '90s. The red fish numbers are the worst of all. We only make enough money for food."

He spat on the sand, letting his eyes roam to the opposite hills, when I asked him about the impact of poaching. "Poaching?" he said finally. "I'm not connected with poaching."

Another fisherman told me that the net they used was 1 kilometer long and 12 meters deep. Each spring the bottom had to be prepared, smoothed by a steamboat trailing a sort of plow, before they could start fishing. Then they worked through the spring, until fishing was halted in June, setting their net for 90 minutes at a time and hauling ten times during the course of a day. "We can catch as much as 20 tons of fish with one set," he smiled. "We can fill one of those skiffs ten times over, but not so far this year."

By then the motorboat had dragged the far end of the net back to the shore, and many of the other fishermen were in the water, kicking up mud and wrestling the float-line into a closed noose that they gradually cinched tighter. A squalling school of bream boiled out of the silt, their flanks flashing like coins in the sun. These were seized one by one and tossed spinning into the narrow skiffs.

I moved closer and saw that beneath the bream there were red fish in the net. I could see them only in coiling glimpses, representatives of a whole different kingdom from the bream, creatures that might have been serpents or dragons: a leathery patch of armored skin here, then the flicking tip of a scimitar tail elsewhere, or a snout nearly as long and sharp as a unicorn's horn. The bream were cleared away, layer by layer, until finally the monsters were revealed in the sun and silt and foam. They were stellate sturgeons, about a dozen of them, their pink scutes flashing like neon lights down their flanks, their Pinocchio snouts making their slender bodies look all the more serpentine.

Later, we would take one of these fish to a sheltered slough somewhere in this maze of reed and water, where Nikolai kept a houseboat. The overhanging willows moved gently in the breeze, as did bunches of vobla tied to the eaves of the boat. Nikolai boiled water over a stove fashioned from a 55-gallon oil drum, butchered his sturgeon, obtained through some sort of transaction at the fish camp, and prepared *ukha,* the famous fish-and-potato soup of tonya fishermen. We ate at a table spread with fresh radishes, cucumbers, and tomatoes and thick-sliced bread spread with homemade currant jelly or crocus-blossom honey. The soup was savory and filling, the meat as sweet as butter. We drank tall mugs of beer and shot-glasses of vodka, and we shared toasts, the last of which was to the health of the Caspian Sea.

Anatoly kept silent, letting Nikolai have his say, while his friend complained that the government was the biggest poacher on the Caspian, that scientists once again were parroting whatever the government wanted them to say, that the disasters to come with Lukoil's development of the north Caspian reserves would be conveniently blamed on natural forces, that the sturgeons would be lucky to last five more years. "But it is normal for government to lack honesty with its people," he said. "And it is always the same—common people are not heard. Only those with money have a voice."

Outside, voices filled the air: a symphonic chorus of mating frogs and nesting birds. Nikolai smiled and poured himself more beer. "But here there are only natural sounds," he sighed. "Here you can eat fish."

We would return to Astrakhan that night, where the Godunovas would put me up in their two-room apartment before my flight to Baku the next day. On the television news there were ghastly film clips taken during a Victory Day celebration the day before in Kaspiysk. A bomb, stuffed with bolts and nails and hidden in roadside bushes, had detonated as a military brass band passed by. Thirty-four died, musicians and spectators, among them twelve children. The camera lingered at the blood-streaked body of a little girl in a jumper and dark ringlets, a stuffed animal at her side. Several feet away a trumpet lay on the pavement. Katya and Galina and I watched in horror. Finally tears fell down Galina's cheeks.

But for a moment at the tonya, that history, and all history, was held in abeyance. The fishermen paused for just an instant, and even the movements of the sturgeons and remaining bream seemed for just that second to have been arrested. Then a pelican—one of the Caspian's white-feathered Dalmatian pelicans—fell spiraling into the river, pursuing a fish, its breast striking the water with a report like a gunshot. At that the fishermen and their quarry were in motion again, the floats bunching up and the stellates rolling about in all their red and fatal beauty. History moved forward as well, even there, where we could eat fish.

~ 12 ~

The Blood of the Earth

i.

Increasingly, there were alternatives. A product called Alexei's Caviar-Like was made from fish fats, vegetable fats, salt, water, and sundry preservatives and stabilizers. Unlike the genuine article, this caviar was kosher, but available only in Israel.

At the Novo-Petrovsky poultry farm near Moscow, a caviar substitute was made from chicken eggs. Technicians mixed the eggs with sunflower oil, salt, fish essence, and Indian tea. The mixture went into a machine that rendered the stuff into droplets that were then deep-fried in oil. The droplets emerged as shiny black pearls. "It looks just like the real thing," enthused a BBC reporter in 2000, "and tastes remarkably similar."

And out of California, from a Glendale-based company called Royal Caviar, comes Kaviar, made from soybeans. "The tiny black and gray beads glistening invitingly atop squares of toast could fool the eye—but the price tag would not trick any true lover of caviar," wrote Florence Fabricant in a July 18, 2001, *New York Times* article. Nor would the taste, she said, but it was better than the traditional cosmetic substitute, dyed black lumpfish roe.

Then there were those who don't desire caviar at all, or who at least conceive of the milk of wonder in terms of something else: a solution to a mystery, maybe, or else another sort of aphrodisiac for which no cosmetic substitute exists: boundless wealth, or unbridled power, or even just fuel for an SUV or a war machine.

For Grigory Palatnikov and Arif Mekhtiev, senior scientists at the Azerbaijan Institute of Physiology, the wonder was in the mystery. We sat in a conference room there on a late weekday afternoon. Dr. Palatnikov was a small, frail man whose eyebrows hung like rain clouds over his eyes. These, together with his glasses sagging to the tip of his nose, gave him a mournful aspect. Dr. Mekhtiev, in a crisp gray business suit, was as efficient in his bearing as Palatnikov was elegiac. But they spoke virtually as one, in a conversation that required hardly any prompting from me.

The first of the Soviet Union's modern hatcheries, those great factories that had reversed the decline of the sturgeon, had been built on Azerbaijan's Kura River as early as 1954, they said. Subsequently fishermen were required to deliver a certain number of broodstock to the hatcheries during a narrowly defined fishing season each spring. There was no thought of drilling into the sea floor for oil, at least not in the north Caspian, and seismic charges used to map undersea oil deposits were prohibited for the sake of the sturgeons. Now the Kura hatcheries were still running, but they were old-fashioned and underfunded. And there was little chance they would be renovated. The World Bank had approved a $9 million loan for a new hatchery. But that was five years ago, and still the hatchery existed only in blueprints. "I think they spend the money instead on presentations and conferences," said Palatnikov.

The Kura itself had silted up. Few sturgeon could get in through the mouth, and those that did wouldn't spawn because the speed of the current was inadequate. The rest piled up in front of the mud and were easy prey for poachers, who pretended to be catching other fish. The poachers took any sturgeon, male or female, adult or juvenile, that they found. Meanwhile, the pneumatic cannons of the oil prospectors were discharged without respite in the shallow waters where sturgeon feed. The repeated shocks, the two scientists said, inflict skeletal damage on a fish whose cartilaginous frame is more delicate than that of bony fish.

The prospecting has led to drilling, and the oil companies—British Petroleum, foremost among them—have convinced the Azerbaijani government that their work is clean, that the mud and sludge brought up by the drills could be harmlessly dumped in the sea. "But as all the studies prove," Palatnikov objected, "there are no harmless substances associated with petroleum extraction." Mekhtiev recited a catalog of the pathogens that appeared with disheartening frequency in the brains, livers, gills, and muscles of sturgeons collected during a Caspian Environment Programme survey the previous winter.

Outside, the traffic raced in crisscrossing bumper-car patterns through the wide, pot-holed avenues of Baku. Over the weekend I had walked many of them, starting with a lap around the crumbling stone parapets at its heart, walls that 600 years ago had contained the entirety of a city since grown to 2 million. Today the living remains of the Persian city that Tsar Alexander conquered in 1806—the scattered mosques and minarets, the flat-roofed houses of sun-baked clay bricks—mingled with brooding Stalinist office buildings and cookie-cutter Soviet apartment blocks. Signs were in Russian or Azeri or both; their letters Latin, or Cryllic, or Arabic, or any two of the three. Satellite dishes sprouted like mushrooms on windowsills, railings, and rooftops.

Saturday night I had dinner with a group of men from the Institute for Social Action and Renewal (ISAR) in Eurasia, a nongovernmental organization (NGO) working for environmental protection and political reform. We ate at Esfane, a restaurant in the heart of the city, sharing shots of vodka and delicious kabobs of lamb and sturgeon in a dark pomegranate sauce, talking about books and films and American jazz.

Then I joined Ibrahim Abdulrahimov, a member of ISAR, at his apartment for a showing of the Andrei Tarkovsky science-fiction film *Solaris* on his videocassette recorder. After the film, Herbie Hancock played in the background as Ibrahim assured me that no one ate caviar in Azerbaijan now except the very rich. "It is too expensive," he said, explaining that the delicacy cost the equivalent of $30 a kilo in Azeri *manat*, for most people an average monthly wage.

Food was cheap in Baku by Western standards, but not by Azeri reckoning. At least it was there, and for sale, along with a wondrous array of electronic goods and pirated CDs and DVDs. The journalist Thomas Goltz was in Azerbaijan in 1991, just after the collapse of the ruble, and found himself a rich man with a few dollars in his pocket. "The sad truth, though, was that there was nothing to buy," he wrote in *Azerbaijan*

Diary (1998). "The exception was caviar. We lived on the stuff, often going through a kilogram a week. It was much easier to get than the condiments that go with it—like butter, and sometimes bread."

Goltz said the name "Azerbaijan" is a distortion of a Greek name given the region during its brief rule by the successors of Alexander the Great. A better source, to my ears, is *azar*, the Azeri word for "fire." The Apsheron Peninsula's fountains of oil and flaming jets, even when they were of more religious interest than economic, illuminate the whole of Azeri history: a land of great natural resources, the lost Eden where apples, grapes, cherries, and maybe also horses were first domesticated, possessing the best harbor on the Caspian as well, but no natural defenses. Hence its violent pageant of conquering armies: the Medes, the Persians, the Greeks, the Romans, the Arabs, the Turks, the Mongols, the Turkmens, the Persians again, and finally the Russians.

Independence from the Soviet Union had not brought peace. The checkerboard boundary lines drawn by Stalin between Muslim Azerbaijan and the Soviet republic of Armenia, which was Orthodox Christian, set a bomb ticking that in 1991 exploded into outright war with an independent Armenia. Since then a million ethnic Azeris had been displaced by a Russian-supplied Armenian military occupying a fifth of Azerbaijan. A 1993 military coup ended in the return to power of Heidar Aliyev, a former KGB officer and Politburo member. For nearly twenty years, Aliyev had ruled Azerbaijan as the first secretary of its Communist Party until fired from his post by Gorbachev for corruption. After Aliyev's return an Azeri counteroffensive brought the war to an unresolved stalemate and cease-fire. Now it festered like a tumor in the nation's belly and made Western investors nervous.

In 1994, a source identified only as a representative of a major Western oil company spoke to the *New York Times* about its negotiations first with Azerbaijan's democratically elected president, and then the Aliyev government. "We are in the business of producing and selling oil for profit," he said in the June 2 issue. "I would like to conclude these agreements this century. Sometimes I wonder why we are here. Then I remember the Caspian; it is more than a gold mine. So we will wait as long as we have to. Believe me, it will be worth the wait."

They didn't have to wait long after all. Over the next three years, as the war with Armenia cooled off, a file-cabinet of lucrative contracts were signed between the Aliyev government and what Goltz described as "a veritable alphabet soup of oil companies." To Palatnikov and Mekhtiev, the contracts spelled doom for the sturgeon. "If the sturgeon are gone," said Palatnikov, "they will leave an empty space not just in the ecology of the Caspian, but of the entire world. This is an organism that has no natural enemies besides man, that emerged in its modern form during the Jurassic, and has reached the present practically un-changed. And they possess a unique genetic device. Most flora and fauna are diploid, which means that they have a matched pair of each chromosome. But sturgeons are polyploid. Their chromosomes come in matched sets of four, eight, or even sixteen. That is one reason why it is difficult to tell one species from another through normal genetic testing procedures. But it may also be a key to their remarkable adaptability and longevity."

Mekhtiev suspected the fish to hold a key to the developmental links between all that eventually descended from fish. "Research shows," he added, "that in a number of different parameters—its embriological de-velopment, physiological as well, and the morphology of the brain, for example—the sturgeon differs greatly from sharks, skates, and from bony animals. In some parameters it is closer to reptiles, in some to am-phibians, and in fact Linnaeus at one point thought that sturgeons were amphibians. But in all respects the sturgeon is closer to the main trunk of evolution than the rest of the fish, and so you see it is not just an object of consumption—it is an irreplaceable clue to the mysteries of evolution."

I was grateful for the help of my translator, Leyla Gamidova, who was good with the technical language of this discussion. Tall and sturdy and blonde, an articulate and opinionated ethnic Russian, Leyla was attached not to the institute but to a private agency offering translators for visitors. She had picked me up at the Hotel Azerbaijan in her flimsy Volga sedan and then taken me at full throttle through the chaotic streets of Baku. Other cars shot by our windows like hazards in a video game as she told me how a recent fender-bender had cost her months in court and much of her savings. When we arrived at the institute, the only parking space available was just a few feet bigger than her car, and on a steep downhill pitch. Leyla asked me to park the car for her, and then we hastened into the institute.

After the interview I arranged with Palatnikov for visits to a pair of hatcheries on the Kura, and then both scientists accompanied Leyla and me out to the street. I asked them about the problem of dividing the sea and its resources, an ulcerous issue that the trans-Caspian nations had been arguing about since 1991. They said that at this point Iran and Turkmenistan were united in opposing the wishes of the other three nations. "The main problem is oil," said Palatnikov, "but sturgeon is an obstacle too. Recently the Iranians refused to sign an agreement on quotas for caviar production. They said that since their hatcheries were producing more fish, they should have a larger quota."

"Is that true?" I wondered.

"I visited one of their plants, and they are indeed working very intensively," he conceded. "And they deal very severely with poachers. Boats are shot at by the coastal sentinels without warning. On the first offense, one hand is cut off."

"They are very cruel," Mekhtiev said.

The two men left on foot, and Leyla looked skeptically at the forward pitch of her car in relation to the Volkswagen parked snugly in front of it. When she asked me to back it out of the space, I cautioned that I wasn't familiar with the feel of the clutch on the Volga. With that, she went to stand between the two bumpers, offering her own thighs as shock absorbers. "You might get hurt," I told her.

"I would rather get hurt."

That told me as much as I needed to know about the justice system in Azerbaijan and the risks I was assuming myself. Nonetheless, I persuaded her to stand somewhere else and managed to back the Volga out of the space without injury or mishap. Leyla resumed the wheel, and we enjoyed another hell-for-leather passage back to the hotel. Along one stretch of the road, a group of four or five uniformed policemen were flagging occasional cars to the curb. "They are all corrupt," Leyla explained. "You either pay them a large bribe or you pay the government an even larger fine."

The Hotel Azerbaijan was an old-fashioned Soviet luxury high-rise gone shabby: nicked paint, spotted rugs, sticky shower panels. A wide plaza in front of the hotel would have been handsome had there been any water for the fountain and had the pavement been repaired. Adjacent to the hotel was Baku's federal ministry building, seven stories tall and a city block long, a vast chimerical structure even bigger than the Hotel Moskva. With its Greek columns, Islamic arches, spiked medieval battlements, state-penitentiary windows, and Aztec-temple outer staircases, it was the most monstrously Kafkaesque piece of architecture I had ever seen.

From my balcony the Caspian Sea looked as it did in a mural in the hotel lobby: a pristine and sun-kissed Mediterranean green. From the tree-lined promenade that extends along the waterfront, an observer has a wider field of vision: a fleet of oil tankers tied up at wharves to the north, and the skeletal frames of old drilling rigs poking up like stubbled wheat over the horizon to the south. If you look down from the seawall, you see that the water is fouled with trash and a surface film of oil. The oil lifts and drops with the motion of the water, catching the light of the sun and reflecting the same spectrum of unearthly colors as in that strange and sentient chemical sea that covered the surface of the alien planet in *Solaris*.

ii.

Marco Polo reported that the Apsheron Peninsula's fountains of oil produced a substance that wasn't good to eat, alas, but was fine for burning and useful for cleaning the mange of camels. Later the Persians scooped petroleum from shallow wells on the peninsula and started something of a modest trade in the stuff.

The industrial use of petroleum, according to food historian Felipe Fernández-Armesto, grew from a crisis in fat supplies in the burgeoning cities of Europe in the 1800s. Colonial ventures were launched for supplies of palm oil, fleets were launched to obtain whale oil, and fossil fuels were skimmed out of the ground in Ontario in 1858, then pumped out of the Pennsylvania earth in 1859. Fossil fuel resisted all efforts to make it edible, but the Americans found another use for it. In displacing water and steam as the fuel of choice for the Industrial Revolution, refined petroleum became almost overnight a global commodity, an elixir of power, and a species of black gold, long before caviar laid its claim to that phrase in the West.

In the 1870s, the Russian government opened the Apsheron Peninsula to private fuel speculators, among them Sweden's Nobel brothers and France's Rothschilds. Within a decade, 200 refineries were at work in Baku, where a new industrial suburb came to be known as Black Town. The refineries tapped not only wells but inexhaustible fountains, gushers with names like Wet Nurse and the Devil's Bazaar. A gusher called Friendship poured forth 43,000 barrels a day, most of it wasted, for five months.

Caspian oil flowed throughout the Russian Empire, nearly matching the production of the United States and challenging John D. Rockefeller's Standard Oil Company for global dominance. But over the next three decades, Baku—one of the most corrupt and poorly run corners of the Russian Empire—also became a hotbed of revolutionary activity. Lenin's newspaper *Iskra* was printed there and then secretly distributed along petroleum supply routes. The most energetic socialist organizer in Baku was a young Georgian named Joseph Djugashvili, whose first alias was Koba, his next Joseph Stalin. A 1903 oil workers' strike in Baku was the match that ignited a wave of labor strife across Russia and the nation's first general strike.

For lack of investment, Baku's wells and refineries declined and went stagnant, but the Caspian remained the most important source of oil on Europe's periphery, and in 1917 Kaiser Wilhelm's Germany signed a peace treaty with the new Bolshevik government in Moscow that promised Caspian oil to the Germans if only they would rein in their allies the Turks, who were advancing on Baku. But the Turks came anyway, laying siege to the city and capturing some of the outlying oil fields. In 1918, just as the Germans were at the gasping end of their oil reserves, a small force of British troops made its way to Baku through Persia. They held the city for only a month before withdrawing, but that was long enough for Germany to despair of any oil and sue for peace. After the armistice in Europe, the director of France's Comité Général du Pétrole boasted that oil, "the blood of the earth," had also been "the blood of victory" in the Great War.

Hitler smelled that blood in World War II and gambled all he had on seizing Baku. His refusal to divert troops from the Caucasus sealed the fate of the Sixth Army at Stalingrad. Then he tried from the other direction, ordering Field Marshall Erwin Rommel to drive his Afrika Korps through Egypt, Palestine, Iraq, Iran, and then to Baku, but the Afrika Korps's defeat at El Alamein in 1942—a defeat largely the result of Rommel's inadequate fuel supplies—doomed that ploy as well. Hitler never got the Baku oil. Instead the Wehrmacht ran dry, and the war was lost.

In subsequent decades, this decisive prize of history's two greatest armed conflicts faded in importance. Production fell across the peninsula, and efforts to meet unrealistic production quotas resulted in countless spills and leaks. By 1991, the Soviet Union was the world's largest oil producer and its second leading exporter, trailing only Saudi Arabia, but that was on the strength of its Siberian fields. Baku and its deteriorating land-based wells contributed only 3 percent of Soviet oil supplies. Although the Soviets ran some offshore facilities near the coast of the peninsula, they were not much tempted to drill into the north Caspian seafloor. Oil was cheaper to get in Siberia, and the north Caspian— where oil deposits are under high pressure and mixed with poisonous hydrogen sulfide gas—presented difficult technical challenges. An accident there would be a conspicuous ecological catastrophe, and the Soviets preferred not to gamble with the sturgeon and its feeding grounds.

But in 1991, as the USSR imploded, surveys of the Caspian's offshore fields reported reserves of as much as 200 billion barrels of crude, matching the combined proven reserves of Iran and Iraq. For the leaders of the poor and newly independent nations of the Caspian—especially one such as Azerbaijan, which for a century had been paid only a pittance for its oil by Moscow, and which needed friends in the West to escape the shadow of Russia—that temptation was rather too much.

As it has been for Kazakhstan, Turkmenistan, and even oil-rich Russia. In April 2002, the heads of state of the five Caspian nations met in Ashgabat, the capital of Turkmenistan. They meant only to define the general principles of the division of the sea's resources, and also set standards of environmental protection. The host was Turkmenistan's former Communist Party chief, Saparmurat Niyazov, who prefers to be called Turkmenbashi, "Leader of the Turkmens," and who has made himself the center of a bizarre personality cult in the most isolated and authoritarian of the former Soviet states.

The summit fell apart, doomed by such bones of contention as the south-central Caspian's Alov oil field, claimed at once by Azerbaijan, Iran, and Turkmenistan. It was there that an Iranian warship had threatened Azerbaijani research vessels the previous summer. Since then, Heidar Aliyev has bought a pair of American-made warships and welcomed Turkish fighter jets into Azerbaijan. In terms of Baku's old gushers, it all had to do more with the Devil's Bazaar than with Friendship, and in the summit's aftermath, the angry Turkmenbashi warned, "The Caspian reeks of blood."

iii.

I remembered that tin of Zukovsky Caviar, a movie prop, that I saw in Ed Grace's office in Valley Stream, New York. In the James Bond film *The World Is Not Enough*, Valentin Zukovsky finds himself stretched thin by all the shady enterprises he runs in Baku. "First the casino, and now the caviar factory," he sighs to Bond as he rushes off to the latter. "I'm a slave to the free-market economy."

I wouldn't care to eat Zukovsky Caviar, since in the movie the finished product is stored in unrefrigerated vats recessed into the floor of the factory. Zukovsky falls into one of these vats during a typically apocalyptic assassination attempt against Bond. The caviar is very soupy, looking more like crude oil than caviar, and Zukovsky nearly drowns in it before being rescued by Bond.

Even in a James Bond film, with opening credits that unfold before the motions of a nude woman slathered in crude, and with a beautiful oil baron named Electra King as Bond's love-interest and antagonist, Hollywood to some degree imitates life. The film overstates the importance of the Caspian in energy terms, claiming that the West will depend entirely on its oil for the next fifty years, but it is on the mark about the still ticklish problem of how to get it out of the Caspian and into the gas tanks of the West. The film is also right about how easily things blow up.

During the 2002 spawning season, the region exported a little more than a million barrels per day—which was not enough. The Russians run pipelines to Novorossiysk, their port on the Black Sea, but the former Soviet republics have no wish to rely on Russia for their export needs, and greater capacity is needed in any event. In 1997, the Azerbaijan International Oil Consortium (AIOC), an alphabet-soup of oil companies led by British Petroleum, built a pipeline from Baku to

Novorossiysk, and the next year another line from Baku to the Georgian Black Sea port of Supsa. But all this was still not enough capacity for the oil that the sea was expected to produce, and it still left tankers waiting in long and vulnerable lines at the Bosporus.

The proposed solution had been an overland line through Turkey, financed by a coalition of Western investors and lending institutions. A thousand miles long and big enough to carry a million barrels per day by itself, the pipeline would connect Baku to Tblisi, in Georgia, and then drop south to the Turkish port of Ceychan on the Mediterranean. Known as the BTC (Baku-Tblisi-Ceychan) line, the $3 billion project was bitterly opposed by Vladimir Putin, who wanted Russia to be the West's sole alternative to Middle East oil. But finally he bowed to the inevitable and elected to join the project, approving the Russian company Lukoil's purchase of a 7.5 percent share.

There is a rosy view that pipelines will promote greater economic and social integration in the region, that while oil may be the death of the sturgeon, it will finally prove to be the blood of peace. But even the big-ticket BTC line was at best a thin plaster over underlying tensions, at worst an additional blister. Turkey had cemented its BTC-driven economic alliance with Georgia and Azerbaijan with a military pact as well, much to the unease of every other nation in the Caucasus. Armenia, the most uneasy of all, had renewed its own alliance with Russia, which believed the Georgians to be aiding the Chechen rebels. The Iranians, meanwhile, were angry that the United States blocked even a discussion of a short supply route through Iran to the Persian Gulf, and that the BTC project had been set in motion ahead of any settlement about property rights to the seafloor. There were stirrings of Islamic militancy throughout the Caucasus and central Asia, and Tehran was widely suspected of fanning those flames.

There was another big spoon stirring the pot as well. The Chinese were at the forefront of an Asian demand for oil that was expected to grow eight times faster than Europe's over the next decade, and they had invested $6 billion in Kazakhstan's oil fields. They had also proposed building several pipelines that would run east, not west, from Kazakhstan. This occasioned heart palpitations among investors in the BTC project, since that line would need at least 100,000 barrels per day from that country to be profitable.

The world's lust for oil and the crashing arrival of the free-market economy had at least made formerly inconsequential places such as Azerbaijan and Kazakhstan into big spoons themselves. The Azeri people could see it coming. Theirs was the poorest country in Europe during the mid–1990s, a place where unemployment was epidemic and 85 percent of its people lived below the official poverty line. But suddenly the Azeris had their own gold mine—"more than a gold mine"—and friends in the West who were prosperous, who were democratic, who ate caviar, and who were writing outrageously big checks to their government. New buildings were going up. A Mercedes dealership opened; McDonald's arrived. Just as Electra King would promise to James Bond, if only he were on her side, the world was to be theirs.

iv.

Aytan, our driver, wondered if I ate chicken legs. A balding, easygoing man, he was also the owner of a well-kept Kia Sportage SUV. "I have a friend in Los Angeles, a Jew, who says that eating chicken legs makes you age faster," he said, swerving around a pothole. "So like other Americans, he only eats chicken breasts, never the legs. Then the American companies bring their chicken legs over here to sell."

I rode shotgun in the Kia, aging faster from the road conditions than from the effects of chicken legs. Dr. Palatnikov and Leyla bounced about in the rear seats. We were en route to the Kura River and its two functioning sturgeon hatcheries. Leaving Baku early in the morning, we had ridden past a wide and dirty sink of old Soviet oil derricks and empty drill frames along the city's south shore. The Caspian washed over the feet of the outermost derricks and surrounded some others in salt ponds. This was the result of a mysterious rise in the sea level, some 8 feet between 1978 and 1994. Neither Palatnikov nor anyone else could explain this or prior fluctuations, since they don't correlate with changes in rates of evaporation or river flow. Tectonic shifts beneath the sea may have something to do with it, but in Baku the chicken-leg rumor mill had another explanation: that in the 1990s the Russians had opened dams on the Volga expressly to flood Azerbaijan's coastal oil installations.

We passed a 10-foot section of wall that hugged the road, the heads of idle oil derricks rearing above the stone in a sort of Jurassic Park effect; then the neat white buildings and red tile roofs of British Petroleum's main office complex; then the walled-off beach-side home of the American consul, with offshore oil platforms squatting on the horizon like an approaching fleet of alien spaceships. As the city yielded to the countryside, there was entropy: dilapidated roadside cafés and stores; half-constructed buildings with no one working on them; randomly located piles of concrete blocks or clay bricks; railroad tracks with idle freight and tanker cars. It all had the naked, unfinished aspect of a construction site where everyone had quit and gone home in the middle of the day, a perestroika monument on a universal scale.

Ten miles outside the city, a wide, sage-colored plain opened to the west, ending abruptly at the dry and sun-streaked parapets of the Gobestan Mountains, a spur of the Caucasus. We stopped at an irrigation canal to talk to a group of leather-faced fishermen in worn sweaters and pants. They were fishing for carp, but not doing well with the spring flooding. There would be more carp later in the summer, they believed. A water snake swam down the center of the canal as we talked, its length fluttering in the brown water like a ribbon in the wind. I bought one of their fish for 12,000 manat, or about $3, as a gift for Leyla.

Leyla's modesty about her driving skills didn't prevent her from asking to relieve Aytan at the wheel of the Kia and then charging ahead at 80 miles per hour. Hitchhikers and herds of sheep were neatly grazed, and only at the last instant did she veer around a ram rooted in the middle of our lane. "He wanted to fight," she laughed. Only when she savagely ground the Kia's gears did Aytan insist on resuming his place.

By mid-morning we were near Kursangi, in the floodplain of the Kura, where ramshackle houses nestled amid neat orchards and gardens. Half an hour later we reached the Kura itself, the river dividing the Greater Caucasus in Azerbaijan's northeast from the Lesser Caucasus of the southwest. It was a sluggish half-mile width of muddy water, framed by shrub-covered levees on either side. We crossed a bridge and took a road that ran west with the river. A pond heron in bridal white flushed from the grass along the road and soared over farmlands greening with young cotton. Flocks of sheep stared from behind wire fences as schoolchildren walked home for lunch, the boys in sport jackets, the girls in ankle-length dresses. "This is very good farmland," said Palatnikov. "The soil is so fertile, if you just shove a stick into the ground, it will grow. But the people are lazy."

"Well, they prefer to fish," Leyla said.

Palatnikov told me that the Mingäevir Hydroelectric Plant was some distance upriver. For the sake of that plant, the Kura was dammed even before the Volga, and that was why the Soviets built the first of their hatcheries here. We crossed the Kura again, skirting its flooded banks, and soon reached a dirt road barely distinguishable from the dry salt marsh, its paste-like mud pocked with cattle prints, that stretched to the levee built along the riverbank.

There was no gate or bright sign to mark the entrance of the Kura Experimental Sturgeon Plant, as there had been at Bios. We drove past the marsh into a complex of buildings sheltered by tall pines, poplars, and rose bushes. The main office had the long and narrow profile, the weathered tile roof and white stucco walls, of a colonial outpost somewhere in Africa. Toward the river newly constructed lengths of tile roof rested on steel poles and slanted over rows of recessed concrete pools or long artificial ponds. Raised pools, 6 meters wide, were unsheltered and unused. Several had been filled with soil and planted with marigolds, which were just blossoming. Beyond these stretched an acre of much larger artificial ponds, framed in concrete, one adjacent to another, like empty building foundations. Those ponds had been drained and left to grow grass. Sunlight moved in dappled patterns across the roofs and neat walkways, while the scents of pine and flowers sweetened the air.

The plant's director, Dr. Rasim Guseynov, sat at his desk amid orderly stacks of papers. His hair was thinning and graying at the temples. We sat with several members of his staff at a conference table drawn lengthwise to his desk, sipping at tea and nibbling hard candies. Guseynov said that his plant was not running at full capacity, that last year it had produced 5.4 million fingerlings but could easily produce more than 7 million. As in Russia, the issues were lack of money and lack of broodstock, but the situation was more desperate here. The Caspian Fish Company, a private enterprise, managed in part by President Aliyev's son Ilham, and the only legal entity for dealing caviar in Azerbaijan, had provided money for roofing to cover the pools and for some equipment repairs, but not nearly enough for a full refurbishment. Nor was the fish company providing enough broodstock: so far this season, only eight stellate sturgeon, a few more Russian, and one beluga, a male.

There was no natural reproduction in the Kura, Guseynov said, and there had been little or none ever since the power station had been built. Nowadays there were very few fish that even came into the river because of silting at its mouth, which had increased with the rise in the Caspian's sea level. "The main channel is blocked," he said, drawing at his cigarette and then folding his hands. "There is a subchannel that is free for shipping, but the sturgeon do not find that. We are working on the problem of opening the main channel, but again, it is a question of government commitment."

Such a question was not raised in Soviet times, nor did it need to be. There was money, there was broodstock, and there was a decent living wage. "There is enough money in our budget for 20 percent raises in salary," Guseynov said, "and the government keeps promising these raises, but they never appear. I am a graduate of a Moscow institute, and I have been here forty-three years. I live here, I have to work here— there is now no other place for me to work. But to be paid such a small amount. . . . " His voice trailed off and he took a long pull at his cigarette. "It was much better in the USSR," he continued. "Everybody could live off their salary."

"They used to add a thirteenth-month salary each year," remarked Palatnikov.

"And a bonus on top of that," Leyla added.

Guseynov took us on a tour of the plant, through the building with the rows of incubator trays, where loaf-shaped containers suspended over the trays filled slowly with piped-in water and then tipped, providing a burst of aerated current to the eggs; then to the operating room, where the eggs were taken from the females. The floor and walls and counters were in an immaculate glazed white tile. A copper pipe for water ran above the counters, with lengths of rubber hose trailing from nipples on the pipe. It had the bare, antiseptic look of an execution chamber, which in fact it was. Palatnikov would tell me later that the plant's methods were outdated, that the staff lacked the expertise to perform cesarean-sections on their broodstock, and that requests for training in such procedures were not funded.

Guseynov showed us the discharge canal, through which twenty-day-old fingerlings swam directly into the Kura, never to return. The river had inched up through the grass at the canal's mouth, and it was only a few inches from swallowing the canal and invading the hatchery. The director said the Kura was 8 to 10 meters deep here and that such an intrusion would be disastrous. Then we went to the ponds beneath the new roofs, where the breeding Russian and stellate sturgeons moved in dim, reticulated shadows beneath the surface.

The lone beluga had a pond to itself. Guseynov had a hatchery worker wade in to corral the beluga into a floating meshed stretcher. It took only a moment for the worker to locate the fish in the shallow water and slide the device under it. The wooden frame floated to the surface, and then so did the beluga in its midst, the fish's dorsal scutes softened to medallions down the lengths of its spine. The beluga was about 6 feet long and estimated by Guseynov to be eighteen years old. It bumped its snout against the frame and then curled to the left and right, unable to turn in either direction. The worker grasped it by the snout and tail, turned it for an instant to expose the mouth, gills, and belly, and then released it from the frame. The great fish burst forward, foaming to the far end of the pond, where it sank back into its solitude.

I considered that its captor felt no less confined and alone, but Guseynov, his eyes trailing after the fish, still had faith in what he did. "Yes, hatcheries like this can sustain the sturgeon, despite the poaching and the oil pollution," he had told us inside. "The current of the Kura extends far into the Caspian, beyond the area of oil development. If the government would support us, we would have no problem increasing the numbers of sturgeons, even under these conditions. It is something that pays for itself. With a minimal investment in a sturgeon plant, one may expect quite large returns. Oil reserves, no matter how large, are eventually used up. But fish are forever, if only you handle them reasonably."

v.

There were no friends of British Petroleum in the Kia. Aytan was sorry that day to be missing a public forum in Baku mounted by BP and several other Western companies. He wanted to be among the many people asking why there were so few Azeris on their payrolls. Leyla mentioned that most of BP's recruiting for Azeri women took place at parties, but then they were certain to be fired if they got pregnant. Palatnikov had done some work for BP, earning $400 per month to carry out an ecological analysis for the firm. But he had been angered to learn that a group of Scottish students assisting him in that project were each being paid $2,500 per month. Nor did BP managers like what they heard from him. Environmental standards suitable for the North Sea, where pollutants are dispersed by oceanic currents, he told them, were not suitable in the Caspian, where they merely accumulate. "Now they bring in their own specialists," Palatnikov concluded. "They do not consult with local experts anymore."

The oil companies have their own complaints in a country where parts might sit for months for lack of enough by way of bribes for officials in charge of transporting them to development sites. Pennzoil was the victim of such a boondoggle in its attempt to build a compressor plant to capture natural gas vented from Oily Rocks, a 48-mile-long city in the sea of abandoned Soviet wells and collapsing platforms. When the parts finally got there, project managers found that the underwater pipes to Baku had never been laid for lack of kickbacks to that set of officials. "Sometimes in my most cynical and gloomy moments," a Pennzoil manager told Thomas Goltz in *Azerbaijan Diary*, "I think that nothing will happen until the existing infrastructure collapses so totally that there is nothing left to steal."

The infrastructure is certainly rotten, but there is still money to steal. At the highest levels, the instrument of choice for accomplishing that is a Production Sharing Agreement (PSA). The first such was signed in 1994 between the Aliyev government and the Azerbaijan International Oil Consortium, the coalition headed by British Petroleum. The PSA granted access to certain oil fields, guaranteed a stable legal and tax framework for the oil companies, and also guaranteed that the terms of the PSA would supersede any present or future laws in Azerbaijan.

The PSA was ratified by the parliament, but its terms remained secret, as have the terms of the twenty-one PSAs ratified since with other companies. Typically the PSAs specify an up-front bonus payment and then additional payments once a certain export level is reached. The secrecy of the agreements makes a truly accurate accounting of Azerbaijan's oil revenues impossible to calculate, but the International Monetary Fund estimates these to be some $1.1 billion from 1996 to 1999. And these would increase: Annual export payments were expected to reach $200 million in 2003 and nearly $1 billion in 2005.

So far, that money had bought a new international airport and a few new buildings in Baku catering to the oilmen and the country's economic elite, but nothing else visible to the public. Despite having a well-educated population, with many native professionals, Azerbaijan is still the poorest country in Europe, a place where the average per capita income is less than half the official poverty line ($89/month), the salaries of teachers and engineers less than a third that amount. One-fourth of the nation's children are malnourished, and two-fifths suffer from anemia. Waterborne diseases have been common because the treatment plants and pipeline networks are steadily deteriorating. According to government estimates, unemployment had held steady at 18 to 19 percent since 1997, but it was almost certainly higher.

Astoundingly enough, Baku suffers regular electric outages in the winter for lack of fuel oil, and elsewhere outages are around-the-clock and throughout the year. Rising world oil prices have made it more profitable for Azerbaijan to sell its oil than to refine it, and the Aliyev government has left the country with not enough oil in its cupboard for its own power plants. Meanwhile, as natural gas continued to vent from Oily Rocks, Azerbaijan imported domestic supplies of that fuel from Turkmenistan. Those imports had just been suspended. Aliyev blamed a budget deficit.

It had always been a dirty business. The rising sea had compounded the sins of the past, flooding not only old Soviet well sites but also coastal sewage plants, utility towers, and communications lines, all of which were adding their chemicals to the Caspian. Now came the oil consortium with a World Bank–approved set of environmental standards called BATNEEC: Best Available Technology Not Entailing Excessive Costs. To Palatnikov and others among the cynical and gloomy, this translated into whatever environmental protections the Western companies found conveniently affordable. In 1998, an Azeri environmental group was funded by BP to help monitor fields southwest of Baku; when the group called attention to a die-off of marine birds around some State Oil Company of Azerbaijan (SOCAR) rigs, the funding ceased. In 2000, an accident at a field in Kazakhstan coincided with massive deaths among Caspian seals. Galina Godunova reported that the eyes of oil-fouled seals dissolved within a few hours.

The oil industry argued that canine distemper was the chief killer of seals that year, but there is no argument that the ecology of the sea is distorted. The jellyfish is considered the pigeon of the seas, an organism that flourishes in marine environments stressed by factors that eliminate other fauna: high water temperatures, excessive nutrients or pollutants, and overfishing, all of which have abetted a sudden infestation by the *Mnemiopsis leidyi* comb jelly. The jellies graze on the zooplankton favored also by such small fish as herring and sprat, which in turn feed the seals. That made the comb jellies likely suspects in the crashing declines of all three species. But the tissues of dead sprat revealed high concentrations of heavy metals and oil products. Sprat were also a crucial prey of beluga. In Astrakhan, harvests for all commercial species were down 30 to 50 percent, prompting authorities there to extend the legal fishing season.

The Caspian Sea, the Champagne region of the caviar industry, has become one of the most polluted water basins on earth, and the United Nations Environmental Program lists 200 species under threat of extinction there. BP has mounted a vigorous public relations campaign stressing safety and trust, and recently it has taken the extraordinary step of publishing its contract payments to the Aliyev government. Yet hardly a week went by that the company wasn't accused of an incident of illegal dumping by one of the region's environmental NGOs. Still, from an environmental perspective, Azeris were glad that it was Western companies doing the bulk of this work, and not SOCAR or the Russians. In the Russian sector, where so much pressurized hydrogen sulfide lurks, Lukoil's zero-tolerance standards touted by Alla Mazhnik at KaspNIRKh were nothing new. The same impossibly high standards existed during the Soviet era, and they were used only as a lubricant for graft.

In Azerbaijan, the great grief of this second oil boom has been the failure of the Western companies to either champion or demonstrate the Western values of accountability and fiscal transparency. The oil companies reply that they are neither governments nor social service agencies, that they must play with the cards they are dealt by the leadership of the countries in which they work. People had shining hopes as well of the Western governments that support BP and Amoco, Mercedes and McDonald's, the United States in the forefront—hopes that such governments would insist on the sort of reforms that support not only a long-term return on their corporate investments, but long-term political stability: a free press, legitimate elections, due process; running water and electricity and health care; jobs for Azeris on the oil platforms and a fair price for the fisherman for his fish.

Instead, the seventy-eight-year-old president, who was in failing health, was engineering more of the status quo. Claiming that the nation's constitution needed updating, the president had scheduled an August 2002 referendum on thirty-nine proposed amendments, the most significant of which concerned the question of presidential succession in the event of death or severe illness. Currently the speaker of the parliament would assume the presidency, but Aliyev has suggested the prime minister instead. It was then expected that Aliyev's son Ilham—known to the citizenry only as an international playboy—would be immediately installed as prime minister. Opposition parties in Azerbaijan and the World Council of Europe have decried the move as an insult to even the pretense of democracy. But the United States, grateful for Aliyev's support in the War on Terror, had done nothing more than mildly suggest that the referendum be rescheduled to allow more public discussion.

Palatnikov mentioned as we drove out of Baku that on Transparency International's 1999 index, which ranks countries by the number of reported experiences with corrupt officials, Azerbaijan was graded a 96 out of a possible 99. A perfect score of 99 would presumably match the level of corruption in Milton's Pandaemonium. Russia scored 82. The only countries that scored higher than Azerbaijan, Palatnikov noted, were Indonesia and Nigeria—two other nations, like Russia, blessed with the "resource curse" of oil. Of course, even by Soviet standards, Heidar Aliyev was notoriously venal. He was installed to restore order, which he did, and then was expected to steal if left to his own devices which he has.

The disappointment that haunts the streets of Baku and roams the countryside—a disappointment gathering to bitterness and rage—has fastened on the Western institutions that had chosen to cooperate in this for the sake of the oil, their profits, their SUVs, and, if you will, their caviar. The U.S. government has claimed to be addressing the many issues in Azerbaijan through what it terms "quiet diplomacy." That process had been inaudible so far to the Azeris, and now that Presidents George W. Bush and Aliyev were wartime allies, the people on the streets knew that such diplomacy would grow even quieter, that the $50 million in U.S. aid this year would get lost somewhere in the federal buildings and do nothing to reform the economy or alleviate poverty. Aldo Leopold, in his 1941 essay "Ecology and Politics," concluded, "Perhaps ethics are too complex to follow automatically in the wake of newer Fords and shinier bathtubs."

The Caspian Environment Programme has estimated that at their peak the sturgeon fisheries were worth $6 billion per year to the region—not an inconsiderable sum even in terms of oil money, and something that could have been forever, as Rasim Guseynov had said. Meanwhile, international proponents of such alternative energy sources as wind or sunlight observe that the economy of oil is false, that its price in dollars and cents doesn't reflect the environmental costs of procuring and burning it. There are social costs as well that seem peculiar to the blood of the earth. The Nigerian writer Ken Saro-Wiwa, who was hanged in 1995 for leading protests against the effects of the hydrocarbon civilization on subsistence cultures in his country, described petroleum extraction as "genocide by environmental means."

One of Gary Larson's *Far Side* cartoons presents a seashore with some mountains in the background, a landscape not unlike the Caspian. But a ship named "Transoil" is sinking into the sea and trailing a black slick. On the shore lies the oil-fouled corpse of an armor-plated dragon. The scene is captioned, "A tragedy occurs off the coast of a land called Honah Lee."

The night before, I'd looked across the Baku skyline at a rare celestial display. All five of the planets visible to the naked eye—Mercury, Venus, Mars, Saturn, and Jupiter—could be seen at once in a string of pearls trailing down the western sky. "How hard to realize that every camp of men or beast has this glorious starry firmament for a roof!" wrote John Muir in *The Yosemite* in 1912, staring upward from a mountaintop in California, and realizing from the breadth of that firmament that wherever or however people happen to live, "we all dwell in a house of one room."

vi.

The gate to the Urst-Kurinski Experimental Sturgeon Plant was locked. We stood at the end of a rutted dirt road. Beyond the gate we could see a beaten-down wood-framed house and some leaning sheds, then a row of whitewashed concrete buildings about a half-mile away. They squatted like pillboxes beneath a spreading sky marked only by some floating puffs of cloud and the crosshatches of the utility poles that marched down the side of the road. Around us bare dirt and starving patches of grass stretched from the hatchery to the huddled homes through which we had just passed.

Palatnikov pulled at the steel gate, stared up the road, pulled again at the gate, and then walked, perplexed, back to the Kia. Finally there was nothing for it but for the frail man to ease himself over the waist-high fence that ran on either side of the gate and set off on foot. In his touring cap and loose coat, he dwindled down the road like the Little Tramp at the end of another adventure. Twenty minutes later, a tall, swarthy man in a striped warm-up jacket walked down from the plant to unlock the gate and bid us welcome.

The director of the Urst-Kurinski plant was the friendly and matronly Mustafayava Gulsura. Her staff was almost entirely women, all of whom had come to work on foot. Many wore neat white lab coats over their long dresses, as did the director, and head scarves over their rich black hair. Gulsura immediately took us outside, where her tanks and ponds stretched to a levee that Palatnikov said marked nearly the mouth of the Kura. Gulsura said that half of the ponds had been lost to the rising Caspian, but that this was only one of the several reasons her hatchery—like Guseynov's—was working well below capacity.

I read once in a fishermen's magazine about a sportsman's trouble-plagued expedition to the mouth of the Ural River, in Kazakhstan, in the early 1990s. He was fishing for beluga and considered all the trouble he took to get there incidental once he found himself in the midst of thousands of the great fish, almost all of them over 6 feet long, their backs creasing the surface in long squadrons as they cruised up the river's channels. The belugas were feeding on other fish as they went, and their prey had fled in panic to the margins of the channels. Some had abandoned the water entirely, flopping on dry land, while the powerful sucking jaws of the dragons, making audible gulping sounds, swept the sand and spat out bloody portions of asp, bream, and carp.

It was a drama that had been enacted for eons at the mouth of this river as well, just on the other side of that levee, but a long time ago now. There were no beluga here, and the surviving ponds were only sparsely populated with Russian and stellate broodstock. Gulsura showed us a 3-meter tank holding ten-day-old Russian sturgeon fingerlings, some ready to feed and coursing about the middle of the tank, the rest swarming fearfully at the tank's edge. The man in the warm-up jacket lifted several out of the water with a swath of sieve stitched by hand to a wire frame and tied to the end of a pole. The Russian sturgeons were black, the length so far of only the space between two knuckles of a finger. They seemed like bits of sand to be thrown into the wind.

We went into a dark and windowless warehouse where the worms were grown that were ground up into feed for the sturgeons. Long rows of racks with spaces for drawers formerly packed with soil and worms stood mostly empty. "There is no money to replace the boxes," said Gulsura. The suggestion of money for commercial feed would have been laughable. Instead, as much of the brick floor space as could be spared was spread with soil. A woman with a bright purple sweater beneath her lab coat smiled as she shone a lamp into one corner and rooted with her fingers through the dirt. The worms were as long as a fingernail and a nearly translucent white. Palatnikov looked on mournfully as the worms, writhing, recoiled from the light and tunneled back into the soil.

∽ 13 ∾

A CAPACITY FOR WONDER

i.

On the other side of the world, several weeks later, Sue Ireland was doing her paperwork—the USF&W form for handling an animal listed under the Endangered Species Act, another such form for importing or exporting fish or wildlife, the CITES permit application for transporting sturgeons across the Canadian border—because one of the captive females might be spawning tonight. That was when she heard the news as it appeared in the *Bonners Ferry Herald* of June 6, 2002.

"'A spokesperson for The Nature Conservancy,'" said Jack Siple, reading from the newspaper's front page, "said that the U.S. Fish and Wildlife Service, the Idaho Department of Fish and Game, and the Kootenai Tribe of Idaho are all in agreement that more wetlands are desperately needed along stretches of the Kootenai River below the Libby Dam.'"

Sue glanced up, stared at Jack for a moment, and then bowed her head, sighing. "Well, isn't that just great?" she said finally. "Now we can all go out on the streets of Bonners Ferry and get shot on sight."

Jack nodded, his mouth stitched tight, his eyes lit up with their own sort of gunfire. "We'd better call the paper and get a correction there."

It was the first week in June 2002, and spring had left the Caspian, inching up rungs of latitude toward the Arctic. The white sturgeons in the lower Columbia River had completed their spawning, and by then only the most northerly surviving populations were still going about their duties: the green sturgeons along the northern Pacific Rim; the kaluga and Amur sturgeons in the Amur River basin; the Siberian sturgeons in Lake Baikal, and in such rivers as the Ob and the Lena that run north to the Arctic Ocean; the short-nosed sturgeons in the St. John River in New Brunswick; the lake sturgeons in the rivers and lakes of Ontario and Manitoba; the white sturgeons in British Columbia's Fraser River, and, in the United States, trapped and isolated populations of whites in a few of the dammed-off sections of the upper Columbia and its tributaries.

This population of white sturgeons, the ones in the Kootenai River below the Libby Dam, had been bottled up that way for 10,000 years. It was the risk they took in spawning in the Kootenai, which wanders lengthily in a maze of mountain ranges before finding its way to the Columbia River. At the end of the Pleistocene, the tail-end of the Kootenai dropped lower than the rest of it, and the result was Bonnington Falls, in southern British Columbia. The fish have been landlocked ever since, one of seventeen such white sturgeon populations in the Pacific Northwest, the rest thanks to hydroelectric projects. These were the only sturgeons that were naturally so, existing solely in the 170-mile stretch between Bonnington Falls and Kootenai Falls near Libby, Montana. And they had been landlocked long enough to become unique in both biology and behavior: smaller than other white sturgeons, less genetically diverse, active at lower temperatures, and accustomed to using British Columbia's Kootenay Lake in place of the Pacific Ocean in their life cycle.

The problem here was that even with no fishing pressure, the Kootenai whites had been disappearing. After holding steady for many years at around 5,000 fish, their numbers dropped precipitously through the 1980s, to only around 880 at the end of the decade. During that time the Kootenai Tribe of Idaho—with 110 members who still had the right to harvest sturgeons, but who chose not to—charged that the sturgeons were suffering from the effects of the Libby Dam, which had been completed in 1972. Then the tribe applied to the Bonneville Power Administration (BPA) for funding to build a hatchery. USF&W opposed the proposal, just as it has opposed hatcheries on the Suwannee in Florida, but this hatchery was to be built on tribal land, in Indian Country, and had political support from the state and the landowners along the river. The funding was secured in 1988, and the first year-class of hatchery-raised fingerlings was put into the Kootenai River in 1991.

By then The Nature Conservancy and several other environmental organizations had determined that still more aggressive action was necessary. Their 1992 proposal that the Kootenai white sturgeon be listed under the Endangered Species Act was approved by USF&W in 1994. With that, the sturgeon joined a bestiary of other animals in these mountains protected by the ESA—the grizzly bear, the gray wolf, the lynx, the mountain caribou, and the bald eagle—and became party to a long-standing grievance on the part of the farmers, ranchers, and miners of this river valley. But Darrell Kerby, the mayor of Bonners Ferry, told me that in his town the response to the listing of the sturgeon was of a different sort.

"People out here have come to view the ESA as one of the biggest reasons it's so hard to make a living in this place," he said later that day in the offices of the Pace-Kerby Real Estate and Insurance Agency in downtown Bonners Ferry. Idaho's Route 95 crosses the river in a four-lane bridge at the site of the old ferry transit. Most of the little town nestles on the south bank of the Kootenai and on the west side of the highway in a grid of wide roads, grain elevators, and old-fashioned two-story storefronts.

"And they don't like being kept out of the process—as they have been, for example, with the grizzly bear," Kerby continued. "The sturgeon, though—well, it may not be warm and fuzzy, but unlike the grizzly, it's an animal that people here love. It was an important food source, and then a popular sport fishery. They admire and appreciate the lineage and the age of the fish, and they want to keep it around. We'd also like to get that sport fishery back, and pull in some tourism money. So with this listing—well, we knew that if we were going to survive in the first place, and if our natural resources were to be sustained, it wasn't going to do any good just being damned mad all the time. We had to engage the relevant agencies, and make local knowledge available to them."

In other words, everybody wanted more sturgeons, and so began a remarkable collaboration between state, federal, and tribal agencies in a part of the country where entities at those levels are more typically at war. The coalition crossed borders as well, including agencies from Montana and Canada, as well as the Bonneville Power Administration. Getting USF&W on board, however, required some adjustment in the role the hatchery would play in the recovery effort, and the coining of a new term in fisheries management: "conservation aquaculture."

This was a different idea from the one showcased by the Russians in the Caspian, which involved raising population levels through sheer force of numbers in mass-produced, artificially propagated fish. Instead, this hatchery would release only a few juvenile sturgeons—less than 4,000 so far since 1990—that as a group were as genetically diverse as wild fish, and in numbers only large enough to ensure that the Kootenai sturgeon didn't become extinct. Meanwhile, Sue Ireland and other scientists on the recovery team searched for why it was, exactly, that the numbers of wild fish had dropped so much, and what systemic changes in habitat might be necessary to restore them and make the hatchery obsolete.

This was the great mystery, though in a sense it wasn't a mystery at all. The fish were disappearing, Sue learned, because there was no natural recruitment—which is to say, there were no young fish, other than those spawned in the hatchery, joining a population dominated by adults twenty-five years old or more. Despite the hatchery, sturgeon numbers now, in 2002, were estimated at 760. Only seventeen wild juveniles had been found in the past ten years, and just one lonely larval sturgeon—and that in the stomach of a predator. The fish were dying off like Shakers.

Yet unlike Shakers, the fish were spawning. So somewhere between the fertilized egg and the two-year-old juvenile, the age at which hatchery fish were released, there was a recruitment bottleneck in the Kootenai. Either the eggs weren't hatching, or the larvae were dying en masse each year. The mystery was where exactly that bottleneck lay. The trick then was to unplug it.

Wetlands, or the lack thereof since the river had been disconnected from its ancient floodplain, might have something to do with it. Farmers began that disconnection when they built dikes along the riverbank to control flooding, and then the Libby Dam finished the job. There were a lot of theories about why the river was no longer the sturgeon nursery it used to be, and one way or another, the dam played a role in all of them. But Sue—who had been employed by the tribe as their fisheries program coordinator since 1996, and who also headed up the ESA recovery team—had to be careful about what she said.

Once she gave a presentation to a resource committee whose membership included the supervisor of the Libby Dam. Sue's name on the agenda for the meeting was misspelled as "Sure." Not a misprint at all, said the dam supervisor, since Sue was reliably "sure" to mention the dam whenever she talked about the sturgeon problem. But the essence of this collaborative conservation effort, this unusual alliance of cowboys and Indians, of local wildlife enthusiasts and regional power providers, was a shared presumption that the dam stayed, that whatever changes were to be made in the ecosystem would be done with the dam as part of the equation.

So she also had to be careful about what words others put in her mouth. In the opinion of the Kootenai Tribe of Idaho, Sue knew, there was no problem with the modern lack of wetlands in the valley, at least in terms of public policy statements. You could post it on billboards around Bonners Ferry, or trail it on banners behind small airplanes: We don't intend to convert farmlands back into wetlands here.

A classic *Far Side* cartoon hung on the door to Sue's office, one that neatly summed up the Kootenai sturgeon's situation. A lost soul stands before two doors, one labeled "Damned if you do," the other "Damned if you don't." A devil stands behind him, poking a trident into his back and saying, "Come on, hurry up—it's one or the other." On both doors, the "n" in "damned" had been inked into an "m."

ii.

Frank Chapman supports the letter and spirit of conservation aquaculture and regarded the progress of this effort on the Kootenai with more than a touch of envy. I asked him over the telephone if he had done any spawning of gulf sturgeon this spring. "We could not spawn, Rick. They said no way, too controversial." Did he at least do any tagging? Yes, but at his own expense. "We tagged for four weeks and we only captured two females with black eggs. One was overripe, and the other too early. I'm sure there's one or two females that might have spawned in the Suwannee, but basically, my conclusion is there was none. So it's pretty pitiful. They still believe the fish will magically recover on its own by 2023."

He listened soberly to my report on the Caspian. I told him how hard it was for scientists there to find broodstock and about the lack of genetic diversity in the fish their hatcheries produced. "Well, what else are you gonna do?" Frank said. "By now, they have no choice."

Did he support Caviar Emptor's demand to have the beluga listed under the ESA? Emphatically not: "Because Caviar Emptor does not support any provision for the aquaculture of beluga in this country. They say it's a dirty industry, but you know it's gonna be the only way to save them. I've been bombarding the feds with letters. I'd never be able to spawn my own belugas, or even keep them."

A month later, at the end of July and after the first deadline had passed for a government ruling on the beluga's status, I spoke with Lisa Speer of the National Resources Defence Council and the coordinator of the Caviar Emptor campaign. "Fish and Wildlife just issued a federal register notice indicating that they're holding off on a final decision pending review of some CITES documents," she told me. But she had no patience with the reiterated arguments of Eve Vega and other caviar industry figures in the newspapers that a legal outlet for beluga caviar provided money for hatcheries and at least a modicum of control over the harvest.

"To argue that we should still be importing huge amounts of beluga caviar to help the fish, to say that somehow that's going to, well . . ." This ended in laughter. Then she added, "It assumes that CITES wields a big stick, when in reality it wields a twig, when in reality CITES is not having a significant impact on reducing the pressure. Restoring the beluga and other Caspian stocks will require a long-term solution involving habitat restoration, better law enforcement, improved management, and some real coordination between the Caspian governments. And it is our experience in fisheries that governments and international agencies respond too slowly to a crisis. So we appeal to other constituencies—to consumers, purveyors, and chefs, who can bring market forces to bear on a conservation issue."

Aldo Leopold would agree with Henry David Thoreau, who never met that philosopher who could show him the difference between a fish and a man. In *Sand County Almanac* (1949), Leopold remarked upon "how like fish we are" in our readiness to seize whatever worldly pleasure comes floating our way: "And how we rue our haste, finding the gilded

morsel to contain a hook. Even so, I think there is some virtue in eagerness, whether its object is proved true or false. How utterly dull would be
a wholly prudent man, or trout, or world!"

A spoonful of caviar is a gilded morsel that contains a multitude of
hooks, one of which is its essence as the opposite of prudence. If there is
some virtue in eagerness, then there was some pathos in the closing, in
July 2002, of the Russian Tea Room, the Manhattan restaurant founded
in 1926 by former members of the Russian Imperial Ballet and celebrated in the *New York Times* on July 3, 2002, as "that storied preserve of
infused vodka, glinting caviar, and buttery blini." The demise of the Tea
Room, which lately had been buying its caviar from Arkady Panchernikov's Caspian Star company, would be part of the changing of the
guard in New York restaurants, one that would see a number of the city's
great French venues close their doors in the next two years. Their classic
Old World elegance, still on display at Petrossian, had been upstaged by
that fusion of New World elegance and home-style unpretentiousness
achieved at California's Chez Panisse and the French Laundry. New
York's newer restaurants were more informal, more contemporary, a little
less pointedly elitist and a little more essentially American. This was
part of a trend that Patric Kuh would see as typical of the genius of
American cuisine: its ability to combine the perfection of *potage Dubarry*
with the warmth of the bare-table luncheonette; its willingness, in other
words, to scatter beads of caviar amid hills and valleys of tapioca.

Those beads now were more and more likely to be American, either
paddlefish or white sturgeon. Another sort of punctuation point was
reached this summer of 2002 when Petrossian, the arch-purveyor of
Caspian caviar, introduced "Tsar Imperial Transmontanus" caviar in its
catalog and on its website. "We now offer a truly glorious Tsar Imperial,
spectacular in size, flavor, and color," ran the website copy. "Thanks to
diligent conservation efforts, and careful supervision by Petrossian, native white sturgeon are once again flourishing in California. Nearly extinct in the last century, these farm-raised fish produce caviar which we
liken to the finest Osetra, with a nutty flavor both smooth and robust."
The Tsar Imperial Transmontanus cost $84 for a 50-gram tin, a little less
than half the price of Petrossian's Tsar Imperial–grade beluga.

Frank Chapman's hopes for an American race of farm-raised beluga,
already dim, would grow dimmer yet one morning late that summer

with the discovery of one of his two belugas floating dead in its tank. The seven-year-old fish was 69 inches long, 75 pounds, and found during its autopsy to be a male. "Apparently flakes of fiberglass were breaking off the side of its tank," Frank told me, broken-hearted. "And he died from ingesting them." He moved his other beluga to another tank, but not in time. That fish was found after its death to be a female that had already reached sexual maturity.

iii.

Jack Siple, the hatchery manager, went out to check on the gravid female, while Sue made a note to call the newspaper and then finished filling in her blanks. Suitably Celtic, she was a pony-tailed, brown-banged spark plug of a woman in her forties who loved her work and who had proven a skilled enough diplomat to sustain—at least so far—the support of all the fractious interest groups involved in this experiment in conservation aquaculture. This was all the more impressive in considering that the tiny Native American nation that employed her was still technically at war with the United States.

At one time, the Kootenai people occupied both sides of the American and Canadian Rockies. Those in the west fished for salmon and sturgeon and hunted mountain caribou, while those in the east relied on buffalo. The Kootenai designed a distinctive double-prowed, flat-bottomed canoe, with opposite ends that jutted forward into the water like a sturgeon's snout, in what is known as a sturgeon-nose design. They hunted the great fish from this with toggle-headed harpoons, dropping a stone tied with cedar bark rope from the stern once their Nantucket sleigh rides began. They sometimes captured exhausted sturgeons by capsizing the canoe, rolling the fish in over the gunwale, and then righting it and bailing.

The Kootenai hold that their signature on an 1855 treaty agreement with the United States was forged, and for that reason they never retired to a reservation, as promised in the treaty. But the rich alluvial soil of the Kootenai Valley ensured that they wouldn't be left in peace, and a century of disease, alcoholism, forced dislocation, and bald government swindling ensued. In 1942, the Grand Coulee Dam put an end to the whole region's salmon runs. The tribe's remaining land base, which existed in a legal limbo, eroded to the point that in 1974 surviving Kootenais declared war against the United States, erecting roadblocks on roads through tribal land and charging ten-cent tolls to finance the war effort.

The only real fighting was in the newspapers. The federal government offered clear title to 12.5 acres of land in Bonners Ferry. The Kootenai, unimpressed, refused to sign, and they maintain only a truce in their state of war even now. But publicity about their grievances led at least to that acreage being placed in trust, and to better access to utilities and social services. At the same time, the tribe's newfound political muscle allowed them to defeat a proposal to build a dam at Kootenai Falls. Then the 1976 Indian Self-Determination Act gave them more power over their own economic affairs, and some savvy management has led to some important additions to the Bonners Ferry economy: the Kootenai River Inn, a part of the Best Western chain; an electronic gaming addition to the inn; and this hatchery, with its staff of twelve and its pipeline to state and federal funds.

The slot machines at the inn are controversial, but not the hatchery, located on a bend of the river 3 miles west of Bonners Ferry. If Darrell Kerby was right, people in this town of 2,400 appreciate it as the means of striking a truce between the irresistible force that is the ESA and the immovable object that is a productive hydroelectric dam. Lately that truce was threatened, however, from both sides. The farmers and ranchers were leery about what changes might be in store now for managing the river, which had just been designated as critical habitat under the ESA. Meanwhile, a large Arizona-based conservation organization, the Center for Biological Diversity, was threatening to sue to have the dam torn down. And USF&W had given this newfangled conservation aquaculture method only until 2009 to provide for delisting the Kootenai sturgeon.

"This is an issue in which you might say the leadership is well out ahead of the rank and file," Kerby had said. "We need some successes, and the sooner the better."

Sue turned to the next form, made a short phone call, looked out the window at the clouds, and laid down her pen. "You know, I always endorsed The Nature Conservancy, always contributed money," she said.

"I'm a dedicated conservationist, but like the Kootenai Tribe, I believe that everything is connected, including human beings—we're part of the landscape too. But the people in environmental organizations like that, they don't live here, and they don't live with the consequences of their decisions." She said the Center for Biological Diversity didn't "have a clue" as to what the situation was in the valley. "And they claim all this knowledge about the Kootenai sturgeon, but they never talked to me, or any of the other biologists involved in this project," she added. "Now that I see what their tactics are, I think there's just got to be a better way."

One of the successes of the sort needed by both Sue and the mayor, albeit a small and incremental one, might happen tonight. We went outside, where the clouds wheeled kaleidoscopically over the forested peaks of the Selkirk Mountains. The hatchery's neat gray and blue buildings were ringed by lodgepole pine, Douglas fir, and cottonwood and sprinkled about with the SUVs and pickups of the staff or University of Idaho graduate students carrying out experiments. I had hoped to get here in time for fishing, which is done from the riverbank by strong men with fishing poles and 50-pound monofilament line. But the population structure here was the opposite of the one at the Caspian. Here, there were plenty of mature fish for broodstock, but all too few juveniles, and Jack and Sue already had all the fish they needed: six females, six males, none of them used before for hatchery production.

We met Jack again in the hatchery's main building. Jack was ponytailed, too, his wispy brown hair, turning gray, pulled tight under a camouflage-pattern baseball cap. His face was well-lined, his eyes snappy with an extra dose of Western independence. He took us to one of the sarcophagus-shaped spawning tanks, 12 feet long and 3 feet wide. The tanks' plywood covers were fastened shut with C-clamps, and 2-inch water hoses were connected to both ends. Jack set about loosening the clamps in a scene that suggested we were about to get our first glimpse of the monster in a science fiction film. "This isn't like California, where you have a complete life history for those domesticated fish," he remarked. "Down there you can predict within the hour when they'll spawn. Here, we look at the eggs, and from then on it's up to the fish. Some fight off the hormone—bigger fish especially. Like humans, they're older and they get a little more set in their ways. But one year we had an

8-footer that spawned well. On the other hand, we've always had fish that didn't perform."

He slid the cover to the floor. In the dim light the water was a cloudy gray, the fish itself a coal-colored torpedo, 7 feet long and a slender 136 pounds. She floated languidly at rest with only faint and sleepy movements of the fins and tail. Her dorsal row of scutes showed like a string of widely spaced pearls cast into a stream. "Sometimes a bigger fish is easier, and sometimes it beats the living snot out of you," said Jack.

He yawned, rubbed his eyes, and then leaned on his hands against the rim of the tank. "I injected her with the hormone at 8 last night, checked her at midnight and 4 A.M., and gave her the second shot at 8 this morning. If it was just one or two of them, great, but I get pretty beat this time of year doing six females. This one could go tonight, but they've been releasing water from the dam and the river temperature has been dropping. So I have a feeling she won't go till tomorrow morning. I'll be checking her every hour. If she starts dropping eggs on the bottom of the tank, I'll call in the crew and we'll put her in the stretcher."

iv.

The Libby Dam is one link in the largest interconnected hydroelectric system in the world. At 422 feet high, and a little more than 3,000 feet across, the dam is literally a mountain of concrete, stitching together the Purcell and the Cabinet ranges in a Great-Wall-of-China sort of battlement that slopes back against its reservoir—called Lake Koocanusa, a stitching together of "Kootenai," "Canada," and "USA"—as it spans the valley. Its 525,000 kilowatts are generated at only 10 percent of the cost of electricity from fossil fuel or nuclear power, 4 percent of that from gas turbines, and at no threat to air quality. This is power, moreover, that can be produced over and over again as a river goes on its way to the sea. There is enough elevation at the dam's place on the river for the same sample of water to spin turbines sixteen times between there and the mouth of the Columbia.

Since the dam was raised, other fish populations besides the sturgeon have swooned: rainbow and cutthroat trout; mountain whitefish; the

kokanee, a species of landlocked salmon; and the Kootenai River burbot, a freshwater cod and yet another candidate for an ESA listing. Biologists for the Idaho Department of Fish and Game believe that the
common denominator in these declines is the nutrient trap created by
the dam. Microscopic plant life, carrying nitrogen and phosphorus, now
settle to the bottom of Lake Koocanusa, just as Soviet dams made the
Volga all too clear. Sue noted, however, that years of mining and lumber milling in these mountains have brought more than just nutrients
to Lake Koocanusa. "The sediment behind the dam is probably unbe-
lievable now in both its quantity and its toxicity," she said. "That's another reason the dam can't be removed."

It has ever been thus, that dams have had immediate and disastrous
effects on anadromous fish populations, insidious long-term effects on
riverine ecosystems. The Bonneville Power Administration is bound by
law to help mitigate these effects, and with the Kootenai sturgeon, this
meant that dam managers were cooperating in experimental adjust-
ments in the timing, volume, and temperatures of the water released
from the dam, hoping that a regimen closer to the river's natural behavior in the spring might unplug that spawning bottleneck.

But the BPA had its own tightrope to walk. In the past several years,
flows of extra water in the spring had not relieved that bottleneck, but
they had caused septic systems to back up and wells to go sour in the
valley. Over the next five years, USF&W wanted to increase the volume of those flows by 40 percent. Valley residents had started a letter-
writing campaign against that idea and were demanding reimbursement
for any property damage. The Center for Biological Diversity, meanwhile, already had its lawyers on the case and was suing USF&W for
even higher flows.

Some valley homeowners wonder why Sue doesn't just put a lot more
juvenile sturgeons into the river and save everybody all this trouble.
That would be a solution thoroughly out of synch with the idea of conservation aquaculture as it was being done here, but one that answered
to an old dream of plenty, a scenario of desire, that has been invoked
thousands of times elsewhere, from the Delaware River to the Caspian,
but no more powerfully than on the American frontier, which began,
after all, 400 years ago in Manhattan. That was where Europeans first
gazed on what Gatsby's friend Nick Carraway described as "the fresh,

green breast of the new world," where "for a transitory enchanted moment man must have held his breath in the presence of this continent,
compelled into an aesthetic contemplation he neither understood nor
desired, face to face for the last time in history with something com-
mensurate to his capacity for wonder."

That wonder assigned qualities of the infinite to the New World's
wildlife and natural resources, but it met its first disillusionment in the collapse of the East's anadromous fisheries. The villains in that scenario—
fishing pressure, water pollution, and dams—moved west with the frontier
and were poised to work the same mischief there until the blossoming of
aquaculture, or so it seemed. In 1872, at an experimental hatchery on California's McCloud River, a tributary of the Sacramento, manager Livingstone Stone described the germination of his Pacific salmon eggs in
language that anticipated Nick Carraway's. "The thrill of excitement that
tingled to our fingers' ends when we first saw the little black speck in the
unhatched embryo, which told us that our egg was alive. It was one of
the dearest sights on earth to us then," wrote Stone. "We can hardly believe that such a commonplace, matter-of-fact affair could ever have
stirred our feelings and our imagination as it did once, when the sight and
sensation were both new, and the world of promise before us was untried
and unknown."

Why not? The fish hatchery looked to be the best-of-both-worlds
combination of the two defining economic inventions of the past 10,000
years, the farm and the factory, and a technology powerful enough to
overwhelm fishermen and pollutants. Best of all, it would work in combination with dams to make rivers as productive of fish as they were of
kilowatts.

But that world of promise has never fully answered Stone's hopes for
it. In the East, hatcheries for both Atlantic sturgeon and Atlantic
salmon failed to return any mature fish. Attempts to establish Pacific
salmon species in the East failed, though transplanted shad and striped
bass from the East thrived in the cleaner, more free-flowing rivers of the
West. Shad flourished again for forty years in the East, were once again
fished to the breaking point, and have not been back.

In the Northwest, for political and economic reasons the salmon
hatcheries haven't been allowed to fail, though they certainly have
failed to perform. Their defenders point out that the technology has

improved and that artificially propagated fish now make up 80 percent of the salmon in the Columbia. They neglect to mention that salmon runs are less than 5 percent of their historical levels, that the fish are extinct in 40 percent of their original rivers in the basin, and that they would certainly be gone entirely if not for the Endangered Species Act. In *Salmon Without Rivers* (1999), biologist and fisheries historian Jim Lichatowich described the linkage between dams and hatcheries as a "partnership that was forged deep inside the heart of the industrial economy," one that "remains the ultimate expression of human domination over nature." His term for the attitude supporting that partnership is "techno-optimism," and the result for salmon in the Northwest has been similar to that of sturgeon in the Caspian, where techno-optimism is all that sustains fish that in various ways have lost their habitats.

It's a dream of plenty older than the New World, this notion of a free lunch and human domination through the right technology. And even as Sue Ireland and her recovery team struggle to redefine the hatchery-dam partnership, it's an optimism that still resists facts. In September 2001, an Oregon federal judge ruled that there was no substantial difference between salmon spawned in the wild and those spawned in a hatchery. Therefore any number of hatchery fish could be counted toward the recovery levels mandated by the ESA, a position supported by the George W. Bush administration. "Since hatchery fish can be raised and added to a river at will," noted the *New York Times* on February 14, 2002, "the whole problem of declining species magically disappears— along with all the annoying steps that have to be taken to protect their habitat."

v.

John Muir's natural habitat, after his walk to Florida and his shipboard journeys to New York and San Francisco, was his revered Yosemite Valley. And he finally died, it would seem, in a vain attempt to protect part of that valley from a dam.

Long before that, in the fall of 1874, he was a guest of Livingstone Stone at his salmon hatchery on the McCloud River. Muir stayed a week, studying the limestone geology of the area and waiting for snow conditions to improve before beginning what would be a successful ascent of Mt. Shasta. That was three years after he had begun his task of exploring every canyon and peak in the Yosemite region, and his discovery of residual glaciers in the Sierra Nevada. Muir challenged the scientific orthodoxy of the day in arguing that Yosemite was the slow result of glacial scouring, and not the sudden prodigy of a geologic cataclysm. It was an argument that Muir finally won, and that established his credentials as a scientist, however self-taught.

Later he fell into environmental activism rather by accident following an 1889 camping tour of Yosemite with a magazine editor. Seeing that herds of sheep were having a baneful effect on the valley's grasslands, they resolved to begin a campaign for the establishment of what would become the Yosemite National Park. Muir was already famous for his magazine articles on the natural beauty of the West, and within a year Congress passed a bill creating that park. In 1891, Congress also passed an act empowering the president to create forest reservations, and the year after that Muir founded the Sierra Club.

But Grover Cleveland's 1897 creation of thirteen such reservations, totaling 21 million acres, provoked a political counterattack by commercial logging and mining interests. In Muir's mind, this was a battle between "landscape righteousness and the devil." The developers persuaded Congress to temporarily nullify most of the reserves, and Muir responded with two magazine articles—one in Harper's Weekly, the other in the Atlantic Monthly—that catalyzed the American environmental movement and thwarted his opponents in their attempt to permanently annul the reservations. In 1903, Muir took President Teddy Roosevelt on a camping trip into Yosemite, and over the next six years Roosevelt doubled the number of national parks, established sixteen national monuments, and set aside 148 million acres of additional forest reserves.

Even by then, however, the American conservation movement had split into two philosophical schools: utilitarians, who believed in the wise and sustainable use of wilderness lands, and preservationists, who defended—in Muir's words—"the great fresh unblighted unredeemed wilderness" (Alaska Fragment, 1890), a natural cathedral untouched by the human stain. Muir was a devout preservationist, and one of the most powerful men in America. His final battle with James D. Phelan, the mayor of San Francisco, would seem to have been an unequal contest, but it wasn't a straightforward matter of the Sierra Club versus unrestrained private commerce. It also involved a dam, and since dams tend to either exist or not, there was no middle ground. And since the ground involved was the Hetch Hetchy Valley, one of the most stunning portions of Yosemite National Park, and the subject of luminous landscapes by the painter Albert Bierstadt, it became literally a battle to the death for John Muir.

Phelan was also a political activist—a populist reformer, an admirer of Muir, and the fiery opponent of the commercial monopolies that had come to dominate the California economy. One such monopoly was the Spring Valley Water Company, which supplied San Francisco's water at high prices and in insufficient quantities. The most practical route around that monopoly, determined Phelan in 1901, was a dam on the pristine Tuolomne River creating a reservoir that would flood the Hetch Hetchy Valley, a place only a few hundred Californians had even seen. Then an aqueduct could carry the Tuolomne's water to the city while the dam produced electricity.

"Dam Hetch Hetchy!" thundered Muir in response to the idea. "As well as dam for watertanks the people's cathedrals and churches, for no holier temple has ever been consecrated by the heart of man." Phelan replied that the 400,000 people of San Francisco were suffering from bad water "and ask Mr. Muir to cease his quibbling."

The quibbling escalated and went on for twelve years. The 1906 earthquake, and ensuing fire, underlined the city's need for more water. A 1908 city referendum carried strongly in favor of the dam. Muir and the Sierra Club hit back with articles, pamphlets, and broadsides against those whom Muir described as "James Phelan, Satan and company." These succeeded in inflaming national sentiment against the project, provoking the *San Francisco Chronicle* to label Muir and his allies as "hoggish and mushy esthetes." Meanwhile, the bitter campaign was draining Muir, who by then was in his seventies. "I'll be relieved when it's settled, for it's killing me," he wrote.

It was settled at last at the end of 1913, when the U.S. Senate passed a bill authorizing the dam with a vote of 46–25. "The American people have been whipped in the Hetch Hetchy fight," lamented the *New York*

Times on December 7, 1913. One year later, on Christmas Eve, 1914, the grief-stricken old explorer died of pneumonia. His remains were laid next to those of his wife on his ranch in the Alhambra Valley.

That epic battle, however, swelled the ranks of the environmental movement and defined the tactics that would later defeat hydroelectric projects in the Grand Canyon and Dinosaur National Monument and effect the passage of the Wilderness Act in 1964, and then the Endangered Species Act nine years later. But in the mystical qualities of Muir's preservationist fervor, it also propagated a view of Yosemite and the American wilderness that wasn't strictly correct.

Yosemite was not just the creation of God and glaciers. Muir had arrived in the valley twenty years after its original inhabitants, the Ahwahneechee Indians, had been murdered or relocated for the sake of gold prospectors. Muir never realized that the Ahwahneechee had used fire at regular intervals to burn away the valley's brush and saplings, which made for lusher stands of mature black oak and better crops of acorns. That also resulted in an airy, park-like sort of forest that European Americans such as Muir, Bierstadt, Teddy Roosevelt, and later the photographers Edward Weston and Ansel Adams viewed as the template for creation, the very Eden that preceded the fruit, the serpent, the curse of thorns and thistles. In reality the thorns and thistles had been removed by the sweat of another people's brows. The righteous landscape of Yosemite was in part the product of human industry.

Yet there was more to it than the valley's beauty. There was also its position at the opposite end of the American continent from Manhattan. The old Dutch colony and Yosemite Valley defined the alpha and omega of that garden where Europe's poor and oppressed went for freedom, equality, wealth, and however else those dreamers lent substance to Jay Gatsby's milk of wonder. In Europe, the existence of the New World had provided a relief valve to its social tensions and environmental constraints, all of which today are part of that simmering political caldron and vortex of extinction, the Caspian Sea. But in America this fresh green breast unrolled to the Pacific, offering a grandeur of possibility that was multiplied as much through the various tools of techno-optimism—the factory and the railroad, the hydroelectric dam and the fish hatchery—as it was through the millions of acres of open space, once those pesky Native Americans were disposed of.

Yosemite was at the end of that space. John Muir's genius encompassed both tool-making and commerce, and if he didn't understand how the Ahwahneechee had applied those to the valley, he knew full well how men of his own race would do the job. He couldn't possibly be a utilitarian, because, though he himself felt no envy for millionaires such as E.H. Harriman, he agreed with Thorstein Veblen's 1899 assertion that "the desire for wealth can scarcely be satiated in any individual instance."

The world, in other words, is not enough. Personal greed, like that on display in Azerbaijan, would inevitably defeat the sustainable use of natural resources. Others might take a more hopeful view of human nature, especially in a society that has so far preserved the rest of Yosemite, passed the Endangered Species Act, and cultivated such grassroots utilitarians as the members of Sturgeon for Tomorrow. But this is also a society committed to steady annual growth in its economy and gross domestic product—a society with systems of manufacture and finance that rely not only on the limitless quantities of resources such as the American frontier once offered but also on ever-multiplying markets, ever-increasing levels of consumption and desire and imprudence.

The economist John Maynard Keynes termed this the "ultimate perplexity" of the capitalist system. "What will you do," he asked in 1935, "when you have built all the houses and roads and town halls and electric grids and water supplies and so forth which the stationary population of the future require?" The answer at the turn of the twenty-first century had been the globalization of this Western system of manufacture and finance, which only postponed an answer to Keynes's query and universalized its ecological costs.

It was the historian Frederick Jackson Turner who first discerned the influence of the frontier in the unfolding of America. Turner also foresaw the consequences of its closing, warning in 1893, a year after the founding of Muir's Sierra Club, and at the height of the sturgeon slaughter of the first American caviar industry, that when the frontier was gone and all the rivers dammed and the houses in place, once Gatsby's orgastic future had dwindled into the present, "the stubborn American environment [would be] there with its imperious summons to accept its conditions."

Sue and I went to visit the Libby Dam while Jack was waiting for his female sturgeon to drop some eggs. Then we stopped at Kootenai Falls on the way back. The parking lot was empty, and there were no other visitors to its trails and vantage points on that weekday afternoon. This was the eastern end of the Kootenai sturgeon's range, though Sue said the fish were such powerful swimmers that sometimes, somehow, and for some reason, one would beat its way past these falls.

We stood in aesthetic contemplation on a wood and steel-cable suspension bridge as the water foamed and thundered beneath us over a series of stone parapets. We wondered how a sturgeon could overcome such stones, while the river ran headlong ahead of us, hastening west to Bonners Ferry to serve the latest of its summons to that town's stationary population.

~ 14 ~

THE GILDED MORSEL

i.

Jack Siple called at 4:30 the next morning. Clouds lay banked in gray stepping stones up the valley to the north as I drove through the empty streets of Bonners Ferry, across the river, and then to the hatchery. To the south the sky stretched wide and pink and vacant.

Whether the result of adrenaline or coffee or both, Jack had an air of hair-trigger alertness that frayed out to weariness just at the edges. Only Chris Lewandowski, the hatchery's assistant manager and its other fisheries biologist, was there besides Jack. In wire-rimmed glasses and seersucker shorts, he sat in the hatchery's control room at a computer. The screen revealed what to expect from the Libby Dam that day. "Thursday, 5 A.M., 13,000 cubic feet per second, up to 18,000 by 5 P.M.," he read aloud. "Looks like they're raising the flow on us."

"Looks like they're trying to flood us," Jack groused. "They were only releasing 8,000 at the beginning of the week. That's up 10,000 in just a few days, and by the time that water picks up some runoff, it's going 20,000 feet per second past here."

"They're doing flood control, not fish control," Chris said.

In other words, it had been a rainy spring, and the reservoir was getting a little high. Bonneville Power wanted to take advantage of the dry weather to lower Lake Koocanusa by a few feet, even if that meant

285

releasing a surge of cooler water that might inhibit sturgeon spawning. Yes, the dam and the hatchery were supposed to be on the same page in these matters, but in reality the BPA had other constituencies and concerns to serve as well (not to mention differing flow regimens for the other troubled fish species). Sometimes things were still out of whack, and this surge of cold water, flushing through a tank that still had its cover clamped to it, might disturb this female Jack had spent the night with.

Others sifted in: Eric Wagner, fiftyish, a hatchery technician in a silver-white goatee and a "Sturgeon for Tomorrow" baseball cap; Bob Aitken, a pony-tailed and big-shouldered Kootenai who was also a technician; then Sue and a couple of graduate students. "I'll never get used to these nights on call," Eric said. "I didn't even get to sleep until 4 A.M."

Jack and Eric reviewed the destinations and numbers for portions of this spawn, if it happened: 10,000 eggs for insurance purposes to the Canadians at the hatchery in British Columbia; 5,000 for a study at the University of Idaho on the effects of different kinds of sediments on the eggs; and several hundred for a white sturgeon iridovirus study. "She dropped her first egg at 3:30," Jack said. "It's been two hours. She should be about ready now."

Chris had put on rain pants and hiking boots. Bob doused the electric lights as Jack undid the C-clamps. The tanks and water pipes behind us disappeared into a gloom lit only by the auroral glow of a door half-open to the outside, and the heartbeat gurgle of the moving water grew louder as Jack moved the lid partway off the tank. The river water smelled like mud and grass. The female floated at the surface, her snout flush against the tank's forward end, like a racehorse about to explode out of its starting block. Chris and Eric slid a stretcher into the tank next to the fish. Its hollow aluminum poles bobbed on the surface. "I'm going to see if I can grab her lip," Chris said.

"Be careful," said Jack. "She's gonna . . . "

The female bucked and rolled, pushing a wave of water over the lip of the tank that sent the rest of us scattering. Chris stood his ground, his hands groping under the surface. He said, "She's gone under the stretcher. She's down at the other end now."

Jack took the lid completely off the tank. Chris kept his hands in the water and motioned for Bob to push the stretcher down to that end, keeping its poles flush to either side of the tank. "That worked pretty slick," he said at last. "I've got her by the lip now."

"Until she turns and breaks your wrist," Jack proposed.

By then Chris was standing in the tank and the stretcher had largely enclosed the fish. "Okay, we're ready," he said. She didn't turn, and he released his hold on her. "Just don't get too frisky on me, girl."

Eric and Sue were ready with a pair of one-by-six boards as four others of us took hold of the stretcher and raised the fish clear of the water. The boards were notched on the bottom to fit over the lips of the tank, and notched on top to hold the poles of the stretcher. Chris positioned the boards across the tank, and we dropped the poles into the notches. The fish offered us her armored back, battleship gray with splotches of white and pink, her scutes smooth and as pale as zinfandel, an old scar scrawled in a chalky signature near her dorsal fin, a cave drawing from before the Permian. We stood for just a moment, dumb and scarcely breathing ourselves, and then Jack suggested that we'd better get going.

ii.

When Elena Zhuravleva, the KaspNIRKh translator, had shown me the 2,000-pound stuffed beluga at the Astrakhan museum, claiming there were still fish of that size in the Caspian and the Volga, and that poachers had recently caught one nearly that big, I accepted that as a beluga-scaled fish story and applied salt.

But in December 2002 Katya Godunova e-mailed me a photograph that proved that at least as recently as 1997 there were giants in the waters of the earth: a crowd of men in a street in Astrakhan hauling the carcass of a beluga that dwarfed even that famous specimen. The fish had been maneuvered onto a long makeshift wooden dolly. One man pulled from the front with a steel cable. Others had run what looked like blankets or bedsheets under the fish's belly. They trotted in jubilant pairs alongside the fish with opposite ends of the sheets clutched like yokes over their necks and backs. The eyes of the beluga were invisible in the photo, its hide slick and gray. Were it not for the gaping mouth and frond-like barbels, the beast could have passed for an ICBM hijacked from an old Soviet missile bunker.

Katya said that this fish—a little over 4,000 pounds, 21 feet and 4 inches long—had been stuffed and mounted and would be unveiled at another museum after Christmas. "Poachers caught this fish, or I'd rather say whale judging by its giant size," Katya wrote. "They delivered 250 kilos [550 pounds] of caviar from the fish and kept it for themselves and then phoned to the museum and offered this rare object together with the mound of meat. As far as I know it was decided to preserve meat for cosmonauts. This fish is approximately 130 years old. Anyway she might be coeval of the abolition of serfdom in Russia in 1861. I attached the photo of the fish. Please, admire."

At the end of June 2002, USF&W had released its "Notice of 90-day and 12-month petition findings" in response to Caviar Emptor's petition on the beluga. "Currently, population estimates for Caspian Sea and Black Sea beluga sturgeon are not available," the report observed. "At the present time, the Caspian Sea population is believed to be so depleted that natural reproduction in the wild may be insufficient to sustain the species. Even hatchery production to augment this stock may no longer be a viable alternative due to the lack of available funding to continue artificial propagation programs and maintain an aging hatchery infrastructure in range countries. Additionally, the number of female sturgeon taken in the Volga River delta was considered insufficient to even support artificial propagation efforts." The notice concluded that listing of this species "may be warranted."

Then began a ninety-day period for collecting public comments, a number of which were Frank Chapman's pleas against an ESA listing without an exclusion for aquaculture. But those three months passed without a decision from USF&W. Then, in September, KaspNIRKh released the results of the intergovernmental census of north Caspian sturgeon stocks that the institute had conducted the previous winter. The number of beluga sturgeon in the sea, asserted KaspNIRKh, was approximately 9.3 million.

That number, accepted at face value by CITES, was based on extrapolations from trawl surveys that scientists from Caviar Emptor and nearly anywhere else, inside Russia or out, found indefensible. Ellen Pikitch, a biologist with Caviar Emptor and the Wildlife Conservation Society, asserted that the number was inflated by a factor of at least twenty-five. Vladimir Ivanov, the former director of KaspNIRKh, agreed, telling the *New York Times* on January 4, 2003, that it was not possible that the beluga population had increased to that level, or that it had increased at all. Vadim Birstein, also speaking to the *Times*, was no less skeptical: "CITES is expecting us to believe that they have performed a miracle," he said. "Corrupt Russian officials are distorting the data to get bigger export quotas."

Ivanov's successor at KaspNIRKh, Mark Karpiuk, didn't respond to interview requests from the *Times*, but papers submitted by him to USF&W opposing the beluga listing were cosigned by Dr. Jim Armstrong, the deputy secretary general of CITES. Armstrong told the *Times* that he was confident at least that the decline in beluga numbers since the 1998 inception of CITES had been reversed. "The point here is the trend, not the numbers," he said.

In Azerbaijan, the point had very much to do with the numbers, whether they were votes or export quotas or beluga sturgeons. In August, according to the nation's Central Election Commission, nearly all eligible voters (88 percent) turned out to vote their nearly unanimous approval (96 percent) of President Aliyev's constitutional amendments, including the new provision placing the prime minister next in line for the transfer of presidential power. Opposition leaders and Western observers termed these numbers fraudulent, but that did nothing to delay the inevitable: Aliyev named his son Ilham as prime minister, the U.S. State Department granted its blessing on the procedure, the elder Aliyev decided not to run for reelection, the younger Aliyev won a landslide electoral victory in September 2003 in another process marred by ballot fraud (but endorsed by the United States), and riots erupted in the streets of Baku during the son's inauguration. By then, Heidar Aliyev lay ill in a Cleveland hospital, where he died two months later at the age of eighty.

Before all that, however, Azerbaijan broke ranks with Russia, Kazakhstan, and Turkmenistan on matters of beluga management. In 1992, those countries had agreed to divide the beluga harvest in the north Caspian in proportion to how much each country spent on hatcheries, an arrangement carried forth under CITES in its division of export quotas. In the summer of 2002, however, Azerbaijan demanded a larger share of that quota based on money it had spent in dredging the mouth of the Kura River. After that demand was rebuffed by the other states, Azerbaijan's minister of environmental protection shocked the whole Caspian community with a letter to USF&W endorsing the ESA listing of beluga. "The population of beluga," wrote the minister, "needs to be restored to healthy levels of abundance with a normal age structure before sustainable fishing can resume."

From the perspective of CITES, Caspian range states working together to produce dubious science was one thing; those states not working together at all was quite another, and in October CITES itself banned all trade in beluga meat and caviar, at least until unity was restored in terms of management policy. The next month I e-mailed Katya, asking her if the CITES ban was having any impact in Astrakhan. Her answer contained that photo of the beluga that was about to be put on display. "I have less information about CITES, rather speculations than information," she went on to say. "Beluga is the most rare to find among the red fish family. This fish is spiting itself by having the most delicious caviar. Poachers hunt for beluga mainly. I have no idea how this taboo might consequent. I only know that those who are going to guard the fish must be brave and bribeless enough to oppose the already existing corrupt system. Much depends on such law-keepers and nature-defenders."

In the United States, the law-keepers and nature-defenders had much to do in the airports and the courtrooms. In August 2002, Russian-born Viktor Tsimbal, president and owner of Miami-based Beluga Caviar, pleaded guilty to conspiracy, smuggling, and money laundering for his role in organizing an operation similar to Gino Koczuk's: that is, using couriers to carry suitcases of contraband caviar through U.S. airports. USF&W began its undercover investigation in 2000 when the agency noticed a large discrepancy between legal imports of beluga caviar and the amount on the retail market. They found that in 1999 alone, Tsimbal had imported 22,700 pounds of smuggled caviar. Nearly 6 tons of that was beluga, enough to exceed Russia's entire export quota for the species that year.

In the Mississippi basin in 2002 legal harvests of shovelnose sturgeon and illegal harvests of paddlefish produced trails of eggs that led to the door of Arkady Panchernikov, who resold the roes as varieties of

Caspian caviars. In May, Panchernikov was indicted on six counts of illegal trafficking in caviar, which included smuggling on behalf of Gino Koczuk during the latter's criminal proceedings. Panchernikov, whose annual sales were estimated at $12.5 million, accounting for a U.S. market share that had grown to 60 percent, entered a plea of not guilty. But Cynthia Monaco was confident. "Mr. Panchernikov is the largest importer of caviar in the United States," she told the *New York Times* on May 25, 2002, "and his indictment is a major step in the efforts of the Fish and Wildlife Service to stop illegal harvesting of sturgeon roe."

In November, Panchernikov changed his plea to guilty in a deal with Monaco, and the following May, in Brooklyn's U.S. District Court, he was sentenced to twenty-one months in prison and fined $400,000 by Judge Charles P. Sifton. In the courtroom, Panchernikov's wife, Irma, moaned loudly when her husband was ordered to pay the first $100,000 immediately, according to the *New York Times* of May 3, 2003.

Regarding the Caviarteria's $100 million lawsuit against USF&W, the one in which Vadim Birstein was to have his opportunity to discredit Steve Fain's DNA test, Ed Grace told me that the case had been on the verge of being settled out of court when Bruce Sobol died in an apparent suicide on July 21, 2003. Sobol had been locked in a legal battle with his brother Eric's widow over control of the business, and five of Caviarteria's seven locations had closed within the past two years.

With its informal and unpretentious atmosphere, Caviarteria would have seemed better suited than Petrossian to flourish among the new wave of New York restaurants. But of course everything that could have gone wrong had gone wrong. The *New York Post* reported on July 23, 2003, that Sobol had overdosed on sleeping pills and had been found in his East Side apartment with a plastic bag tied over his head. Eve Vega told me that once again there was speculation within the industry about a suicide that might have been a murder instead. In either event, his death derailed that out-of-court settlement.

Back in December 2002, after Panchernikov had entered his plea bargain, Ed Grace sent me an e-mail from Chicago. He said that over the previous two months he had made more than twenty flights to New York and back to work on the Panchernikov case, and he was relieved that it wouldn't be going to trial after all. "I am also sort of lucky that I was single during the last two years," he added. "I am not sure how a family would have handled all the traveling and late nights." He remembered slogging with assistant U.S. district attorneys Monaco and Peter Norling down the middle of the street in Brooklyn during a snowstorm on New Year's Day 2001 to get to their offices. The storm had shut the city down. "But we had to get the Koczuk appeals brief done and out the next day to the Circuit Court of Appeals," he wrote. "Brooklyn was covered in over a foot of snow and there was no traffic anywhere because the streets had not been plowed, and we were walking to work. In the end it turned out very well, but I am sure it was a big sacrifice for Monaco's and Norling's families. We won the appeal and now a lot of the cases are pleading in this country before they go to trial because the defendants don't want to lose at trial and face very large prison sentences."

He mentioned that Vladislav Tartakovsky, the former head of a firm called Caviar Supreme, had just been apprehended in New York. "He was working with Koczuk and is the last one to come out of the Koczuk investigation, which will then end a five-year investigation," Grace wrote.

Grace knew that also marked the end, probably, of that portion of his career devoted to chasing caviar smugglers. "It's funny," he wrote. "I was watching the end of *The Untouchables* last night (I have to—it was filmed in Chicago), and the last scene is where Elliot Ness (No, I am not Elliot Ness) is putting all the news clippings in a file and packing his things up. I did the same thing last week with the news clippings from the caviar cases in New York, and had a very surreal moment. Eve Vega's favorite quote to give the newspapers is that if we list sturgeons as endangered species, it will cause the caviar industry to be just like Chicago, Capone, and liquor. But Eve, I think it has already been like that for some time."

iii.

The female had been turned, and a hose to feed water to her gills fitted into her mouth. The white mantle of her belly, laced with tracings of gray, had a glow of tenderness and innocence among the metallic overtones of the fluorescent lights. The tips of her fins were brushed in mauve, like fingernail polish. Jack Siple stood hunched over her breadth, a white plastic ladle held in supplication against her vent. Chris

Lewandowski, with both hands in white latex gloves, worked his fingers down the length of her belly, pressing and releasing and pressing again. The skin rippled in a wave ahead of his fingers. "Here's your first scoop," Chris said.

Her vent was the length of a fingertip, extending horizontally across her abdomen below an iodine-colored cut, sewn with stitches. The cut had been made several weeks ago to assess the condition of her eggs. Jack said forty eggs had been needed for the sample, but with this particular fish he had a heck of time finding any. Finally he made do with thirty-nine. The sample eggs were boiled, fixed in formalin, sliced for viewing under a microscope, and sent to Joel Van Eenennaam at UC-Davis. Joel confirmed Jack's conviction that she was ready for the hormone that induces ovulation. Now the vent's lips were swollen and even whiter than her belly. A crystalline spurt of ovarian fluid, like water from an underpressurized water fountain, fell into the ladle. "Nothing," Jack said. "No eggs. I can't believe that."

Chris and Sue stared into the ladle, which might have been empty, the fluid was so clear. Chris returned to his massage, grumbling, "They're all on the bottom of the tank."

Jack emptied the fluid into a stainless steel basin just in time to catch a second spurt. A single drop of darkness floated in the midst of the ladle. Jack said, "Well, we got one egg."

"When did she start dropping eggs?" Sue wondered.

"That was 3:30," Jack replied. "So it's been two hours."

Chris found several more eggs with a swipe of his hand into the water below the fish. "There's at least two or three thousand eggs in this tank," Chris ventured. "Maybe more. Maybe she dumped 20,000 before we could get to her."

That was an issue that could be settled right away with a cesarean section, but Sue only needed some of her eggs, not all of them. What Chris and Jack were doing instead of a c-section was called hand-stripping. Chris said the method had been discovered here accidentally when Larry Aitken, one of Bob Aitken's several brothers, happened to rub the belly of an ovulating female. The method yielded nowhere near the quantity of eggs of a c-section or sacrifice, but more than enough for the modest goals of conservation aquaculture, and with none of the trauma or risks of surgery.

"I can't believe there's just one egg," Jack murmured, to himself this time, as Chris moved his hands up and down both flanks of the fish.

"No, she's got a lot of eggs," Chris said at last, "if we can just get them."

Chris went back to his hand-stripping, which produced another spurt of fluid. "Here they come," Jack said. He swore under his breath to find that again his ladle held only a single lonely egg.

"She hasn't dilated yet," Eric offered.

"Well, she's pumping fluid," said Chris. "She's pushing herself."

Jack said, "I'm thinking about turning her over, but . . . "

Chris's hands were working a point up and to the right of her vent. "It feels like she's got a lump or obstruction right here. Something feels solid."

He looked into the basin that held the fluid, which was being saved for a project at the university, and wondered if there was enough fluid yet for that. "Yep," Jack nodded gloomily. "That stuff may be all we get."

"This fish is what—sixty, seventy years old?"

"Maybe eighty, maybe older," Jack nodded.

"I think some of these fish are just a little too far past their prime." Chris pressed his right hand against that solid spot and looked at Jack. "Want to try a controlled shake?"

"Can't do worse."

They turned her gently onto her stomach, then lowered the stretcher back into the tank. As soon as she was submerged, but still enclosed, she lunged left, then right, then left again, throwing sheets of water from both sides of the tank. Sue and the rest of us skipped backward, but Chris and Jack stood at the stretcher and took their soakings. "There you go," Jack cried.

Chris smiled and freed one hand to wipe his glasses against his T-shirt. "If that doesn't break her loose . . . "

The fish came streaming out of the water again. They turned her on her back once more and refitted her with the hose. Chris had barely touched her before another spout of fluid issued forth. "Oh, yeah, here we go now," Eric said.

"Probably one more egg," Jack suspected. He glanced into the ladle. "Yep—what did I tell you? That's three now." At that moment the fluid blackened and clumped into a stream of eggs. "Uh-oh, here we go." The ladle filled to overflowing almost instantly. Sue hastily provided the basin intended for the eggs. Several fell onto the fish's belly and skittered down her sides as Jack emptied the ladle. He held the ladle beneath her vent again, but the eggs thinned out, though the fluid kept coming. Chris was puffing with the effort of working her belly. "Sorry you're working so hard," Jack said.

"Well, I'm just afraid of hurting the fish."

"I tell you, I've never seen so much ovarian fluid."

"Is that good or bad?" asked one of the graduate students.

"It's good. It keeps the eggs moist."

The fluid went black again, coming in spurts of watery jam. The first basin had been filled, and Bob Aitken was at Jack's side with the second. Sue was taking several 2-milligram samples from the first batch of eggs. These she spread in a petri dish, and then she set to counting the eggs in each sample, one by one, in order to get an average count for 2 milligrams. From that she would be able to generate an estimate of the total number of eggs from this female. Jack's ladle was filled and emptied, filled and emptied, sometimes trailing strings of slime from its lips. "She's going like an oil well now," Chris said.

By 6:15, three Canadians had arrived from the BC hatchery. Traci Jensen, the tall and angular lead scientist with the Canadian contingent, told Sue that the CITES permits were in order for them to carry 10,000 fertilized eggs across the border. Sue estimated that the fish had yielded about 30,000 eggs by then. Jack glanced up and whistled. "Man, you'd be surprised," he said. "It doesn't look like much, but all of a sudden you've got a lot."

"Maybe we should give her a rest," Chris suggested.

They turned her around and dropped her into the water again, where she floated placidly, her fins just stirring. After a few minutes she was on her back in the stretcher. Chris, with his fingers aching, renewed his encouragement, but the oil well had stopped, offering neither eggs nor fluid. Jack stood up and rubbed his back. Chris grumbled, "That's what I get for being a nice guy. Let's put her in the water again, let her kick."

Which is what she immediately did, as Eric leaned over the tank, her tail lashing within a hair's-breadth of his goatee. She took a few more exploratory swipes with her tail as Eric looked on from a safer distance. Traci asked Chris if the fishing had been slow this spring. "It's been muddy, but you can see we're spawning," he replied. "We actually could have spawned last week. We had the fish already. But we have naturally high run-off this time of year. The banks are falling in with the road run-off, and the water was so muddy last week it overwhelmed the sediment filters."

Bob Aitken had been joined by his brother Ralph, also a hatchery technician, also a big man with a gentle manner. He had Bob's high-strung Husky trailing at his heels. "We could do better if the dam was more cooperative," Ralph said. "But they've got other species to worry about, and they never used to cooperate at all."

He wondered if the eggs were cold. "They're pretty cool," Eric told him, "but they're not broken or anything."

By 6:45 the fish had been raised and turned again. She surrendered more eggs, but only at intervals in occasional clumps. "She's drying out, isn't she?" said Jack.

Chris straightened, making fists with his tired hands and then stretching his fingers. He wondered how long she had been out. Eric looked at his watch: "An hour and twenty."

Chris didn't think that was too much, but that she could be allowed another break. "She's just pushing so hard," he said, feeling her girth once more. "There are eggs still in there, but they're deep. That lump is gone, though."

I asked Sue what the lump might have been. "Maybe a tiny bit of water got in through that cut when we sampled her a few weeks ago," she said. "If that happens, it'll make some of the eggs sticky and they'll clump. That's a theory, anyway."

The fish's next turn yielded only a few more eggs, and the skin around her vent and stretching up her belly had grown pink. At 7:15, Chris said, "That's enough abuse for this fish. We don't want to hurt her." He spread antiseptic jelly on her vent, on the surgical cut, and on the skin surrounding both. Then she was lowered back into the tank and the stretcher slipped from beneath her. She floated motionless for a moment as the river water pumping through the tank coursed over and around her. Finally she eased forward, in slow motion, before resting her snout again against its wall.

Sue already had the complete batch weighed and a production figure available that she had passed on to Jack. "Fifty-five thousand, seven hundred eggs total for this girl," he announced to the group, rather in the manner of the proud father.

Chris had already joined Sue and Jack and various Canadians, graduate students, and hatchery technicians in carrying out the next step, the process of mixing spoonfuls of Fuller's Earth, a fine silt used for rock polishing, into basins full of roe.

"We did a c-section here once in '92, and we're never going to do that again," Eric told me. "We were told that hand-stripping wasn't practical, that at most we'd get 20,000 eggs, but we've actually gotten as many as 120,000. . . . It just depends on how long you want to keep her in the stretcher."

This somewhat elderly fish, #262 in the registry of a race numbering in no more than three-digit figures, had done her job. She would be returned to the river and not taken again to be put in a stretcher except in the event of a catastrophe. Her 55,700 offspring, a few of them anyway, once the silt had stripped them of their adhesive jelly and they had been fertilized with sperm, and once they had bubbled in an incubating jar for a few days, hatched into larvae, and waxed into fingerlings, would be part of the next annual attempt to find and unplug the spawning bottleneck in the river. They would serve as insurance as well for as long as the bottleneck—and the collaborative will to do something about it—persisted.

Sue was getting milt out of refrigeration and making it available to those who stood opposite each other along a harvest table, all using the quill-end of turkey feathers to keep the eggs and silt circulating. The scraping of the feathers mixed with the murmur of conversation and the heartbeat of the water as Jack eased the sheltering cover back into place over the exhausted fish.

iv.

I was flying home the next morning, but that evening, around 7:30, Jack Siple phoned me in my room at the Kootenai Inn, telling me to come down to the hatchery again. In a room off the inn's main lobby, the slot machines, with their bright lights and happy chimes, were already in motion, but outside the sun shot in slivers of rose and peach across the Selkirks. The streets of Bonners Ferry had already gone empty and silent, and the river, in shadow, ran in hues of deep violet beneath the bridge.

I turned off Route 95 and made my way through thinning houses and spreading fields to the river once more, and then the hatchery. Jack had told me earlier that day that he had worked many years for Idaho Fish and Game, but it had not been a good marriage, and he had ended it abruptly one day by retiring. "Retiring?" his supervisor said over the phone. "You can't do that without the paperwork."

"Check your FAX machine," Jack suggested.

Then he had been lured out of retirement by the Kootenai Tribe to manage the spawning and oversee the grunt work at this hatchery. That meant more trouble with Fish and Game, which at first was opposed to a hatchery on the river. "But then Sue got here and she smoothed things down. She's good at that," Jack recalled.

He had admitted earlier today that he was getting old for this, that sometime soon he would have to step back and let someone else pilot these fish through spawning. He admitted also that he was as uncertain as anybody as to the success of this project. "We know we're doing all we can, but is it enough?" he wondered. "Did we start soon enough? Or is it already too late?"

Then there was that other part of him that wanted to wait for that answer, even if it meant setting his clock by sturgeon time. Last winter Idaho Senator Mike Crapo had come to the hatchery with a TV news crew, and the broadcast report on the visit had included a video clip of Jack releasing a juvenile sturgeon into the river the previous spring. "Take care of yourself," Jack had called after the fish. "See you in twenty-five years, I hope."

He was alone at the hatchery that night. He had gone thirty-six hours without sleep, and the lines on his face had deepened into arroyos and dry gullies. The dam, he mentioned, was about to release a lot of very cold water over the next six hours, and it was lucky we had gotten our work done today. He was jubilant over the fertilization rates of the eggs: 98 percent for the batch to be kept here, 71 percent for the university's batches, 76 percent for Traci Jensen's. But what he wanted me to see before I left was on a slide beneath a microscope.

During the afternoon Jack had set up just a pair of eggs in a petri dish beneath that same microscope. I had bent down to the eyepieces and my breath had caught in my throat. The eggs were identical, except that one was tipped slightly. Both showed the stunning shifts in pigmentation that occur in sturgeon eggs immediately after fertilization. There were round and inky orbs at the tips of their raised ends, as black as wormholes through time; these were ringed in a sort of mineral beige. Then there was another ring of black that faded into an iridescent umber lit with undertones of gold and rose.

Livingstone Stone, regarding his salmon eggs at the McCloud River hatchery, had been thrilled by the "world of promise" he saw in "the little black speck in the unhatched embryo." This was too soon for that sort of promise, but not for this opalescent beauty that took me completely by surprise, that in concert with the eggs' vulnerability and perfection made my eyes nearly sting with tears. Their coatings of fluid encased them in a glass that gleamed in the light flooding up from below. Even the minuscule cracks and stress lines in the plastic of the petri dish suggested these were gems at rest on a setting of quartz.

Now, ten hours later, the promise had arrived as well. The cleavages had commenced, that process of cell division that proceeds at such a furious pace even with sturgeons. Jack had put seven eggs under the microscope, all at various stages of cleavage and polarization. The black orbs at their upper poles had disappeared, replaced in two or three of the eggs by tan puzzle-pieces of interlocking lobes. These seemed to rise on pedestals, to be about to burst through the glass. In others the lobes at one side had broken down into smaller sections, creating a sort of shingled and pebbled effect. In one egg, the most advanced, the lobes had dissolved entirely into a starburst of lighter and darker pixels.

The eggs were as lovely as they had been before, and no less vulnerable, but now were full of portent and purpose, full of a rampant energy, its spark struck somewhere in the bowels of the sun when—as Jay Gatsby conceived it—the rock of the world was being balanced on a fairy's wing.

This was the pap of life, the milk of wonder, both the food of the gods and its seed. I rose from the eggs, my eyes welling with tears, my mind poised for only a transitory moment over the continents and rivers of a world without sin.

EPILOGUE

On April 20, 2004, the U.S. Fish and Wildlife Service ruled—under the terms of the Endangered Species Act—that the beluga sturgeon was threatened, but not endangered. The service pledged to rule within six months whether imports of beluga caviar to the United States would be reduced or eliminated. The agency also ruled that the aquaculture of beluga sturgeon in the United States was prohibited.

In July, Caviarteria settled its suit against the federal government. "The government gets the caviar and Caviarteria gets one dollar," wrote Ed Grace. "What a strange ending to a very strange event. After six years nothing really gets decided on the DNA."

As of October 2004, USF&W still had not ruled on the status of beluga caviar imports to the United States. But in the previous month CITES had temporarily halted the export of all caviar—beluga, osetra, and sevruga—from the Caspian range countries. Dr. Jim Armstrong, the deputy secretary general of CITES, explained that the countries had failed to live up to an agreement signed in 2001 that pledged an accurate accounting of how much sturgeon was harvested illegally.

On the Kootenai River, the 2003 and 2004 spawning seasons passed with no evidence yet of successful natural recruitment of young sturgeons into the wild population. By 2003, the adult population had dwindled to 600 fish. USF&W has extended its timeline on the project, targeting sometime between 2020 and 2030 as a point at which the adult population would stabilize at 3,000, with—if still necessary—infusions of hatchery-spawned fish.

ACKNOWLEDGMENTS

All the singular hours spent at a keyboard during the composition of a book tend to obscure the degree to which such a project is a cooperative endeavor. Without the help, encouragement, and forward momentum of the following, this particular project could never have gotten off the bottom of the river:

My former editor Chris Carduff, who conceived this book in the first place, and Amanda Cook, who for a time carried on ably in Chris's place;

A host of good friends or relatives, all of whom alerted me to stories or references I might otherwise have missed, foremost among them Tom Carey, Doug White, the late Brian Gibbons, David and Susan Lyons, John and Rosemary Winslow, and Sam Pierson;

My brothers-in-law Dave Sherman and Brad Sherman, both of whom helped plug gaps in my office technology, and the Alaskan writer Jeff Fair, who provided companionship from afar during all those singular hours, as did Katie Goodman and the trustees of the New Hampshire Writers Project;

Ron Davidson, archivist of the Sandusky Library in Sandusky, Ohio, and the Illinois author and naturalist Joel Greenbaum, both of whom provided important materials or references on the history of the Midwest's lake sturgeon fisheries;

David Sleeper, now of the Hubbard Brook Research Foundation, who was the first champion of my writing in his days as an editor at *Country Journal* magazine, and who remains a friend, advocate, and pro bono editor;

The author and naturalist Dick Russell, who provided a wealth of contacts among conservationists in both Russia and North America, and who recommended the services of San Francisco travel agent extraordinaire Debbie Chapman (it was thanks only to Debbie that my travel to Eurasia went as smoothly as it did);

The documentary film-maker Beth Solomon, who provided valuable advice for my research around the Caspian;

Many members of the Institute for Social Action and Renewal in Eurasia (ISAR)—among them Kate Watters, Michelle Kinman, and Eliza Klose in Washington; Aleksey Knizhnikov in Moscow; and Stephanie Rust, Enver Safar-zade, and Zamina Shikhiyeva in Baku—all of whom generously extended their help, and in Aleksey's case his hospitality as well, throughout my research in Russia and Azerbaijan;

Phil Peck, Head of School of the Holderness School and a scholar of Russian culture and history, who provided not only a valuable introduction to his areas of expertise, but support and cheerleading throughout the duration of this project;

Mary Kietzman, librarian of the Holderness School, who over and over again managed to find the hard-to-find book or reference, and who of all people was the most invaluable to my print-media research effort;

All the people who graciously volunteered their time, their confidence, and some portion of their privacy in order to play roles in this book, though several did even more than that: Ed Grace of the U.S. Fish & Wildlife Service, who kept me abreast of all developments regarding law enforcement throughout the duration of this project; Dr. Vadim Birstein, who sought out contacts for me in Eurasia, who kept me particularly informed of developments in the Caspian, and who so conscientiously coached me through the intricacies of his own work; Dr. John Waldman of the Hudson River Foundation, who generously reviewed the entire manuscript of this work, offering necessary corrections and Galina and Katya Godunova, who made me feel at home when I was farthest from home.

My friend and mentor Jim Brewer, now retired from the Holderness School, who also read the entire manuscript, and on every page found ways to tighten and clarify my writing;

My agent Gary Morris of the David Black Literary Agency, who struck the spark that set this in motion;

Of the Perseus Books Group, my editor Megan Hustad, whose insight and sensitivity allowed her to find the beating heart of a rather bloated first draft of this manuscript; copy editor Kathy Streckfus, who so skillfully pared the manuscript down to that heart without injuring a single major artery; and project manager Iris Richmond, who patiently kept everything on track, on schedule, and on target;

My children, Ryan Adams Carey and Kyle Anne Carey, who not only endured the many inconveniences and absences occasioned by this project, but did so with humor and unfailing encouragement;

And my wife, Susan Atwood Carey, who endured the same inconveniences and absences, who responded with her own measures of humor and encouragement, who patiently listened to each chapter as it rolled out of the printer and was read aloud, and who served as this story's first and most fundamental guiding spirit.

BIBLIOGRAPHY

Angier, Natalie. "Cooking and How It Slew the Beast Within." *New York Times,* May 22, 2002.

Asimov, Eric. "C'est la fin! Lutèce Closing After 43 Years." *New York Times,* February 11, 2004.

Askerov, F.S., Y.Y. Zaytsev, R.Y. Kausmov, and Z. Kuliyev. *Amazing Caspian Fishes.* Baku, Azerbaijan: Print Studio, 2001.

Askerov, Faik, Yuliy Zaytsev, and Sissel Tresselt. *Wonderful Wildlife of the Caspian Sea.* Baku, Azerbaijan: International Operating Company, 1999.

Associated Press. "Baku Riots as Aliyev Ascends." November 4, 2003.

Avers News. "Fishing of Sturgeon in Russia and Trade in Them." London: TRAFFIC Europe, 2000.

Bain, Mark B., Nancy Haley, Douglas L. Peterson, Kristin K. Arend, Kathy E. Mills, and Patrick J. Sullivan. "Shortnose Sturgeon of the Hudson River: An Endangered Species Recovery Success." Paper presented at the Annual Meeting of the American Fisheries Society, St. Louis, August 23–24, 2000.

Bain, M., N. Haley, D. Peterson, J.R. Waldman, and K. Arend. "Harvest and Habitats of Atlantic Sturgeon *Acipenser oxyrinchus* Mitchill 1815 in the Hudson River Estuary: Lesson for Sturgeon Conservation." *Bulletin of the Spanish Institute of Oceanography* 16, nos. 1–4, 2000.

Bainard, J. "DNA Fingerprinting to Track Caviar." Science News On-Line, sciencenews.org, August 22, 1998.

Balon, Eugene K., ed. *Environmental Biology of Fishes* 48, nos. 1–4, March 1997.

Bates, Marston. *The Forest and the Sea.* New York: Random House, 1960.

Beauvoir, Simone de. *The Ethics of Ambiguity.* Paris: Gallimard, 1947.

Bellafonte, Ginia. "Avoiding Overt Sensuality in a Time of Vulnerability." *New York Times,* October 16, 2001.

Bemis, William E., and Eric Findeis. "The Sturgeons' Plight." *Nature* 370, August 25, 1994.

Berniker, Mark. "Azerbaijan Confronts Myriad Risks in Economic Development Efforts." Eurasianet.com, February 6, 2003.

Billington, James. *The Icon and the Axe: An Interpretive History of Russian Culture.* New York: Knopf, 1966.

Binder, David. "Biologists Breathe New Life into Sturgeon's Ancient Habitat." *New York Times,* July 2, 2002.

Birstein, Vadim J. "New Perspectives for Monitoring Migratory Animals." *Environmental Policy and Law* 29, no. 5, 1999.

_____. "Sturgeons and Paddlefish." In *Endangered Animals: A Reference Guide to Conflicting Issues,* edited by Richard P. Reading and Brian Miller. Westport, Conn.: Greenwood, 2000.

_____. *The Perversion of Knowledge: The True Story of Soviet Science.* Boulder: Westview, 2001.

_____. "Sturgeon Species and Hybrids: Can Hybrids Produce Caviar?" *Environmental Policy and Law* 32, no. 5, 2002.

Birstein, Vadim J., and Phaedra Doukakis. "Molecular Identification of Sturgeon Species: Science, Bureaucracy, and the Impact of Environmental Agreements." In *Monitoring Migratory Animals.* Bonn, Germany: Federal Agency for Nature Conservation, 2001.

Birstein, Vadim J., Phaedra Doukakis, and Rob DeSalle. "Molecular Phylogeny of Acipenseridae and Black Caviar Identification." *Journal of Applied Ichthyology* 15, 1999.

_____. "Polyphyly of mtDNA in the Russian Sturgeon, *Acipenser gueldenstaedtii:* Forensic and Evolutionary Implications." *Conservation Genetics* 1, no. 1, 2000.

Bishop, Jerry E. "Something Fishy." *Wall Street Journal,* May 17, 1996.

Bober, Phyllis Pray. *Art, Culture, and Cuisine: Ancient and Medieval Gastronomy.* Chicago: University of Chicago Press, 1999.

Boeckmann, Susie, and Natalie Rebeiz-Nielsen. *Caviar: The Definitive Guide.* London: Octopus.

Bogue, Margaret Beattie. *Fishing the Great Lakes: An Environmental History, 1783–1933.* Madison: University of Wisconsin Press, 2000. Citing W.B. Scott and E.J. Crossman. *Freshwater Fishes of Canada.* Ottawa: Fisheries Research Board of Canada, 1973; and Records of the Joint Commission Relative to the Preservation of Fisheries in Waters Contiguous to the United States and Canada. Record Group 22. Great Lakes Materials, 1893–1895.

Booth, Chris. "Russian Pigs' Caviar Treat." BBC News, January 26, 1901.

Bowles, Samuel. *Our New West.* Hartford, Conn.: Hartford Publishing, 1969.

Boyle, Robert H. *The Hudson River: A Natural and Unnatural History.* New York: W.W. Norton, 1969.

_____. "The Cost of Caviar." *Amicus Journal,* Spring 1994.

Brillat-Savarin, Jean Anthelme. *The Physiology of Taste: Meditations on Transcendental Gastronomy.* New York: Liveright.

British Columbia, Ministry of the Environment, Department of Fisheries. Miscellaneous correspondences; annual reports; BC Fisheries Reports. Coqualeetza Archives and University of British Columbia special collections library.

Brock, Pope. "RFK Jr.'s River of Trouble." *Talk*, October 2000.

Brozan, Nadine. "Bill Murray, Sturgeon Friend." *New York Times*, July 30, 1994.

Bruch, R.M. "Management of Lake Sturgeon on Winnebago System: Long-Term Impacts of Harvest and Regulation on the Population Structure." *Journal of Applied Ichthyology* 15, 1999.

Burgess, Robert. "Florida's Sturgeon Spree." *Outdoor Life*, March 1963.

Burkard, Hans-Jurgen. "Black Gold." *LIFE*, February 2000.

Burnhill, Tim. "Pillars of Fire, Poison Gas—and Gobs of Oil, Too." *Science* 295, January 18, 2002.

Burros, Marian. "Unraveling a Caviar Mystery." *New York Times*, February 7, 2002.

Campton, Donald E., Anna L. Bass, Frank A. Chapman, and Brian W. Bowen. "Genetic Distinction of Pallid, Shovelnose, and Alabama Sturgeon: Emerging Species and the US Endangered Species Act." *Conservation Genetics* 1, no. 1, 2000.

Canon, Scott. "Insatiable Hunger for Caviar Spells Trouble for Missouri Sturgeon." *Kansas City Star*, November 26, 2002.

Carr, Archie. *A Naturalist in Florida: A Celebration of Eden*. New Haven, Conn.: Yale University Press, 1994.

Carr, S.H., F. Tatman, and F.A. Chapman. "Observations on the Natural History of the Gulf of Mexico Sturgeon (*Acipenser oxyrinchus de sotoi* Vladykov 1955) in the Suwannee River, Southeastern United States," *Ecology of Freshwater Fish* 5, 1996.

Caspian Revenue Watch. "Caspian Oil Windfalls: Who Will Benefit?" Open Society Institute, 2003.

Catesby, M. *The Natural History of Carolina, Florida, and the Bahama Islands*. Vol. 1. London, 1731.

Chapman, Frank A., and Stephen H. Carr. "Implications of Early Life Stages in the Natural History of the Gulf of Mexico Sturgeon, *Acipenser oxyrinchus de sotoi*." *Environmental Biology of Fishes* 43, 1995.

Clarkson, Jesse D. *A History of Russia*. New York: Random House, 1961.

Clugston, J.P., A.M. Foster, and S.H. Carr. "Gulf Sturgeon, *Acipenser oxyrinchus de sotoi*, in the Suwannee River, Florida, U.S.A." In *Proceedings of the International Symposium on Sturgeons*, edited by A.D. Gershovich and T.I.J. Smith. Moscow, September 6–11, 1993.

Cobb, John N. "The Sturgeon Fishery of the Delaware River and Bay." Report of the State [PA] Commissioners of Fisheries for the Years 1892–94, U.S. Commission of Fish and Fisheries, Washington, D.C., 1895.

Coleman, C.W. "Sturgeon Fishing in the James." *Cosmopolitan*, 1892.

Collins, Judy. "Goodbye to Buttery Blini." *New York Times*, July 30, 2002.

Conte, Fred S., Serge I. Doroshov, Paul B. Lutes, and Elizabeth M. Strange. *Hatchery Manual for the White Sturgeon*, Acipenser transmontanus *Richardson*, *with Application to Other North American Acipenseridae*. Cooperative Extension University of California, Division of Agriculture and Natural Resources, Publication 3322, Oakland, 1988.

Crawford, Matt. "Sea Lamprey Hitting Sturgeon Hard." *Burlington Free Press*, Vermont, April 15, 2001.

Cullen, Robert. "The Rise and Fall of the Caspian Sea." *National Geographic*, May 1999.

Demac, Nancy Churnin. "Here's Who's Cooking." *San Francisco*, March 1985.

De Salle, Rob, and Vadim J. Birstein. "PCR Identification of Black Caviar." *Nature*, April 22, 1996.

Doland, Angela. "Three Caspian States Agree to Halt Sturgeon Fishing for a Year." *San Francisco Chronicle*, June 21, 2001.

Doyle, Clare. "Tension Brewing in Azerbaijan over Planned Constitutional Referendum." Eurasianet.com, July 12, 2002.

Dubinin, Maksim, and Nikolai Maleshin. "The Green Referendum." *Russian Conservation News* 24, Fall/Winter 2000.

Duke, S., P. Anders, G. Ennis, R. Hallock, J. Hammond, S. Ireland, J. Laufle, R. Lauzier, L. Lockhard, B. Marotz, V.L. Paragamian, and R. Westerhof. "Recovery Plan for Kootenai River White Sturgeon." *Journal of Applied Ichthyology* 15, 1999.

Dumas, Alexandre. *Le Grand Dictionnaire de Cuisine*. Vol. 3, *Poissons*. Payré, France: Edit-France, 1995 [1873].

Dunn, J.P., Jr. *Massacres of the Mountains*. New York: Harper and Brothers, 1886.

Eaton, Leslie. "A Family Tale of Infidelity." *New York Times*, January 20, 2003.

Faber, Harold. "Cornell Biologist Studies Sturgeon's Steep Decline." *New York Times*, July 25, 1994.

Fabricant, Florence. "A Credible Soy Stand-In for Caviar." *New York Times*, July 18, 2001.

———. "La Caravelle, a French Legend, Is Closing After 43 Years." *New York Times*, May 21, 2004.

Fakler, John T. "Eggs a la O-Town: Fishy Business to Reap Roe." *Orlando Business Journal*, June 23, 2003.

Fernández-Armesto, Felipe. *Near a Thousand Tables: A History of Food*. New York: Free Press, 2002.

Figes, Orlando. "Who Lost the Soviet Union?" *New York Times*, January 20, 2002.

Filipov, David. "Poaching Spawns the Caviar Mafia." *Boston Globe*, May 26, 2002.

Fisher, Patricia. "New Caviar Measure to Protect Imperiled Sturgeon." U.S. Fish and Wildlife Service, March 25, 1998.

Fitzgerald, F. Scott. *The Great Gatsby*. New York: Charles Scribner's Sons, 1925.

Flannery, Tim. *The Eternal Frontier: An Ecological History of North America and Its Peoples*. New York: Atlantic Monthly Press, 2001.

Fletcher, Jane. "The Great Caviar Caper." *San Francisco Chronicle*, June 5, 1996.

Frantz, Douglas. "Iran and Azerbaijan Argue over Caspian's Riches." *New York Times*, August 30, 2001.

_____. "Pipeline to the Past Is a Gift from Oil to Archeology." *New York Times*, September 19, 2001.

Friedman, Robert I. *Red Mafiya: How the Russian Mob Has Invaded America*. Boston: Little, Brown, 2000.

Friend, Tim. "How Sturgeon Eggs Take the DNA Test." *USA Today*, March 31, 1998.

Fulmer, Melinda. "Cultivating a Niche for Farmed Caviar." *Los Angeles Times*, May 13, 2001.

Gershanovich, Andrew D, and Theodore I.J. Smith, eds. *Proceedings, International Symposium on Sturgeons, September 6–11, 1993*. Moscow: VNIRO, 1995.

Gibson, Gail. "Caviar Scheme Nets Record Fine." *Baltimore Sun*, July 20, 2002.

Glaberson, William. "Caviar Seller Faces Charges of Illegal Distribution and False Records." *New York Times*, May 25, 2002.

Glavin, Terry. *A Ghost in the Water*. Vancouver: New Star Books, 1994.

Godunova, Galina. "Massive Die-Off of Caspian Seals—A Warning Sign for Human Beings." *Give & Take: A Journal of Civil Society in Eurasia* 3, no. 4, Winter 2001.

_____. "Where the Volga Meets the Caspian." *Moscow Today & Tomorrow* 10, no. 1, January 2001.

Goldstein, Darra. "Caviar Dreams." *Saveur*, January–February 1998.

Goltz, Thomas. *Azerbaijan Diary: A Rogue Reporter's Adventures in an Oil-Rich, War-Torn, Post-Soviet Republic*. Armonk, N.Y.: M.E. Sharpe, 1998.

Golubov, Boris. "The Caspian: Receptacle for Radiation." *Give & Take: A Journal of Civil Society in Eurasia* 3, no. 4, Winter 2001.

Goode, George Brown. *The Fisheries and Fishing Industry of the United States*. Washington, D.C.: Government Printing Office, 1884.

Gorman, James. "Yosemite and the Invention of Wilderness." *New York Times*, September 2, 2003.

Grace, Ed, and Diana Weaver. "Caviar Smuggler Pleads Guilty." U.S. Fish and Wildlife Service, March 30, 2001.

Grant, Mark. *Roman Cookery: Ancient Recipes for Modern Kitchens*. London: Serif, 1999.

Gravitz, Lauren. "Rare-Species Backlog." *Discover*, January 2002.

Greenburg, Joel. *A Natural History of the Chicago Region*. Chicago: University of Chicago Press, 2002.

Hamilton, Anita. "The Beluga's Blues." *Time* 161, no. 2, January 20, 2003.

Handelman, Stephen. *Comrade Criminal: Russia's New Mafiya*. New Haven, Conn.: Yale University Press, 1995.

Hansen, Dan. "Group to Sue for Libby Dam Water Release." *Spokesman Review,* Spokane, May 8, 2002.

Hauserman, Julie. "US Warning Cans Plan to Eat Rare Fish." *St. Petersburg Times* (Florida), February 21, 2000.

Herald, Earl. *Fishes of North America*. New York: Doubleday, 1972.

Hildebrand, Samuel F., and William C. Schroeder. *Fishes of Chesapeake Bay*. Neptune, N.J.: Smithsonian Institute, TFH Publications, 1972.

Hoffman, David. *The Oligarchs: Wealth and Power in the New Russia*. New York: PublicAffairs, 2002.

Hofman, Mike. "Dossier: The Sturgeon General." *INC.COM*, March 2002.

Holliday, J.S. "The California Gold Rush Reconsidered." In *Probing the American West: Papers from the Santa Fe Conference*. Santa Fe: Museum of New Mexico Press, 1962.

Holloway, Margeurite. "Caviar on the Hudson." *Audubon*, May-June 1994.

Hoover, Aaron. "A Century of Sturgeon: The History, Biology, and Future of the Gulf of Mexico Sturgeon in Florida." Thesis, Department of Fisheries and Aquatic Sciences, University of Florida, 2002.

Hopkirk, Peter. *The Great Game: The Struggle for Empire in Central Asia*. New York: Kodansha, 1992.

Horvath, Stephanie M. "Caviar Industry Fights Efforts to Add Fish to Endangered List." *Wall Street Journal*, August 12, 2002.

Hosking, Geoffrey. *Russia and the Russians: A History*. Cambridge, Mass.: Belknap, 2001.

Ingwerson, Marshall. "Ancient Fish of the Caviar Trade Now Faces Smugglers, Oil Drills." *Christian Science Monitor*, August 19, 1997.

Ireland, Susan C., Paul J. Anders, and John T. Siple. "Conservation Aquaculture: An Adaptive Approach to Prevent Extinction of an Endangered White Sturgeon Population." In *Biology, Management, and Protection of North American Sturgeon*, edited by W. Van Winkle, P.J. Anders, D.H. Secor, and D. Dixon. American Fisheries Society Symposium 28. Bethesda, Md.: American Fisheries Society, 2002.

Irving, Washington. *History, Tales, Sketches*. Edited by James W. Tuttleton. New York: Library of America, 1983.

Ivanov, V.P. *Biological Resources of the Caspian Sea*. Astrakhan, Russia: Caspian Fisheries Research Institute, 2000.

Ivanov, V.P., S.I. Nikonorov, and Yu N. Perevaryukha. "May Caviar of Siberian Sturgeon Be Present in Sturgeon Caviar Supplied from the Volga River?" World Conservation Trust, IWMC.org.

Johnson, Kirk. "PCB Cleanup in Upper Hudson River Delayed Another Year." *New York Times*, March 11, 2003.

Kahn, Joseph. "Why West's Billions Failed to Give Russia Robust Economy." *New York Times*, November 2, 2000.

Kakutani, Michiko. "Underground Economics Equal Money to Be Made." *New York Times*, May 21, 2003.

Kaliyev, Roustam. "Russia's Organized Crime: A Typology." *Eurasia Insight*, Eurasianet.org, January 31, 2002.

Kaplan, Robert D. *Eastward to Tartary*. New York: Random House, 2000.

Keller, Bill. "Arise, Ye Prisoners of Starvation!" *New York Times*, February 23, 2002.

Keynes, John Maynard. *The General Theory of Employment, Interest, and Money*. San Diego: Harcourt Brace, 1935.

Khodorevskaya, Raissa P., et al. "Present Status of Commercial Stocks of Sturgeon in the Caspian Sea Basin." *Environmental Biology of Fishes* 48, 1997.

Kochladze, Manana. *Pocketing Caspian Black Gold*. Georgia: CEE Bankwatch Network, April 2002.

Kootenai Nation, Elders of. *A Century of Survival: A Brief History of the Kootenai Tribe of Idaho*. Bonners Ferry, Idaho: Kootenai Tribe of Idaho, 1990.

Kootenai Tribe of Idaho. "Hatchery and Genetic Management Plan." Bonners Ferry, Idaho: Kootenai Tribe of Idaho, December 15, 2000.

Kotkin, Stephen. *Armageddon Averted: The Soviet Collapse, 1970–2000*. New York: Oxford University Press, 2001.

Kuh, Patric. *The Last Days of Haute Cuisine*. New York: Penguin, 2001.

Kurata, Phillip. "Caspian Ecosystem Menaced by Pollution." Environmental News Service, April 4, 1999.

Kynard, Boyd, Martin Horgan, and Micah Kiefer. "Habitats Used by Shortnose Sturgeon in Two Massachusetts Rivers, with Notes on Estuarine Atlantic Sturgeon: A Hierarchical Approach." *Transactions of the American Fisheries Society* 129, 2000.

Lavender, David. *California: A Bicentennial History*. New York: W.W. Norton, 1976.

Lelyveld, Michael. "Will a New Formula for Sharing Caspian Riches Work?" Radio Free Europe, November 28, 2001.

Leopold, Aldo. *Game Management*. New York: Macmillan, 1933.

_____. "Engineering and Conservation." In *The River of the Mother of God and Other Essays by Aldo Leopold*, edited by Susan L. Flader and J. Baird Callicott. Madison: University of Wisconsin Press, 1991 [1938].

_____. "Ecology and Politics." In *The River of the Mother of God and Other Essays by Aldo Leopold*, edited by Susan L. Flader and J. Baird Callicott. Madison: University of Wisconsin Press, 1991 [1941].

_____. *A Sand County Almanac*. New York: Oxford University Press, 1949.

Lester, Toby. "New-Alphabet Disease?" *Atlantic Monthly*, July 1997.

LeVine, Steve. "What? No Caviar?" *Wall Street Journal*, June 6, 2001.

Lewis, Paul. "Fred Danback, 79, a Pioneer in Fighting Pollution on Hudson." *New York Times*, March 12, 2003.

Lichatowich, Jim. *Salmon Without Rivers: A History of the Pacific Salmon Crisis.* Washington, D.C.: Island Press, 1999.

Llosa, Mario Varga. "Out of Many, New York." *New York Times*, December 11, 2001.

Logan, Samuel H., Warren E. Johnston, and Serge I. Doroshov. "Economics of Joint Production of Sturgeon (*Acipenser transmontanus* Richardson) and Roe for Caviar." *Aquaculture* 30, 1995.

Maddocks, Kevin. "Expedition Beluga—Tribulation in Russia." *In-Fisherman*, n.d.

Massie, Suzanne. *Land of the Firebird: The Beauty of Old Russia.* New York: Simon and Schuster, 1981.

McCaffery, Jen. "The Great Caviar Bust." *Dish*, Columbia School of Journalism, Spring 1999.

_____. "Bad News Belugas." *New York Observer*, August 2, 2000.

McClane, A.J. *McClane's Standard Fishing Encyclopedia and International Angling Guide.* New York: Holt, Rinehart and Winston, 1965.

McPhee, John. *The Founding Fish.* New York: Farrar, Straus, and Giroux, 2002.

Meier, Andrew. "Russia in the Red." *Harper's Magazine*, June 1999.

Mellart, L. "The Earliest Settlements in Western Asia from the Ninth to the End of the Fifth Millennium, B.C." *The Cambridge Ancient History.* Vol. 1. Cambridge: Cambridge University Press, 1970–1975.

Minai, Leanora. "What Was a Sturgeon Doing in Tampa Bay?" *St. Petersburg Times* (Florida), March 19, 2002.

Miner, Steven Merritt. "Where the West Begins." *New York Times Book Review*, July 8, 2001.

Mitchell, Joseph. *The Bottom of the Harbor.* New York: Modern Library, 1994.

Moiseev, A. "Total Allowable Catch Estimation for Sturgeon Species in the Caspian Sea." Management Authority for Sturgeon of Russian Federation, 2002.

Morris, Roger. "Fish, Flood, and Foolishness." *Western News*, May 8, 2002.

Muir, John. *The Story of My Boyhood and Youth.* Madison: University of Wisconsin Press, 1965 [1912].

_____. *The Yosemite.* New York: Century, 1912.

_____. *A Thousand-Mile Walk to the Gulf.* Atlanta: Cherokee, 1990 [1916].

Myers, Steven Lee. "Landmark Buildings Tumble, Creating a Dust-Up." *New York Times*, October 16, 2003.

New York Times. "Fish Wars," editorial. *New York Times*, February 14, 2002.

_____. "A River Reborn," editorial. *New York Times*, October 2, 2002.

Newman, Andy. "Caviar Dealer Is Sentenced for Falsifying Sales Records." *New York Times*, May 3, 2003.

Nichols, G.G. "Sandusky of To-Day." Sandusky, Ohio: I.F. Mack, 1888.

Nikonorov, Sergei. "Conservation and Sustainable Use of Sturgeon in the Russian Federation." IWMC World Conservation Trust, IWMC.org.

Nixon, Rob. "A Dangerous Appetite for Oil." *New York Times*, October 28, 2001.

Norman, Barbara Makanowitzky. *Tales of the Table: A History of Western Cuisine.* Englewood Cliffs, N.J.: Prentice Hall, 1972.

Olmstead, Marty. "Pioneers of the New American Caviar." *Mainliner*, August 1980.

O'Neill, Molly. "For Caviar, a New World Order." *New York Times*, December 23, 1998.

Ono, R. Dana, James D. Williams, and Anne Wagner. *Vanishing Fishes of North America.* Washington, D.C.: Stone Wall Press, 1983.

Pala, Christopher. "Is This Really the End of Caviar as We Know It?" *St. Petersburg Times* (Russia), July 3, 2001.

———. "Environmentalists Claim Victory in Caviar Clash." *Moscow Times*, November 4, 2002.

———. "Multiplication Problem Threatens Stock of Sturgeon." *New York Times*, January 6, 2004.

Pala, Christopher, and Florence Fabricant. "World's Caviar Faces a Ban." *New York Times*, September 1, 2004.

Paragamian, Vaughn L., and Gretchen Kruse. "Kootenai River White Sturgeon Spawning Migration Behavior and a Predictive Model." *North American Journal of Fisheries Management* 21, 2001.

Paragamian, Vaughn L., Gretchen Kruse, and Virginia Wakkinen. "Spawning Habitat of Kootenai River White Sturgeon, Post-Libby Dam." *North American Journal of Fisheries Management* 21, 2001.

Pares, Bernard. *A History of Russia.* New York: Dorset, 1953.

Passy, Charles. "Caviar on the Cheap." *Wall Street Journal*, February 23, 2001.

Paustovksy, Konstantin. *The Black Gulf.* Westport, Conn.: Hyperion, 1977.

Peimani, Hooman. "Caspian Sea Divide No Closer to Closure." *Asia Times*, April 18, 2002.

Pèpin, Jacques. "A Delicacy's Delicate Future." *New York Times*, July 3, 2001.

Peterson, D., M. Bain, and N. Haley. "Evidence of Declining Recruitment of Atlantic Sturgeon in the Hudson River." *North American Journal of Fisheries Management* 20, 2000.

Pohl, Otto. "New Jellyfish Problem Means Jellyfish Are Not the Only Problem." *New York Times*, June 25, 2002.

Reading, Richard P., and Brian Miller, eds. *Endangered Animals: A Reference Guide to Conflicting Issues.* Westport, Conn.: Greenwood, 2000.

Reichl, Ruth. "Caviar by the Mother-of-Pearl Spoonful." *New York Times*, October 29, 1997.

Reisner, Marc. *Game Wars: The Undercover Pursuit of Wildlife Poachers*. New York: Viking, 1991.

Rosenberg, Steven. "'Fowl' New Caviar for the Masses." BBC News, February 8, 2000.

Rosenblatt, Roger. "In Search of the Beauty and Mystery of Home." *Time*, August 2, 1999.

Roznik, Sharon. "Opening Day Sturgeon Harvest Way Down." *Fond-du-Lac Reporter*, February 10, 2002.

Ruhlman, Michael. *The Soul of a Chef: The Journey Toward Perfection*. New York: Penguin, 2001.

Rundquist, Jane. "Fishing and Utilization of the Sturgeon by the Aboriginal Peoples of the Pacific Northwest." Unpublished manuscript, 1994.

Saffron, Inga. *Caviar: The Strange History and Uncertain Future of the World's Most Coveted Delicacy*. New York: Broadway Books, 2002.

Saradzhyan, Simon. "'Caviar Mafia' Invades Caspian Guard Station." *Moscow Times*, April 18, 2001.

Schoonmaker, Frank, and Tom Marvel. *American Wines*. New York: Duell, Sloan, and Pearce, 1941.

Schriek, Daan van der. "Azerbaijani President Determined to Press Ahead with Referendum." *Eurasia Insight*, Eurasianet.org, July 24, 2002.

Schulenberg, E. Von. "What." Sandusky, Ohio: I.F. Mack, 1903.

Schwarz, Benjamin. "A Job for Rewrite: Stalin's War." *New York Times*, February 21, 2004.

Scott, W.B., and E.J. Crossman. *Freshwater Fishes of Canada*. Ottawa: Fisheries Research Board of Canada, 1973.

Secor, David H. "Atlantic Sturgeon Fisheries and Stock Abundances During the Late Nineteenth Century." In *Biology, Management, and Protection of North American Sturgeon*, edited by W. Van Winkle, P.J. Anders, D.H. Secor, and D. Dixon. American Fisheries Society Symposium 28. Bethesda, Md.: American Fisheries Society, 2002.

Secor, D.H., P.J. Anders, W. Van Winkle, and D. Dixon. "Can We Study Sturgeons to Extinction? What We Do and Don't Know About the Conservation of North American Sturgeons." In *Biology, Management, and Protection of North American Sturgeon*, edited by W. Van Winkle, P.J. Anders, D.H. Secor, and D. Dixon. American Fisheries Society Symposium 28. Bethesda, Md.: American Fisheries Society, 2002.

Secor, David H., and John R. Waldman. "Historical Abundance of Delaware Bay Atlantic Sturgeon and Potential Rate of Recovery." American Fisheries Society Symposium 23. Bethesda, Md.: American Fisheries Society, 1999.

Shoumatoff, Alex. "Lives of the Naturalists: A Profile of Vadim Birstein," dispatchesfromthevanishingworld.com.

Sierra Club. "Hetch Hetchy-History," sierraclub.org.

Sloan, Allan. "Consumption, Conspicuous or Not." *New York Times*, February 12, 2003.

Smith, Barbara Sweetland, and Redmond J. Barnett. *Russian America: The Forgotten Frontier*. Tacoma: Washington State Historical Society, 1990.

Sohbetquizi, Nailia. "Pragmatism Guides Russian-Azerbaijani Deal Making." *Eurasia Insight*, Eurasianet.org, January 15, 2002.

Specter, Michael. "Azerbaijan, Potentially Rich, Is Impoverished by Warfare." *New York Times*, June 2, 1994.

———. "Pollution Threatens World's Caviar Source." *New York Times*, July 7, 1994.

Speer, Lisa, Liz Lauck, Ellen Pikitch, Susan Boa, Lisa Dropkin, and Vicki Spruill. "Roe to Ruin: The Decline of Sturgeon in the Caspian Sea and the Road to Recovery." Natural Resources Defense Council, Wildlife Conservation Society, Sea Web, 2000.

Stabile, John, John R. Waldman, Frank Parauka, and Isaac Wirgin. "Stock Structure and Homing Fidelity in Gulf of Mexico Sturgeon (*Acipenser oxyrinchus desotoi*) Based on Restriction Fragment Length Polymorphism and Sequence Analyses of Mitochondrial DNA." *Genetics* 144, October 1996.

Stedman, Michael. "Charting a Course for the Mighty Volga's Future," strana.ru, March 20, 2002.

Sternin, Vulf, and I. Doré, *Caviar: The Resource Book*. Moscow: Cultura, 1993.

Sternlieb, Leslie. "California's Cultured Pearls." *The Wine News*, December-January 2000–2001.

Stewart, Barbara. "Come On In, the Hudson's Fine." *New York Times*, October 1, 2002.

Stille, Alexander. "Using Genetic Matchmaking to Save Endangered Species." *New York Times*, February 12, 2000.

Stone, Livingstone. "Some Brief Reminiscences of the Early Days of Fish Culture in the United States." *Bulletin of the U.S. Fish Commission*, no. 22, 1897.

Stone, Richard. "Caspian Ecology Teeters on the Brink." *Science* 295, January 18, 2002.

Stout, Ray. "Biologists Release 75,000 Sturgeon Larvae." *Western News* (Libby, Montana), June 16, 2000.

———. "Idaho Biologist Proposes Nutrients for Kootenai River." *Western News* (Libby, Montana), March 23, 2001.

Strom, Stephanie, and Constance L. Hays. "In Tougher Times, It's a Life of Affluence Minus the Trimmings." *New York Times*, October 23, 2001.

Sulak, K.J., and J.P. Clugston. Letter to Kane Metcalf and Paul Zajecek in the Florida Division of Aquaculture, re: Comment on broodstock acquisition, February 23, 2000.

Sulak, Kenneth J., Randy Edwards, and Gary Hill. "Why Do Sturgeons Jump? Insights from Acoustic Investigations of the Suwannee River, Florida." Poster paper 95, Fourth International Sturgeon Symposium, Oshkosh, Wisconsin, July 8–13, 2001.

Tagliabue, John. "From Spotted Owls to Caviar." *New York Times*, December 30, 2000.

Tannahill, Reay. *Food in History*. New York: Stein and Day, 1973.

Tayler, Jeffrey. "Russia Is Finished." *Atlantic Monthly*, May 2001.

_____. "The Caviar Thugs." *Atlantic Monthly*, June 2001.

Teale, Edwin Way, ed. *The Wilderness World of John Muir*. Boston: Houghton Mifflin, 1976 [1954].

Thompson, Stith. *Tales of the North American Indians*. Bloomington: Indiana University Press, 1929.

Thoreau, Henry David. *A Week on the Concord and Merrimack Rivers*. New York: Penguin, 1998 [1849].

Toussaint-Samat, Maguelonne. *A History of Food*. Cambridge, Mass.: Blackwell, 1992.

Traynor, Ian. "Jostle to Plunder Caspian Riches Turns Nasty." *Guardian* (London), April 25, 2002.

Turner, Frederick Jackson. *The Frontier in American History*. New York: Henry Holt, 1947 [1893].

United States, *Bulletin of the U.S. Fish Commission for 1888*. Vol. 8. Washington, D.C.: Government Printing Office, 1890.

United States, *Transcript of Criminal Cause for Resentencing, U.S.A. vs. Eugeniusz Koczuk*. Docket #98-cr–1140, U.S. District Court, Eastern District of New York, January 7, 2002.

United States, *United States of America against Andrzei Lepkowski, Eugeniusz Koczuk, Wieslaw Rozbicki*. Brief and Appendix, U.S. Court of Appeals for the Second District, 00–1504 (L). [January 2002.]

Van Winkle, W., P.J. Anders, D.H. Secor, and D. Dixon, eds. *Biology, Management, and Protection of North American Sturgeon*. American Fisheries Society Symposium 28. Bethesda, Md.: American Fisheries Society, 2002.

Veblen, Thorstein. *The Theory of the Leisure Class*. New York: Dover, 1994 [1899].

Vehling, Joseph Dommers. *Apicius: Cooking and Dining in Imperial Rome*. New York: Dover, 1977 [1936].

Verhovek, Sam Howe. "Arguing That a Fish Born in a Bucket Is Not Endangered." *New York Times*, February 4, 2002.

Wakeford, Anne. *State of Florida Conservation Plan for Gulf Sturgeon* (Acipenser oxyrinchus desotoi). Florida Marine Research Institute Technical Report TR–8, 2001.

Waldman, John R. "The Mystery of Why Sturgeon Leap." *New York Times*, October 21, 2001.

Waldman, John R., John T. Hart, and Isaac I. Wirgin. "Stock Composition of the New York Bight Atlantic Sturgeon Fishery Based on Analysis of Mitochondrial DNA." *Transactions of the American Fisheries Society* 125, 1996.

Waldman, John R., and Isaac I. Wirgin. "Status and Restoration Options for Atlantic Sturgeon in North America." *Conservation Biology* 12, no. 3, June 1998.

Walsh, Nick Paton. "'Mutant Fish' Fear for Caspian Caviar." *The Observer*, August 10, 2003.

Weihman, Ted. "China Making Diplomatic Push in Central Asia." *Eurasia Insight*, Eurasianet.org, June 9, 2003.

Weir, Fred. "Russia Today Froze Fishing for Endangered Sturgeon." *Christian Science Monitor*, July 20, 2001.

Wharton, J. *The Bounty of the Chesapeake: Fishing in Colonial Virginia.* Charlottesville: University of Virginia Press, 1957.

Williams, Selina. "Caspian Summit Failure Not Seen Deterring Investors." Dow Jones Newswires, April 6, 2002.

Williamson, Douglas F. "Caviar and Conservation: Status, Management, and Trade of North American Sturgeon and Paddlefish." TRAFFIC North America, May 2003.

Williamson, Douglas F., George W. Benz, and Craig Hoover. *Proceedings, Symposium on the Harvest, Trade, and Conservation of North American Paddlefish and Sturgeon: Chattanooga, Tennessee, May 7–8, 1998.* TRAFFIC North America/ World Wildlife Fund, Washington, D.C., 1999.

Wines, Michael. "The Worker's State Is History, and Fashion Reigns." *New York Times*, November 6, 2001.

———. "Bomb Blast at a Crowded Parade Kills at Least 34 in Russian Town." *New York Times*, May 10, 2002.

Wolff, Lisa. "Fishing Freeze Targets Illegal Caviar Trade." *Gourmet News*, June 2001.

Yeltsin, Boris N. *Against the Grain.* New York: Summit Books, 1990.

Yergin, Daniel. *The Prize: The Epic Quest for Oil, Money, and Power.* New York: Simon and Schuster, 1991.

INDEX

Abdulrahimov, Andrei, 243
Acipenser baerii (Siberian sturgeon), 107, 266
Acipenser fulvescens (lake sturgeon), 14, 76, 90, 145–55, 160–64, 266
Acipenser gueldenstaedtii (Russian sturgeon), 23–24, 71, 110, 116, 185
Acipenseriformes, 3–4, 8, 122
Acipenser medirostris (green sturgeon), 177–78, 266
Acipenser nudiventris (ship sturgeon), 49
Acipenser oxyrinchus de sotoi (Gulf of Mexico sturgeon), 3
Acipenser persicus (Persian sturgeon), 71, 110–11
Acipenser ruthenus (sterlet sturgeon), 102, 173
Acipenser schrenckii (Amur sturgeon), 52–53, 107, 185, 266
Acipenser stellatus (stellate sturgeon), 38, 61
Acipenser sturio (European sturgeon), 12, 64, 123
Adams, Ansel, 281
Aeroflot airlines, 33, 36, 37, 50, 51, 212, 230
Against the Grain (Yeltsin), 210
AIOC. *See* Azerbaijan International Oil Consortium

Air France airlines, 51
Aitken, Bob, 286, 293, 295–96
Aitken, Larry, 293
Aitken, Ralph, 296
Alabama, University of, 111
Alabama sturgeon (*Scaphirhynchus suttkusi*), 9, 14, 34
Alaska, 168
Alexander, Tsar, 243
Alexander III, 57
Alexei's Caviar-Like, 241
Alexis, Tsar, 63, 205
Alger, Horatio, 48
Aliyev, Heidar, 244–45, 250, 257, 260, 261, 289
Aliyev, Ilham, 254, 260, 289
American Airlines, 189
American Museum of Natural History (AMNH), 35, 99, 103, 104, 112, 114, 117, 119, 128
Amnesty International, 101
AMNH. *See* American Museum of Natural History
Amoco, 260
Amur River, 52
Amur sturgeon (*Acipenser schrenckii*), 52–53, 107, 185–86, 266
Anaconda Wire & Cable, 124, 125, 135
The Antiquary (Scott), 200
Apalachicola River, Fla., 16, 20–21, 27

Apicius, 199, 200
Aquaculture, 175
aquaculture
    in California, 19, 165–82, 184–85,
        191–96
    in China, 184–86
    CITES and, 84–85
    conservation, 268–70
    ESA and, 288
    in Florida, 21–23
    Kootenai white sturgeon and, 265–69
    in Russia, 23–24, 77, 92–94, 218–24,
        225–29, 252–56, 287–90
    USF&W and, 21
Aquamar Gourmet, 65
Archambo, Brenda, 75, 76, 77, 80, 86
Armstrong, Jim, 289
Arrowhead Fisheries, 165
Ashcroft, John, 135
Astrakhan, Russia, 5, 63, 208–9, 212–15,
        221, 226
Astrakhan Caviar, 14
Atlantic Monthly, 279
Atlantic States Marine Fisheries
        Commission, 128
Atlantic sturgeon, 14, 17
    behavior of, 87
    in Delaware Bay, 3
    ESA and, 141–43
    feeding specialization of, 7
    Gulf of Mexico sturgeon and, 10
    in Hudson River, 122–30, 173
    poaching of, 42
    size of, 5
Austria, 3
Aytan, 252, 256–57
Azerbaijan, 58, 68, 82, 93, 204, 220,
        225, 228
    aquaculture and, 289–90
    caviar production in, 243–47
    oil production and, 251–52, 256–61
Azerbaijan Diary (Goltz), 243–44, 257
Azerbaijan Institute of Physiology, 242
Azerbaijan International Oil Consortium
        (AIOC), 250–51, 257

Babrovsky, Anatoly, 205, 212, 213,
        215–16, 218, 233, 236, 238
Bain, Mark, 142–44
Baker, Josephine, 57
Baker River, Wash., 3
Baku, Azerbaijan, 58
Baku-Tblisi-Ceychan (BTC) line, 251
Balducci, 108, 159, 190
Baldwin, Alec, 132
BATNEEC. *See* Best Available
        Technology Not Entailing
        Excessive Costs
Bay Company, 151
Beard, James, 184, 196, 197, 198, 200
Beer, Ken, 167–68, 174, 175, 181,
        182, 189
Beluga Caviar, 290
beluga sturgeon, 3, 68–69, 85, 185,
        270, 289–90
benthic cruising, 7
Berg, Leo, 102
Bermuda, 123
Best Available Technology Not Entailing
        Excessive Costs (BATNEEC), 258
Beyer, Malcolm, 130–31
Bierstadt, Albert, 280, 281
Binkowski, Fred, 77, 90, 154, 155
Bios, 218–19, 222, 224, 228, 234
Birstein, Jacob, 100, 226
Birstein, Kathryn, 104
Birstein, Vadim, 35, 65, 67, 128, 131,
        135, 291
    CITES and, 289
    DNA testing program of, 100–120
    KaspNIRKh and, 234
    Koczuk lawsuit and, 49
    restocking and, 224
    Russian aquaculture and, 227
    Russian economy and, 210–11
Birstein Computer Services, 99
Bismarck, 151–52, 155
The Black Gulf (Paustovsky), 217
Black Sea, Russia, 12, 62, 63
Block, Frederic C., 42, 46–47, 134,
        136–40, 159–60

Blohm, Benedict, 14
Blum, Kenneth, 40–41
Bogue, Margaret Beattie, 151
Bond, James, 33, 250
Bonners Ferry Herald, 265
Bonneville Power Administration
    (BPA), 266, 268, 276, 285–86
The Bottom of the Harbor (Mitchell), 121
Bowman, Andrew, 47, 139, 159–60
Boyle, Bob, 104, 124–25, 128, 130–33,
    141, 144, 156, 171
BP. *See* British Petroleum
BPA. *See* Bonneville Power
    Administration
Bracco, Lorraine, 132
Braun, *Wernher* von, 165, 176
British Airways, 98
British Columbia, 170, 266
British Petroleum (BP), 242–43, 250,
    256–57, 259, 286
Brokaw, Tom, 131
Browne Trading Company, 189
Bruch, Ron, 80, 154
BTC line. *See* Baku-Tblisi-Ceychan line
Bulletin of the U.S. Fish Commission
    (1888), 13, 174
Buraczynski, Kathryn, 101
Burgess, Robert, 16
Bush, George W., 21, 261, 278

Caen, Herb, 196, 197
California
    aquaculture in, 19, 165–82, 184–85,
        191–96
    cuisine in, 196–202
    Gold Rush in, 168–70, 181, 197
    Russian, 165–82
    white sturgeon in, 5, 18–19
California, University of, 165
California-Davis, University of, 18–19,
    172, 185
California Department of Game and
    Fisheries, 171
California Sunshine Fisheries, 184
Canada, 5

Cape Codder, 17
Carr, Archie, 2, 27–28
Casper, Bill, 75–80, 87, 124, 126
    California aquaculture and, 174
    lake sturgeon and, 146, 148, 158
Caspian Environmental Center
    (CEC), 214
Caspian Environment Programme,
    243, 261
Caspian Fish Company, 254
Caspian Fisheries Research Institute
    (KaspNIRKh), 92, 93, 212,
    215–18, 226–28, 234, 288
Caspian Sea, Russia, 12, 62, 203–5
    beluga sturgeon of, 5
    as caviar source, 34–35
    oil production and, 248–52
    Russian aquaculture and, 23–24,
        218–24
    Russian caviar and, 67–69, 71–72
    wildlife of, 204–5
Caspian Star, 33, 42, 48, 58, 65, 69,
    97, 271
Catherine the Great, 63
caviar
    bargain, 59
    beluga, 37, 61, 69–71
    black, 23
    black market in, 99
    cost of, 37, 190–91
    early history of, 13–14
    faux, 14, 46, 241
    flavor of, 61, 70–71
    international trade in, 33–43
    malossol, 57, 95–96
    in New York, 56–74
    osetra, 23, 49, 61, 71
    pike, 225
    post-World War I and, 55–58
    pressed, 95–96, 98
    Russian, 13, 14, 56–74
    salmon, 186–87, 225
    salt and, 58
    serving of, 61–62
    sevruga, 61, 72–73

caviar *(continued)*
  smuggling of, 33–43
  in United States, 34, 95–99
  white sturgeon and, 23
Caviar, N. J., 14, 15
Caviar Aristoff, 108
Caviar Direct, 108
Caviar Emptor campaign, 84, 85, 118,
    122, 190, 194, 270, 288
Caviar Russe, 33
Caviar Supreme, 292
Caviarteria, 34, 42, 48–49, 66–67, 116,
    117, 159, 190, 291
Caviar: The Resource Book (Sternin), 81
CEC. *See* Caspian Environmental Center
Center for Biological Diversity, 273,
    274, 276
Central Election Commission, 289
Chapman, Frank, 46, 58, 78, 81, 82, 86,
    88–90, 104, 122, 222
  Florida aquaculture and, 1–4, 8, 10,
    17–24, 27, 166, 167, 269–72
Chechnya, 86
Chesapeake, 15
Chesapeake Bay, 124, 126
Chesapeake Biological Laboratory, 16
Chez Panisse, 196, 198–99, 200, 271
Chile, 176
China, 78, 184–86
Chondrosteidae, 7–8
Christians, 12
Citarella, 108
CITES. *See* Convention on International
    Trade in Endangered Species of
    Wild Fauna and Flora
Claiborne, Craig, 183, 184, 196
Clark, Jamie Rappaport, 114
Clark, Wallis, 172–73, 174, 176
Cleveland, Grover, 279
Clinton, Hillary, 136
Close, Glenn, 132
Clugston, Jim, 10, 19–20
Coco, Chris, 78
coelacanth, 16–17, 102
Coleman, C. W., 27

Columbia River, Wash., 3, 15, 266
Comité Général du Pétrole, 248
Con Ed. *See* Consolidated Edison
Conference of the Parties to CITES, 109
Connoisseur Brands, 34, 48, 108, 159
Conservation Biology, 104
conservation laws, 15
conservation movement
  growth of, 157–58
  Muir and, 278–82
Consolidated Edison (Con Ed), 125
Convention on International Trade in
    Endangered Species of Wild Fauna
    and Flora (CITES), 65, 92, 96,
    104, 108–9, 111, 270
  Appendix II of, 34, 35, 51
  Appendix I of, 51, 68, 85
  aquaculture and, 84–85
  beluga sturgeon and, 289–90
  caviar industry and, 82, 83
  enforcement and, 83–86
  goals of, 68
  importing caviar into U.S. and,
    34–35
  international trade in caviar and, 34
  price of caviar and, 37
  TRAFFIC and, 84
Cosmopolitan, 27
Cossacks, 63, 96
Crapo, Mike, 298
Cretaceous, 6, 8
Cronin, John, 125, 131, 132, 133
Czech Republic, 109

Dagestan, 86, 215, 232–33
Dallas, Tex., 58
D'Amato, Cus, 131
Danback, Fred, 124, 135
Danube River, Austria, 3
Darnell, Stephen, 45–46
Dean & DeLuca, 48, 108, 159
de Beauvoir, Simone, 202
Delaware Bay, 3, 13, 14, 15, 49
Delaware River, 123
Delta airlines, 33

DeSalle, Rob, 35, 65, 99, 103, 104,
106–7, 110, 112–17, 119, 135
Dieckmann, Johannes, 63–64
Dieckmann & Hansen, 13, 14, 33, 43,
44, 48, 57, 58, 68, 208, 213
Djugashvili, Joseph. *See* Stalin, Joseph
DNR. *See* Wisconsin Department of
Natural Resources
Doroshov, Serge, 78, 83, 131
aquaculture and, 19, 77, 165–67
California aquaculture and, 172,
174–77, 182, 192, 221
sturgeon feeding and, 7
Drobenko, Walter, 41, 43, 47, 49, 116,
119, 136, 138
Dumas, Alexandre, 79

East India Company, 12
"Ecology and Politics" (Leopold), 85, 261
Edward II, King, 62
Edwards, Chuck, 194–95
Endangered Species Act (ESA) of 1973,
68, 281
aquaculture and, 288
beluga sturgeon and, 85, 270, 290
Gulf of Mexico sturgeon, 8, 21
salmon and, 277–78
short-nosed sturgeon and, 34, 141–44
white sturgeon and, 267
Engstrom, Dafne, 197
California aquaculture and, 171–73,
175–76, 183–89
Engstrom, Mats, 79, 81, 82, 86, 92, 96,
194, 197, 202, 234
California aquaculture and, 171–73,
175–76, 183–89
ESA. *See* Endangerd Species Act of 1973
Escoffier, Auguste, 196
Esenink, Serge, 218
The Ethics of Ambiguity (de Beauvoir),
202
European sturgeon (*Acipenser sturio*), 12,
13, 34, 57, 64, 123
Evergreen Eagle, 51
Exxon, 125

Fabricant, Florence, 241
Fain, Steve, 113–16, 119, 291
Far Side cartoon, 261, 269
FBI. *See* Federal Bureau of Investigation
Federal Bureau of Investigation (FBI), 44
Federal Refuse Act (1899). *See* Hudson
River Fishermen's Association
Fernández-Armesto, Felipe, 62, 247
Finn airlines, 33, 39
Fisher, M. F. K., 198, 200
The Fishery, 167, 182
Fishing the Great Lakes (Bogue), 151
Fiske, Dwight, 29
Fitzgerald, F. Scott, 57, 202
Fitzgerald, Zelda, 57
Fleming, Ian, 73
Florida
aquaculture in, 21–23
Gulf of Mexico sturgeon of, 7
Muir and, 17
sturgeon fishing in, 15, 16, 25–29
Florida, University of, 2, 8, 17, 19
Fond du Lac, Wisc., 75, 77, 149
Fond-du-Lac Reporter, 78, 158, 163
Foster, Stephen, 2
Four Seasons, 196
Fourth International Symposium on
Sturgeon, 75–94
Fox River, Mich., 75–76, 77
France, 57–58, 248
Fraser River, Canada, 5, 15, 170, 266
French Laundry, 199, 200, 201, 271
The French Menu Cookbook (Olney), 196

Gallo brothers, 198
Game Management (Leopold), 81
*Game Wars: The Undercover Pursuit of
Wildlife Poachers* (Reisner), 32
Gamidova, Leyla, 245, 252–55, 257
Garbo, Greta, 66
Gatsby, Jay, 43, 122, 202, 276, 281, 299
General Electric, 124, 125
Georgia, 1–3
Germany, 14, 63–64
Ghana, 78

A Ghost in the Water (Glavin), 170
Gino. *See* Koczuk, Eugeniusz
Gino International, 34–36, 40–43, 47,
    52, 58, 65, 67, 135, 136, 138
Glavin, Terry, 170
Godunova, Galina, 205, 212, 213–14,
    228–29, 239, 259
Godunova, Katya, 205–6, 212, 215, 217,
    218, 230, 239, 286–87
Goebel, Ron, 161–62
Gold Rush, 168–70, 181, 197
Goltz, Thomas, 243–44, 245, 257
Gorbachev, Mikhail, 101, 119, 186, 206,
    210, 211, 232, 244
Grace, Ed
    Koczuk sentencing and, 135–40
    USF&W enforcement and, 32–33, 45,
        48, 50–53, 59, 66, 67, 95, 97, 116,
        250, 291
Grace's Marketplace, 108
Grand Dictionnaire de cuisine (Dumas), 79
Greater Verplanck Caviar
    Company, 130
Great Lakes, 15, 75, 152–53. *See also*
    lake sturgeon
Greeks, 62
Green, Seth, 173–74
Greenland, 78
Green Revolution, 201
green sturgeon (*Acipenser medirostris*),
    177–78, 266
Guide Culinaire (Escoffier), 196
Gulf of Mexico, 2
Gulf of Mexico sturgeon (*Acipenser
    oxyrinchus de sotoi*), 3, 14, 16
    artificial spawning of, 10
    CITES and, 34
    as endangered species, 8
    feeding specialization of, 7
    restoration of, 17–24
    in Suwanee river, 7
    water temperature and metabolic
        rate of, 10
gulf sturgeon. *See* Gulf of Mexico
    sturgeon

Gulsura, Mustafayava, 262–63
Guseynov, Rasim, 254–56, 261, 262

Hancock, Herbie, 243
Hansen, Johannes C. F., 63–64
Hansen Caviar, 33–34, 44, 46
Hansen-Sturm, Arnold, 33–34, 43–46,
    64–65, 108, 127
Harper's Weekly, 279
Harriman, E. H., 170, 282
Harry & David, 159
hatcheries. *See* aquaculture
Hawaii, 58
Helfrich, Rich, 191, 193, 194,
    194–95, 201
Hemingway, Ernest, 57
Hitler, Adolf, 205, 225, 248–49
Holland America Cruise Line, 44
Holloway, Jamie, 8–9, 18, 25–26,
    28–29, 178
Holmes, John A. S., 182
Hosking, Geoffrey, 210
HRF. *See* Hudson River Foundation
HRFA. *See* Hudson River Fishermen's
    Association
Hudson, Henry, 12, 123, 151
Hudson River, 14, 42, 121–30
    Atlantic sturgeon in, 173
*The Hudson River: A Natural and
    Unnatural History* (Boyle), 125
Hudson River Fishermen's Association
    (HRFA), 86, 125
Hudson River Foundation (HRF), 86,
    104, 122, 125, 127–28, 131
Huso dauricus (Kaluga sturgeon), 52, 185

ICIA. *See* International Caviar Importers
    Association
Idaho Department of Fish and Game,
    265, 276
Illinois, University, 32
Importers' Association, 86
inc.com, 159
Indian Self-Determination Act
    (1976), 273

Industrial Revolution, 155, 201, 247
INDWIZ Trading & Taxidermy, 51
Institute for Social Action and Renewal
    (ISAR) in Eurasia, 243
International Caviar Importers
    Association (ICIA), 68
International Sturgeon Symposium
    (1993), 104
Iran, 43, 44, 69, 189, 229
Ireland, Sue, 265, 268, 272, 273–74, 283,
    286–87, 296–97, 298
Irving, Washington, 123
ISAR. *See* Institute for Social Action
    and Renewal
Iskra, 248
Israel, 78, 241
Italian sturgeon (*Acipenser naccarii*), 111
Ivanov, Vladimir P., 92–93, 226,
    233, 289
Ivan the Terrible, 62, 67, 209, 217
Izvestia, 214, 230

Jensen, Traci, 295, 298
JFK. *See* John F. Kennedy International
    Airport
John F. Kennedy International Airport
    (JFK), 33, 36–41, 95
Johnston, Warren E., 175
Journal of Applied Ichthyology, 107
Jurassic, 3, 5, 245

Kalmykia, 215, 232–33
Kaluga sturgeon (*Huso dauricus*), 52, 185
Kapperman, Kevin, 182
Karpiuk, Mark, 289
KaspNIRKh. *See* Caspian Fisheries
    Research Institute
Kazakhstan, 48, 68, 69, 82, 83, 97–98,
    228, 249, 251–52
Keeper Springs, 132
Keller, Thomas, 199–201
Kelly's Katch, 190
Kennebec river, 12
Kennedy, Robert F., Jr., 42, 131–33
Kerby, Darrell, 267

Keynes, John Maynard, 282
KGB, 100, 101
Khan, Batu, 62, 204, 217
Khan, Ghengis, 62, 204, 209
Kitanov, Alexander, 218, 219, 221–22,
    223, 224
Kliuev, Nicholas, 218
Klyuchevsky, Vassily, 210
Knight, Anthony, 191, 192
Koba. *See* Stalin, Joseph
Koczuk, Eugeniusz, 58, 116, 118, 209
    caviar smuggling and, 33, 34, 40–43
    sentencing of, 134, 135–40, 159–60
    trial of, 46–47
Koczuk, Helena, 40
Kodyakov, Nikolai, 205, 206, 235–36,
    238–39
Kolstov Institute of Development
    Biology, 100, 101
Kootenai River, Idaho, white sturgeon in,
    265–69, 272–78
Kootenai Tribe of Idaho, 265, 266,
    269, 272
Koz, 290
Krohn, Randy, 161
Kuh, Patric, 197, 199, 271
Kura Experimental Sturgeon Plant, 254
Kura River, Russia, 93, 246,
    252–56, 290
Kynard, Boyd, 142

Lacey Act of 1900, 45
Lake Erie, 152
Lake Michigan, 75, 77, 151, 153
lake sturgeon (*Acipenser fulvescens*), 14,
    76, 266
    caviar and, 79
    size of, 90
    spawning of, 154–55
    spearfishing for, 145–55, 160–64
    wasting of, 151–53
Lake Winnebago, Wisc., 75, 76–78, 82
    spearfishing in, 145–58
"The Land Ethic" (Leopold), 158
Larson, Gary, 261

The Last Days of Haute Cuisine (Kuh), 197
Las Vegas, Nev., 34, 66, 159
Lauk, Liz, 84
Le Cirque, 33
Lenin, Vladimir, 57, 64, 205, 210, 217, 231–34, 248
Leopold, Aldo, 81–82, 85–86, 156–58, 261, 270–72
Le Pavillon, 196, 198, 199
Lepkowski, Andrzej, 40
Lewandowski, Chris, 285–87, 292–97
Libby Dam, Idaho, 265, 268–69, 275–76, 283, 285–86
Lichatowich, Jim, 278
LIFE magazine, 235
Linares-Casenave, Javier, 177–82
Linnaeus, Carolus, 4, 26, 102, 245
Linville, Regina, 178, 181
Lithuania, 37, 49
Logan, Samuel H., 175
Lolavar, Hossein, 47–48
London Company, 12
Longfellow, Henry Wadsworth, 151
Los Angeles, Ca., 58
LOT airlines, 33, 40
Louis XV, 57
Lufthansa airlines, 33
Lukoil, 228
Lysenko, Trofim, 100

Madonna, 73
Manchuria, 185
Mansfield, Mike, 173
Marky's, 108
Marquis, Roland, 36, 38–39, 51–53, 95
Maryland Fish and Wildlife, 47
Mazhnik, Alla, 227–29, 259
McCafferey, Jen, 50
McClane's Standard Fishing Encyclopedia and International Angling Guide, 130, 171
McDonald's, 211, 252, 260
Mekhtiev, Arif, 242, 243, 245, 246
Melendez, Joe, 193–94

Memorial, 101
Menominee tribe, 89–92, 146
Mercedes, 260
Meridien Shipping, 41
Merrimack river, 12
Mexico, 168
Miami, Fla., 34, 58, 66, 159
Milner, James, 152
Miner, Steven Merritt, 210
Mingäevir Hydroelectric Plant, 254
Mishe-Nahma, King of Fishes, 151
Mississippi River, 9
Mitchell, Joseph, 121, 122, 144
Monaco, Cynthia, 42, 47, 48, 135–40, 159–60, 292
Mondavi, Robert, 198
Mongols, 12, 62, 63, 204, 217, 230, 291
Moore, Brendan, 192
Moore, H. F., 153
Moscow, Russia, 211–12
Moscow Times, 67
Moscow University, 100
Muir, John, 81, 86, 89, 140–41, 144, 261
    California and, 169–70
    conservation movement and, 278–82
    Florida and, 17
    Suwanee River and, 8
    Wisconsin spearfishing and, 155–58
Mullis, Kary, 105
Murray, Bill, 104, 110

Napoleon, 13, 57, 209
National Geographic, 226
National Marine Fisheries Service, 45, 141, 144
National Park Bill of 1890, 81
National Resources Defense Council, 42, 270
Naturalnaya, 226
A Naturalist in Florida (Carr), 2, 27
Natural Resources Defense Council (NRDC), 68, 122, 133
Nature, 106, 107, 113
The Nature Conservancy, 265, 267, 273
Neilson, Philip, 153

New Jersey, 14
Newman, Paul, 132
The New School University, 56, 156
New York, 13, 14, 121–30
  caviar in, 56–74
New York, N. Y., 34, 58
New York Aquarium, 114
New York City, N. Y., 14
New Yorker, 115, 121
New York Observer, 50
New York Post, 66, 291
New York Times, 84, 86, 89, 155, 183,
  189, 241, 244, 271, 278, 280–81,
  289, 291
New York Times Book Review, 210
NGOs. *See* nongovernmental
  organizations (NGOs)
Ninneman, Gary, 145–51, 154, 155, 158,
  160–63, 174, 190, 237
Ninneman, Todd, 148, 162–63
Niyazov, Saparmurat, 249–50
Nobel brothers, 248
Noe, Rob and Jen, 148, 150, 155, 163
nongovernmental organizations
  (NGOs), 243
Norling, Peter, 292
Noroozi, Ken, 47–48
North Korea, 186
Northwest Airlines, 52
NRDC. *See* Natural Resources Defense
  Council (NRDC)

oil industry, 242–53, 256–61
Oily Rocks, 257, 258
Ojibwa tribe, 76, 145, 151, 163
Olney, Richard, 196–97, 198, 200
O'Neill, Molly, 189–90
Oregon, 13

Pace-Kerby Real Estate and Insurance
  Agency, 267
paddlefish (*Polyodon spathula*), 7–8, 47
paedomorphosis, 4, 5, 8
Palatnikov, Grigory, 242, 245–46, 252,
  255, 257, 262

Paleozoic, 4
Panchernikov, Arkady, 33, 48, 49–50, 58,
  65, 69, 83, 136, 271
  California aquaculture and, 174
  USF&W investigation of, 97–98,
    290–91
Paraguay, 78
Paris, France, 56
Park, Chulhong, 17, 18, 21, 22, 24,
  78, 81
Parker, Blaine L., 182
Parkyn, Daryl, 1, 3, 8–11, 18,
  25–29, 178
Passy, Charles, 190, 194
Paustovsky, Konstantin, 217
PCR. *See* polymerase chain reaction
  (PCR) method
Penn Central Railroad, 125
Pennsylvanian Age, 4
Pennzoil, 257
People Magazine, 44
Pépin, Jacques, 84
peramorphosis, 4, 8
Persian sturgeon (*Acipenser persicus*), 71
Persian sturgeon (*Acipenser persicus*),
  110–11
*The Perversion of Knowledge:
  The True Story of Soviet Science*
  (Birstein), 119
Peter the Great, 57, 63, 217
Petrossian, Armen, 58, 68, 84–86, 92,
  104, 107
Petrossian, Melkoum, 56, 64
Petrossian, Mouchegh, 56, 64
Petrossian Paris, 33, 44, 47, 56, 58–61,
  65, 66, 68, 69, 95, 96, 158–59, 176,
  202, 208, 213
Petrossian Restaurant, 55, 99
Phelan, James D., 280
Picasso, Pablo, 73
Pikitch, Ellen, 288–89
Playboy, 44
Pleistocene, 266
Poland, 37, 40
Polo, Marco, 204, 247

polymerase chain reaction (PCR)
  method, 105–20
Polyodon spathula (paddlefish), 47
Production Sharing Agreement
  (PSA), 257–58
PSA. *See* Production Sharing
  Agreement (PSA)
Putah Creek, Cali., 166
Putin, Vladimir, 211, 215, 228

Radits, Matthias, 190
Rainbow Room, 44
Raymakers, Caroline, 83, 84, 93–94, 105
Razin, Stenka, 205, 207, 230
Reisner, Marc, 32, 45
Ritz, Cesar, 57, 58, 64
Riverkeeper, 42, 125–26, 131–34
Rockefeller, John D., 248
Rockie's, 197
Romania, 222
Romanoff Caviar, 43, 44, 65, 70
Romans, 62, 82
Rommel, Erwin, 248–49
Roosevelt, Theodore, 279, 281
Rory, 8–11, 25–26, 29
Rothe, Rob, 36, 39, 40, 50–53, 95, 116
Royal Caviar, 241
Rozbicki, Wieslaw, 40
Ruhlman, Michael, 199–200
Russia
  aquaculture in, 23–24, 92–94,
    218–24, 225–29, 252–56, 287–90,
    289–90
  black market in, 231–34
  California aquaculture and, 165–82
  caviar and, 13
  caviar in, 14, 56–74, 208–9, 212–15
  cuisine in, 209
  history of, 208–11
  oil industry in, 242–52, 256–61
  organized crime in, 67, 232–33
  Thieves World and, 231–34
Russia and the Russians: A History
  (Hosking), 210
Russian-American Company, 168

Russian Czar, 49
Russian Fisheries Committee, 227
Russian Revolution, 185
Russian sturgeon (*Acipenser
  gueldenstaedtii*), 23–24, 71, 110,
  116, 185
Russian Tea Room, 33, 271
Russia's Secret Rulers (Timofeyev), 231
Russkaya Ikra, 208, 221, 225
Ryder, John, 174, 180

Sabena airlines, 33
Sacramento River, Cali., 169, 170, 176
Sakharov, Andrei, 101
salmon, 277–78
Salmon without Rivers (Lichatowich), 278
A Sand County Almanac (Leopold),
  81, 270
Sandusky Register-Star, 153
San Francisco, Ca., 58, 79
San Francisco Bay, Cali., 18, 167–68
San Francisco Chronicle, 196, 201, 280
Sar-Wiwa, Ken, 261
Scaphirhynchus platorynchus (shovelnose
  sturgeon), 47, 111, 290
Scaphirhynchus suttkusi (Alabama
  sturgeon), 9
Schact, Siemon and John, 152, 153
Scherbatova, Tatyana, 223–24
Schoonmaker, Frank, 198
Scott, Sir Walter, 200
Sea of Azov, Russia, 62, 100
Sea Web, 68
Secor, David, 16
September 11, 96, 97, 115, 140, 158
SFT. *See* Sturgeon for Tomorrow
Shedd Aquarium, 24
ship sturgeon (*Acipenser nudiventris*),
  49, 107
short-nosed sturgeon (*Acipenser
  brevirostrum*), 22–23, 266
  CITES and, 34
  in Delware Bay, 3
  early history of, 14
  ESA and, 34, 141–44

Shoumatoff, Alex, 115

shovelnose sturgeon (*Scaphirhynchus platorynchus*), 47, 111, 290

Siberian sturgeon (*Acipenser baerii*), 107, 266

Sierra Club, 81, 279, 280, 282

Sifton, Charles P., 291

Simple French Food (Olney), 196

Simpson, O. J., 105

Siple, Jack, 265, 272, 274, 285–87, 292–99

Smith, John, 12

Sobol, Bruce, 49, 66, 159, 291

Sobol, Eric, 34, 49, 66–67, 116, 119

Sobol, Louis, 66

SOCAR. *See* State Oil Company of Azerbaijan

Solaris, 243, 247

Soulé, Henri, 200

The Soul of a Chef: The Journey Toward Perfection (Ruhlman), 199

South Carolina, 22

    Soviet Union aquaculture and, 77

    Bolshevik Revolution and, 56

    collapse of, 34, 49, 67, 232

See also Russia

Spawning

    artificial, 10

    of lake sturgeon, 154–55

    temperature and, 168

    See also aquaculture

Speer, Lisa, 85, 270

Sports Illustrated, 124, 131, 134

Spring Valley Water Company, 280

Stalin, Joseph, 100, 207, 244, 248

Standard Oil Company, 248

State Oil Company of Azerbaijan (SOCAR), 259

stellate sturgeon (*Acipenser stellatus*), 38, 61

Stepanyan, Svetlana, 216

sterlet sturgeon (*Acipenser ruthenus*), 102, 173

Sterling caviar, 190, 193–94

Sternin, Vulf, 4, 7, 62, 81, 91, 120

St. John's River, Fla., 22

Stolt Sea Farm, 92, 182, 187, 189–90, 190–96

Stone, Livingstone, 299

The Story of My Boyhood and Youth (Muir), 156

St. Petersburg Times, 21, 219

Struffenegger, Peter, 81, 83–84, 92, 186–88, 192–93, 194–95

Strugeon Society, 99

sturgeon

    Alabama, 9, 14, 34

    Amur, 52–53, 107, 185–86

    Atlantic, 3, 5, 10, 14, 17, 42, 87, 122–30, 141–43, 173

    behavior of, 27–28, 75–76, 86–90

    beluga, 3, 68–69, 85, 270, 289–90

    communication and, 88

    DNA testing program for, 100–120

    European, 12, 13, 34, 57, 64, 123

    fishing for, 11–17, 25–29, 145–58, 160–64

    green, 177–78, 266

    Gulf of Mexico, 3, 8, 10, 14, 16, 34

    Italian, 111

    Kaluga , 52, 185–86

    lake, 14, 76, 90, 145–55, 160–64, 266

    oil industry and, 242–52, 256–61

    Persian, 71, 110–11

    Russian, 23–24, 71, 110–11, 116, 185

    ship, 49, 107

    short-nosed, 3, 14, 22–23, 34, 141–44, 266

    shovelnose, 47, 111, 290

    Siberian, 107, 266

    stellate, 38, 61

    sterlet, 102, 173

    white, 3, 5, 18–19, 77, 165–82, 265–69, 272–78

Sturgeon for Tomorrow (SFT), 76, 77, 79, 80, 89, 126, 146, 150, 153, 154, 282

Sturgeon Quarterly, 104, 112, 117

Sturgeon Society, 104, 112, 117, 131, 135
Sturgeon Specialists Group, 104, 108, 111, 117
Sulak, Ken, 20, 25, 86–89
Sutter, John, 168
Suwanee River, 1–3, 8–11, 13, 19
    Gulf of Mexico sturgeon in, 7, 17–18
    sturgeon fishing in, 15
    sturgeon population of, 20–21
Sweden, 248

Talk magazine, 132
Tampa Bay, Fla., 7
Tartakovsky, Vladislav, 292
Teale, Edwin Way, 170
Teleosteidae, 7–8
Tennessee Aquarium, 24, 78
The Theory of the Leisure Class (Veblen), 32, 61
Thieves World (*vorovskoi mir*), 231–34
Thoreau, Henry David, 270
A Thousand Mile Walke to the Gulf (Muir), 156
Timofeyev, Lev, 231
Tocqueville, Alexis de, 209
Tolstaganova, Larissa, 88
Trade Records Analysis of Flora and Fauna (TRAFFIC), 83, 105, 108, 109, 115, 209
Trader Joe's, 159
TRAFFIC. *See* Trade Records Analysis of Flora and Fauna
Transparency International, 260
Treaty of Guadalupe Hidalgo, 168
Trotter, Charlie, 190
Tsar Nicoulai Caviar, 79, 81, 82, 91, 183–84, 190
Tsimbal, Viktor, 290
Turkmenbashi. *See* Niyazov, Saparmurat
Turkey, 37
Turkmenistan, 68, 82, 111, 249, 258
Turner, Frederick, Jackson, 282
Tyson, Mike, 131

United Airlines, 44
United Arab Emirates, 37, 47, 49
United Nations Environmental Program, 259
United Nations Food and Agriculture Organization, 172
United States
    caviar industry in, 95–99
    conservation movement in, 278–82
    importing caviar into, 33–43
U.S. Caviar & Caviar, 47–48, 65
U.S. Customs, 36, 74
U.S. Department of Agriculture, 37
U.S. Department of Commerce, 106
U.S. Fish and Wildlife Service (USF&W), 19
    aquaculture and, 21
    beluga sturgeon and, 290
    California aquaculture and, 173
    Caviarteria raid by, 66
    DNA testing program of, 85, 115–16
    enforcement and, 31–43, 95–98
    Kootenai white sturgeon and, 266–68, 276
    lawsuits against, 48–49, 159, 291
    restocking and, 10–11
U.S. Fish Commission, 7, 13, 14, 15, 173
U.S. Food and Drug Administration, 74
U.S. Geological Survey, 20, 86
U.S. State Department, 44, 289
Upper Cretaceous, 3, 6
Ural River, Kazakhstan, 48
Urbani Truffles, 41
Urst-Kurinski Experimental Sturgeon Plant, 261–62
Uruguay, 176
USA Today, 115
USF&W. *See* U.S. Fish and Wildlife Service
Uzbekistan airlines, 33

Van Eenennaam, Joel, 165–68, 174, 177–82, 293
Vasilyeva, Lydya, 221

Veblen, Thorstein, 32, 61–62, 157, 206, 282
Vega, Eve, 33, 84, 156, 270, 291
    California aquaculture and, 174
    Russian caviar and, 56–74
    U.S. caviar industry and, 95–99
Vehling, Joseph Dommers, 199
Venezuela, 123
Vinegar Factory, 108
Volga River, Russia, 5, 62, 203–6, 235–39

Wachtel, William, 43, 138–39
Wagner, Eric, 286, 294–95
Waldman, John, 86, 87, 88–89, 104, 121, 126, 127, 129
Waldorff-Astoria, 44
Wallenberg Committee, 101
Wall Street Journal, 65, 69, 107, 190, 194
Washington, 3
Washington, University of, 172
Wegner, William, 132–33
Weston, Edward, 281
white sturgeon, 3, 18, 77
    in California, 18–19
    California aquaculture and, 165–82
    caviar and, 23
    early history of, 13
    feeding specialization of, 7
    in Kootenai River, Idaho, 265–69, 272–78
    size of, 5
Wilderness Act of 1964, 281
The Wilderness World of John Muir (Teale), 170

Wildlife Conservation Society, 68, 84, 288
Wilhelm, Kaiser, 248
Wisconsin, 75, 76–78, 82, 145–58, 160–64
Wisconsin Department of Natural Resources (DNR), 76, 77, 89, 148, 150, 153, 163
Wolf River, Wisc., 89–91, 146, 154
World Bank, 228, 242, 258
World Conservation Union, 104, 107, 108, 117
World Council of Europe, 260
The World Is Not Enough, 33, 250
World War I, 15, 55
World War II, 248–49
World Wildlife Federation, 24
Wright, William, 178–79, 181

Yazbak, Alfred, 34, 48, 159
Yellowstone Park, 105
Yeltsin, Boris, 210, 211, 221, 232
The Yosemite (Muir), 169, 261
Yosemite National Park, 279–80

Zabar, Ann, 34
Zabar, Eli, 138
Zabar, Saul, 34, 107
Zabar's, 34, 41, 42, 43, 108, 136, 138, 140, 159, 190
Zambia, 78
Zhuravleva, Elena, 212, 215–18, 218–19, 226, 227, 286
Zimbabwe, 34–35, 51, 104
Zukovsky, Valentin, 250
Zukovsky Caviar, 33, 250